For Jack, Jonah, Kim, Martha and Sam

And in memory of a wet Whalley Range

Urban Theory

'Just when we need it most, urban theory seems to be failing us. This book explains why we need it.'

Jamie Peck, University of British Columbia

'Harding and Blokland address the vaunted "crisis" in urban theory with a thoughtful assessment of extant theories in terms of performance, commensurability, and critical engagement. In a conversational and lively tone, they view theories of inequality, public space, identity, power, agency, and culture through the lens of "relaxed urban theory." Excellent overview for scholars and engaging classroom material.'

Susan E. Clarke, University of Colorado

'Inspired by Peter Saunders's non-spatial urban thinking, Harding and Blokland's book provides a provocative, wide-ranging and comprehensive treatment of concepts geared to understand cities, and is a compulsory addition to any urban student's intellectual arsenal in a period of renewed interest in urban theory.'

Roger Keil, York University

'Urban theory is said to be in a mess. Proceeding with great analytical clarity, this book introduces a relaxed definition of urban theory that enables the reader to make sense of the non-linear, variegated world of urban theory as it has developed over time and through the application of different disciplines, methods and epistemologies. In reviewing all the major conceptualisations of urban theory, Harding and Blokland provide clear insights into recent developments and the controversies and critiques they have provoked. The book is a pedagogical tour de force for students and scholars alike.'

Patrick Le Galès, CNRS Research Professor at Sciences Po's Centre d'Études Européennes and Professor at Sciences Po, (Paris)

Alan Harding & Talja Blokland

Urban Theory

A critical introduction to power, cities and urbanism in the 21st century

Los Angeles | London | New Delhi
Singapore | Washington DC

Los Angeles | London | New Delhi
Singapore | Washington DC

SAGE Publications Ltd
1 Oliver's Yard
55 City Road
London EC1Y 1SP

SAGE Publications Inc.
2455 Teller Road
Thousand Oaks, California 91320

SAGE Publications India Pvt Ltd
B 1/I 1 Mohan Cooperative Industrial Area
Mathura Road
New Delhi 110 044

SAGE Publications Asia-Pacific Pte Ltd
3 Church Street
#10-04 Samsung Hub
Singapore 049483

© Alan Harding and Talja Blokland 2014

First published 2014

Editor: Robert Rojek
Editorial assistant: Keri Dickens
Production editor: Katherine Haw
Copyeditor: Richard Leigh
Proofreader: Dick Davis
Marketing manager: Michael Ainsley
Cover design: Francis Kenney
Typeset by: C&M Digitals (P) Ltd, Chennai, India
Printed and bound by CPI Group (UK) Ltd, Croydon, CR0 4YY

Library of Congress Control Number: 2013951657

British Library Cataloguing in Publication data

A catalogue record for this book is available from the British Library

MIX
Paper from
responsible sources
FSC
www.fsc.org   FSC® C013604

ISBN 978-1-4462-9451-2
ISBN 978-1-4462-9452-9 (pbk)

Contents

About the authors

Alan Harding is Professor of Public Policy and Director of the Heseltine Institute for Public Policy and Practice at the University of Liverpool Management School in the UK. Previously, he held posts at Manchester, Salford and Liverpool John Moores universities. His research interests are in urban and regional development, governance and policy and he has acted as an advisor on these issues for a wide range of leading agencies with interests in this field.

Talja Blokland (1971) is an urban sociologist who has worked at Yale University, the University of Manchester and various Dutch universities. Since 2009, she has held the chair of Urban and Regional Sociology at Humboldt University in Berlin. Her publications include *Urban Bonds* (Polity 2003), *Networked Urbanism* (edited with Mike Savage, Ashgate 2008) and various articles on race and ethnicity in the city, poor neighbourhoods, urban violence, gentrification, urban middle classes and neighbourhood relations and everyday interactions.

Foreword

This book provides an introduction to 'urban theory' for an audience that does not necessarily have any prior knowledge about this interesting but ill-defined and, some would say, controversial area of academic study. It has been a long time in the making. One of the co-authors started it over a decade ago, when he was fortunate enough to be awarded a UK Economic and Social Research Council (ESRC) Professorial Fellowship that, ideally, should have been enough to see the job through. Unfortunately, at the same time, he assumed additional responsibilities for building up a self-funding research centre at Salford University. Times were relatively good. Research funding was plentiful. The book therefore remained half, rather than fully, written at the end of that award. These things happen. The end-of-award report was less enthusiastic than it might have been, but nobody died.

There followed a frustrating few years, book-wise, during which time this same co-author moved to the University of Manchester to head up another self-funding research institute. Times were hard. A combination of global financial crisis and intermittent national (UK) economic recessions saw the virtual disappearance of the sorts of 'soft' (*sic*) money that has been known to make such a job tolerable. Sometime in 2010, however, this co-author, approaching his wits' end about how this book would ever be finished, had a brainwave. He invited his fellow co-author to join him and contribute strands of analysis that he would have been incapable of formulating, far less providing, alone. This co-author had been teaching urban theory classes for a couple of years and was dissatisfied with the textbooks available, yet knew she would never have the competence or the motivation to do anything about this unaided. She therefore welcomed the offer to board this train. But then her life, too, changed. Amongst other things, she became Head of Department and spent much time acquiring the bureaucratic skills needed within a German university. Further delay was inevitable. Nonetheless, three years on, various life-changing events to both participants and too many sleepless nights later, here it is.

In writing the book, we have set ourselves the objectives to inform, to challenge and to make complex ideas accessible. A rapidly changing world brings with it a rapid turnover of ideas. The task of staying abreast of contemporary changes is made that much easier if the reader does not have to track each of them from countless individual sources; a journal article here, a book chapter there. The first challenge we took on, therefore, was to identify, assemble, and describe the body of work that best captures the evolution of urban theory, historically, with a particular focus on the most important contributions, as we see them, that appeared either side of the millennium.

But we also wanted to go beyond the genre of the textbook. Textbooks and readers perform an invaluable service in pooling and communicating broad bodies of knowledge, but they often suffer from two drawbacks. On the one hand, they can be dry and descriptive, adding little to the source material upon which they draw. A second challenge was therefore to offer a critique of the changes we describe and to draw them together in ways that had not been attempted before. By being critical, we sought to help readers take issue with some important interpretations of the contemporary urban world as well as know and understand them. On the other hand, textbooks and readers can sometimes place unreasonably heavy demands on their audiences in assuming they are familiar with most of the concepts, and much of the jargon, upon which new understandings are built. The third challenge was therefore to treat readers as intelligent people who are interested in extending their knowledge but without assuming they have enormous amounts of prior information and training to draw upon.

The task of realising these aspirations with respect to 'urban theory' proved easy in some respects but difficult in others. Strangely enough, it is easier to be critical than to describe in some respects. As we make clear, the field of urban studies ranges over a vast canvas that could never adequately be covered in a single book, but urban *theory*, paradoxically, is often held to be in short supply, to be of limited utility or to be insufficiently applied. Urban researchers are often charged with not drawing upon theory remotely as much as they should, and it is not uncommon to hear it argued that urban studies have become, or risk becoming, almost a theory-free zone. One of the arguments often advanced to explain that tendency is that relatively narrow urban *policy* issues have established an unhealthy stranglehold over debates about the conditions and futures of cities. It is certainly true that descriptions and critiques of urban policies and programmes have accounted for a significant urban literature in which overt theoretical considerations are absent, lie implicit or else seem to be tacked on only as an afterthought.

Why should this be the case? One common explanation over the years has been that a substantial proportion of urban research is conducted under contract to 'real-world' clients. Government departments, local authorities and other public agencies, traditionally some of the biggest purchasers of contract research, are not exactly renowned for their enthusiasm for abstract conceptual debate. Their needs are generally for 'practical', 'objective' commentary and advice that can provide them with the ammunition to lobby for, establish, change, extend or abolish particular programmes. In one sense the idea that 'the state' somehow exerts a stranglehold over urban research, and by extension over opportunities to develop new theories and concepts, might seem compelling. There is no doubt, for example, that the tight spending climates in which many universities work, along with performance metrics that increasingly emphasise 'impact', 'engagement' and 'relevance', encourage academics to seek out external funding to supplement the more direct sources of support that have, in many cases, failed to keep pace with increasing demands upon their services. One obvious result is that the research agendas of at least some academics have become more closely tied to those of policy-makers and practitioners. As the role of universities in supporting the development of the 'knowledge economy' has come into sharper focus, it is also the case that governments have increasingly favoured applied research over 'blue-skies thinking' on the somewhat simplistic assumption that this will best serve the interest of 'user communities' and society as a whole.

But to see this trend as dominant is to misrepresent a much more complex process and to oversimplify and overstate the ostensible malaise of urban theory. The 'state control' argument implicitly assumes three things: that urban policy issues take up much of the space devoted to debates about our towns and cities because more money is spent on research in this field; that there is no external support for more abstract and theoretical work in urban studies; and that academics can only engage in effective theory-building if they are specifically paid to do so. On examination, none of these assumptions is particularly persuasive. Working backwards through them, the latter holds least water. Theory-building is cheap and relatively unreliant upon external patronage. It need not cost any more than the time that academics are prepared to devote to it. Of course it helps if that time, along with the costs of related empirical research, is paid for. But there is no reason, in principle, why the production of works in urban theory should not continue even if there were no external support for urban studies at all. There is certainly no lack of outlets for such work, be it through specialist journals or specific series of books in the lists of major publishers.

And the fact is there *is* external support, from various sources. The second assumption, that theory-resistant practitioners and policy-makers are the main funders of urban research, is not accurate. Indeed, they are by no means the sole supporters of urban research, even within the public sector. Within the UK, for example, government-funded research councils have supported significant programmes, over a long period, touching upon a range of urban themes: the inner cities; relations between central and local governments; urban economic development; the changing urban and regional system; local governance; economic restructuring and social change within particular localities; urban sustainability, the economic competitiveness and social cohesion of cities and the development of urban technologies. It is undeniable that applicants to these programmes have increasingly been asked to demonstrate the actual or potential applicability of their work. But they are also routinely required to demonstrate, to highly discerning peer reviewers, that their projects will develop new conceptual insights and improve the sophistication of research methods. Charitable foundations and trusts, too, have put significant resources into relatively open-ended urban research.

The first assumption is also flawed. There is no doubt that some of the exposure achieved by urban policy debates is in some small way related to the volume of publicly funded research which has been put into this area. But two things have to be recognised. First, a great many academic contributions to policy debates, including many of the most critical ones, are made by scholars who are neither major beneficiaries of urban research funding nor urban theorists in any significant sense. These commentators usually make their interventions for no more sinister reason than that they are interested in the subject. The fact that they do so shows that academic concern with urban development issues is not just a matter of funding and, more significantly, that those policy analysts who are not externally funded show no greater interest in urban theory than their colleagues who are. Second, it is clear that the interest shown by academics in 'the urban' is reasonably widely shared. Politicians, journalists, public servants, business leaders, voluntary sector bodies, community activists and lay people all use urban debates to air their concerns about the state of contemporary societies of which they form such an important part. Policy debates touch a popular nerve more fundamentally than abstract theorisation, whether or not it attracts or deserves the label 'urban', has typically been able to do.

Taking these various observations together, it appears that if urban studies can be considered to have become a theory-free zone in recent years, as critics allege, this cannot be put down to the lack of external support or to the preponderance of forms of support which do not prioritise abstract debate. Nor does it reflect a more general disinterest in urban studies and policy debates. In reality there are other, more mundane but powerful considerations that should be borne in mind when accounting for what we feel is the mythical 'crisis' in urban theory. Two are particularly noteworthy. One is that it is very difficult, some would say impossible, even to define the field of urban theory. It is not surprising, therefore, that academics with a passion for theory-building sometimes gravitate to other fields. As we make clear, in a predominantly urbanised world, it has become extremely difficult to distinguish 'urban' experiences and processes from 'non-urban' ones. That being the case, it is easy to see how 'urban theory' can struggle to demonstrate its distinctiveness and become indistinguishable from 'theory' in a more general sense. The evidence in this book shows that many leading scholars who initially acquired their reputations on the basis of urban research have been content to remain within the nebulous field of urban theory. Many, having begun making theoretical contributions on the basis of their empirical work in or on cities, have 'outgrown' urban studies and chosen instead to engage in wider debates within their particular academic disciplines. However, it also shows that urban theory, as we understand it, continues to proliferate.

The second consideration, and the most basic of all, is that theory can be desperately hard going. It demands a great deal of effort and application from its readers, let alone its authors. The urban geographer David Harvey, one of the most diligent of urban theorists over the last forty years, consistently warns his readers about the sacrifices that are needed to master difficult concepts. He is fond of quoting Marx (1948), who said in his introduction to the French version of *Das Kapital* that '[t]here is no royal road to science, and only those who do not dread the fatiguing climb of its steep paths have a chance of gaining its luminous summits'. Many urbanists, faced with the unusually large degree of uncertainty that surrounds the exercise, are disinclined to put the necessary level of investment into reaching Olympian heights in urban theory-building. The hardier souls who try run two risks. One is that the understandings they gain from attaining such rarefied perspectives are not always easy to apply to actual events in real places. Concepts that help us understand patterns as seen from the mountain top are not always so useful when we are trying to make sense of the world from street level. Another is that theorists elect, from personal preference or simple lack of time, to continue to deal in abstractions rather than apply them. Having gained their luminous summits, they are not always inclined to descend or offer a helping hand to fellow climbers. Even if academics are not put off by the difficulties, then, their efforts in theory-building can still become detached from empirical and policy questions.

There is little this book can do to solve any of the dilemmas of urban theory and its relationship to urban studies. Part of the motivation for writing it, however, is to clarify those dilemmas and to help readers coming to the subject for the first time to understand and pick their way through them. As scholars who, during the course of their careers, have sought to move between the worlds of theory and practice in very different ways, we wish to hold fast to our belief that 'there is nothing so practical as a good theory'. This book will have done its job if, by the end of it, readers are reasonably convinced of three things. First, that despite all the difficulties with definitions, there is something to be gained from understanding how various theories have informed the study of urban development and change. Second, that theories need to be applied, or to be capable of application, and therefore of refutation, if their potential value is to be maximised. And finally, that the development or application of theory need not be an entirely academic exercise, of interest only to a small elite group. It should, and can, be an enterprise that grapples with some fundamental issues in a way that helps the widest possible audience understand two critical things: first, the forces that create and re-create our cities and what happens within and between them; and second, the potential that exists for people to help create the sorts of cities they want.

It is normal, in these circumstances, to offer a word of thanks to all those who helped in the production of The Work. We are far too humble and conservative to ignore tradition and reject precedent. We thank Jenna Büchy, Carlotta Giustozzi, Tilman Versch and Louise Zwirner for early support in collecting the literature; Ruth Scott-Williams, for recovering references that had gone astray; and Carlotta Giustozzi, Anna-Katherina Dietrich, Katherine Kruse, Suzanna Raab, Hannah Schilling, Vojin Szerbedzija, and Robert Vief for their help in preparing the manuscript, which was not an easy task given the huge number of references we have used. Julia Nast shared her literature review on neighbourhood effects with us, for which we are thankful. Students taking the BA class in urban theory at Humboldt University in the summer semester of 2013 and those who attended the RTN Urban Europe summer school in Urbino in 2005 provided excellent forums for us to try out some of our arguments at different stages of their development. If there is anyone standing at ESRC who has custody of the folk memory of Award No. R00027194, entitled 'Institutions, coalitions and networks for urban and regional development: theory and practice', he or she is due Alan's sincere and belated thanks for the Council's kind support.

As is always the case, there are many people to thank, but it is the authors alone who are to blame for what follows.

Talja Blokland, Berlin
Alan Harding, Liverpool
September 2013

1

What is urban theory?

Learning objectives

- To understand the conceptual dilemmas that come with attempts to define 'the urban'
- To see how classical scholars have thought about the urban and rural in the context of modernity
- To understand what 'theory' is and learn about the various epistemological and ontological perspectives that inform theory

Urban studies and urban theory

People are entitled to be confused, even a little intimidated, by the way towns and cities are studied today. Contemporary courses in urban studies cover just about every conceivable aspect of the urban experience. Some approaches are relatively self-contained and coherent, but most tend to shade into each other. In an age in which more than half of the global population is living in urban areas for the first time in human history, there are no easily defined conceptual boundaries that can allow us to designate everything on one side of an imaginary line as urban studies and everything on the other side as something else. Neither are urban studies the property of a single academic discipline. Claims are made for a distinctive urban sociology, an urban politics, geography, economics, planning and so on, but in practice it is hard to distinguish one from another. The 'urban' components of these disciplines are not very self-contained either. It is difficult, for example, to say what differentiates urban geography from human geography, or urban sociology from more general social theory. And it is far from clear which of the standard academic disciplines 'owns' the more specific subject matter that often surfaces in the literature; urban archi-tecture, conservation, design, ecology, economic development, environment, landscape, management, morphology, policy and so on.

Urban subdisciplines

Urban studies are eclectic; they bring together and build upon knowledge, understandings and approaches from a wide range of subject areas. Recounting his experience of urban sociology as an undergraduate in 1970, Peter Saunders could remember little coherence in his chosen course of study other than the fact that 'if you could find it happening in cities, then you could find it discussed somewhere in the ... literature' (Saunders, 1986: 7). Little has changed since Saunders' undergraduate days in this respect. If anything, urban studies have become still more eclectic and fragmented. So, for example, it has been argued that Saunders' field concerns itself with the following: how the urban experience feels; if and how places acquire distinctive identities; how urban life is affected by a person's gender, class, and ethnic group or the sort of housing he/she lives in; the effect of different urban environments on social relationships and bonds; the history of urbanisation; the 'spatial structures' of cities; the nature of, and solutions to, urban problems; and political participation and local governance (Savage, Warde & Ward, 2003: 2–3). And that is just urban sociology.

A list of issues claimed to be central to urban geography is equally eclectic and shows a fair degree of overlap: the causes of urbanisation; the national and international urban hierarchy; the 'urban system'; the determinants of land use within cities; urban investment patterns; town planning; urban transport; social and residential areas within cities; the role of social class, gender, ethnicity and sexual identity in urban affairs; the problems of inner cities, peripheral urban areas and suburbs; urban policy 'solutions' to urban problems; images of cities; and cities in the developing world and post-communist eastern Europe (Carter, 1995; Short, 1984, 1996; Herbert & Thomas, 1982; Johnston, 1980). Urban politics, on the other hand, spans issues such as the role of elites and regimes in urban development, intergovernmental relations and urban policies, the role of bureaucratic and political leadership in urban change, the autonomy of city governments, citizenship, urban social movements, gender and race relations in cities, and the design and operation of the institutions of urban governance (Judge et al, 1995; Davies & Imbroscio, 2009). A resurgent urban economics, on the other hand, concerns itself with the urbanisation process, alternative approaches to locational analysis, the characteristics of urban markets (housing, transportation, facilities), urban labour markets, the behaviour of urban govern-ments and their implications for urban public economics, and the quality of urban life (Arnott & McMillen, 2006; Mills, 2004).

The fact that urban studies do not have an obvious centre of gravity or an essential and shared core of ideas has occasionally been seen as a source of concern by some scholars, particularly amongst those who argue that they should play a role in underpinning desirable economic, social, environmental, cultural or political change, however defined. For at least the last 40 years there have been sporadic but fierce debates about the nature, status, relevance and usefulness of urban studies. It has been argued, particularly following periods of economic crisis and social and political upheaval, that urban studies, and by implication the conceptual tools on which they draw, are 'in crisis'.

Thus, for example, some of the most noted contributions to the evolution of 'urban theory' (e.g. Castells, 1972; Harvey, 1973) have resolutely rejected what their authors perceived to be the dominant, pre-existing paradigm(s) within urban studies and argued for fresh thinking that could overturn the scholarly status quo and, ideally, help transform the broader conditions that gave rise to them. The (urban) impacts of the global financial crisis in 2008, and the wave of austerity budgeting by national governments that followed in its wake, witnessed a similar outpouring of (self-) criticism along the lines that 'theory', and the work based upon it, no longer seemed to underpin the political action that is necessary to achieving substantive change, even when it aspired to do so (see Swyngedouw, 2009: 603–4). Similarly, as noted in the Foreword, claims have occasionally been made that urban studies are somehow 'captured' by public funding that is only made available for 'practical' research that is unthreatening to policy elites (Forrest, Henderson, & Williams, 1982) and that some of its key exponents are therefore 'neutralised' and incorporated into closed, elite policy circles, thereby providing legitimacy rather than knowledge that may challenge received wisdoms and conventional practices (Boland, 2007).

It must be noted, however, that neither the eclecticism of urban studies nor the concerns that are sometimes expressed as to whether they are effective in fulfilling a perceived 'mission' seem to affect their popularity. Their appeal to students and their importance for academics and policy-makers has, we would argue, continued to grow.

Metaphorical cities

Urban studies do not just cover a broad canvas. They utilise many different concepts in exploring their wide-ranging subject matter. One indication of the sheer variety of approaches upon which they draw is the range of characterisations and metaphors academics have used to understand and describe cities and processes of urban change. Cities are analysed in terms of their size and status. There has been work on global (Sassen, 1991), world (Hall, 1984; Friedmann, 1986) and mega-cities (Gilbert, 1996), as well as regional (Calthorpe & Fulton, 2001), provincial (Skeldon, 1997), intermediate (Bolay & Rabinovich, 2004), small and medium-sized cities (Erickcek & McKinney, 2006). Cities are seen as characterising different epochs and stages of development. There are old (Ashworth & Tunbridge, 1999), new (Mullins, 1990), modern and postmodern cities (Watson & Gibson, 1995); imperial and postimperial, colonial and postcolonial cities (Driver & Gilbert, 1999; Betts, Ross, & Telkamp, 1985); pre-industrial, industrial and postindustrial cities (Savitch, 1988); yesterday's, today's and tomorrow's cities (Hall, 2002); 'successful' cities in the sunbelt and 'declining' cities in the rustbelt. Cities and their neighbourhoods are distinguished according to location. There are inner cities, outer cities, suburban or edge cities (Garreau, 1991), central and peripheral cities, frontier and border cities. Cities are said to specialise in different functions: there are technopoles (Castells & Hall, 1994); commercial, manufacturing, tourist (Judd & Fainstein, 1999) and service cities; airport, maritime and university cities. Politically and ideologically, cities are characterised as communist or capitalist (Smith & Feagin, 1987), socialist and post-socialist, liberal, progressive (Clavel, 1986), conservative or pluralist. There are public and private cities. On the outer edge of our perceptions there are symbolic or virtual cities and 'the city as text' (Donald, 1992).

The variety of city types described in the urban literature is matched by the range of experiences cities are claimed to undergo. We hear, for example, about urban crisis (Cloward & Piven, 1975), decline, decay and poverty. Cities are said to be divided (Fainstein, Gordon, & Harloe, 1992), unequal (Hamnett, 2003), sick, unfairly structured (Badcock, 1984), heartless, captive (Harloe, 1977), dependent (Kantor & David, 1988; Kantor, 1995), dispossessed, ungovernable (Cannato, 2001), unheavenly (Banfield, 1970) and contested (Mollenkopf, 1983). They are, or have been, in recession, in stress (Gottdiener, 1986), in trouble, in revolt, at risk or under siege (Graham, 2011). At the same time, we hear of urban innovation (Clark, 1994), redevelopment, regeneration, renewal, renaissance and revitalisation. Cities are, or can be, healthy (Ashton, 1992), liveable, intelligent (Komninos, 2012), humane (Short, 1989), just (Fainstein, 2010), ideal (Eaton, 2001), safe, creative (Cooke & Lazzeretti, 2008), accessible, good, free, compact (Jenks & Burgess, 2000) or sustainable (Haughton & Hunter, 2003). There are cities that have shrunk (Glock, 2006; Hannemann, 2003; Galster, 2012a) but refused to die (Keating, 1988), and others that have been reborn (Levitt, 1987), saved or transformed. There are utopian possibilities: cities that are perfect (Gilbert, 1991), heavenly, ideal, magical (Davis, 2001), beautiful, triumphant, radiant or visionary. In between urban heaven and hell, cities have more prosaic attributes: they are ordinary (Robinson, 2006), planned (Corden, 1977), informational (Castells, 1989), cultural, rational, organic, developing, globalising (Marcuse & van Kempen, 2000), emerging or evolving. There are cities in transition, in competition (Brotchie, 1995) or on the move.

This brief illustration of the enormous variety in the way cities and urban processes are characterised is enough to warn us that there is no consensus in urban studies, not just about what is the appropriate focus for analysis but on the broader question of whether towns and cities are 'good' for human life. On the one hand, cities are seen as quintessential sites where freedom of lifestyle or subcultures can be practised; as places where multiple ways of being can each find their own niches. On the other, they are also seen, in what Lofland (1998) describes as the anti-urban discourse, as places of problems, of vice and moral decay. Especially in the US, the countryside, with its natural wilderness and its ostensible freedom, provides a pastoral image in contrast to the cold, anonymous, rational city, as is visible in the Hudson River landscape paintings of artists such as Thomas Cole (Figure 1.1).

Partly this can be explained by the different places that the process of urbanisation occupies within distinct national histories. In both the relatively 'young' US and the older UK, the city has tended to be associated, rightly or wrongly, with industrialisation and with the 'shocking' and socially dislocating aspects of early industrial cities such as Manchester and Chicago. In areas of the world with longer, pre-industrial urban histories – Greece and China are good examples, as are the principle pre-industrial trading centres of Europe – the absence of such a strong association between urbanity and industrialisation encourages a different 'take' on the city as a centre, variously, of democracy, enlightenment,

Figure 1.1 *A View of the Mountain Pass Called the Notch of the White Mountains (Crawford Notch),* Thomas Cole, 1939

Source: Wikimedia Commons:
http://upload.wikimedia.org/wikipedia/commons/9/93/Thomas_Cole_-_A_View_of_the_Mountain_Pass_Called_the_Notch_of_the_White_Mountains.jpg

innovation and technological and artistic development. Partly, though, it is about radically different ways of seeing. Storper and Manville (2006: 1269) summarise the persistence of double vision when suggesting that:

> Urban studies have always been shot through with a curious mix of pessimism and utopianism. For almost as long as we have had cities, we have had predictions of their decline and, for almost as long as we have had talk of decline, we have had prophecies of resurgence.

In using metaphors to describe the conditions of cities and how they change, urban commentators necessarily draw upon a more or less coherent set of concepts; that is, upon one or more theories. Take the notion of the 'dependent city'. Having invented this label, Paul Kantor (Kantor & David, 1988; Kantor, 1995) naturally had to say what he meant by cities and who or what he considered them dependent upon. In fact Kantor equated cities with city governments. He explained how decision-makers in US city governments cannot do as they please but are dependent in the sense that their choices are constrained by their need to take into account the actions and preferences of other decision-makers in the business community and in state and federal governments. Kantor's argument therefore drew upon theories about the relationship between levels of government ('intergovernmental theory') and between the public and private sectors ('political economy'). In Kantor's case, the choice of theoretical perspectives was made explicit. He made reference to a number of theories he felt could not entirely answer the questions he posed but, in combination, shed helpful conceptual light upon them.

The role of theory in urban studies

Not all commentators within urban studies are as obliging as Kantor when it comes to outlining the theoretical foundations of their work. Indeed urban studies, especially in the UK and Europe, are sometimes saddled with a reputation for occupying a 'theory-free zone' by some critics precisely because their exponents are said not to draw explicitly or fruitfully upon relevant theories and concepts, or at least not enough. It is also argued that literatures which conceptualise the urban form and change on a theoretical level find little resonance with either the literature that studies social problems in the city or those scholars who work outside of academia in policy-oriented professions. Here, research is being used, and this research is increasingly conducted by consultancy firms and semi-commercial university research institutes or foundations. As far as there is urban theory, then, we signal a distance between those who do 'urban theory' and those who draw on empirical studies, often commissioned, for actual practice of urban policy. This division seems to be on the rise and creates two issues. First, it makes part of urban studies obsolete, and the world would not look any different if their theories did not exist. Second, it creates poor knowledge about the urban world, as nothing is as practical as good theory (Pawson, 2003). Unreflexive data-collection and report-writing may legitimise specific policies, but will not provide much of an understanding of the processes and mechanisms one would need to understand in order to be able to strive for social change to begin with – in policy, but also in non-governmental organisations and activism.

These three key features of the urban studies literature – the limited degree of explicit theorisation, the wide range of subject matter covered and the disconnection between urban theory and empirical research – do not appear to put academic researchers and students off the subject. They nonetheless generate questions about the role of theory in urban studies. Can we even talk of urban theory in any meaningful sense? Can urban theories be distinguished from broader theoretical developments in the social sciences, or do they simply entail the application of general theories to urban phenomena? Are there even such things as distinctively urban phenomena? If not, what objects do urban theories focus upon? How have urban theories developed and how do they relate to one another? Is there such a thing as *contemporary* urban theory and, if so, what differentiates it from previous approaches? How are urban theories used, by whom and for what purpose? Do they have any impact upon popular debates about cities? These are the central questions this book grapples with. Before proceeding to them, however, we need to elaborate a little on the term 'urban' and on the general nature of theory, whether or not it is described as urban. This discussion helps clarify what is and can be meant by 'urban theory'.

What is urban?

The *Oxford English Dictionary* defines *urban* as 'of, living in, or situated in, city or town'. For everyday purposes that is a perfectly adequate definition. Like most dictionary entries, however, it only begs further questions. In this case the first obvious question is what is meant by a city or town, and how do they differ from other sorts of place? Whilst the average Briton might intuitively know when he or she passes through Loughborough or Mansfield that they are towns, not cities, and that Liverpool (Figure 1.2) or Manchester certainly do qualify as 'cities', what exactly makes him or her *know* that this is the case? A related but more searching question concerns what 'of' means in the above definition. How do we define what is 'of' cities and towns? What is specifically urban? What is urban different from? All of these questions cause problems for social scientists, but the difficulties presented by the first are overcome rather more easily than the latter.

Figure 1.2   Liverpool Skyline with HMS Ark Royal docked at cruise terminal

Source: Wikimedia Commons
http://commons.wikimedia.org/wiki/File:Liverpool_Skyline_with_HMS_Ark_Royal.jpg.

Figure 1.3   Plauen skyline

Plauen, Germany. Picture taken from the Bärensteinturm., Christopher Voitus, 2006.
Source: Wikimedia Commons: http://commons.wikimedia.org/wiki/File:Plauen-Overview.JPG.

If the (Anglo-Saxon) meanings of city and town are probed further, they are found to depend upon arbitrary categorisations that only make sense relative to other, equally arbitrary ones. A town, for example, is defined as a collection of dwellings bigger than a village that, in turn, is bigger than a hamlet. A city, meanwhile, is either an important town or a town awarded privileged status by charter, especially if it also contains a cathedral (although, just to confuse matters, not all cities have cathedrals, nor have all towns with cathedrals become cities!). Different definitions apply in different countries. In Dutch and German, no linguistic distinction is drawn between city and town (with *stad* and *Stadt* meaning both town and city, and defined by rights of government and tax-collection of the feudal times, so that the contract between *land* and *stad* is derived from the power division between the European gentry and merchant citizens). German and Dutch added *Großstadt* and *grote stad* when the industrial revolution and accompanying demographic growth of cities started to set them apart from other towns. In some cases, Australia being one example, messy conceptual dilemmas are sidestepped through conventions whereby a minimum population size or density is defined, above which a settlement is automatically classified as a town or city (Carter, 1995: 10–12). As with most 'technical' methods of designating towns or cities, this convention provides the categorical clarity needed by national states, but it does not always make sense in people's daily experiences.

The way social scientists have dealt with issues concerning the definition of cities and towns is a good example of how empirical work often proceeds in the absence of precise concepts. Academics have not let the fact that there are no universally agreed, watertight definitions of city and town prevent them from undertaking urban research. For the most part they have simply lived with a particular society's conventional labels, drawing attention to their limitations as necessary. Political scientists, for example, have tended to proceed on the basis that cities can be defined, however imperfectly, by the boundaries that are relevant to political decision-making; that is, by areas covered by a local or metropolitan government. Studies that required a broader focus have embraced other definitions such as a 'travel-to-work area', a 'standard metropolitan statistical area', a conurbation, a 'functional urban region' or other territories defined for the purposes of statistics.

Urban sociologists have tended to eschew geographical definitions of cities and often taken the city as a container of other sociological phenomena and questions studied within the city, contributing to the common understanding that cities pose 'urban problems'. In US English, 'urban' and especially 'inner city' have taken on the connotation of referring to minorities, especially African-Americans and Latinos, and refer to crime, drugs, pregnancies out of wedlock among teenagers and other forms of behaviour labelled in mainstream discourse as 'deviant', if not 'immoral'. 'Urban music', usually referring to one or other form of hip-hop, and 'urban clothing' associated with this subculture spring from an understanding of 'urban' as linked to certain types of neighbourhoods in cities which are seen as both the stage and the site that generates an 'urban' subculture.

The second set of questions, about what is urban and how it differs from the 'non-urban', goes to the heart of what urban studies and urban theory are and can be about. The answers, again, are disappointing for those who prefer clear definitions and solid conceptual platforms on which to build. The simplest answer to the question 'what is urban?' is 'that which is not rural'.

Rural and urban

The urban–rural distinction has a long tradition within social science and there is no doubt that at one time it drew attention to some crucial differences between town and country. Most leading social theorists recognise the critical place of towns and cities in the process of industrialisation and the transition from the largely agrarian feudalist system to the largely urbanised capitalist one (Saunders, 1986: 13–51). Weber (1958), for example, argued that the characteristics of certain medieval European cities stood in stark contrast to those of rural population centres in that they contained concentrations of alternative political and economic power and had very different social structures based on comparatively complex divisions of labour. Moreover, Weber identified the market place as the crucial element that differentiates the city from other forms of settlements. In his view, the social action of exchange created an equality among partially integrated actors based on accidental and superficial contacts and hence organised the earliest form of 'public space', sociologically meant (see also Bahrdt, 1998).

Marx agreed on the importance of the division of labour. Indeed, he positively welcomed the destructive effect urbanisation had on pre-existing social structures and the fact that it freed the labouring classes from 'the idiocy of rural life'. Marx and Weber saw conceptual benefits in the use of the terms 'urban' and 'rural' in the period before the industrial age, a time when the city was a relatively distinctive and fruitful unit for analysis.

The usefulness of the urban–rural distinction for social scientists, however, declined steadily with increasing industrialisation. Sociologists became increasingly critical of the bipolar juxtaposition of the urban and the rural, not least because 'the rural', as discussed in the work of Ferdinand Tönnies and others, was associated with a romanticised vision of social life that sociologists wanted to move away from (e.g. Mazlish, 1989). Urbanisation in the Global North came to be seen as synonymous with, but dependent upon, industrialisation so it was the latter concept that dominated explanations of social change.

An everyday distinction between urban and rural persisted because the two terms still conjure up contrasting visions of the way space is used; dense, built-up, 'man-made' areas on the one hand, sparsely populated, 'natural' countryside on the other. But the utility of 'urban' as an everyday term has been devalued too. Urbanisation does not just mean that the great majority of people come to live in or near towns and cities whilst 'ruralism' is concentrated into ever-smaller geographical areas inhabited by proportionately fewer people. It affects rural life in much more profound ways. The countryside is fundamentally shaped by and managed for the benefit of urban populations, be it through servicing their demand for food through intensive agricultural production methods or the provision of homes or retail and leisure opportunities for city workers and residents. Whatever happens in cities also happens outside them and it has become virtually impossible to isolate urban from rural ways of life. Ray Pahl's (1970: 209) comment that 'in an urbanised world, "urban" is everywhere and nowhere; the city cannot be defined' summarises the conventional wisdom about the universal nature of 'the urban' and the redundancy of the urban–rural distinction, at least in the 'developed' world.

Two important consequences flow from the doubts that have been cast on the importance of the urban–rural dichotomy. One is that it has become very difficult to define 'urban' in a way that is sufficiently distinctive for it to be useful for social scientists. If 'urban' is everywhere, isn't 'urban geography' simply 'geography', 'urban politics' just 'politics' and so on across subject areas? The line advocated by the likes of Pahl is now accepted by most academics, even if they are convinced of the importance of urban studies. Savage, Warde and Ward, for example, felt motivated to write an urban sociology textbook but had to concede that 'there is no solid definition of the urban. ... The label "urban" sociology is mostly a flag of convenience' (Savage et al., 2003: 2). Similarly, Carter accepted that urban geography 'cannot claim to be a systematic study' but simply 'considers [economic, socio-cultural and political] processes in relation to one phenomenon, the city' (Carter, 1995: 1). Dunleavy, on the other hand, opted for a relatively arbitrary 'content definition' of the urban field, based upon particular social and political processes, because he adjudged as failures alternative attempts to define it geographically or institutionally (Dunleavy, 1980: 21–55).

The other implication is that the town or city, as an entity, long ago ceased to be particularly distinctive for social scientists. As Saunders (1986: ii) argued:

> [t]he city is not a theoretically significant unit of analysis in advanced capitalist societies ... Marx and Engels, Weber and Durkheim ... saw the city as important historically in the development of industrial capitalist society, but none of them saw it as significant for an analysis of such societies once they had become established.

Evidence for this argument can be found in a curious contemporary paradox. Whereas the more general concepts developed by those path-breaking social theorists in their analyses of industrialised societies continue to exert an important influence on many aspects of urban studies, those parts of their work that dealt specifically with cities are ignored by all but a few commentators (e.g. Elliott & McCrone, 1982, on Weber), with the exception of Georg

Simmel (1950), whose essay on the 'mental life' of cities has seen a revival especially since what we will later discuss as the cultural turn in urban studies. What is left is, first, a rather abstract discussion on space, including arguments that space is produced and therefore not a container concept (Gottdiener & Hutchison, 2011), which has consequences for defining 'city', and second, a large field of studies called 'urban' that focuses on social questions located in cities, but not addressing the specificity of the urban of these questions in any great theoretical depth.

What is theory?

Dictionaries generally define *theory* as a body or system of ideas that explains one or more aspects of reality. This conjures up a picture of the theorist as someone with throbbing temples who spends his or her time dreaming up and applying formalised sets of rules through disciplined, abstract thought. Social science theory would, however, stop being social science the moment it lost all connection to the empirical, that is, to the realm of experienced reality (in contrast to metaphysics).

   We are all theorists at some level. We use theory routinely and flexibly, even if we are not always aware of it. As Charles Lemert (1995: 14–15) writes, 'everyone knows, beyond much reasonable doubt, that there is a sphere of social things out there that affects human life in powerful ways', and theory in its everyday sense is little more than the stories we tell about what we have figured out about our experiences in social life. In order to analyse or to act, we need to process large amounts of information such that the focus for our analysis or our practical options are simplified and made manageable, and in order to do so, we draw, often though not always, on theories of what matters, how things work and what causes what.

   Not just in academia, but also in the fields of policy and practice, nothing is as practical as a good theory (Zijderveld, 1991: 15). Theory is derived from the Greek *theorein*, meaning 'observing' or 'considering' (ibid.). Theories, then, are the outcomes of reflection that sharpen our understanding of the world. They use relatively coherent, connected concepts and statements about the social that help us understand what matters, how things work and what causes what. In philosophical parlance, we make use of two tools that help us impose order on our experiences: an ontology and an epistemology.

Ontology and epistemology

An ontology is a view about 'essences'; about what are the basic, indivisible building blocks from which our understanding of ourselves and the world we inhabit is constructed, about what is 'real'. 'Humans are naturally co-operative' is an ontological position that makes a substantial difference to the way people who share it see the world. It leads to particular ways of behaving or interpreting events that contrast in potentially fundamental ways with those of people who believe humans are essentially competitive. An epistemology, by contrast, is a view about the nature of knowledge; about how we know what we know and what counts as evidence in confirming or refuting claims to knowledge. One simple epistemological position is that we can only truly know that which we experience through our physical senses, whereas the interpretations of such experiences, for example how we make sense of them, are assumed to be more or less similar to different individuals. This position has very different implications from one which has it that the same physical sensations mean completely different things to different people, depending upon the way they have come to understand and conceptualise them. Within the social sciences, more than in the natural sciences, different ontological and epistemological positions have given rise to a great variety of theoretical approaches.

These different approaches can be reconciled with one another to some extent, depending on what sort of questions we want to pose, utilising a particular theory. If we are mainly concerned with 'what' questions, for example, we will be drawn to exploratory, descriptive and evaluative approaches that present the fullest possible picture of the issue we are interested in. Such approaches, however, do little to help understand how and why things work. If 'why' questions are uppermost, then we will more likely look to explanatory approaches that grapple with the issue of causation in some, possibly mild, form. It can be argued that as nobody can describe everything social, description involves theories about what matters and what does not, behind which lie ideas about how things work. Interpretations of the social, however, imply a more visible, stronger presence of theory. If 'how' is the primary question, we will gravitate toward normative and prescriptive approaches, that is, those dealing with the way things should be and the best ways of ensuring they are as we would want them. The degree to which theoretical perspectives can be combined and integrated, however, is strictly limited. Whilst some theories are readily acknowledged to perform better than others, for example in answering 'what' as opposed to 'why' questions, by their very nature theories claim that their particular knowledge is universally true. Even the claim that 'no truth is universal' is itself universal; it is true everywhere, at all times, or it is meaningless. It is 'truth claims', and the evidence upon which they rest, that fuel the many internal disputes within social science.

Urban studies, for all their eclecticism, concentrate upon analysing various aspects of a particular historical form of *human* settlement. They therefore fall squarely within the *social* sciences. As a result, urban theory has inevitably been touched by the major controversies within social science more generally about its epistemological status.

Epistemological questions include whether social sciences can legitimately draw upon the ideas and methods of the natural sciences or must develop their own; what counts as knowledge and how it is gained; whether the main aim of inquiry should be understanding or prediction; whether objectivity is possible; what, if anything, is the difference between facts and values and which are the more 'real'; what is the relationship between researcher and researched, and so on. To enumerate all the possible approaches to these issues would mean trawling through a huge variety of 'isms' – from Althusserianism, through materialism, to Weberianism – which might claim the status of theory. To simplify, however, let us start from the observation that the key schools of social science since the beginning of the twentieth century have stemmed from, or can roughly be linked to, three overarching approaches; positivism, hermeneutics and realism (Bhaskar, 1993). These approaches make different claims about what is real and about the nature of knowledge and how it should be gained.

Positivism

Positivism draws most directly on the natural sciences. It has traditionally formed the basis of most social science, although its pre-eminence has declined over time as its relevance to the study of human affairs – and even its dominance within the natural sciences – has increasingly come under attack. For positivists, theories are laws that accurately describe regularities in events and phenomena. They explain things in that they might show, for example, that event B always follows event A but never happens when A does not. They also facilitate predictions; positivists would expect B to follow A in the future just as it has in the past. Positivist theories therefore suggest causation, but A could be said to 'cause' B only in so far as B's relation to A is regular and predictable. Positivist theories do not involve an understanding of *how* A causes B, only a demonstration that it appears to do so. If A were not followed by B under certain circumstances, the theory would fall and another would be needed. It comes as no surprise that the attempts to create a social science modelled after the natural sciences came up during the high days of industrialisation and the expansion of industrial capitalism, in turn related to modernity with its core element of rationalisation: the turn towards a world of *Entzauberung* (disenchantment: Weber, 1988: 594) opened up the possibility of seeing the world as having a rational rather than divine order to it, an order that humans hence could understand and explain thoroughly without having to draw on the metaphysical. While this stream of thought of course as an intellectual project found its basis in the Enlightenment, its social consequences became most pronounced in the times of rapid urbanisation in the Global North, to which industrial capitalism was closely related. The belief in a rational social science was based on the positivist premise that scientific knowledge about the world is possible and can be based on the non-normative, rational registration of facts.

For positivists, the only phenomena about which scientific knowledge is possible are those that can be observed directly. Such phenomena are 'facts', whereas those that cannot be observed are 'values' or abstractions that can have no scientific status. Consequently, positivists have no scientific interest in the motivations underlying human actions or in abstract concepts – God, justice, love, and so on – that have no observable form. They are only concerned with the actions themselves and the effects that abstract concepts have on observable behaviour. In principle, positivist theories should be based only upon 'value-free' observations gathered from experiments or comparisons by objective and disinterested observers. Strictly speaking, they should also rely upon inductive research methods; that is, they should start with the particular (empirical observations) and move to the general (theoretical statements).

The commitment to inductive methods reflected positivism's original mission to avoid two perceived weaknesses in pre-existing social inquiry. One was the tendency to 'prove' pet theories with reference only to a few examples. The other was reliance upon non-verifiable religious or metaphysical arguments. However, critiques of early positivism resulted in the role of abstractions in theory-building being recognised even within broadly positivist schools of thought. As a result, the commitment to base everything upon empirical facts, however defined, softened over time. The critical rationalist school inspired by Popper, for example, provided a powerful case for using deductive rather than inductive research methods. Deduction – the move from the general (theory) to the particular (evidence) – demands that researchers put forward hypotheses and see whether 'facts' corroborate them. It allows researchers to guess what they might find before they look for it and to amend their hypotheses if they do not find it. All that is required for scientific truths to emerge deductively, Popper argued, is that theoretical statements can be proven wrong by empirical evidence – that they are falsifiable. If we agree with Popper, however, we must accept that all 'truths' are tentative since all scientific 'laws' are simply hypotheses that have yet to be falsified (Popper, 1934).

Positivist-inspired approaches within social science are many, varied and by no means mutually compatible. However, all attribute great importance to objectivity on the part of researchers and their methods, a distinction between facts and values, and a central role for observable empirical evidence in the development of theory. For positivists, a social 'science' that lacks these characteristics is not truly scientific. Ranged against this view are alternatives that insist that social science is only possible if it is based upon a different view of science than that borrowed by positivism from the natural sciences.

Hermeneutics

Positivism has long been counterposed to hermeneutics, whose principal characteristics are in many respects the negation of the fundamentals of positivism. Whereas positivists attempt to explain and predict human action by observing behavioural outcomes, hermeneutic approaches look to understand human actions and events with reference to the interpretations people apply to them; that is, by looking at the reasons underlying behaviour. Rather than assuming, as do positivists, that the vagaries of human consciousness can safely be ignored when formulating theories, hermeneutics puts it at the very centre of its concerns.

The hermeneutic theorist/researcher does not merely observe and record 'external' events. He/she must understand both the meanings of actions and events for those involved – as influenced by their desires, beliefs and intentions as well as their memories from previous, similar experiences that provide the scripts for interpreting new encounters – and the context within which participants act and the way this affects their desires, beliefs and intentions. The role of theory, then, is to make sense of events and processes by developing a full understanding of how the meanings that underpin them come to be attributed within particular contexts. Theories developed from such a perspective put much more emphasis upon interpretation and understanding than upon explanation and prediction. Prediction, in particular, is seen as virtually impossible in the social sciences because people are part of 'open systems', where change is constant and the combination of circumstances leading to particular actions and events is rarely repeated, rather than the 'closed systems' of the natural sciences where many fundamental factors do not vary.

Hermeneutics sees no sense in a distinction between facts and values because the meaning of all things, whether they are directly observable or not, is necessarily a matter of interpretation. People do not simply receive raw sensory data; they experience things and interpret them simultaneously. 'Reality', within hermeneutics, is therefore inseparable from subjective human perceptions. It is not something independent of human experience. The importance of subjectivity and interpretation within hermeneutics helps explain its strong focus upon issues of communication, be it through language, texts or behaviour. More important to this discussion, it also raises questions about whether objective knowledge is possible. Can one person or group's subjectivity be 'right', scientifically, and another's 'wrong'? If not, what distinguishes 'theory' from 'opinion' and how can we adjudicate between theories that are based upon subjective meanings but contradict one another? There are two schools of thought, here.

Both concede that theorists are no more objective than those they observe and that their prejudices will always inform their observations. Both suggest, though, that the choice of research methods can minimise any theoretical bias that results from this fact.

Both strands within hermeneutics tend to subscribe to what have been called abductive research strategies (Blaikie, 1993: 176–90). Abduction involves four stages. First, so as not to impose their own view of reality on their task, researchers ask 'how are things perceived?' and try to understand the everyday concepts and meanings that are attached to the particular issue or phenomenon they are interested in. Second, they ask 'so what?' and examine the actions and interactions to which these meanings give rise. Third, they ask 'what does this mean for participants?' and gather subjective accounts of how perceptions and actions are linked in everyday life. It is at the fourth stage – that of theory-building, when the observer stands back and attempts to impose order upon the results of the first three stages – that the two strands diverge. The first believes that the hermeneutic method, because it encourages the theorist to resolve the creative tension between the subjective accounts of those he/she observes and his/her own prejudices, results in understandings which transcend both and can therefore claim to be objective. The other argues that 'truth' can only lie in a clear, codified and intelligible rendering of subjective views. The latter is a *relativist* position which forces the theorist to accept there are no universal criteria that can adjudicate between different 'truths' and alternative 'realities'.

Realism

Realism is a relatively new rival to positivism and hermeneutics. It tries to marry positivism's commitment to causal explanation and the possibility of prediction with the hermeneutic principle that much of what is important within the social sciences cannot be directly observed. Realists agree with positivists that there is a reality that is independent of human perceptions. Proceeding from this position, they have to argue that objective knowledge of that reality is possible; otherwise their position would be meaningless. (Scientifically speaking, it would be less than helpful to suggest that something other than our subjective perceptions exists but we cannot know what it is.) Realists therefore challenge at least one strand within hermeneutics in arguing that subjective perceptions might not only fail to grasp reality, but also grasp 'realities' that do not exist; in other words, they can be wrong. At the same time, realism also challenges the positivist view that only that which can be observed is real. Realists therefore have to come up with a way of knowing and understanding reality that is not just based on empirical observations.

The realist approach to 'facts and values' that emerges from this basic position is a complex one. On the one hand, realists insist that empirical observation has an important role to play in developing and testing theories. On the other hand, they accept that abstract concepts are fundamental to the way we all view the external world. This circle is squared in two ways. First, it is argued that the realist theorist/researcher's job is to link empirical observations with abstract arguments in such a way that he/she gains privileged insights that are denied to those who rely upon empirical observation or subjective interpretation alone. Second, the rather indeterminate status of facts and values is linked to the argument that there are different levels of reality that are perceived in different ways and provide different elements of 'truth'. On the surface there is the *empirical* domain of observable experiences. At a deeper level is the *actual* domain consisting of events, whether or not they are observed. At the deepest level is the *real* domain that is made up of the structures and mechanisms that cause events.

The primary job that realist theory sets itself is to identify the unobservable but nonetheless 'necessary' and 'real' mechanisms which underlie and cause events in particular circumstances. Realist explanation therefore attempts to go a stage further than positivism. It aims to show *how* A causes B and not just to describe patterns that indicate there are causal relations between the two. This goal is achieved, realists argue, through the use of retroductive research strategies that combine empirical and theoretical forms of inquiry. Retroduction proceeds in three stages. In the first, empirical observations are made, as in positivist approaches, which identify patterns in the particular events or actions that require explanation. In the second, theory-building stage, the theorist/researcher asks 'what sort of mechanisms would be necessary to bring about these patterns?'. He/she then comes up with conjectures about these mechanisms that stand as a tentative theory. In the third stage, an attempt is made to establish the validity of the theory by checking whether a larger body of evidence, conceptual and empirical, is consistent with the existence of the theoretical mechanism(s).

There is enormous controversy within the social sciences as to the strengths and weaknesses of these three approaches. There is no agreement about which, if any, is most consistent, has superior methods, or is most useful. The picture is complicated still further by the fact that different theoretical traditions and the schools of thought that develop around particular theorists do not necessarily fall entirely within any one of the three overall approaches. For instance, Weberianism – the concepts and theories associated with the sociologist Max Weber – draws upon hermeneutic and positivist approaches. By contrast, critical theory – an approach associated with the 'Frankfurt School' in general and with Jürgen Habermas in particular – draws upon insights and methods from hermeneutics and realism. Variants of Marxism, on the other hand, would be 'claimed' by positivists and realists. Boundary disputes within social theory represent a fascinating field of study in themselves, but they need not detain us. All we need note here is that there are some fundamental differences within the social sciences when it comes to defining what theory is and how it should be constructed and used, and that these differences are inevitably reflected in urban theory.

And so what on earth is urban theory?

Combining the definitions we have unearthed so far, we might describe urban theory as 'a body of ideas explaining one or more aspects of reality within, or of, towns and cities'. We have seen, however, that towns and cities in themselves are no longer seen as particularly useful units for social scientific analysis. It is also apparent that 'urban' is defined in such general terms that it is difficult to contrast it with anything. It therefore cannot help us greatly in isolating a field of study. What, then, does this simple definition of urban theory mean? The history of the last hundred years of social science provides two answers to that question. The more relaxed view is that it is perfectly permissible to say there are theories on the one hand and urban areas on the other and that urban theory is simply the first applied to or deduced from aspects of the second. The alternative view takes the much stricter line that each school within social science must clarify its core concepts and define its field of study carefully. If 'the urban' is not specific enough to define such a field then the theorist must come up with definitions that identify the 'theoretical object' of urban studies more precisely.

Nowadays the relaxed position is by far the most common. It is typified by Savage et al. (2003: 2) who claim that 'the fact that the urban cannot be defined in a general way does not mean that important things cannot be said about specific processes in particular cities!' The implication of this position is that urban theories are generated in one of two ways. In the first, theories that concern themselves with general social processes are applied – by the original theorists or others – to (or within) towns and cities. In the alternative, theories grow out of specific and consciously chosen 'urban' observations. There is no reason to believe, though, that theories derived from this second route will necessarily be any more 'urban' than those generated by the first. As we shall see, cities are sometimes seen as microcosms of societies, and there are examples of theoretical debates that had their origins in urban observations becoming more general and universal in scope.

No distinction is generally made between these two forms of urban theory. Michael Peter Smith's (1980) review of urban social theory, for example, discusses theorists such as Wirth, who devoted much of his time to urban analysis and research, and Simmel, who wrote specifically (but only in one of his many publications) on cities as the ultimate expression of modernity, where his main interests lay, in a relatively minor part of his contribution to the development of sociological theory more generally. But it also includes Freud, whose work made very few references to cities and towns or to urbanism. Smith justifies the latter choice by arguing that when Freud talks of civilisation, he is not just referring to an advanced state of social development but is dealing specifically with *urban* civilisation: 'Freud treats as indicators of "civilization" a variety of different ... socio-economic developments that originated or occurred almost exclusively in cities' (Smith, 1980: 50).

If Freud can be considered an urban theorist, or if Freudian psychoanalytic theory can at least be considered 'urban' when refocused and adapted by the likes of Smith, it is clear that the relaxed approach to the definition of urban theory – that it encompasses any application of concepts to urban phenomena – results in it covering a very broad canvas indeed. If we adopt this first position, though, such an eventuality cannot be avoided. The decision not to impose a tighter, limiting definition on 'the urban' means the range of issues that might be covered by urban theory is huge. The field expands every time there is a novel meeting between theory and urban phenomena and there are no conceptual boundaries other than those that theorists as a group effectively choose, through their work, to accept. Judge, Stoker and Wolman found this to be the case even within the single subdiscipline of urban politics: '[t]here are now *so many* theories that it is increasingly difficult for scholar and student alike to keep pace with them' (Judge et al., 1995: 1; emphasis in original).

The second, less relaxed position offers the prospect of a more restrictive and, arguably, more manageable focus for urban theory. Saunders (1985; 1986: 52–182) identifies a number of attempts to provide urban studies with a distinct theoretical focus. Each of them is reviewed briefly in the next chapter. Saunders concludes (1986: 51), however, that '[t]he result has, in most cases, been conceptual confusion and a series of theoretical dead-ends'. Not everyone would agree with this conclusion. Nor would it be fair to argue that conceptual confusion and theoretical dead-ends are limited to explorations within urban theory. For the purposes of this book, though, we will accept the view of Saunders and others that urban theory is not adequately defined by those attempts to provide urban studies with its own distinctive theoretical object. Such a focus would be too restrictive. In particular, it would exclude many recent theoretical debates that have important implications for cities but were not designed primarily as contributions to urban theory.

Accepting the relaxed position on the nature of urban theory, however, means a choice has to be made about which theories the book should cover and which should be excluded. Ultimately, this choice has to be based upon personal values and preferences about what is important. Nonetheless, it is easier to make with regard to older, more established theoretical approaches than it is with recent contributions. Previous reviews of the various urban subdisciplines impose a semblance of order upon theoretical debates that occurred up until the early 1980s. History has not pronounced so conclusively on more recent debates, however. The choice here will therefore need to be justified on the basis of some key propositions about what separates recent debates from previous ones. We return to this issue in the latter part of Chapter 2. In the first sections of that chapter, though, a brief review of the historical development of urban theory helps put the choice made here into perspective.

Questions for discussion

- Urban sociologists have tended to avoid geographical definitions of the city. Discuss the advantages and disadvantages of doing this.
- This chapter has identified a gap between urban theory and applied urban studies. What elements should theory include, in your view, to overcome this gap?
- Some scholars have argued that the urban is everywhere and that the rural or country has become obsolete as a concept. What arguments can you think of in favour or against this position?

Further reading

The philosophy of science/social science

The literature in this area is notoriously hard going. Blaikie's *Approaches to Social Enquiry* (1993) is an unusually lucid and readable introduction to the field and would be a good starting point for the uninitiated. Outhwaite's *New Philosophies of Social Science* (1987) offers a good overview of recent developments but is less user-friendly. Delanty's *Social Science* (1997), similarly, is up to date and includes useful sections on positivism and hermeneutics. Readers interested in learning more about one of the three approaches outlined above might start with Bryant's *Positivism in Social Theory and Research* (1985), Bauman's *Hermeneutics and Social Science* (1978) or, on realism, Sayer's *Method in Social Science* (1992).

Overviews of urban theory

As reported in the text, the better contributions tend to focus upon a single academic subject area rather than present an interdisciplinary picture. Saunders' *Social Theory and the Urban Question* (1986) is comprehensive and clearly written, but concentrates upon urban sociology and is now somewhat out of date. For those interested in the way individual theorists' understandings evolve over time, the 1981 version of that book provides interesting reading. Saunders' work might usefully be read in conjunction with Savage and

Warde's *Urban Sociology, Capitalism and Modernity* (2003) which is more eclectic but covers more recent material. Judge, Stoker, and Wolman's *Theories of Urban Politics* (1995) is a comprehensive, more up-to-date, edited volume covering the urban politics subfield. The early chapters of Dunleavy's *Urban Political Analysis* (1980) also contain a good, if dated, review of theoretical literature and discuss the validity of the urban' from a political science perspective. Theoretical approaches within urban geography can be covered by a selective reading of Carter's *The Study of Urban Geography* (1995), Herbert and Thomas' *Urban Geography* (1982), Hall's *Urban Geography* (2007), Johnston's *City and Society* (1980) and two books by Short, *An Introduction to Urban Geography* (1984) and *The Urban Order* (1996). Various recent readers assemble diverse writings from different disciplines. LeGates and Stout's *The City Reader* (2011) is a collection of twentieth-century writings on cities, grouped thematically, that includes some key theoretical contributions. Fainstein and Campbell's *Readings in Urban Theory* (2011) is more contemporary and explicitly theory-based but narrower in its coverage and dominated by US writers and has a focus on urban planning.

2

Urban theories under conditions of modernity

Learning objectives

- To understand the evolution of urban theory and the main theorists who have shaped its development
- To learn how the community power debate, humanistic geography and 'radical' approaches developed in reaction to the Chicago School and what their strengths and weaknesses were
- To examine the challenges urban theory has faced, subsequently, in a more globalised, interconnected and urbanised world

Introduction

This chapter provides an overview of the evolution of urban theories, beginning with what are often thought of as the 'founding fathers' – they were all men – of urban sociology at the University of Chicago. Through discussing the subsequent influence of neo-classical economics, we show how spatial analysis, in particular within geography, grew. While these perspectives tried to examine how people (and firms) responded to changing environments, the literature then moved to the question of why they did, bringing about the early perspectives, particularly in political science, on decision-making, for example the early community power debate. The 1960s and 1970s, generally seen as a turning point, then brought a form of radicalism into urban studies as well as a humanistic geography and a new urban sociology, arguing against the positivist perspective of earlier times. This cleared the ground for the turn to postmodernism that followed, which we will address briefly in the next chapter.

The task of tracing developments in urban theory over the course of a century, even within a single discipline, is not straightforward. Savage et al.'s (2003: 2) comment that 'the history of urban sociology is discontinuous, unamenable to an account of its linear evolution around a single theme' could easily be applied to developments within other disciplines. Given that subdisciplines do not develop logically, it is unsurprising that the theories they draw upon do not exhibit much more order. In the terms used in Chapter 1, we do not find, for example, that positivist approaches gave way at a critical juncture to others drawing upon hermeneutics and that these, in turn, were supplanted by realism. Paradoxically, though, the fact that the boundaries between urban disciplines are so fuzzy and that each is influenced by wider debates within social science makes the job simpler than might be expected. In fact there is a surprising measure of agreement on the key schools and landmark debates in geography, politics and sociology that have had most impact on the way urban areas are viewed and studied. These are briefly examined in turn.

The Chicago School and urban ecology

The work of the Chicago School of urban sociology in the inter-war years is generally seen as the first significant flowering of urban theory. Park, Burgess, and McKenzie (1925) borrowed from biological sciences, just as early European sociologists such as Herbert Spencer and August Comte had done (Mazlish, 1989, Collins, 1985: 121–36). They had developed a social Darwinism or social evolutionary thinking, where principles from the natural world were thought to work for social facts as well. Their inspiration stems, in particular, from Charles Darwin's (1859) arguments about (a) the competition that occurs between and within species for access to life-sustaining features of the natural environment, and (b) the process of natural selection – interpreted by Spencer (1864) as 'the survival of the fittest' – that results from this competition. Urban ecologists used the biological concepts of competition, selection, invasion, succession and dominance to explain two central aspects of urban life: first, how adaptation to urban environments by a city's population is shaped by competition between the communities and interests within it; and second, how processes of adaptation, in turn, affect the environment – that is, the physical form cities take. Park described the city as a mosaic of social worlds, where each group would find its natural habitat among equals, the idea being that various groups live in close proximity but are separated into their own environments. The image he had was of a smooth, conflict-free, peaceful coexistence. This sifting and sorting produced an urban morphology with a hierarchical structure, as Burgess described.

Burgess' concentric zone model

Burgess' (1924, 1925, 1927) famous 'concentric zone model' of the city, based on the city of Chicago, makes conceptual links between a particular physical form and the quasi-biological processes of sifting and sorting. It presents a simple picture of the morphology of the city in which rings of successively higher-status housing are found as one travels further away from the central business district and the inner-city 'zone in transition' that surrounds it. This pattern is then explained through a process of 'invasion and succession' that stems from population expansion and economic growth. On one hand, poor newcomers constantly arrive in the inner city. On the other hand, the central business district expands and its relatively high rents displace lower-value commercial, industrial and residential uses. These two factors encourage a progressive out-movement of population – suburbanisation – in which each city ring is colonised by inhabitants of the one inside it whilst the most affluent residents create new outer rings. Within each of the areas, cultural homogeneity occurs, while at the same time these areas are thought to generate their own cultures, determining the behaviour of their residents. As we will see in Chapter 6, what later developed as cultural understandings of the ghetto and even neighbourhood effect studies can be traced back to this particular assumption about the spatiality of community and culture.

Burgess' work, like that of most of his Chicago School colleagues, is classically positivist social science. It clearly draws upon the natural sciences. Urban ecology's concern with urban morphology also lends itself well to quantitative measurement and to forms of theorisation that deal with the outcomes of human behaviour – patterns of migration, of social segregation, land use and so on – rather than what causes them or their meanings for those who take part.

Criticism

It is these features of urban ecology, rather than the questionable relevance of models such as Burgess' for the experience of other cities, that proved most controversial. Members of the Chicago School were accused, for example, of representing the urban social processes they observed as organic and 'natural', so that they failed to acknowledge that they were the product not of 'blind' biological imperatives, but of human choices whose contexts could feasibly be altered by collective acts of will. Moreover, they failed to pay attention to unequal power positions and the role of politics in the way in which the city was socially organised.

Urban ecologists were therefore easily derided as apologists for the status quo who saw urban inequality and social segregation as inevitable, even necessary for the preservation of urban populations. Such criticisms acquired a more legitimate target with the development of 'structural functionalism' in sociology (Parsons, 1951), another quasi-biological mode of sociological explanation. Structural functionalists *are* conservative in so far as they tend to argue that anything that does not lead to disorder and destabilisation is functional to the preservation of a given social system. Society will always move, they assume, towards an equilibrium that is 'natural'; conflicts are seen as distortions and those diverting from the mainstream as 'deviant'. In the study of deviance and crime, the so-called social disorganisation thesis developed by Shaw and McKay (1942), both members of the Chicago School, for example, explained youth crime by arguing that the concentration of migrants and poverty in inner-city areas created a living environment that lacked the basic cohesion and social control (hence the term disorganisation) needed for a healthy community. From that starting point, functionalist approaches to crime and deviance flourished.

The charge of conservatism sticks less easily to urban ecologists, however, who always acknowledged that human communities were the product of culture and co-operation as well as biology and competition. Park and Wirth, in particular, were prominent reformists, and Park's belief in a better, more equal society becomes most obvious in his writings on race and prejudice, which he thought of not as functional, but as a temporary state that could be overcome by information and education (Park, 1950: 250). Both believed biological analogies played an important role in social scientific explanation but readily advocated public sector intervention in many of the processes they studied in order to correct 'man-made' urban problems. Indeed, one of the aims of the Chicago School was to provide just such a productive link between scientific analysis and policy-making. Their strong focus on communities, geographically understood but defined by ethnicity and class, and the ecological determinism that their approach invited are, however, problematic, especially for urban policy. Ecological determinism occurs when variables such as high poverty rates that are attributed to a district become ascribed to individuals within that area – people who come from an area with high poverty must be poor – which of course becomes particularly salient when areas are seen as 'containing' cultures, including morals.

Important for the development of urban theory is that the Chicago School as a whole cannot, however, be pigeon-holed as positivist. Its 'ethnographic' work – for example, *The Polish Peasant* (Thomas & Znaniecki, 1918–20), based on life-history interviews with Polish immigrants – lay firmly within the hermeneutic tradition and generated very detailed accounts of the lives and perceptions of Chicago's different ethnic and racial groups, as well as social groups such as the bohemians in *The Hobo* (Anderson, 1923) and the female dancers dancing with patrons for money in *The Taxi-Dance Hall* (Cressey, 1932). These Chicago

School researchers were amongst the first to use 'participant observation' – a technique in which the researcher shares, as far as possible, in the day-to-day experiences of research partners and tries to understand the world as he/she sees it – in an urban setting.

These empirically oriented strands of the Chicago School produced urban theory of the sort identified by our more relaxed definition. That is, they either based theoretical statements on what were considered specifically 'urban' observations or they applied more general concepts to urban phenomena. However, with Park, McKenzie (1924) and Zorbaugh's (1930) writings on urban ecology, and especially with Louis Wirth, the School also contributed to urban theory in the stricter sense. Wirth initially worked within the intellectual framework of his PhD advisor, Robert Park, on a famous study, *The Ghetto* (1928), which dealt historically with the ways of life of Chicago's newly arriving Jewish immigrants (of which Wirth's family was one) and the origins and characteristics of the ghetto. Besides his work on mass communication and socio-psychological analysis, he continued to work on the city and urban ecology. His attempt to specify the theoretical concerns of the School is probably the most famous urban theory article ever written.

Wirth's urbanism thesis

In 'Urbanism as a way of life', Wirth (1938) made what turned out to be the last major attempt to demonstrate the theoretical value of the urban–rural distinction. He isolated three characteristics of 'urbanism' that, he argued, were central to towns and cities and therefore provided the basis of a distinctive urban way of life: size, density and heterogeneity. For Wirth, differences in these three factors accounted for all the major contrasts between different types of human settlement. Those differences, however, would not be so stark that 'urbanism' would cease and 'ruralism' begin at an arbitrary city boundary. Rather, places could be more or less urban or rural; that is, they would range along a continuum between ideal types of urbanism and ruralism, neither of which would necessarily be found, in pure form, in reality.

Wirth argued that a number of personal, social and organisational traits flow from the fact that cities are big, dense, socially heterogeneous places. His city was an uncomfortable, alienating and socially fractured place. Drawing upon Simmel (Wolff, 1950), he saw urbanism as characterised by individual anonymity and personal relationships that lacked intimacy and were more likely to be superficial, transitory or based upon financial transactions. In contrast to Simmel (1950), for whom the freedom that the anonymity of the city provided was most important, Wirth saw anonymity as isolating and the cause of social pathologies. Socially, urbanism was associated with high levels of mobility, instability and insecurity within communities, but at any one point in time people tended to reside within segregated 'natural areas' that were glaringly different in terms of lifestyles and life chances. Institutionally, urbanism was argued to depend upon formal and repressive, rather than informal, social controls and on the mass provision of services by government. Urban citizens were seen as individually powerless, their only influence over the society in which they lived being through membership of organised groups. Wirth talked rather less about ruralism, but some of his followers lent credence to his arguments by finding characteristics that were the obverse of his ideal type of urbanism in rural areas (Redfield, 1947).

Wirth's deductive theory is nonetheless adjudged a failure, if a glorious one. Initial criticisms suggested his generalisations were empirically inaccurate and that 'urbanist' traits were common in rural areas, as was 'ruralism' in the city, for example within some of the close-knit, homogenous 'urban villages' discovered by Gans (1962). Given that there is constant movement and migration between country and town, however, it was not surprising that urban and rural characteristics – assuming they were really distinct – became spatially intermingled. Saunders (1986: 104–5) defends Wirth against such criticisms and makes the point that, strictly speaking, they could not invalidate his theory anyway. Urbanism, as an ideal type concept, would not be 'disproven' even if the characteristics it defined turned out to be found only in rural areas. Such empirical evidence would, however, mean the conceptual value of 'urbanism' was questionable as the city would not be the cause of the urban way of life. In fact it is the usefulness of Wirth's categories, rather than any shortcomings of his ideal types, that is the main problem with his analysis. Gans (1968), for example, argues persuasively that many of the characteristics Wirth deduced from the attributes of size, density and homogeneity (a) were arguably relevant to inner-city areas but not beyond, (b) could be 'caused' by other urban attributes such as high residential turnover, and (c) applied only to the least mobile urban groups. Gans argued that differences in lifestyle were compositional differences, following not from the city as such but from the composite characteristics of city residents.

The Chicago School legacy

For all its limitations, the Chicago School left a substantial legacy that is not just confined to its influence on later generations of (urban) ecology. It made at least three more significant contributions. First, it established positivist and hermeneutic traditions within urban theory and research. Second, it suggested that a geographical definition of cities was inadequate for social scientific purposes and that others based upon some key attributes of urban areas, whether or not they followed Wirth's lead, might be more appropriate. Third, it established research interests in urban morphology, social segregation, and communities, culture and ethnicity within cities. Each had an impact on the way subsequent urban studies were conducted and what they focused upon.

Urban geography and spatial analysis

The Chicago School was dominated by sociologists, but its concern with the morphology of cities was primarily taken forward by the discipline that has most interest in the spatial patterns associated with human behaviour – human geography. However, urban geography established a niche for itself within human geography, not by building upon approaches based on evolutionary biology, but by drawing heavily upon neo-classical economics and, to a lesser extent, geometry. This change of orientation is not as pronounced as it might seem. In fact there are strong conceptual parallels between evolutionary biology and neo-classical economics.

Both approaches see competition as the major source of change in the 'universes' they study but argue, at the same time, that economies and populations tend towards a 'natural' equilibrium. For neo-classical economists, the competition is for profit and takes place between different economic producers. The equilibrium represents the most efficient use of resources within an economy (not to be confused with the fairest use of resources, however defined). For approaches that draw upon evolutionary biology, the competition is for territories that best sustain life and takes place between or within species (for natural scientists) or between different social groups (for social scientists). For urban ecologists, equilibrium is represented by a pattern of land use in which different urban groups have sorted themselves into the local environments to which they are best suited. Both approaches accept that equilibria are prone to disturbance by external shocks – a sudden influx of population, say, or a steep rise in the cost of raw materials – but argue that such upheavals trigger off new processes of competition which lead, in turn, to new equilibria.

The difference between the two approaches is in what is seen to drive the process of competition. For evolutionary biologists, it is the survival instinct. For neo-classical economists it is *utility maximisation*. The essential building block of neo-classical economics is 'economic man' [sic] who bases every choice he makes upon rational calculations about what is good for him, economically; that is, upon his 'personal utility'. All neo-classical predictions about markets and economic behaviour rest upon the assumption that all individuals are utility maximisers and, although not meant in a biological way, that this is natural, essential human behaviour. Urban geographers borrowed the idea of utility maximisation but gave it a spatial twist. Economic approaches within urban geography thus adopted the 'nearest centre assumption'; that is, the proposition that utility-maximising individuals will always minimise the distance they travel to satisfy their wants and needs.

The influence of neo-classical economics on geography

The influence of neo-classical economics enabled geographers to expand the focus of urban studies from the Chicago School's concern with the spatial patterns made by human activities *within* urban areas to one that also examined the patterns made *by* urban areas. The focus upon patterns within cities continued in studies of the economics of urban land use (Alonso, 1960), social area analysis (Shevky & Bell, 1955) and factorial ecology (Davies, 1984) where factors related to housing and socio-economic characteristics are worked out and used to divide the city into a number of distinctive, smaller areas with the use of the technique of factor analyses.

A concern with the patterns made *by* urban areas developed from 'central place theory' (Christaller & Baskin, 1966). This focused upon the development of 'urban systems' and attempted to explain what determines the number, size and distribution of urban centres within a larger territory. Geometry played a substantial part in the analysis of urban systems, as it did in the wider 'spatial analysis' or 'spatial science' movement of which central place theory formed an important part (Haggett, 1965). Other branches of spatial analysis specialised in various aspects of location theory (Lösch, 1965) and generated 'laws' to explain, for example, the distribution and siting of particular types of industrial plant and retail outlet.

The various approaches within spatial analysis dominated post-war urban geography into the 1970s and generated an enormous literature that cannot be summarised here. However, they shared some common characteristics. First, spatial analysis was more technologically driven than other conceptual approaches in urban studies. It played a central part in geography's 'quantitative revolution' that was made possible by the huge technological strides taken in data-collection capacity and data-manipulation techniques during the 1950s and 1960s (Johnston, 1979: 41–111). Second, it represented the high water mark of positivist approaches within urban studies (Harvey, 1969). Improvements in data storage and handling made it possible to use much larger volumes of information for research and theory-building. This made the use of quantitative methods, and inductive approaches in particular, much easier (Isard, 1960; Bunge, 1962). Third, spatial analysis was closely linked to developments in urban and regional planning. It peaked at a time when there was much more confidence than there is today that rational, technical solutions could be found for all of society's major problems. Spatial analysis, with its claims to be able to model the present and forecast the future, complemented this world-view perfectly, with the result that positivist urban geography dominated the conceptual agenda of planners for many years (Hall, 1988).

Criticism

Ironically it was these three characteristics of spatial analysis that critics later used to question it (Harvey, 1973; Cox, 1995). Even before the 1970s, however, when positivist approaches came under greatest attack, the limitations of spatial analysis were apparent even to theorists who were broadly sympathetic to positivism. The reliance upon neo-classical economic assumptions, in particular, was seen as too restrictive and attempts were made by behavioural geographers to provide urban geography with more sophisticated conceptual foundations. Behavioural approaches in the social sciences are generally amongst the most positivist in their orientation. They typically reject approaches that are based upon the theorist's notion of how people *should* behave in favour of one that analyses how people *do* behave in response to various stimuli. Being positivist, they are, of course, less interested in *why* people behave as they do. Behaviourism generally assumes that the social sciences should only be concerned with behaviour that can actually be observed, not with underlying motivations, ideas or emotions. It shares with functionalism the assumption that people behave the way they do because it is beneficial to them.

The first behavioural geographers followed in the positivist tradition and remained within the confines of spatial analysis (e.g. Pred, 1967; Toyne, 1974). They borrowed an argument – this time from organisational theory (Simon, 1957) – that proclaimed the archetypal 'economic man' of neo-classical economics to be a misleading fiction. No real individual, argued Simon, has the time, knowledge, capacity or inclination to consider every factor that could be shown to be relevant to even a single utility-maximising (or distance-minimising) decision. Since perfect knowledge is impossible, individuals decide on the basis of 'bounded rationality'. Rather than maximise their utility, they 'satisfice'; that is, they make choices from a restricted number of easily available alternatives on the basis of what will do rather than what is best.

The idea that satisficing was the basis of 'real' decision-making was supported by a new generation of locational analysts. Initially the notion that people satisfice rather than maximise their utility was simply used as an alternative behavioural assumption on which to base positivist research. Soon, however, researchers were examining not only *how* people and firms responded to environmental stimuli through their locational behaviour but also *why* they made the choices they did; that is, they studied processes of decision-making. In time, the concern with individual perceptions and choices meant certain behavioural geographers moved away from both spatial analysis and positivist explanation altogether. They formed one strand of humanistic geography that is sceptical of any theoretical approach that assumes, rather than examines, human perceptions and motivations. Just as they had within the Chicago School, then, positivist approaches in urban geography ultimately brought forth rival traditions more influenced by hermeneutics.

The community power debate

Urban ecology's interest in 'communities' was taken up in numerous sociological community studies that focused upon anything from city neighbourhoods to entire small towns (Bell & Newby, 1971), with a tradition evolving in Britain in the Institute of Community Studies through the work of Young, author of various studies on East London with Willmott (e.g. Young & Willmott, 1979). These studies had in common that they approached the places they studied as bounded, within the borders of which social phenomena could be understood (Stacey, 1969), often treating the community as the life-world of individuals as if they had no relations or interdependencies with people elsewhere (Blokland-, 2003a; Wellman & Leighton, 1979). Generally speaking, '[t]he theoretical input into these studies was extremely crude' (Dunleavy, 1980: 28). However, they provided the context for one of the major conceptual and methodological controversies in urban studies; the community power debate of the 1950s and 1960s. The idea that community studies should focus more precisely upon the issue of power was a reaction to studies based upon ecological and economic principles that made it seem that human activities in cities were ordered not by the actions and decisions of individuals, but by intangible mechanisms, be they 'the hidden hand of the market' or 'impersonal competition' arising from biological programming. For all their differences, the main protagonists in the community power debate – pluralists and elite theorists of one form or another – agreed on one thing: that power was a property of people, not of abstractions. They were 'methodologically individualist'; that is, they saw individuals as the basic explanatory unit for all social phenomena in the last instance.

Community power: elite theory versus pluralism

The community power debate began when Hunter (1953), a sociologist, asked 'who runs Atlanta?' In attempting to answer that question, he adopted what became known as 'reputational analysis'. First, he tested the extent to which 'four groups that may be assumed to have power connections ... [in] ... business, government, civic associations, and "society" activities' (Hunter, 1953: 11) were reputed to be powerful by their peers. Having ranked the responses and identified a long list of perceived 'community influentials', Hunter then interviewed the top-ranked individuals to ascertain who amongst them was seen as most powerful, how they interacted, how they grouped themselves in relation to key 'community projects' and how their influence over these projects was channelled. Using this method, Hunter claimed to identify a small clique of 'policy-makers' that collectively were said to determine all the major decisions taken within the city. The clique was overwhelmingly dominated by senior executives of the city's key businesses. Only one member – Atlanta's mayor – held public office. Hunter was therefore able to offer 'scientific proof' that local representative democracy provided a smokescreen for dominant economic interests and that nothing in the governance of Atlanta moved if it did not originate within, or gain the approval of, a business-dominated elite. This conclusion about the urban 'power structure' established Hunter as the father of US urban elite theory.

Hunter was criticised by pluralist scholars, largely political scientists, who argued that a methodology that relied on reputations could not possibly prove anything about power. What was needed was evidence of the way power was *actually* used in particular decision-making situations. Dahl (1961) applied 'decisional analysis' in a classic study that asked 'who, if anyone, runs New Haven?' and came to the conclusion that no one did in an absolute sense. Having examined decision-making in a number of policy areas, Dahl argued that whilst some individuals were particularly influential within one area, none had influence across the board. In other words, power, although by no means equally shared across all social groups, was sufficiently diffused for rule by an elite – particularly an unelected one – to be impossible. Other pluralist community power studies (e.g. Banfield, 1966) supported Dahl's argument that local representative democracy worked in that many different groups could influence decisions and there were enough checks and balances within the system to prevent the centralisation or abuse of power.

Pluralists were attacked, in turn, by neo-elite theorists who did not favour Hunter's reputational method but insisted that decisional analysis was also inadequate for the purposes of measuring power. Neo-elitists argued that the decision points studied by pluralists were purely arbitrary and that decisional analysis was blind to the way policy agendas were set. Pluralists could not prove that the decisions they studied represented the most important points at which power was exercised, nor that the issues those decisions dealt with were critical to the city's most powerful people. For neo-elitists, the power used to make concrete decisions represented only one face of power. A second face, involving 'non-decision-making', sees the powerful act to ensure that only those issues that are comparatively innocuous to them ever reach the point of decision. Thus the weak mini-elites identified by pluralists in different policy areas may have been decisive in disputes over issues that were on the agenda laid before them, but that agenda could already have been neutralised so as to be unthreatening to the 'real' elite (Bachrach & Baratz, 1962, 1970).

Moving urban theory forward: gains and criticisms

The community power debate began as a struggle between opposing approaches in urban theory, but it quickly outgrew its urban origins. It triggered an unresolved and ever more abstract debate about power that was taken up by political and social theorists who had no academic interest in urban studies (Lukes, 1974; Foucault, 1980). That community power theorists did not have the last word on the issue of power is therefore unsurprising. They can, however, take credit for moving urban theory on in at least three ways. First, in emphasising decision-making, they, like certain behavioural geographers, underlined the importance of 'human agency' and moved away from the idea that patterns of human activity were somehow determined by impersonal forces alone, or were simply 'natural' and explained by their function. Second, they raised important issues about 'who benefits' from urban decision-making and demonstrated that urban theory could be critical and normative as well as analytical and descriptive. Third, in being unusually transparent about their concepts and methodologies, they encouraged an informed and open, if ultimately frustrating, theoretical debate.

The way in which the debate about power developed was nonetheless suggestive, again, of the limits to positivist urban theory. Community power theories drew upon very different forms of 'observable' behaviour. Reputational analysis, on its own, proved unsatisfactory because it inferred rather than proved the use of power. Decisional analysis, on the other hand, claimed to observe the use of power directly, but was able to do so only in situations where there was evidence of a conflict of interest over a specific decision; that is, when the powerful clearly triumphed over the less powerful. Pluralist methods could not cope with the idea that the use of power may not be associated with conflict and that people may be quiescent for reasons other than their satisfaction with decisions. In trying to allow for such possibilities, subsequent theories of power had to delve deeper into abstractions, such as the role of ideology and the difference between 'real' and perceived needs, which are not readily observable and are therefore beyond the purview of positivist approaches.

The conceptual and methodological difficulties associated with the 'power' side of the community power equation were the main focus for critics of urban elite and pluralist theorists. However, there was also concern with the 'community' side. Hunter and Dahl were urban theorists in the relaxed sense of the term, but, as advocates of particular approaches and methods, they were theorists first and urbanists some way behind. They were not terribly interested in making specific arguments about Atlanta and New Haven. Rather, they assumed those two cities were microcosms of (US) society and went on to draw general conclusions about the pros and cons of (US) liberal democracy. In seeing cities as relatively self-contained social systems, however, they played down the influence that external decisions – for example, by non-local investors and higher levels of government – had over the nature of local power and the scope of decisions made locally. They treated the cities they studied as if they existed in a social and political vacuum where only local actors were involved. The 'localism' of the community power debate set precedents for urban theory that were not critically re-examined for some time.

Humanistic (urban) geography

The late 1960s and early 1970s are generally seen as a turning point in the social sciences. The crisis is usually characterised as a struggle by 'radical' approaches – particularly those drawing upon Marxism – to challenge and overturn dominant, largely positivist orthodoxies. The form that radicalism took with respect to urban theory is examined below. As in other fields, however, it grew out of frustration with the fact that social science theory did not appear to recognise, far less articulate or support, the grievances of those groups who shared least in the fruits of capitalist economic expansion. It is an irony of Marxist approaches that an analysis that usually originates in a concern for 'oppressed' people invariably ends up according little or no role to 'human agency'. There were other critics, however, who were less interested in material inequality but *did* challenge positivists on the issue of human agency, expounding a belief that social sciences had to turn away from finding the objective truth and should pay attention to subjectivism. Berger and Luckmann (1966), for example, pleaded for a social constructivist approach to the social sciences. They were concerned with the functionalist assumption that social order reached an equilibrium if all went well, as this perspective hampered social change, including politically progressive change. Such scholars argued that positivism simplified or ignored the complexity of people as individuals; for example, by making assumptions about human motivations and representing collective behaviour simply by dots and lines on maps in the case of spatial analysis. This current of thought is central to humanistic geography and social constructivist sociology which take 'meaning' and 'subjectivity' particularly seriously and therefore gravitate toward forms of analysis that are closely related to hermeneutics.

Post-positivist approaches

Humanistic geography, within which we include cultural geography, is a collection of disparate 'post-positivist' approaches rather than a single approach and, as such, is not easily summarised. Cloke, Philo, and Sadler (1991: 57–92), however, argue that it can roughly be divided into two groups that have contrasting reasons for taking an interest in subjectivity. The first is concerned with the subjectivity of the *researcher* and the implications that follow for the status of 'truth' and how it can be established. The second is more concerned with the subjectivity of the *researched* – 'real' people in the 'real' world – and what that means for the focus and methods of research. The first group tends to emphasise ontological and epistemological issues, whilst the second concentrates more upon methodological ones. Since the debates that have taken place within and between these two groups are not especially 'urban', and since urban subject matter is incidental to humanistic geography, we will consider them only briefly. They nonetheless demonstrate, once more, how approaches allied to hermeneutics offered challenges and alternatives to positivism.

Both groups within humanistic geography are primarily interested in two things: how people – researchers and researched – experience and understand the everyday 'life-world'; and the way particular places acquire 'meaning' from the subjective interpretations attributed to them. The differences between them mirror the alternative hermeneutic approaches to subjectivity identified in Chapter 1, in that one tends towards relativism whilst the other argues that objective conclusions can be based upon subjective raw material. Debate within the first group is particularly abstract and dense. It generally starts from the phenomenological argument that the realm of subjective meaning cannot be compared with the positivist world of empirical facts but it can and must still be amenable to 'scientific' study. This argument presupposes an alternative, non-positivist approach, hence much of the debate concerns the philosophical ramifications of such a position. Some phenomenologists argue that perceptions have their own 'essences' that exist independently of individuals and can be uncovered in various ways by the theorist (Relph, 1970). Others, including some existentialists (Entrikin, 1976), reject the notion of universal essences but propose that a fuller understanding of the meaning of places can be gleaned by synthesising the 'objective'/scientific knowledge of the researcher and the 'subjective'/everyday views of the researched. In both cases, subjective perceptions are seen as useful in so far as they facilitate the discovery of important features of places but to have no intrinsic value in themselves (Pickles, 1985).

Other, less abstract approaches are more interested in understanding the 'life-worlds' of the researched as an end in itself. Idealists (Guelke, 1974) take this line because, they argue, the only 'theories' worth examining if one is interested in human behaviour are those in the heads of the researched rather than the researcher. Pragmatists (Frazier, 1981; Jackson & Smith, 1984) adopt a similar position in arguing that people basically come to understand by doing; that is, they extend or modify their theories of the way the world works by periodically re-evaluating their 'taken-for-granted worlds' in the light of 'real' experiences which throw them into doubt.

Consequences for methods

In practical terms, humanistic geography is primarily associated with research into small localities which traces the relationship between 'place, group and life-world'; that is, how places acquire 'meaning' and the extent to which people's understandings are shaped by the types of place they inhabit and the shared social experiences they have within them. It is even more localist in its orientation than community studies were.

The work which resulted from these interests bears a close resemblance to ethnographic studies conducted by members of the Chicago School, a debt acknowledged by exponents such as Geertz (1993) and Jackson (1985). In contrast to that earlier generation of studies, though, more recent ethnographic work has rarely been undertaken as a self-conscious attempt to improve understandings of *urban* life and tends to consist of studies of phenomena and groups that happen to be in the city, but where the question of how the city may be relevant has almost completely disappeared. Excellent ethnographies in sociology and urban anthropology such as Liebow's (1967) *Tally's Corner*, Williams' (1990) *Cocaine Kids*, Newman's (1999) *No Shame in My Game* (on the working poor) and Jones' (2009) *Between the Good and Ghetto* (on girls' deviance) have been produced, but have contributed little to urban theory.

A notable exception in geography is the contribution of Ley, who in his empirical and theoretical work and his evaluations of other theorists has invariably retained a focus upon the city and its neighbourhoods. Ley's work is eclectic and draws upon many of the approaches discussed in this chapter (Ley, 1983). However, his contribution to humanistic geography includes some pioneering work (Ley, 1974) in which he used a variety of 'people-sensitive' techniques – including participant observation, analyses of social networks and the 'mapping' of cultural phenomena such as graffiti that had previously been ignored by geographers – to understand the life-worlds of various groups within the black community in inner-city Philadelphia. Other exceptions lie outside geography, with scholars like Loïc Wacquant (2008), Philippe Bourgois (1995), Mitch Duneier (1999) and Elijah Anderson (1990a, 2000). Ley's work is less abstract and more accessible than that of many humanistic geographers, but it does not escape the two major, if paradoxical, criticisms levelled at this sub-field as a whole. One is that, in concentrating on micro-scale studies designed to do least damage to the complexity and integrity of individuals who (they say) should always be the ultimate focus for research, humanistic geographers escape the simplifying generalisations of positivism only by retreating into triviality. Cloke et al. (1991: 84), for example, note ironically that Rowles (1978) goes 'beyond the "navel-gazing" of ... existing ... literature' by exhaustively studying 'the geographical experience of five elderly people living in Winchester Street, an inner-city neighbourhood of an eastern US city'(!) The opposite criticism is that humanistic geography does not really escape the straitjacket of positivism because it takes subjective experiences at face value and is therefore unable to penetrate through to the 'real' but unobservable forces that influence them. To complete this review, we turn to 'radical' approaches, some of which claimed to be able to do just that.

'Radical' approaches

Radical approaches in urban theory are one academic expression of the strong 'anti-establishment' movement of the late 1960s. The landmark year of 1968, in particular, witnessed profound demonstrations of dissatisfaction with the post-war order across the Western industrialised world. 'Radical' social scientists who were part of the 'post-'68 generation' channelled this critical spirit in many different ways but were united in two important respects. First, they found positivist social science profoundly conservative in that it theorised about and described how things were but gave few indications that they could be different, far less better. For some followers of Karl Marx, in particular, this made social science as it was then predominantly practised 'ideological' in at least two senses. On the one hand, it helped propound an ostensibly 'objective' world-view that effectively legitimised the narrow interests of those in power. On the other hand, it failed to get below the surface of events and therefore gave a distorted picture of 'reality'. Second, radicals saw the reformulation of theory as a step on the road to fundamental social change.

The goal radicals set themselves, then, was to develop a social science which was simultaneously more penetrating and more supportive of the liberation of humankind in a general sense. In practice, these two objectives were not always easy to reconcile and the liberatory intent and potential of some theories was often difficult to discern. In principle, though, radicals followed Engels in seeing the point of academic endeavour as being not so much to understand the world as to change it. In urban theory, the radical movement was heavily influenced by Marx but it also drew upon Max Weber. Neo-Marxists, neo-Weberians and their sympathisers acquired strong profiles in urban geography (Peet, 1977), urban sociology (Pickvance, 1976; Saunders, 1979; Harloe, 1981; Elliott & Maccrone, 1982), urban politics (Dunleavy, 1980) and urban planning (Dear & Scott, 1981) and came to dominate the pages of 'radical' journals such as *Antipode*, founded in 1969, and the *International Journal of Urban and Regional Research*, founded in 1977. Whilst they share a critical predisposition, though, theorists within these two traditions differ in important respects. We begin with neo-Marxism.

Neo-Marxism

Followers of Marx have a *materialist* view of society in which production – the way humans organise to satisfy their material needs and desires – plays the dominant role. Depending on which reading of Marx one favours, the 'mode of production' operating in any given society either determines the way it is organised, socially and politically, or is the single most powerful influence. Marx recognised that various modes of production have existed in history but concentrated upon the one that dominated his era (and every successive one), capitalism. Capitalism, for Marx, is characterised by relations of production in which a privileged group of capital owners generate profits for themselves by exploiting the mass of people who must sell their labour power in order to survive. However, capitalism is inherently crisis-prone and contains the seeds of its own destruction. On the one hand, antagonism between capital owners and their increasingly organised workforces finds expression in the class struggle that, for Marx at least, could ultimately have only one winner. On the other hand, the rapacious competition between producers is self-defeating as it inevitably leads to crises of 'over-accumulation' in which too many goods or services are produced, prices fall, levels of profit decline and firms are driven out of business. Thus capitalism is characterised by a process of 'creative destruction' (Schumpeter, 1944) in which firms constantly try to steal a march on their rivals – through introducing new technologies, shedding labour, and reducing costs – but cannot maintain their competitive edge indefinitely.

Neo-Marxists accept this basic analysis but, with the benefit of more than a century's worth of hindsight, they are more sceptical than Marx about capitalism's self-destructive tendencies and pay considerably more attention to its durability. Indeed, two major attempts to adapt Marx's thought for the purposes of 'radical' urban theory – through the work of David Harvey (1973) in geography and Manuel Castells (1974) in sociology – can be interpreted as analyses of how certain 'urban' features help stabilise capitalism and dampen down, if not avert, its crisis tendencies. Harvey and Castells, however, adopt very different approaches and draw upon alternative strands within the Marxist tradition. For

Harvey, at least in his early Marxist work, the critical issue is how cities contribute to the preservation of capitalism by offering investment opportunities for 'spare' capital. Castells, by contrast, is – or rather was – primarily interested in the way the public sector helps manage capitalism by supporting the reproduction of the labour force.

Harvey's pre-Marxist work was firmly in the positivist tradition. His radicalisation, however, saw him turn to Marx and draw, in particular, upon his analysis of the institution of land ownership and the notion of rent. Harvey finds these concepts useful in examining the way capital becomes tied to the fortunes of particular places but he extends and translates them into a contemporary urban context (Harvey, 1973, 1982, 1985a, 1985b). His best-known argument is that over-accumulation crises can be displaced or averted because investment can be switched between different 'circuits of capital'. Harvey sees industrial production – the main focus for Marx's analysis of capitalism – as only one aspect of the productive process. It represents the primary and most important circuit of capital. When there is over-accumulation in this primary circuit, however, investment can be switched into a secondary circuit in which profits depend more upon rent than production. The secondary circuit comprises 'fixed capital', which includes aspects of the built environment linked to production (offices, etc.), and the 'consumption fund', which includes aspects of the built environment linked to consumption (houses, etc.). Harvey also identifies a tertiary circuit of capital that comprises investments in the labour force – 'human capital' – and science and technology, both of which indirectly support production.

The three circuits of capital offer alternative investment possibilities, but each is prone to over-accumulation crises. If profitability cannot be maintained by 'playing' the three circuits within a given territory, there remains the option of the 'spatial fix' in which investments in the built environment of particular places are written off entirely, capital is shifted to new locations and the whole process of crisis management begins again. Harvey's analysis offers useful insights into the uneven 'production of space'; that is, how urban areas around the globe grow and decline at different rates at different times in a capitalist system. It highlights the tension between businesses' restless search for profit and the ties to particular locations that result from the investments businesses sink into their built fabric. It also provides a plausible account of the cycles of boom and bust in urban property development. Although he claimed to produce a 'theory of urbanisation', however, Harvey is an urban theorist only in the relaxed sense of the term. He accords analytical priority to the general process of wealth creation and sees the characteristics of urban areas as dependent upon it. Other radical urban theorists went further and, like Wirth, attempted to provide the field of urban studies with its own 'theoretical object'.

Castells is the key neo-Marxist in this respect. Rather than draw directly upon Marx, Castells, in his early work at least, adopted the approach of another neo-Marxist, Louis Althusser. Althusser is a 'structuralist' Marxist who takes very seriously Marx's assertion that the 'truth' about capitalist societies cannot be understood by examining 'surface' phenomena. What he considers necessary, instead, is an appreciation of the underlying 'structures' – essential relations between things – that order surface appearances. Structuralism, then, is a close relative of realism. At least in Althusser's version, however, it departs from realism in two respects. First, it allows no role whatever for empirical 'facts'. Structures, for Althusser, can only be discovered through a process of intellectual production that builds upon but transcends existing abstract concepts. They cannot be identified inductively or deductively with the aid of observation. Second, Althusser did not just claim superiority for structuralist Marxism. He declared it a science and contrasted it with all other social science approaches that were deemed mere ideologies (Althusser, 1969; Althusser & Balibar, 1970).

Castells Mk I initially followed Althusser's non-empirical, anti-positivist lead and did his best to demonstrate that all previous urban theory was ideological whereas his was scientific (Castells, 1977). He also borrowed from Althusserian structuralism a rejection of any role for human agency in the analysis of social change. Structuralists see humans as conductors for social relations over which they have no control, not as significant agents in their own right. Their theories therefore deal with the relations, understood in the abstract, not the agents. Castells used an Althusserian approach to contribute to a debate about the role of 'the state' in managing and preserving capitalism, an issue which exercised many neo-Marxists at that time. Orthodox Marxist analysis, it was argued, had concentrated too much upon issues of market production and wage labour and overlooked two important features of contemporary capitalist societies. First, the public sector, as an employer and service provider, was more and more central to people's lives and life chances. Second, mobilisation and protest by 'progressive' groups increasingly concentrated upon home and neighbourhood, rather than workplace, issues.

In analysing urban aspects of the role of the state, Castells claimed to provide urban sociology with its one legitimate theoretical object. He argued that urban areas have no significant, independent roles in politics, ideology or economic production. In all these respects they are indistinguishable from the wider society. However, they do play a specific role in consumption. For Castells (1977: 236–7), 'urban units' are to the reproduction of the labour force what firms are to the production of commodities. It is at urban level that public services are provided, in fields such as transport, education, housing and social services, which the private sector is unable or unwilling to provide but are necessary to the replenishment of the workforce. For Castells, such services – which he termed *collective consumption* – are what make 'the urban' distinctive. Thus collective consumption is the essential theoretical object of urban sociology and its main theme is the reproduction of labour power.

So defined, urban sociology provided fertile ground for neo-Marxists to develop their preoccupations with 'contradiction' (i.e. issues on which tensions within capitalism are greatest) and 'praxis' (i.e. theoretically informed 'progressive' action). The contradiction resided in the fact that local public services subsidise 'capital' in that they provide firms with adequately housed, educated, healthy and disciplined workers. But they also drain some of the energy from the capitalist system by reducing demand for market products, by withdrawing money from the economy through taxation, and by breaking the link between wage labour and the power to consume. In terms of praxis, Castells saw collective consumption as providing a 'site of struggle' for 'urban social movements' that challenge the state to improve and expand non-market services. Initially, he argued that urban social movements provide support for the class struggle by extending its scope beyond traditional workplace-based concerns with wages and conditions of employment. Once Castells Mk II had examined various urban social movements empirically, however, he conceded that they bore no necessary relation, and could even be antagonistic, to the politics of class and workplace (Castells, 1983).

Problems with neo-Marxist approaches

Neo-Marxist approaches to urban theory proved hugely controversial inside and outside 'radical' circles. The most fundamental criticisms took issue with features of Castells' initial analysis, many of which were shared by the avowedly non-Althusserian Harvey (1987). However, whereas Harvey continued to defend neo-Marxist analysis against its critics, Castells, by the early 1980s, had conceded its vulnerability. The first step of Castells Mk II, from which much else followed, was to admit that in his early 'empirical' work (Castells, Godard, & Balanowski, 1974) he had done little more than file 'facts' into conceptual boxes already provided by his theories. (Harvey, incidentally, is also charged with 'proving' theoretical statements only through selective examples.) The alternative, Castells decided, was to undertake research on urban social movements that was sufficiently open-ended that answers to major questions were not settled before empirical work began. This led him to abandon 'the useless construction of abstract grand theories' (Castells, 1983: xviii) and completely reconsider his approach. In so doing, he neatly illustrated many of the problems with neo-Marxist analysis, particularly in its structuralist guise.

In his first post-Althuesserian phase Castells (1983) insisted that urban theory must be founded upon structured empirical observation. That meant doing things that critics claimed neo-Marxists routinely failed to do. First, it meant testing propositions that were not pitched at such a high level of abstraction that they could not be falsified. Second, it meant accepting that social change is brought about, in part, by human agency and does not simply reflect abstract, structural forces. (Otherwise, what purpose could empirical observation serve?) Third, it meant abandoning a 'functionalist' view of the state that asserts, rather than demonstrates, that government at all levels supports the long-term survival of the capitalist system and the interests of the ruling class that has the greatest stake in it.

Castells' change of heart posed difficult questions even for non-structuralist neo-Marxists. Harvey's theorisations, for example, struggle to satisfy the criteria set out above. In Harvey's work it is abstractions, rather than any clear decision-making units, which 'act' and 'need'. He talks, for example, of 'capital' seeking x or y without feeling it necessary to specify who, exactly, is doing the seeking, how and of whom. Similarly, the theoretical existence of three circuits of capital is little more than interesting speculation unless they can be identified empirically and it can be demonstrated that particular agents actually switch capital between them, as predicted, in precisely defined and verifiable circumstances. Otherwise, just like the idea that the state extends public service provision at one point in time and reduces it at others because this is 'what capital requires', the theory fits all evidence but explains nothing.

Whilst Castells Mk II differed substantially from the younger incarnation, he nonetheless continued to see collective consumption as the central theoretical concern of urban sociology and urban social movements as its main object of study. (That is, until his metamorphosis into Castells Mk III, of whom we learn more in Chapter 3). This, too, proved controversial. Some critics raised relatively petty definitional issues and argued the toss about what should be termed collective consumption and what represented an urban social movement. Others unfairly suggested that Castells discounted production issues too readily. In fact all he claimed was that production issues, though important, were not peculiar to urban areas in the way consumption issues were.

The simplest and most damaging criticism, however, was that collective consumption services, in the way they were designed and delivered, were not really specific to urban areas. The public services Castells identified were *local* in so far as they were invariably delivered by local governments or other local agencies. However, the fact that such services were inextricably linked to the development of national welfare states meant two things, virtually by definition. First, and most obviously, such services were delivered universally and not just within towns and cities. Second, and more importantly, they were not just matters for 'urban' decisions, as affected by the pressures generated by urban social movements, but reflected national priorities. Thus Castells' designation of a theoretical object for urban sociology was ultimately no more convincing than Wirth's. Just like Wirth, Castells identified an interesting theme for urban theory and research but failed to demonstrate that it was more than one among many.

Neo-Weberian approaches

We must mention one further attempt to provide urban sociology with a specific theoretical object that emerged from debates within neo-Weberianism, neo-Marxism's 'radical' rival. Like Marx, Weber was interested in issues of conflict, power, and domination. However, his approach contrasted with Marx's in at least four key ways. First, in emphasising the growing roles of rationality and bureaucracy in all modern societies, not just capitalist ones, Weber was a more fruitful source than Marx for theorists interested in the growth of the modern state. Second, he rejected the orthodox Marxist idea that all social divisions could be reduced to conflicts between two social classes. Third, he was committed to methodological individualism and hence dismissive of anything that might resemble structuralist analysis. Fourth, his approach was not compatible with a distinction between 'superior' science and 'inferior' ideology. On the one hand, he insisted that social scientists cannot produce 'truth' but must content themselves with providing adequate, and necessarily partial, explanations of phenomena. On the other hand, he argued that social scientific 'laws' should not be confused with moral and political judgements, that the latter would, or at least should, always guide the former but that the methodology of the social sciences should be value-free.

This package of attributes made Weber particularly attractive to those who wished to be critical of contemporary society and to produce work that might contribute to solving its problems whilst avoiding some of the pitfalls of neo-Marxism. The revival of Weberian ideas in urban studies can be traced back to Rex and Moore's (1967) pioneering study of housing and race in Birmingham (UK). Rex and Moore drew heavily upon urban ecological models that, as we saw, suggested the city was divided into rings of progressively more desirable housing as one travels further from the centre. But they did not view the distribution of different standards of housing between different areas of the city and different social groups as a 'natural' product of quasi-biological or economic processes. For Rex and Moore, patterns of segregation were actively managed by human agents. They argued that the black community faced double discrimination in Birmingham's housing market and that this found physical expression in a contrast between the crumbling inner city, where black residents were over-represented, and the more desirable suburbs which were dominated by white middle-class owner-occupiers and white working-class tenants of local authority housing.

Discrimination was found to operate in both public and private sectors in an indirect but powerful way. On the one hand, the rules for allocating public housing, in stipulating a minimum period of residence before those on the waiting list became eligible for homes, effectively excluded black newcomers. On the other hand, the newcomers' relative poverty meant their purchasing options, too, were very limited. Because they were usually unable to obtain mortgage finance from established lenders, black newcomers were forced to accept punitive borrowing rates from less reputable dealers when buying cheap, low-standard inner-city properties. The resulting financial pressures meant many owners had to subdivide their properties and become landlords to people much like themselves. Poorly maintained houses thus became overcrowded, too, bringing landlords into conflict with the local authority. Thus the local authority unwittingly ended up portraying one of the symptoms of the city's housing problem – 'slum' landlords – as its cause.

Rex and Moore's careful empirical research showed how a particular set of circumstances influenced institutional and household decisions in such a way that they ended up producing the sort of neighbourhoods that nobody really wanted or designed. In trying to pinpoint the most important influence over the whole process they settled upon the local authority and building society managers who were most directly involved in determining who got access to what housing. In choosing that focus, Rex and Moore effectively invented *urban managerialism*, an approach within urban sociology that focused upon the role of 'gatekeepers' in allocating scarce urban resources. Pahl developed this concept and argued that 'urban sociology should be concerned with the social and spatial constraints on access to scarce urban resources and facilities as dependent variables and the managers or controllers of the urban system, which I take as the independent variable' (Pahl, 1975: 210).

Like Castells, then, Pahl gave urban sociology an 'essential' theoretical object and a substantive focus for research. Adopting his guidelines, a number of neo-Weberians were better able than their neo-Marxist colleagues to cast useful light on the processes and effects of certain sorts of decision-making in cities through empirical research. However, just as community power theorists faced criticism about the way their 'localist' orientation tended to ignore important non-local considerations, so urban managerialist researchers found it hard to demonstrate that the gatekeepers they focused upon were really the most important influences over the phenomena they sought to explain. On the one hand, it proved difficult to define who was a gatekeeper with respect to a particular issue, given the multitude of gates that always seemed to be involved. On the other hand, a focus on gatekeepers did not help researchers address the fundamental question of who built the gates.

The evolution of Pahl's work exemplifies these difficulties and illustrates the costs, to urban theory, of trying to overcome them. His earliest attempt to define the managers and controllers of the urban system was a somewhat arbitrary list of 'local' occupations and professions. Urban managerialist research, he suggested, should attempt to understand the way in which the ideologies, value systems and practices of people who occupied such positions affected the way in which the resources entrusted to them were allocated. Pahl soon recognised, however, that the level of resources available to these gatekeepers and the degree of freedom they had over the way resources were used were rarely entirely 'urban' matters. It was apparent that the world-view of gatekeepers was only one aspect of an analysis which also needed to examine the way external decisions shaped the context in which they worked; for example, how decisions at central government level affected the resources available for municipal housing and the way local authorities used them. In other words, urban managerialism had to come to terms with the limited *autonomy* of local gatekeepers and the fact that they were not independent variables, but intervening or even dependent ones with respect to many significant urban decisions (Saunders, 1986: 122–39). In adjusting his analysis accordingly, Pahl (1977) had to move his analysis to the national level. Once more, urban theory had to lose its specifically urban focus if it was to justify an interest in a theme that was still no more than one among many.

Radicalism reappraised

Radical approaches within urban theory attracted heavy criticism. Partly this was because of the difficulties in reconciling the practical and theoretical ambitions that often accompanied them and the apparent arrogance with which some of their advocates dismissed the approaches of others. Even Harvey, who has remained true to his mission to revitalise Marxist urban studies, has accepted that 'there is a good deal of intellectual baggage (to say nothing of dogmatism) within the Marxist tradition which hinders rather than helps in the search for penetrating analyses and viable alternatives' (Harvey, 1989b: 126). Doubts were also voiced about whether analyses of social divisions based on Marxist categories of social class or Weberian notions of class and status groups adequately addressed disadvantages deriving from race, gender and sexual orientation.

Ultimately, radical approaches were no more able to provide urban studies with a persuasive theoretical object or a distinctive and superior set of analytic tools than their rivals. However, they did galvanise urban theory considerably by challenging comfortable relations between theory and practice, introducing a stronger moral and political dimension to social scientific inquiry, putting issues of power and inequality centre-stage and proposing various forms of realist analysis as rivals to those based on positivism and hermeneutics. Each of these concerns found echoes in later approaches, if not always in the form that radicals themselves would necessarily have approved of or anticipated.

The legacy of previous theories and their challenges

We have completed our brief, selective journey through the history of urban theory up until the early 1980s. It does scant justice to the positions covered, but it helps us understand the somewhat messy context into which more recent theoretical developments fit. Urban theories have clearly not developed in a self-contained, logical or linear way. Some conform to the strict definition outlined in the previous chapter, but most are 'urban' only in the relaxed sense of the term, to the point where their connections with towns and cities can appear almost incidental. At times an approach has achieved ascendancy because it built successfully and advanced upon its predecessors. At other times, new approaches have fundamentally rejected what went before and employed concepts that previously played little part in urban theory. Theories have risen and fallen in popularity without ever disappearing entirely. Thus there were later versions of, for example, ecological approaches (Hawley, 1950), many urban ethnographies (e.g. Jackson, 1985; Hannerz, 1969; Venkatesh 2000; Duneier & Carter, 1999) and other qualitative studies on place-making (Savage, Bagnall, & Longhurst, 2005), spatial analysis (Macmillan, 1989; Wilson, 1989), positivist behavioural geography (Golledge & Couclelis, 1984), consumption theory (Saunders, 1990) and so on.

Enduring tensions in urban theory

Urban theories clearly employ a variety of approaches in attempting to cover a bewildering range of subject matter. For all the variety of approaches, though, urban theorists have had to engage with two overarching debates that are central to their interests and to social science more generally. The first, what we might call the *place–process debate*, requires the theorist to adopt a defensible position on two questions that are actually opposite sides of the same coin. Is there something intrinsic to the nature of places – towns and cities in particular or in general – which determines the processes that take place within them? Or, alternatively, do processes that operate at a much larger scale than that of the individual urban area effectively determine all the major features of towns and cities? Or, as another possibility, are there processes that may find expression in places but are actually not spatial by nature, an argument made regarding the relevance of class and gender for ways of life rather than that life being urban or not? The second, generally referred to as the *structure–agency debate*, is also associated with two contrasting positions. The first, remarked upon briefly in our discussion of 'radical' theories and also evident in the functionalism that followed in the ecological approaches after the Chicago School, is the structuralist position which argues that the structure of a given system or organisation determines all the significant behaviour exhibited by its component parts. The alternative, usually known as voluntarism, argues that the component parts create the structures, not vice versa. Thus individual human agents, pursuing freely chosen courses of action, have to lie at the root of all causal explanation. This discussion remains unresolved in the social sciences and influences much theorising about the city. For example, when we discuss segregation in Chapter 6 we will see that the extent to which the separation of racial groups and social classes in specific parts of the city is a matter of discrimination and inequality or a choice on the side of the residents remains subject to fierce debate.

The reason why these two debates have proven so intractable has to do with the fact that although it is very hard to defend any of the poles in the debate, it is just as difficult to justify taking what appear to be more reasonable in-between positions and even more difficult to apply that to doing empirical work. Theorists and non-theorists alike instinctively feel that place *and* process are important, as are structure *and* agency. To give a simple example, we would expect the nature of health and personal social services everywhere to be affected by the general tendency of people to live longer, whereas we would be surprised if the nature of local entertainments provided in mining areas was the same as that found in the stockbroker belt. In one instance the generality of a process outweighs the particularities of places, whereas in the other the particularity of a place makes it difficult to speak in terms of a general process. Similarly, most of us feel we are autonomous agents up to a point. Notwithstanding the argument of relational theorists that individuals are not self-propelling essences (Tilly, 1998), the narratives we construct about our lives are very prone to be stories of autonomous free agents. Whilst we know the impact of our personal choices will vary according to the scale of the effects we are trying to achieve, we struggle to make sense of the idea that all our significant actions are 'structurally determined'.

There has been an enormous amount of discussion about the prospects for reconciling the respective poles in the place–process debate (Gregory & Urry, 1985; Soja, 1989; Johnston, 1991; Benko & Strohmayer, 1997) and the structure–agency debate (Giddens 1979, 1981, 1984; Abrams, 1982; Tilly, 1998). Both rest upon the argument that the poles are more apparent than real; for example, that human beings are part of structures that shape their thoughts and actions, but at the same time their actions, intentionally or unintentionally, modify those structures. Hay (1995: 200–1) attempts to colonise this middle ground, and demonstrates the dense nature of the debate, when he argues that people engage in 'strategic action [which] is the dialectical interplay of intentional and knowl-edgeable, yet structurally-embedded actors and the preconstituted (structured) contexts they inhabit'. Marx (1978: 9) put things much more simply when he suggested that 'men [*sic*] make their own history, but ... they do not make it under circumstances chosen by themselves'. Bourdieu's theory of praxis and his notions of dispositions and habitus (Bourdieu, 1977; see also 1984) goes very much in the same direction.

But arguing that reconciliation between different forms of explanation is pos-sible or necessary does not overcome theoretical problems. A horses-for-courses approach to explanation may seem attractive in a pragmatic sense, but the danger is that it can make the explanation of anything in particular harder to achieve. It is one thing, for example, to try and justify a structuralist or a vol-untarist position with respect to phenomenon z. However, the argument that z is the product of both structures *and* human agency will always lack explana-tory power unless clear evidence can be produced which shows that structural forces pointed in direction x, human agency in direction y and the outcome was z. This may sound simple in principle but it is much more difficult in practice (Gregson, 1989).

The problem of applying approaches that claim to reconcile place and pro-cess, or structure and agency, is that, in arguing that two forms of explanation are compatible, they reduce the conceptual power of both. In that respect they share the dilemma faced by neo-Marxists who attempted to demonstrate theo-retically that the state was 'relatively autonomous' from the forces of capital. The relative autonomy position tried to reconcile the structuralist argument that the state acts as the long-term guarantor of the capitalist system with the more voluntaristic position that the class struggle can result in governments awarding concessions to groups other than capital owners. In trying to demonstrate that these two observations are not contradictory, however, the relative autonomy position was able to 'explain' every conceivable action of government whilst being unable to demonstrate whether the needs of capital or the pressures exerted by the working class took precedence in any particular case.

Debates about the place–process and structure–agency controversies tend to be very dense and abstract and to operate at a rarefied conceptual level. There is little in them that could be termed urban theory in either of the senses we have identified. One of the tests we can apply to more recent theories, however, is the extent to which they grapple with these age-old dilemmas in the social sciences.

Assessing 'relaxed' urban theory

The key question that remains is where urban theory has gone since the early 1980s, the point at which this review ends. That question dominates the remainder of the book. As we saw in Chapter 1, the potential range of urban theory is so vast that the answer has to be a selective one. One thing is clear, however. There have been no further developments in urban theory in the more exacting sense of that term. The most recent period has not seen any more attempts to designate a particular theoretical object for urban studies to concentrate upon. Saunders (1986: 289–351) proved, at least for a while, to be a partial exception in that he continued to argue that consumption as a whole – and not just services delivered locally by the public sector – provides a distinctive and compelling object for sociological analysis. However, he does not argue it is the only focus for urban studies, nor does he claim consumption is quintessentially urban. He uses the phrases 'urban sociology' and 'the sociology of consumption' interchangeably, but it is the latter which most accurately described his interests. The former, he admits, was retained only 'as a matter of convention … so as to maintain the intellectual continuity of the field' (1986: 289).

If the supply of urban theory in the strict sense of the term has dried up, however, one could fill twenty books with accounts of developments in theories that could be described as 'urban' in the more relaxed sense. It will only be with hindsight that future commentators will agree upon what the main theoretical developments of the last fifth of the twentieth century and the early years of the twenty-first have been in a way that is comparable to this chapter's treatment of earlier periods. However, we can give some structure to the choices we have made about the content of Chapters 3–7 here by highlighting what appear to us to be the main challenges facing urban theorists in the last 30 or so years.

Key challenges for modern urban theory

We now know enough about urban theory to appreciate that material 'realities' and our ways of perceiving them are not easily separated. The way things appear is not just affected by 'real' changes in the 'empirical' world that positivists and realists claim to inhabit and study. As hermeneutics-inspired and related approaches insist, and realists also accept, appearances mean different things depending upon the theories and concepts we employ in perceiving and understanding them. If our theoretical perspectives change, the world changes with them irrespective of material circumstances. This point may seem pedantic but it is relevant because there is a fair amount of controversy about whether the way urban theory, and social scientific theory more generally, has developed in recent decades is driven by substantive change or is the result of the 'reframing' of the way theorists perceive the world.

Two relatively uncontroversial claims can be made about the recent history of global urbanism in terms of substantive change. First, the world has clearly become more urbanised, as the process of industrialisation has found its way into all corners of the globe, triggering urban population growth on an unprecedented scale and at a speed which far exceeds that associated with the industrial revolution. Second, the implications that follow from explosive urbanisation, for urban settlements and urban life in both the old and newly industrialising worlds, have been profoundly shaped, as well as linked together, by processes of globalisation. We take up the theme of globalisation, and the implications that follow for patterns of urban change, in Chapter 3. At the same time, however, it is argued that these substantive changes, and the bewildering variety of implications they have for different places, demand that theorists see the (urban) world in different ways. This current of thought is particularly strong amongst advocates of what has been called 'the cultural turn' and the development of 'postmodern' theory.

We return to the claims made for both of these departures within the social sciences, the way they have been taken up in urban theory and their impact upon urban studies, in Chapter 3, when we look in particular at the 'Los Angeles School' and the argument that has been made for that city as an emblematic example of the postmodern urban form, and again in Chapter 6, which examines their impact on the way urban lifestyles and cultures have been understood. In essence, though, both build upon what we believe to be a controversial claim that 'modernity' has somehow been transcended.

Put in the simplest terms, modernity is seen as an attitude to the world which took root in (Christian) Europe in the seventeenth and eighteenth centuries and saw faith placed in the notions of freedom, progress, rationality and science. It is not the case that popular, or even elite, understanding of what these notions signified was ever unambiguous, or that there was ever consensus about the way their ostensible pursuit was manifested at any one time. Kumar (1995: 85–100), for example, contrasts modernity with 'modernism', whose various movements, in his account, effectively acted as the conscience of modernity and subjected its overarching belief system to every manner of challenge, but generally with the intention, or at least the effect, of making it more 'modern'.

Postmodernity, by contrast, is seen to lack any remotely unifying set of core beliefs or sense of direction. Ostensibly driven by greater fragmentation, pluralism and individualism within global societies, it is seen as an attitude to the world, after modernity, in which '[r]eality is compartmentalized ... [and] ... made up of distinct and overlapping features which cannot be aggregated or integrated … Post-modernity is expressed in the language of "discourses" and "voices" rather than of falsifiable propositions' (Kumar, 1995: 163).

Whilst it is clearly the case that the debate over the notion of postmodernity has caused greatest excitement and controversy within the social sciences since the period at which the historical review we have presented in this chapter ends, in terms of contemporary studies of 'the urban', we tend to side with Kumar (1995: 176) who, when paraphrasing Berman, states that: 'The main drama on the world stage is still modernity … We are, in fact, most likely still in … [its] … early stages … Large sections of the world are just beginning to feel its full impact." We take this position because we feel that, when the phase of urban theory we deal with in the remainder of the book is evaluated in retrospect, it will be on the basis not of whether the urban world experienced a transition to a putative, and as yet poorly defined, postmodern state, but whether it provided a compelling analysis of how it was that the world became 'spiky' and what that means for the future of cities and urban life.

Urban theory in a spiky world

Since the period we have covered in this chapter, the world has clearly become more urbanised and its urban areas have become more interrelated and more differentiated. In the words of Friedman (2005), the world became 'flatter' as the process of (capitalist) wealth creation became more diffused and the productive capacities of more and more parts of the globe were integrated into international systems of innovation, production and exchange. This undeniably began to reduce the stark differences in wealth between different regions of the world, however they are characterised (e.g. by continent or through such notions as the 'developed' as against 'developing' worlds, 'Global North' versus 'Global South', etc.). During the same period, however, the world became more 'spiky' (e.g. Florida, 2005a) in the sense that the development gains associated with a more globally dispersed pattern of wealth creation have been unevenly distributed. This applies equally to rapidly developing countries, where industrialisation has been associated with huge variations in patterns of subnational spatial develop-ment, and to the older developed world, in which the benefits derived from the transition to a knowledge-based, if not entirely 'post-industrial', economy have been shared unequally, subnationally. The net effect has been a stretching of national and international urban hierarchies, the continuation of which would lead, to paraphrase Glaeser (2011), to a future 'flat world with tall cities'.

During the same period, a combination of the refashioning of the interna-tional division of labour and the restructuring of occupations within the labour market have been associated with rising income disparities in the vast majority of countries. Urban spikiness, as a result, has increasingly been experienced both *between* and *within* urban areas. It is the performance of urban theories in accounting for and understanding this spikiness that we concentrate on in the next four chapters. Chapters 3 and 4 look at inter-urban spikiness. Chapter 3 focuses upon accounts that deal with the impact of globalisation processes on the differential patterns of growth (and decline) experienced by different sorts of urban area. Chapter 4 then goes on to examine theories that purport to explain how it is that cities themselves, or rather decision-makers acting within or on behalf of them, are understood to have affected development paths. Chapters 5 and 6 deal with intra-urban spikiness. Chapter 5 examines theories that have attempted to explain patterns of intra-urban inequality, whilst Chapter 6 looks at accounts that see intra-urban differentiation more as an expression or consequence of diversity. In Chapter 7, we review the strengths and weaknesses of the theories examined in these four chapters against a series of criteria that help us understand the current health and future potential of urban theory.

Questions for discussion

- Community power scholars have different understandings of power. How do they compare, and which understanding of power do you find most fruitful?
- Neo-Marxists and neo-Weberians differ in their understanding of inter- and intra-urban inequalities. What conceptual tools do they provide and which appear most useful to you for what type of research questions?
- Discuss the methodological consequences of humanist geography. What do these consequences mean for the research questions humanist geography can or cannot address?

Further reading

Chicago School

The key source texts are Park, Burgess, and McKenzie's *The City* (1925) and Wirth's 'Urbanism as a way of life', *American Journal of Sociology* (1938). The School's overall contributions to urban sociology are covered in Blumer's *The Chicago School of Sociology* (1984), Kurtz's *Evaluating Chicago Sociology* (1984), Matthews' *Quest for an American Sociology* (1977), and Smith's *The Chicago School* (1988). The work of Park and Wirth is briefly reviewed in Saunders' *Social Theory and the Urban Question* (1986). Wirth is given more extended treatment in Smith's *The City and Social Theory* (1980) and Morris' *Urban Sociology* (2007). Abu-Lughod (1991) in *Changing Cities* does an excellent job in showing how urban ecological approaches developed after the Chicago School and gives a concise overview of the criticism of the Chicago School. The value of the Chicago School for the development of urban anthropology can be found in Hannerz's *Exploring the City* (1980). A good reader with a selection of texts that by and large follow the categorisation of the literature we have applied here can be found in Lake's *Readings in Urban Analysis* (1983). Most readers in urban theory contain the crucial articles of Wirth, Simmel and Burgess, which have been reprinted many times.

Urban geography/spatial analysis

The main sources here are well covered by urban geography textbooks (see the further reading at the end of Chapter 1). Key source texts include Christaller and Baskin's *Central Places in Southern Germany* (1966) and Lösch's *The Economics of Location* (1965). Discussions, from a variety of viewpoints, can be found in Isard's *Location and Space Economy* (1956), Haggett's *Locational Analysis in Human Geography* (1965), Beavon's *Central Place Theory* (1977), and Massey's chapter in Peet's *Radical Geography* (1977). The importance of the quantitative revolution in geography is given extended treatment in Johnston's *Geography and Geographers* (1991) and Gregory's *Ideology, Science and Human Geography* (1978).

Community power debate

The background to the debate is traced in Bell and Newby's *Community Studies* (1971). Their (1974) collection of excerpts of significant community studies, *The Sociology of Community*, is a helpful addition to this overview. The key source texts are Hunter's *Community Power Structure* (1953), Dahl's *Who Governs?* (1961), and Bachrach and Baratz's 'Two faces of power' (1962). The debate is discussed extensively in Polsby's *Community Power and Political Theory* (1980). Briefer discussions can be found in the chapters by Harding and Mossberger in Davies and Imbroscio's *Theories of Urban Politics*, 2nd edition (2009). The contributions of pluralists and elite theorists to the understanding of power are critically reviewed in two books entitled *Power*, one by Lukes (1974), the other by Dowding (1996).

Humanistic (urban) geography

The chapter on humanistic geography in Cloke, Philo, and Sadler's *Approaching Human Geography* (1991) is a good starting point on theoretical discussions in this field. Ley's *A Social Geography of the City* (1983) is a key source text.

Radical approaches I: Neo-Marxist

The evolution of Castells' approach to urban theory can be traced through his *La Question Urbaine* (1972) or its English version *The Urban Question* (1977), *City, Class and Power* (1978), and *The City and the Grassroots* (1983). It is discussed in an accessible way by Lowe in

Urban Social Movements (1986). For a parallel journey through the work of Harvey, see his *Social Justice and the City* (1973), *The Limits to Capital* (1982) and *The Urbanization of Capital* (1985b). Harvey's early work is reviewed in Gottdiener's *The Social Production of Urban Space* (1985). The work of both theorists is reviewed in Saunders' *Social Theory and the Urban Question* (1986). A wider selection of neo-Marxist source material can be found in two edited collections: Pickvance's *Urban Sociology* (1976) and Harloe's *New Perspectives in Urban Change and Conflict* (1981). Geddes reviews neo-Marxist approaches in his chapter for Davies and Imbroscio's *Theories of Urban Politics* (2009). Katznelson covers similar ground, at greater length, in *Marxism and the City* (1993).

Radical approaches II: Neo-Weberian

The key source texts referred to in this chapter are Pahl's *Whose City?* (1970) and Rex and Moore's *Race, Community and Conflict* (1967). Their approaches are based on Weber's *The City* (1958) and various ideas contained in his *Economy and Society* (1968). Both are critically reviewed in Saunders' *Social Theory and the Urban Question* (1986). The edited volumes by Pickvance and Harloe (see above) contain chapters based on neo-Weberianism as well as neo-Marxism. Weber's contribution to urban theory, and his influence on urban neo-Weberians, is discussed in Elliott and McCrone's *The City* (1982).

Modernity and postmodernity

For a thorough treatment of the putative shift from modernity to postmodernity, see Kumar's *From Post-Industrial to Post-Modern Society* (1995).

3

From the urban crisis to the 'triumph of the city'

Learning objectives

- To grasp how concepts and theories have been employed to understand the transition from an industrial to an information-based economy
- To appreciate the role that globalising processes have played in that transition, and their differential impacts upon different sorts of cities
- To develop an understanding of why urban scholarship, as a whole, became less pessimistic about the future of cities but interpreted renewed urbanisation and a putative 'urban renaissance' very differently

Cities as actors in a globalising economy

Chapter 1 demonstrated that the city was regarded as a compelling unit for analysis by leading social scientists who studied the transition from feudalism to capitalism. European cities in particular were considered, for example by Weber (1968), to be important, relatively autonomous centres of economic and political power in the period before the dawn of the industrial age. Urban institutions such as city corporations and craft guilds played a critical role in wresting power away from aristocratic landowners who had dominated economic relations in the feudal period and in creating the conditions in which independent production and trade could flourish. They played an important part in the governance of urban life by helping mobilise investments in the built environment, organise new forms of production, regulate the urban labour market, and manage relations between town and country. They were even involved in facilitating and regulating the 'international' flow of goods through inter-city trading networks such as the Hanseatic League (Dollinger, 1999).

The transition to industrial capitalism that urban institutions helped bring about, however, paradoxically triggered a long-run decline in their autonomy and power. In the economic sphere, the growth of limited liability companies trading at ever larger geographical scales gradually dissolved the close links that had once existed between city elites, city-based institutions, the local ownership and organisation of production, the urban market for goods and services, and locally generated urban investments. In the process key economic interests, whilst they might have remained *in* cities, or at least their wider metropolitan areas, increasingly became less dependent upon – and therefore especially concerned about or committed to – a single urban environment. In the political sphere, the autonomy of urban institutions declined in parallel with the development of nation states and more centralised, national systems of governance (Le Galès, 2002). Indeed, a number of urban historians see the process of nation-building – particularly in Europe – as a history of the subordination of cities and their absorption into national urban hierarchies (Braudel, 1986; Hohenberg & Lees, 1995; Tilly & Blockmans, 1994). The effects of these broad economic and political changes upon the autonomy of urban institutions and processes help explain why social scientists increasingly focused less upon cities and more upon the general process of industrialisation on the one hand and the role of national governments within a political, economic and social order dominated by nation states on the other.

There is a growing sense, however, that the course of history has moved against nations and nationally based systems of economic and social management and towards arrangements in which what happens, economically and politically, at both supranational *and* subnational level is assuming greater importance. Whilst there is broad consensus about the growing importance of supranational institutions and decision-making, though, the debate focusing upon the subnational level has been more speculative. For much of the late twentieth century it also tended to focus more upon the regional than the urban scale (e.g. Keating, 1997; Le Galès & Lequesne, 1998). Thus, for example, the notion of a 'Europe of the regions' (Laughlin, 1996) became a popular short-hand way of combining a relatively negative reading of the future powers and functions of nation states in an increasingly integrated Europe with a relatively positive appraisal of the potential importance of regional economies and regional institutions.

Such assessments were by no means confined to Europe. Speaking of the cultural implications of a world in which nations are less and less self-contained, Appadurai (1996a: 19) argued that '[n]ation states, as units in a complex inter-active system, are not very likely to be the long-term arbiters of the relationship between globality and modernity'. Specifically with respect to economic change, the business economist Ohmae (1993: 78), noting the evolution of supranational trading blocs in Asia and the Americas as well as Europe, argued that:

> [t]he nation state has become an unnatural, even dysfunctional, unit for organizing human activity and managing economic endeavor in a border-less world. ... On the global economic map the lines that now matter are those defining what may be termed 'region states'.

Such claims should be treated with caution, not least because nation states, whilst their borders have undeniably become more permeable, have been the principal architects of new, international institutions and forms of regulation. They also continue to exert huge, explicit or implicit influence over the forms, functions and activities of subnational levels of governance (Harding & Le Galès, 1997; Le Galès & Harding, 1998; Brenner, 2004). Of immediate concern here, however, are the potential implications for cities.

When late twentieth-century commentators discussed the 're-emergence of regional economies' (Sabel, 1989; Amin & Robins, 1990; Storper, 1997), they were more often than not referring to the role played by urban areas in regional economic transformation. Bailly, Jensen-Butler, and Leontidou (1996: 165) drew attention to this when arguing that '[t]oday, the successful region has really become the urban region'. Pierce et al. (1993: 2), in similar vein, suggested that 'national economies are ... constellations of regional economies, each with a major city at its core, each requiring specific and customized strategies'. Scott (2001: 1), describing the emergence of 'global city-regions' – that is, diffuse ter-ritories comprising administratively defined cities, the larger, continuously built-up metropolitan areas that invariably surround them and the broader area over which the metropolitan core exerts significant influence – argued that the 'new regionalism' of which they are a central component 'differs ... from an older regionalism in which individual [city-]regions were ... apt to be much more subservient to the dictates (but also shrouded from outside turbulence by the protective cloak) of the central state'.

In other words, just as it has been argued that any future Europe of the regions would, in reality, be a Europe of the cities or city-regions (Frêche & Lapousterle, 1990), so one scenario for cities – globally, and not just in Europe – involves a potential movement 'back to the future', to an age when cities and urban regions might reclaim some of their former importance in the organisation of economic and social life (Castells, 1997: 269–73).

The idea that cities can be characterised as actors in a global economy is con-troversial (Le Galès, 2002: 8–29) and has been conceptualised in many different ways. Some commentators, for example, have referred to an incipient trend towards 'entrepreneurial cities' whilst others have referred to – or, more usually, lamented – the way a 'new urban politics' or 'new localism' reinforces the importance of urban economic development. For the purposes of organising this chapter, however, let us refer to the possibility of 'competitive cities'. The notion of competitiveness can be interpreted as referring both to the characteristics of a particular entity and to its relationship with, or stance towards, others. A firm, for example, can be seen as competitive in the former sense if it has a substantial or growing market share and produces high-quality and popular goods or services more efficiently than its rivals. But it is also competitive if, irrespective of its current trading performance, it seeks out competition with others, for example by producing for new markets and/or acquiring and rationalising firms active in its own or other sectors.

Extending this analogy to cities breaks an understanding of 'urban competitiveness' down into two distinct strands. A city can be characterised as *economically* competitive if it contains significant concentrations of successful producers and can offer the sort of environment, in the widest sense, that can retain and attract key firms and enable them to develop and grow. But a city – or, more accurately, key interests active within a city or on its behalf – can also be considered *politically* competitive if it competes with others. Competitive behaviour might entail overt attempts to attract particular footloose investments, firms, entrepreneurs or institutions. Or it might be indirect and entail a competitive search for improvements to the general environment in which these things can flourish. The core distinction, then, is between the city as *competitive* and as *competitor*. Whilst being competitive should help the competitor in whatever field he/she competes, it is also theoretically possible for the relatively uncompetitive 'player' to choose, or be compelled, to compete.

Later sections of this chapter review the evidence for the argument that cities – or at least *some* cities, types of city, or areas of cities – have become more competitive, in one or other senses of that word, in recent decades. The key to understanding the context within which both sets of changes have occurred, however, is 'globalisation' and, in particular, the effects that globalising processes are argued to have both on the economic vitality of some, but certainly not all, urban areas and on the perceived need amongst key 'urban actors' to respond to economic change. A brief discussion of the much debated and imprecise notion of globalisation therefore precedes the later discussion.

Before that, though, we need to note just how much of a change there has been for a serious discussion about 'urban competitiveness' to be taking place at all. Had this book been written in the 1970s, for example, the idea of the competitive city would have been greeted with surprise, even derision, by many commentators within urban studies, particularly in the US and the UK. Analyses of urban change in the period between the mid-1960s and mid-1980s, at least when they focused upon cities in the 'developed' world, were dominated by the notion of urban decline. Recent changes in the tone of urban debate are even more surprising if we recognise that the conceptual work which underpinned the earlier, pessimistic view of cities also provided many of the building blocks upon which analyses of a putative urban renaissance have been constructed. On our way to the competitive city, then, we need to detour through the 'uncompetitive city' that ostensibly preceded it. That means beginning with the literature on deindustrialisation and continuing through accounts that anticipated the 'death' of the city as we had known it.

Urban decline and obsolescence

Economic change versus the city

The work of the Chicago School was based, implicitly, upon two assumptions about the development trajectories of urban areas. First, urban populations would continue to grow as new immigrants arrived, from rural areas or other countries, and the gap between birth and death rates grew, and life expectancy expanded, in line with growing affluence. Second, employment opportunities for city residents would expand at a pace that would enable the absorption of economically active people into the urban labour market, notwithstanding periodic fluctuations in the economic cycle and temporary hikes in the level of unemployment. These assumptions reflected circumstances operating in the US during much of the inter-war period in which most Chicago School writing appeared. They continued to hold true, across much of the then developed world, well into the period after the Second World War.

The dominant image of the city in industrialised nations up to the mid-1960s, then, was predicated on growth. It was also assumed that cities would continue to benefit from *agglomeration*; that is, the tendency for productive activities to group themselves together in those places which provide an environment wherein the things producers need – good communications infrastructures, a large and varied workforce, an extensive market for company products, a wide array of suppliers and business services – are in greatest supply. The combination of population growth and agglomeration, it was generally argued, had resulted in two main phases of urban expansion.

In the first – *urbanisation* – there was absolute growth in population and economic activity within urban centres, however defined. In the second – *suburbanisation* – overall population and employment opportunities in the wider urban area continued to expand. But residential patterns became more dispersed, and cities 'hollowed out', as new suburbs, initially containing only a limited amount of local economic activity, appeared on the city fringe. The degree and timing of suburbanisation differed across advanced industrial nations and was not universally welcomed. There was a great deal of Anglo-American debate, in particular, about how to limit or manage 'urban sprawl' (Hall, Thomas, Gracey, & Drewett, 1973) and deal with the 'inner-city problem' which resulted from the selective out-movement of more affluent households and the 'imbalance' this created within the population that remained behind; see Evans and Eversley (1980) and Hall (1981) on the UK. But the underlying assumption about growth was widely shared.

From the mid-1960s onward, however, a further phase in the demographic development of mature, industrialised cities became increasingly apparent. *Counter-urbanisation*, first identified in the US in the early 1970s (Berry, 1976) and subsequently in the UK (Champion, 1991) and other, older industrialised areas of Europe, saw the populations of the older metropolitan areas shrink and those of small urban centres and rural areas grow. Initial attempts at explaining this phenomenon centred mainly upon the relative attractiveness of the latter purely as places to live. It quickly became apparent, however, that counter-urbanisation was closely associated with *deindustrialisation* (Bluestone & Harrison, 1982; Martin & Rowthorn, 1986) and the massive shake-out of employment from established manufacturing sectors based predominantly in the older urban centres. The pattern of residential decentralisation which demographers identified was found to have close parallels in the pattern of employment change, with small, free-standing towns and rural areas gaining job share whilst the larger metropolitan areas – particularly the inner cities – lost it (on the UK, see Hasluck, 1987; Turok & Edge, 1999). It was in this context that the notion of urban decline came to dominate the agenda of academics and policy-makers, particularly Anglo-American ones (Banfield, 1970; Blair, 1974; Lees & Lambert, 1985).

The challenge for theorists was to provide explanations for the changing spatial distribution of employment and to relate it to patterns of population change; in other words, to understand what *caused* urban decline. The novel step forward in providing such explanations entailed focusing not upon the *manifestations* of decline, but upon the *processes* that accompanied it; that is, upon what was happening within the productive sphere. Two conceptual developments, in particular, launched what became known as the 'restructuring' debate (Bagguley, Mark-Lawson, & Shapiro, 1990) and provided a context for subsequent approaches to the role of economic change in the pattern of urban development. Both challenged the positivist orthodoxies of traditional locational theorists and their tendency to look for the causes of employment decline *within* the worst affected areas. They focused instead upon the strategies that firms adopt to maintain or increase output and productivity. The first, concentrating specifically on the UK, was Massey and Meegan's work on the geography of employment decline. The second, operating on a much broader geographical canvas, was the new international division of labour (NIDL) thesis.

Massey and Meegan (1982) examined the 'how, why and where of employment decline' in the UK by using a form of realist analysis. They proceeded upon three basic assumptions: that firms in a market economy constantly review their production strategies in search of higher profits; that the consequences of their decisions for employment inevitably favour some locations and penalise others; but that both the form and timing of new production strategies, and their geographical employment implications, vary. Rather than examine firms' decision-making directly, they identified three in-principle strategies that would result in job loss. These 'causal mechanisms' were: *intensification*, which entailed making a smaller workforce work harder and/or more efficiently; *rationalisation*, which entailed the closure or reduction of productive capacity on some sites and its relocation to or concentration in others; and *investment and technical change*, that is, the introduction of technologies which save labour and potentially change the nature of the goods firms produced.

They then examined data on a range of industrial sectors in which employment was declining and, by looking at what was happening to output and productivity, made judgements as to which of the three strategies was most important in each case. The third stage of their analysis was to establish what effect the three strategies had upon the geography of employment. Although they mainly concentrated upon changes in regional employment levels, Massey and Meegan (1980) also contributed to the 'urban decline' debate by pointing out that company deaths and job-shedding rationalisations were disproportionately concentrated within the mature industrial sectors of the older urban centres. Their explanation of this process, however, differed in important respects from behavioural approaches which took at face value the reasons offered by companies for their preferences for non-metropolitan, and particularly non-inner-city, areas and the argument that regional policies and subsidies were responsible for denuding cities of economic activity (e.g. Fothergill & Gudgin, 1982).

For Massey and Meegan, declining employment in manufacturing in the older urban centres could not necessarily be taken as evidence of generalised industrial decline, since many of the firms in the sectors they looked at used restructuring strategies in an attempt to retain competitiveness and guarantee survival. Nor could it be put down entirely to specific features of metropolitan and inner-city environments. Whereas others argued that major cities declined economically because they suffered from a lack of suitable sites, high land costs, and outmoded transport infrastructures – the downside of agglomeration – Massey and Meegan argued that this only made sense if it could be shown that firms were relocating to other areas in large numbers. Their research showed this not to be the case. Rather, certain firms were shedding jobs in the major cities whilst others were starting up, or increasing production, elsewhere. Two additional factors were identified as important to explaining this pattern. On the one hand, the age and stage of development of many firms in metropolitan areas, and the sectors they operated in, were said to mean they would have lost employment *wherever they were located* as a result of fiercer – often international – competition. On the other hand, it was argued that labour considerations (wages, levels of trades union organisation, the militancy or docility of the workforce) were often critical when firms were looking at investment options. In all these respects, it was metropolitan workforces, rather than the broader urban environment, that were less attractive to employers. Massey (1984) later took this analysis further and argued that industrial restructuring, particularly the introduction of new technologies, effectively destroyed skilled jobs in the older industrial zones – that is, in particular regions and metropolitan areas – and enabled firms to locate in other areas where the cheaper and less skilled employees they needed were in greater supply and/or less organised and more compliant. In other words, the characteristics of 'greenfield workforces' were more important than those of greenfield *sites* in explaining the locational preferences of employers.

The cost of labour and its implications for the locational preferences of firms also lies at the core of the NIDL thesis (Frobel, Heinrichs, & Kreye, 1980). The NIDL thesis started from the observation that multinational corporations (MNCs), which were overwhelmingly headquartered in the advanced industrial nations and traditionally employed the vast majority of their workforces there, controlled a significant and growing share of world trade and employment. In their search for increased profits MNCs were able to use new technologies to shed skilled manual jobs and replace them with a smaller number of professional and administrative white-collar and lower-skilled manual jobs. Combined with the fact that they wished to service markets on a global scale, this meant MNCs were both able and keen to shift basic production – but rarely their more complex management, research, and co-ordination functions – to areas of the globe where labour was cheap and less organised. Such decisions were often facilitated by 'foreign' government policies on issues such as health and safety, environmental protection, corporate taxation, and subsidies to companies which offered MNCs a better financial deal and a less regulated business environment than was common in their host countries.

Both approaches added to the analysis of urban decline in the core industrial countries by focusing upon the 'logic of accumulation' adopted by manufacturing firms operating in an increasingly internationalised economy. The NIDL in particular implicitly supported the arguments of the likes of Harvey that the pattern of production – and hence of urban change – takes different forms in different places at different times depending on the connections between a particular locality and the changes taking place in the wider economy. The NIDL thesis suggested that the losers, certainly in terms of jobs, were the 'core' industrial countries and particularly manual workers in the older industrial cities in those countries. The winners were MNC shareholders, professional workers in 'core' countries and, in a more ambiguous way, lower-paid production workers in the growing urban centres of the 'developing world'. In concentrating upon manufacturing industries, however – and in the case of Massey and Meegan only upon manufacturing sectors that were in crisis in the UK – they told only part of the story. We should therefore mention one further conceptual innovation which put change within manufacturing into a broader perspective: Daniel Bell's postindustrial society thesis.

Bell's (1973) prescient analysis was not a contribution to urban theory in any direct sense but became much cited by urbanists interested in spatial economic and labour market change. He suggested contemporary society was undergoing an economic revolution of a magnitude similar to that which triggered the transition from the agrarian to the industrial society. At the centre of that revolution, he argued, was a new factor of production – knowledge – that was rapidly becoming more important than land, labour and capital as the key to economic organisation and development. In postindustrial society, according to Bell, the production of services would be more important than the production of goods. The occupational structure would be transformed as manual work progressively disappeared and the importance of knowledge-based jobs grew, within both services and manufacturing. In the process, the relevance of antagonism between capital and labour would decline and a new professional and technical class would be created which would provide the basis of a new technocracy, in government as well as business.

The implications of the postindustrial society thesis were not picked up within urban studies for some time. It was only when many of the trends outlined by Bell became more clearly established that urban scholars began using the prefix 'postindustrial' to refer to cities in which professional, administrative, managerial and technical occupations, along with lower-skilled jobs in personal services, came to dominate urban labour markets in the developed world (Savitch, 1988). This delay is not entirely surprising. It took considerable time for urban commentators to realise that deindustrialisation did not mean the end of job-creation in cities and that counter-urbanisation was neither inevitable nor necessarily permanent. Indeed, it could be succeeded by 'reurbanisation' (Champion, 2001) in which the number of people and jobs in cities/metropolitan areas began to grow once more. In the words often used to describe urban economic change in the US during the 1970s and 1980s, 'sunbelt' cities (Perry & Watkins, 1977) certainly prospered but at least some 'rustbelt' cities (Cooke, 1995) began to recover. Taken together, however, the three conceptual literatures outlined here clearly influenced subsequent approaches within urban theory. In particular, they identified a number of characteristics that became important to the analysis of spatial economic change.

First, they emphasised the role of the firm – and especially MNCs – in reorganising production on an international scale. Second, they paid attention to the way in which the internal structure of firms – for example, how routine production activities such as assembly were divided from research and management tasks – contributed both to strategies for raising output and productivity and to changes in geographical employment patterns. The latter consideration, in particular, implicitly suggested that the 'new geography of production' might be linked to a new international urban hierarchy and to the concentration of different sorts of functions in different cities (Cohen, 1981). Third, they identified a critical role for new technology, particularly in the restructuring of manufacturing sectors, the contraction of their workforces, and their changing occupational structures. Fourth, they anticipated the growing importance of the service sector, and of white-collar occupations more generally, for future employment. Fifth, they emphasised the role of information and specialised knowledge in the production of goods and services, implicitly granting them greater importance than more traditional factors of production. All these issues were taken up, in various ways, in subsequent theoretical work.

Understanding globalisation

The authors referred to in the previous section recognised, to varying degrees, that the key processes they described could not be understood within a single national frame of reference but had to be analysed in relation to a set of broader changes, operating cross-nationally. In short, they understood the importance of globalisation. The intervening period, however, has seen conceptual claims about the importance of globalisation grow to the point where it is routinely perceived not just as a contextual variable which merits acknowledgement but as a central factor in the analysis of a wide range of economic, political and cultural changes. We therefore need to appreciate how globalisation is understood before we can begin to trace through the implications for urban theory.

Writing on globalisation became a major growth industry within social science from the late 1980s onwards, spanning many disciplines, including political science (Luard, 1990; Held, 1991; Held & McGrew, 1993), economic and political geography (Harvey, 1989a; Peet & Thrift, 1989; Wallerstein, 1991), sociology and cultural studies (Featherstone, 1990; Sklair, 1991; King 1996; Robertson, 1992; Waters, 1995; Albrow, 1996), and international relations (Czempiel & Rosenau, 1989). Commentators in each of these fields shared a concern to highlight the limitations of theories that are 'methodologically nationalist' (Beck, 2002;

Wimmer & Glick-Schiller, 2002) and take nations, nation states or (national) societies as their basic units of analysis. But the fact that the word 'globalisation' has become ubiquitous does not mean there is any clarity about, far less agreement upon, what it represents (Scott, 1997). As Albrow (1996: 85) pointed out, 'time and again [globalisation] is used as explanation, rather than as something to be analysed, explored, and explained'. In other words, globalisation is too often seen as a cause of other things in the absence of a clear understanding of what, precisely, are the agents of change.

In trying to unpack the term, let us start with the simple statement that globalisation is 'the process of becoming global' and ask how this phrase has been understood and what is involved in the process. For Waters (1995: 3), globalisation is 'a social process in which the constraints of geography on social and cultural arrangements recede and in which people become increasingly aware that they are receding'. For Robertson (1992: 8) it is an 'intensification of consciousness of the world as a whole'. For Giddens (1990: 64) it is 'the intensification of worldwide social relations which link distant localities in such a way that local happenings are shaped by events occurring many miles away and vice versa'. None of these definitions assume that globalisation is new – indeed all three authors are at pains to stress that globalising processes are of very long standing – but they do imply that something has happened in recent times to cause a deepening and speeding up of global interconnections. Harvey (1989a: 260–307) has characterised this extra ingredient as 'space-time compression'; that is, an increase in the pace of changes that affect all places, irrespective of their particularities. These commentators have different views about what has driven globalisation, but they all see it as a multi-faceted process that has taken place simultaneously in economic, political, and cultural spheres.

Appadurai (1996b) illustrates the breadth of change involved in globalisation when referring to increased circulation and movement within various 'scapes'. He identifies: *ethnoscapes*, that is, the flows of tourists, immigrants, refugees, exiles and guestworkers; *technoscapes*, the movement of machinery and plant resulting from the expanding operations of business corporations and national governments; *finanscapes*, the flow of money in global currency markets and stock exchanges; *mediascapes*, the flows of images produced and distributed by newspapers, TV, film, the internet, advertising, etc.; and *ideoscapes*, the diffusion of ideologies supportive or critical of core ethical and political values such as democracy, freedom and rights. Appadurai's typology allows us to speculate that the growing circulation of people, goods, services, money, images, and ideas makes it ever more likely that people's awareness of the world as a whole is increased and that their decisions and actions, and even the values that underpin them, have global reference points rather than, or in addition to, national or local ones.

Appadurai's typology usefully reminds us that globalisation, rather than being a single, easily identified process, is better seen as an umbrella term for a number of economic, political and cultural processes which, although they interlink in complex ways, operate through rather different mechanisms. Some of the cultural aspects of globalisation are covered in Chapter 6 when the impact of the 'cultural turn' and postmodernism on urban studies is discussed. For the purposes of this chapter, though, we are primarily interested in the economic and political aspects of globalisation. If we are to understand the broad implications for cities, we first need to examine the mechanisms through which globalisation in these spheres is said to have been achieved.

Beginning with the former, it has been argued that the globalisation of economic activity has been facilitated by a number of mutually reinforcing changes that have heightened the well-established trend for production, distribution and exchange to take place across national borders. Amin and Thrift (1994: 2–4) and Waters (1995: 65–95) identified a number of salient factors that, not altogether coincidentally, closely match those mentioned in connection with urban decline. First, there is the growing spatial 'reach' and importance of the international finance system and the enhanced capacity that financiers and speculators have to quickly organise transactions on a global scale.

Second, there is the growth and expanding influence of transnational corporations, able to switch investments between areas depending upon the potential returns available. The term 'transnational', rather than 'multinational', is used deliberately here to distinguish corporations that are relatively free-floating in geographical terms – and, indeed, like high-wealth individuals, take advantage of global tax havens to limit the impact of national taxes on their profitability – from those that engage in international trade but are clearly rooted within a particular 'host' country. The development of *trans*nationals, controlled from a number of centres in different countries, is said to be one of the key changes in the global organisation of production (Dicken, 2010: 109–62).

Third, there is the importance of 'knowledge' as a factor of production and the high premium that is increasingly attached to learning and innovation, within society in general and the productive process in particular.

Fourth, there is the development and diffusion of new technologies and the capacity they create to organise and co-ordinate economic activity on a global scale and transmit information virtually instantaneously between remote locations. Each of these factors, it is argued, has facilitated the constant expansion of international, as opposed to domestic, trade in goods, services, information and, to a lesser but still significant extent, labour. On the one hand, they have helped put in place physical and electronic communications infrastructures that enable all manner of global interconnections to be made more easily. On the other hand, they have helped bring into existence a growing cadre of people whose jobs, movements, lifestyles, and values are arguably no longer unambiguously associated with a single country. In trying to capture this change, Featherstone (1993: 174) referred to a global 'third culture', distinct from the traditional 'us' and 'them' categories derived from national boundaries. More specifically, Sklair (1991: 62–71) identified the development of a transnational capitalist or business class that effectively oils the machinery of global interdependence.

The factors underpinning economic globalisation do not entirely account for what we might call the politics of globalisation, but they do play a very important role within it. Literatures on the politics of globalisation address the way in which issues and dilemmas that do not respect national boundaries – for example, environmental pollution, the potential effects of nuclear or chemical war, international terrorism, or the supply and abuse of proscribed drugs – are or are not recognised and dealt with politically. Attention is therefore paid to the actions or demands of a wide range of international organisations that play a part in raising and dealing with those issues and dilemmas. But one type of 'player', in particular, has dominated discussion. In essence, the politics of globalisation debate, as suggested earlier, is about the future of nation states. In particular, it entails asking what happens when individual nation states, acting alone, lack the capacity to respond effectively to global political issues.

The commonest response to this question is that the scale at which decisions are made invariably grows to match that of the issue under consideration. In other words, when the territories covered by nation states are not big enough for particular policy issues and dilemmas to be fully addressed within them, decision-making tends to become supranational. Thus the political issues raised by globalisation are addressed through the 'supranationalisation' of politics, a process that is as much driven by national governments as imposed upon them. Luard (1990), for example, described how a 'global polity' developed as nation states recognised their limited autonomy and co-operated in the development of supranational political and functional institutions in the fields of security, welfare, the environment, and human rights. However, it is with respect to the other field he mentions, economic management, that the ostensible limits of the nation state have occasioned most discussion.

It is now almost axiomatic that 'national economies', to the extent that they can be said to exist in a globalising age, are so dependent upon international trade flows that traditional macro-economic management strategies, at least as they were practised by individual national governments, can have only limited effect. It is widely accepted, in particular, that the Keynesian demand management techniques that dominated national economic policies in the industrialised countries for much of the post-war period are ineffective when practiced in just one country. This is because it can no longer be assumed with any certainty that any attempt by a national government to manipulate aggregate domestic demand for goods and services will lead to desired changes in production levels by home-based firms rather than, for example, a surge in imports.

One response by national governments to such dilemmas has been to increase the volume of economic decision-making that is brokered at supranational level via collaboration in international 'club' institutions. Many such institutions – the World Bank, the International Monetary Fund, the General Agreement on Tariffs and Trade, the Organisation for Economic Co-operation and Development and, later, the G7/G8 group representing the world's largest economies – already existed as a result of the legacy of World War II and a concerted attempt by the major post-war powers to facilitate reconstruction and prevent the kinds of economic instability that had played a role in triggering both world wars. Late twentieth-century developments, however, brought intensification in the development of international trading blocs. Thus, for example, the Single European Market was expanded, bringing greater co-ordination of the economic policy decisions of European national governments through the formation of the European Central Bank and the adoption of the euro, and a steady expansion in the number of countries in the European Union. In the process, European institutions and policy networks assumed roles that previously were the exclusive preserve of individual nation states. Similar developments took place in North America (the North American Free Trade Agreement) and through the creation of Asia-Pacific Economic Cooperation, the Cairns Group (of agricultural trading nations) and the G20, representing rapidly developing countries including Brazil, China and India.

The fact that supranational institutions and policies have become more important to macro-economic management clearly does not mean that national governments need no longer be interested in issues of economic competitiveness. But it does mean the search for 'national' competitiveness has to be pursued through different routes. It is here that the main implications for cities lie. The role of key cities and urban regions in securing competitiveness has become a much more important part of many national governments' agenda. As Peirce's remark above suggests, there has been significant debate about the place of subnational policy initiatives – promoted by subnational agencies as well as national governments – in improving competitiveness. In the process, questions have been raised as to whether 'the nation', as well as being too small a unit for the purpose of addressing certain questions, has at the same time become too big for addressing others (Castells, 1997: 273).

This brief discussion of globalisation suggests that we cannot expect to be able to identify a single process which affects all areas – and hence all cities – in straightforward and predictable ways. Whilst commentators have increasingly talked about the 'effects of globalisation' on particular cities and regions (e.g. Marcuse & van Kempen, 2000) it is evident, on closer examination, that those effects, and the processes that are said to produce them, vary substantially, in space and over time (Knox, 1996). Globalisation is not a single external force that affects all places similarly and simultaneously but rather a combination of different processes that result, overall, in higher levels of interaction between places and the people and organisations located in them (Amin & Thrift, 1994). What is therefore needed is an understanding of the way in which the urban implications of globalising economic and political processes have been analysed.

The much exaggerated death of the city

We have noted how, during the early part of the period covered by this and subsequent chapters, conceptual debate about cities – particularly in the US and the UK but also elsewhere in the 'postindustrial' world – saw globalising processes as being associated primarily with urban decline. It can legitimately be argued that this was always a parochial, 'developed world' view of urban change. The twenty-first century is, after all, 'the urban century' during which, for the first time, a majority of the world's population lives in towns and cities, the result of rapid economic growth in parts of Asia and Latin American either side of the millennium and continuing high rates of urbanisation in parts of Asia and Africa. It is easy to forget, from a North American or European perspective, that 'the urban agenda' across large parts of the world continues to be dominated by the challenges of managing urban growth rather than decline.

However, there is one strand of analysis that is equally relevant, in principle, to 'old' and newly developed worlds alike, and challenges some core received wisdoms about whether urbanisation need any longer be closely associated with economic innovation and growth. The critical issue here is the extent to which technological change necessarily favours agglomeration in the same way as it has in the past or whether, if it does not, we might witness the 'end of cities' as we have known them. One example of this school of thought, from Pascal, rehearsed factors that were seen to underpin urban decline in the developed world – reductions in domestic employment in manufacturing, the availability of cheaper labour elsewhere in the world, the alleged preference for suburban, amenity-rich housing – and added speculation that communication technologies would increasingly enable remote working, in support of the stark claim (Pascal, 1987: 599, 600) that '[i]n the future … many will be able to work virtually anywhere … [F]urther depopulation of cities seems inevitable. Because the city specializes in the advantages of proximity, its attractiveness as a focus for human interactions will continue to decrease.'

A more nuanced and better-articulated version of this line of thought can be found in the later work of Castells. Castells Mk III is very different from the two incarnations discussed in Chapter 2. In later works he abandoned his earlier preoccupations with the importance of socialised consumption and 'radical' urban social movements. Instead, in a series of books (Castells, 1989, 1996, 1997, 1998) he set himself the task of providing 'an exploratory, cross-cultural theory of economy and society in the information age, *as it specifically refers to the emergence of a new social structure*' (Castells, 1996: 27; emphasis in original). It is the implications for cities of that new social structure that mainly concern us here, but to appreciate Castells' position on this issue we must first understand the rudiments of his larger argument.

The focus of Castells' later work is upon the implications of the 'Information Technology Revolution' (ITR) which, he argues, was driven, from the 1950s onward, by developments in micro-electronics, computer hardware and software, telecommunications and broadcasting, opto-electronics and genetic engineering. Following Bell – a debt he acknowledges (Castells, 1996: 26) – Castells argues that contemporary society is undergoing economic transformation on a scale at least equal to that experienced in the transition from the agrarian to the industrial age. In extending and 'urbanising' Bell's analysis, which focused upon an undifferentiated US, he further asserts that the effects of that transformation are experienced more widely – if not in the same way, in all places, simultaneously – and at a faster pace than those associated with industrialisation.

Castells (1989: 531) also agrees with Bell that knowledge and information, and the capacity afforded by new technologies to assemble, process and diffuse them, lie at the core of the recent transformation and have steadily become more important to the production of goods and services than more traditional factors (manual labour, capital, energy, physical communications). Thus, for example, he argues (Castells, 1996: 31) that '[i]nformation technology is to this revolution what new sources of energy were to the successive Industrial Revolutions' and (Castells, 1989: 311) that:

> In the same way that railroads were the indispensable infrastructure for the formation of a national market in the US in the nineteenth century, so the expansion of information systems, based on telecommunications and computers, has provided the technological medium for the formation of a world economy functioning in real time on a day-to-day basis.

At the centre of Castells' analysis, then, are technological change and the effects it has had on the nature of production. He sees the 'informational mode of development' as a radically new way of producing goods and services that needs to be distinguished from industrialism and the forms it took in both market-based, capitalist and 'planned', state-orchestrated economies. Whilst he acknowledges that technological innovation has always played a critical part in economic change, Castells argues that, in contrast to industrialism, which was based upon technologies that enable cheap inputs of energy, 'informationalism' is based upon technologies that enable cheap inputs of information. A second critical difference between the two is that whereas under industrialism new technologies were adopted specifically to promote economic growth and expand output, 'informationalism is oriented toward ... the accumulation of knowledge and ... higher levels of complexity in information processing' as ends in themselves (Castells, 1996: 17). Thus, for example, the internet was established as a means for cheaper, less regulated communication long before its commercial potential was recognised or acted upon.

If technological innovation is the starting point for his analysis, however, Castells insists that 'technology does not determine society' in any simplistic manner and '[n]either does society script the course of technological change' (Castells, 1996: 5). Rather, technological innovation always develops within a particular economic and social context but then goes on to play an important part in shaping further change in its original context and beyond. It is in developing this argument that Castells begins to assess the role of location in the development of new economic activities. He does so by first arguing that the technological innovations that underpinned industrialisation, although they were eventually diffused across much of the globe, were first developed within highly localised 'milieux of innovation' in certain British towns and cities in the late eighteenth century and in Berlin, Boston and New York in the late nineteenth and early twentieth centuries. The ITR, he suggests, was just as geographically concentrated to begin with – this time within the US, and particularly parts of California, during the 1950s, 1960s and 1970s.

Of course there is no necessary correspondence between the particular local conditions which give rise to innovations and those which enable their application. This distinction is not lost upon Castells, who is clear that it is the wide *diffusion* of new technologies – into manufacturing and service industries, global systems of communication, even processes of government – which illustrates the real impact of the ITR. He nonetheless makes two general observations that have direct and indirect implications for urban change. First, and least surprisingly, the process of diffusion, he argues, has produced a global economy that continues to be characterised by 'variable geometry', that is, by radically uneven spatial economic development. But second, this variable geometry is different from that of the preceding period, whether it was based on distinctions between First, Second and Third World countries (Castells, 1996: 92–147) or the pattern of dominant cities and regions in the industrial age (ibid.: 376–428). Rather, the ITR has changed the essential features of urban economies in ways that generate new 'winners and losers' amongst cities.

Having brought his readers thus far, however, Castells is equivocal when it comes to specifying who the winners and losers are. This reluctance stems from his insistence that organisations in the information economy operate within a new and evolving 'space of flows' rather than the old 'space of places' (Castells, 1989: 167–71, 348–53; 1996: 366–428). The ITR, he argues (1996: 471), has resulted in the development of a new, global network infrastructure for transacting business; '[t]he new economy is organised around global networks of capital, management, and information, whose access to technological know-how is at the roots of productivity and competitiveness'. As a result, '[p]resence or absence in [a] network and the dynamics of each network *vis-à-vis* others are critical sources of domination and change in our society' (1996: 469). In other words, what matters for firms in the information economy is not so much *where* they are as *how connected* they are.

Castells hints at the broad spatial implications of an evolving information economy by revisiting the NIDL thesis. The *newest* international division of labour, he argues, is the result of the unequal distribution of four main types of producer that have different relationships to the information economy; producers of high value, of high volume, of raw materials, and redundant producers. How these producers are distributed, he argues, no longer follows the pattern described by the NIDL when, broadly speaking, high-value production was concentrated in the 'command and control' centres of the developed world, high-volume production was rapidly being decentralised to low-cost, developing countries, raw material production was largely a matter of geographical chance and production was most likely to become redundant within peripheral economies and sectors that were unable to compete globally. Instead, for Castells (1996: 147), 'the newest international division of labour does not take place within countries but between economic agents placed in the[se] four positions … along a global structure of networks and flows'. Thus even 'marginalized economies' increasingly contain some high-value production whilst redundant production has become more common within the most powerful economies, 'be it in New York, … Osaka, … London, or … Madrid'. Amin and Thrift (2002: 76) make a similar point when they argue that:

> [C]ities have to be seen as a site in distanciated economic networks... Whatever power they exert occurs through firms and institutions located within them, but not necessarily working for them. Their economic life is constituted through the role they play in a wider global space of circulatory flows and economic organisation.

What is not dealt with particularly persuasively by any of these authors is just how radical the impact of a space of flows upon the space of places might prove to be; in other words, if and how contemporary patterns of urbanisation are likely to change very substantially in the future. Given that the creation of new, virtual communications networks and the technologies that enable connection to them have been essentially 'bottom-up' processes, led by individual firms and governments seeking to enhance their own competitive advantages and those of their territories, it is inevitable that some places were 'wired up' more quickly, remain more connected than others and play host to greater levels of innovation. The infrastructure that has created Castells' 'space of flows', in other words, is likely to have been superimposed upon an earlier 'space of places', hence some places have been better able than others to connect to and capture the benefits of an information-driven economy. The best we get from Castells, however, even though his analysis is replete with references to mega-cities that he considers to be important nodes within the 'space of flows', is that it is too early to say what the geographical implications of 'the creative chaos that characterizes the new economy' (1996: 147) might be. In according primacy to the space of flows, and in stressing the freedom of locational choices opened up by the ITR, his analysis leaves open the 'death of the city' scenario that others posited in a cruder way.

Urban economic renaissance

Post-Fordist urbanism

The later 1980s and 1990s witnessed explosive growth in conceptual literatures that took the main components of economic globalisation – the development of an integrated, 'real-time' worldwide financial system, the growth of transnational corporations, the centrality of 'knowledge' in the production of goods and services and the evolution and diffusion of new communication and information technologies – and attempted to understand their influence upon the changing geography of economic activity and employment in ways that were compatible with the idea that the mature conurbations of the industrial age were in decline but also emphasised that industry was not in crisis everywhere in the developed world (e.g. Amin & Thrift, 1994; Amin & Malmberg, 1992; Aydalot & Keeble, 1988; Castells & Hall, 1994; Dunford & Kafkalas, 1992; Gordon & McCann, 2000; Hall & Markusen, 1985; Markusen, 1996; Markusen et al., 1986; Storper & Scott, 1992; Sternberg, 1996; Storper, 1997). This literature spans a number of disciplines, including economic geography, institutional economics, 'socio-economics', sociology and political science, and is enormously varied. In essence, though, it tends either to focus upon one or more so-called 'propulsive' economic sectors and to examine the locational behaviour of firms active within them, or to begin with particular territories within which particularly high levels of economic innovation and growth occurred and to analyse the variety of conditions that can help explain their 'success'.

Out of this work on the spatial economic implications of globalisation and technological change came a number of controversies about the nature and consequences of a 'new' economy, the most prominent of which focused on how much change there had been between the 'old' – and at one time commonly labelled 'Fordist' – economy and its alleged 'post-Fordist' successor (Piore & Sabel, 1984; Lipietz, 1987). The term 'Fordism' dates back to the 1930s when it was used by the classical Marxist Antonio Gramsci (1982) in his analysis of why the American economy was outperforming European competitors. Gramsci put the superior productivity of American industry down to the 'scientific' mass production methods pioneered in Henry Ford's car factories. But Fordism, as a system of industrial organisation, proved durable, he suggested, only because various carrots and sticks were introduced which made 'the whole life of the nation revolve around production' and helped produce a new type of worker amenable to physically demanding, uncreative, routinised assembly-line work. The carrots offered to the industrial workforce included high wages, which fuelled mass domestic consumption and high product demand, and social benefits which paved the way to the welfare state. The sticks included prohibition and other puritanical measures to encourage discipline, monogamy and sobriety amongst workers. It was this regime of mass production and consumption that was held to have broken down in the 1970s.

For some, post-Fordism was interpreted, narrowly, as a distinctively new system of production – often termed 'flexible specialisation' – whereby firms utilised advanced technology to tailor their products more quickly to niche markets, utilising 'economies of scope', that is, extensive variations in product lines, as opposed to the economies of scale that dominated Fordist mass production. Post-Fordist firms were argued to be less hierarchical and to encourage high levels of creativity from their skilled workforces. In many cases, they were also seen to operate within dense networks of innovative producers whose interdependencies and export potential arguably provided the potential for the reinvigoration of local and regional economies.

For others, though, post-Fordist production methods could only take root within a broader 'regime of accumulation' that was characterised by a range of economic, political, social and cultural support mechanisms and was as supportive to them as the earlier Fordist regime had been to mass production. This new regime was argued to be based upon a rather different virtuous circle in which: substantial technological advances, based upon new information technologies, underpinned product and process innovations in firms geared up to servicing global markets; huge rewards, less regulated by the state, became available to core groups of highly skilled, flexible, and mainly non-unionised workers; demand grew, amongst affluent consumers, for highly differentiated consumer products and personal services; and investment flowed back into research and development to support further technological innovation. In the post-Fordist mode of regulation, the state was said to support a new accumulation regime by emphasising supply-side improvements to economic competitiveness, often at the local and regional scale, rather than through national demand management, and via national policies that emphasised labour market 'flexibility' and a remodelling of the welfare state to provide only residual support for the economically inactive and pathways into employment for the economically active.

In linking 'new' forms of production to changes in national and subnational forms of investment, regulation and governance, writers on post-Fordism provided plausible explanations for the ways in which countries in the developed world responded to the economic pressures generated by globalisation. In terms of what was seen to drive differential urban economic change, however, there was little consensus on, for example, whether the investment behaviour of transnational corporations was more important than that of governments – for example, through high-tech military spending programmes – or, alternatively, more sophisticated market-seeking behaviour by smaller firms – see, for example, the contrasts between Amin (1989), Saxenian (1996) and Markusen (1991). There was no agreement, either, about whether growing innovation and productivity was associated with relatively 'hard' economic 'inputs' (Porter, 1990) or 'softer' ones, such as the 'untraded interdependencies' that were argued to arise from relations of trust and non-monetary exchanges between firms (Storper, 1997; Cooke & Morgan, 1998; Amin, 1989) or the impact that various local political institutions or more open and accountable forms of subnational government have on economic performance (Putnam, 1993; see also Hirst, 1994). Doubts therefore remained as to whether ostensibly similar patterns of economic innovation occurred, for different reasons, in very different contexts, and hence whether 'success factors' could be understood generically and transferred from place to place (Storper, 1993).

What these literatures have in common, however, is that they tend, at best, to leave implicit the particular roles that cities and metropolitan areas – as opposed to 'regions' or even less geographically distinct entities such as 'industrial districts' (Markusen et al., 1986) or 'clusters' (Porter, 1998) – play in an emerging, more globalised economic order. The literature on post-Fordism captured some of the tendencies towards intra-urban polarisation that are addressed in Chapter 5 by examining transformations in labour markets and occupational levels, but its reliance on a relatively small number of illustrative examples of accelerated economic growth in (mainly) non-metropolitan areas, such as the so-called Third Italy, Baden-Württemberg in Germany and high-tech freeway strip developments in America, made it appear, for some time, that the geography of urban economic development, at least in the developed world, was shifting more rapidly than it really was.

Global and world cities ... and Los Angeles

A quite different strand of analysis, which emphasises continuity rather than disjuncture in national and international urban hierarchies, can be found in the literature on global and world cities, within which Los Angeles occupied a prominent, if (arguably) short-lived, position.

World cities

The phrase 'world city' dates back to the early twentieth century when Geddes (1915: 46) used it in a chapter title of his *The City in Evolution* when setting out his impressionistic view of the cities that seemed set to dominate the 'second industrial revolution'. In the hands of Hall (1966), fifty years later, a rather loose approach to the identification of world cities was tightened up considerably.

Hall's 'world cities' were drawn from a list of the world's largest metropolitan areas, by population, on the basis not of size but a set of key characteristics which, he argued, were intrinsic to 'great' cities in the advanced industrial world and whose influence, implicitly, extended beyond their national contexts. Hall's world cities contained: key political and related functions (national governments, professional organisations, trades unions, employers' federations, headquarters of major companies); major centres of trade (via major ports, road, rail and air travel infrastructures); key commercial functions (banks, insurers etc.); concentrations of professional services (health, law, higher education, research, media); and luxury consumption and entertainment functions. On this basis, albeit without presenting any comparative data that distinguished 'his' cities from others, Hall identified London, Paris, Moscow, New York and Tokyo, as well as the multi-city areas of Randstad (Holland) and Rhine-Ruhr (Germany) as world cities. In a later edition of the book (Hall, 1984), he added Hong Kong and Mexico City to the list and omitted the (deindustrialising) Rhine-Ruhr. Hall's main concerns, writing from a planning perspective, were the challenges world cities faced and how their growth had been, and might be, managed. He was less inclined to describe links between them or to analyse the 'world' roles they played.

These concerns featured more prominently in the work of Friedmann (1986; see also Friedmann & Wolff, 1982), whose world cities were argued to be 'basing points for global capital ... [within] ... an economy that seems oblivious to national boundaries' (Friedmann, 1986: 69). His 'world city hypothesis', comprising seven sub-theses, was an exploration of the roles key cities played within 'the spatial organization of the new international division of labour' based upon 'the *presumed* nature of their integration with the world economy (1986: 71; emphasis added). He attempted this by adopting the World Bank's (then) distinction between the 'core' and 'semi-peripheral' countries of the capitalist world. This meant he excluded countries in the so-called 'peasant periphery' – including (remarkably, in retrospect) China and India – and the then Soviet-influenced eastern Europe from his analysis on the basis that they were 'only weakly integrated with the world market economy' (ibid.: 72).

Using various selection criteria, 'not all [of which] were used in every case' (ibid.) – the presence of major financial centres, corporate headquarters, international institutions, high-level business services, important manufacturing centres and major transportation nodes – Friedmann devised a list of primary world cities and a 'suggestive' list of secondary cities, the differences between which were not convincingly explained. The 11 'primary' cities he identified were mainly in the US and Europe but included Tokyo, São Paulo and Singapore. Of the 19 secondary world cities he identified, four were in Europe, four in North America, four in central and south America, five in Asia, one in Africa (Johannesburg) and one in Australasia (Sydney). He then mapped these 30 cities, schematically, and posited links between them in an attempt to illustrate how three international economic 'subsystems', based on Asia, the Americas and western Europe, might be linked together via world cities across the globe.

The remainder of Friedmann's sub-theses dealt mainly with a number of loosely specified (and empirically uncorroborated) labour market characteristics of world cities, as a group, including their impacts upon international migration patterns and the extent to which their specialisation in high-level economic functions was associated with labour market polarisation and growing intra-urban inequalities. What Friedmann intended as an agenda for research on world cities was never followed up systematically. His main contribution to debate on the role of key cities in a globalising economy, based on the idea that certain cities 'articulate' economic relationships across extended territories was, however, taken up in the literature on global cities, which looked more forensically at what it meant to articulate, who it is that does the articulation, and where.

Global cities

Saskia Sassen's *The Global City* (1991) is probably the most celebrated contribution to urban theory in the period covered by our review in Chapters 3–6. In it, she analyses how a 'combination of spatial dispersal and global integration has created a new strategic role for major cities' (Sassen, 1991: 3). She does so by looking in detail at how New York, London and Tokyo function as principal 'command and control' centres within a globalising economy and at the implications that playing such a role has for those three cities' economic base, spatial organisation and social structures. At the core of her analysis is the argument that the overwhelming importance of finance capital and the managerial capacity that is needed to co-ordinate economic activity on a global scale demands the development of 'central places where the work of globalisation gets done' (Sassen, 1994: 1).

Beginning with an analysis of the growing importance of foreign direct investment and the growing proportion of world trade accounted for by producer services and markets in equities and pensions, she goes on to describe how the growth of employment in finance and producer services that support these activities within the US, UK and Japan became 'acutely' concentrated in New York, London and Tokyo, domestically, and on a scale that had no parallel in other major cities, internationally. Her account is empirically richer than those of Friedmann and Hall when it comes to identifying the differences that mark her case study areas apart, but, like both, she deals relatively little with the connections between the cities she studies or with others.

Sassen does, however, deal with other aspects of connectivity when claiming that the global orientations of New York, London and Tokyo mean they are, in important respects, disconnected from the broader geographical territories in which they sit. She also follows Friedmann in linking the labour market polarisation that is associated with the creation of significant numbers of 'high-end' jobs, and the demand they create for personal services, to a trend toward 'divided cities' (Fainstein et al., 1992). It is in these respects that her work has been most contested.

In the latter case, it has been pointed out that sectoral and occupational change are only one part of the explanation for income polarisation, which also needs to take account of the role of government in attenuating divisions via, for example, progressive taxation and the provision or subsidy of collective goods for poorer urban residents (Hamnett, 1994, 1996). In the former, notwithstanding the fact that what happens in global city financial and business service communities clearly has far-flung impacts, Sassen herself later argued that, at least at the scale of global city-region (or 'mega-region'), the relationship between global city functions, largely housed within the central urban core, and other, often less globalised economic activities, was not antagonistic and they could interpenetrate one another to mutual benefit (Sassen, 2007: 95–9). In short, whilst lower-value economic activities may be driven out of global cities by market dynamics, they might also benefit substantially from proximity to a global city.

The work on world and global cities spawned a growing literature which, amongst other things, continued to examine the implications of globalising processes for a broader range of cities (e.g. Marcuse & van Kempen, 2000; Robinson, 2002; Gugler, 2004), attempted to establish the nature and intensity of global flows and linkages between such cities empirically (e.g. Taylor, 2004;

Taylor, Derudder, Saey, & Witlox, 2006) and traced the ways in which crises and shocks that have their origins in one part of the globe are transmitted to and have an impact upon others (see the series of articles in the *International Journal of Urban and Regional Research* introduced by Keil, 2010). As a result, much more is known about the ways in which a huge range of cities experience and are linked together by globalisation. There is one city, however, that has attracted a level of scholarly attention which, on the surface, seems out of proportion to its size and importance, and to which we now turn.

And so to Los Angeles...

In one respect, the sprawling city-region in southern California centred upon Los Angeles (LA) is but one of the places that can be seen as interesting examples of the processes considered important from the variety of perspectives covered by this chapter. It has, for example, been argued to be a global city (Abu-Lughod, 1999) on the basis of its size, its explosive growth in the later twentieth century, its strong economic links with the Asian Pacific and its strength in 'postindustrial' sectors, not least in terms of its dominance within English-language film production. Whether that means it deserves the title of 'the capital of the late 20th century' (Scott & Soja, 1996), however, rests upon the argument that it is not only important but also somehow emblematic of urban development processes towards the end of the last millennium and beyond. This is precisely what certain members of the self-proclaimed 'LA School of Urbanism' (Dear, 2003) claimed, noting that many of the characteristics of LA/southern California that had once been considered exceptional had, by the end of the century, become the norm.

Claims for the growing representativeness of LA have three main elements. (Soja, 2000). First, never having been a dominant centre of 'Fordist' industry, it was arguably characterised by a post-Fordist system of 'flexible accumulation' rather earlier than other (US) cities. Second, in its demographic make-up, it is comprised of minorities. Los Angeles County, for example, having been 80% white in 1960, by 1990 contained minority white (41%), Hispanic (38%), Asian (11%) and black (11%) communities (Dear, 2000: 15). This, it might be claimed, is likely to be reproduced in more and more places in a spiky world that encourages more and more labour migration. Third, its urban form is highly fragmented and decentralised, with multiple commercial centres mixed in with endless suburbs that are only bound together by an extensive network of freeways. Together, these characteristics make it a physically and culturally fractured place, marked by huge disparities and fractious politics (Dear & Dahmann, 2008), whose 'reality' is so diverse and compartmentalised as to be difficult to comprehend. It is perhaps not surprising, therefore, that some members of the LA School see it as 'the archetype of an emergent post-modern urbanism' (Dear, 2000: 99) in the same way that Chicago was argued to be *the* emblematic 'modern' city.

Whether the loosely integrated LA School can be regarded as a source of 'postmodern' urban theory, though, is a moot point. Whilst some of the authors who align themselves to the 'school' find it useful to use the postmodern label to signify that urbanism in LA, in their view, represents a break with the past (see, especially, Dear, 2000), others do not. And even those who do, find it possible to write extensively on the city and its region as if its essential features are legible and understandable, rather than from an avowedly partial viewpoint. Indeed, it is not entirely clear in what sense the LA School is a school. As two of its apologists (Dear & Flusty, 2002: 13) observe:

> [T]he LA School is pathologically anti-leadership ... [and its] ... program-matic intent remains fractured, incoherent and idiosyncratic even to its constituent scholars ... [S]uch a school will be ... always on the verge of disintegration – but then again, so is Los Angeles itself.

There are a number of ironies in the fact that the twentieth century, in many ways 'the American century', was bookended by two schools of urban theory that considered themselves, implicitly or assertively, to be engaged in work that was critical to an understanding of contemporary urbanism everywhere. One is that neither looked far beyond the shores of the US, or even beyond their own metaphorical back yards, for examples of emblematic urban change. Another is that the LA School, in stark contrast to its Chicago predecessor, appeared unable and unwilling to consider the possibility of 'grand narratives' that might help explain how urban life and processes of urban development were changing.

Perhaps the ultimate irony, though, is that the core, pragmatic message of the LA School, that the city somehow 'works' despite the dystopian view that many of them have of it (Davis, 1990), was losing traction even during the peak period of its key authors' most prodigious writings. The claims made for the iconic status of LA and southern California were undermined as some of the driving forces that had underpinned the area's boom years – not least the enormous federal spending on defence-related technologies it attracted – lost momentum (Curry & Kenny, 1999). Indeed, with the benefit of hindsight, the city-region focused upon LA's less-studied and less-celebrated neighbour, San Francisco, whose urban structure would be far more legible to Chicago School theorists than that of LA (see Figures 3.1 and 3.2), emerged as the more 'successful' on a range of economic indicators over the 40-year period from 1970 (Storper et al, forthcoming).'

Figure 3.1   The San Francisco region: a relatively dense urban form

Reproduced with the kind permission of the NASA Earth Laboratory

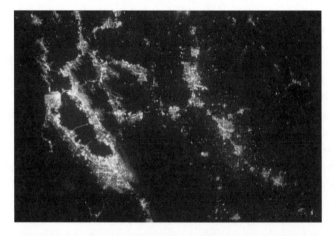

Figure 3.2   The sprawling Los Angeles region

Reproduced with the kind permission of the NASA Earth Laboratory

The new economic geography versus urban neo-liberalism

To complete this review of key conceptual literatures that speak to issues of urban competitiveness, we need to include reference to two strands of theoretical work that depart from those we have considered thus far in the sense that they are not built up, primarily, from observation of particular cases but attempt instead to develop overarching explanations of why it is that the urban world has become more 'spiky'. These approaches emerged out of radically different traditions and come to very different conclusions about what has driven spatial economic change. They are considered within the same section here because they deal with similar phenomena but are, in many respects, polar opposites of one another.

New economic geography

The new economic geography (NEG) is a slightly misleading label in that it refers to a view of geography by economists rather than of the economy by geographers. In essence, it is characterised by a rediscovery of the importance of agglomeration by a new generation of economists. There is nothing new about the notion of agglomeration, which has been a key concept in urban economics and geography for a long time.

Much of the work on agglomeration economies, historically, has focused upon providing an explanation of why firms group together rather than spread out, geographically, in order to serve spatially differentiated markets (Marshall, 1890). This form of agglomeration, which gives rise to what are usually referred to as 'localisation economies', is seen to depend upon 'input sharing', that is, the benefit accruing to firms from being located close to suppliers and purchasers of intermediate goods, and to 'knowledge spill-overs', through which firms are able to gain access to the tacit intelligence and understandings that circulate through formal and informal contact between economic agents with similar interests in particular localities and territories.

The benefits of agglomeration are not seen as accruing only to firms, however. A second form of agglomeration, giving rise to 'urbanisation economies', also provides benefit to workers and residents and is as much about demand as supply-side factors. The focus, here, is on the economic advantages of city size and diversity. Thus, for example, the extensive labour pools that are found in large urban areas not only provide employers with a high degree of choice when hiring staff, but also offer a large number of options to workers and potential workers and provide them, compared to other sorts of place, with a high level of insurance against under- and unemployment. At the same time, the high demand for finished goods, personal and consumer services and homes generated by a large and comparatively discerning residential population drives innovation and competition amongst producers for domestic urban markets. A fascination with the economic effects of urbanisation economies led authors such as Jacobs (1969, 1984) to argue that it is the classical attributes of cities noted by an earlier generation of sociologists – density, heterogeneity and the interpersonal mixing that arises from social encounters as well as employment-based contacts – rather than the sector-specific advantages associated with localisation economies that both attracts and produces economically innovative people and behaviour.

Economists have long recognised that there is a positive relationship between productivity and density – that big cities, in other words, generate bigger economic returns per head of population than smaller ones – and a number of studies show that an increase in the urban population is positively correlated with productivity gains (Ciccone, 2002; Melo, Graham, & Noland, 2009). The difficulty economists have faced is in trying to explain why. Cities, as Fujita, Krugman, and Venables (1999: 1) have noted, have long represented a puzzle for mainstream economists 'to such an extent that most textbooks in economic principles still contain literally no reference to the existence or role of cities and other geographic concentrations of economic activity'. The problem, as they see it, is that the role of increasing returns (Krugman, 1991), upon which the superior productivity of cities is seen to rest, has remained impenetrable to most economic theory, based as it is on an assumption of constant returns and notions of equilibrium which should, in principle, reduce differences between cities over time.

It is only recently that mainstream economists have begun to develop a deeper formal understanding of how it is that 'the dramatic spatial unevenness of the real economy … is … the result not of inherent differences between locations but of some set of cumulative processes … whereby geographic concentration can be self-reinforcing' (Krugman, 1991). In trying to tackle this theoretical conundrum, new economic geographers (e.g. Fujita & Thisse, 2002) have developed new models of agglomeration processes and set in train unprecedented interest in the persistent economic disequilibria that sustains cities. They have been joined by a range of other social scientists who have identified further reasons why, in the transition to the financialised, service driven economy identified by Sassen, big, dense, heterogeneous, well-connected city-regions achieve high levels of productivity and growth (Scott, 2001), leading to a future 'archipelago' economy that arguably is likely to be organised around leading city-regions rather than leading nations (Veltz, 1996).

The particular contribution that new economic geographers have brought to the debate is a neo-classical economist's suspicion of public sector intervention in the market processes that ostensibly drive these changes. Glaeser (2011: 9), for example, whose work on the analysis of the 'new' agglomeration has been highly influential, argues that:

> The hallmark of declining cities is that they have *too much* housing and infrastructure relative to the strengths of their economies. With all that supply of structure and so little demand, it makes no sense to use public money to build more supply. (emphasis in original)

Such advice is not unusual amongst a new generation of spatial economists who routinely argue against place-specific economic interventions and for policies that allow 'successful' places to grow and enable greater labour mobility so that workers can gravitate to economic 'hotspots'. Their influence can be seen in analyses underlying the policies of international organisations (e.g. World Bank, 2008) and individual national governments (e.g. BIS, 2010).

Urban neo-liberalism

In stark contrast to the new economic geography, a strand of analysis that posits a decisive role for government and public sector intervention in creating a spikier urban world emerged from a group of critical scholars, largely drawn from geography, sociology and political science, who have linked the rise and impact of 'neo-liberalism' to the tendency for national and international urban hierarchies to become stretched. Neo-liberalism, in essence, is a preference for market solutions to all human wants and needs, founded on the assumption that market provision will always prove more efficient than the provision of goods or services by the public sector. According to key figures who have been at the forefront of the study of the urban impacts of neo-liberalism, neo-liberalisation, the process through which neo-liberal ideas are ostensibly translated into practice, 'represents an historically specific, unevenly developed, hybrid, patterned tendency of market-disciplinary regulatory restructuring' (Peck et al., 2010: 330).

This somewhat vague definition, which does not lend itself very easily to empirical investigation, comes after more than a decade of research on urban neo-liberalism which draws heavily upon historical analysis. Peck (2010), for example, traced the intellectual history of neo-liberal thought and the way it has been proselytised by key US and other think-tanks. Brenner, on the other hand, focuses on policy shifts by national governments in Europe in support of his argument (2004: 101) that:

> Since the 1970s ... the project of promoting spatial equalisation at a national scale has been largely abandoned. Instead, [western European] national states have attempted to rechannel major public resources and infrastructural investments into the most globally competitive cities and regions within their territories.

Neither Peck nor Brenner suggest that neo-liberalisation takes the same form, at the same time, across the world, nor that the agents who are said to introduce it – particularly transnational institutions and national governments – do not encounter resistance. What they suggest, however, is that neo-liberalisation supports particular, privileged (urban) territories and has a disciplining effect on others. The former are enabled to compete, the latter forced. Peck and Tickell (2002: 392), largely on the basis of observations of the UK and US, summarise the latter thus:

[C]ities ... are induced to jump on the bandwagon of urban entrepreneuri-alism, which they do with varying degrees of enthusiasm and effective-ness. And ultimately, their persistent efforts and sporadic successes only serve to further accelerate the (actual and potential) mobility of capital, employment, and public investment. In selling themselves, cities are there-fore actively facilitating and subsidizing the very geographic mobility that first rendered them vulnerable, while also validating and reproducing the extralocal rule systems to which they are (increasingly) subjected.

In contrast to the world perceived by new economic geographers, then, in which cities compete but should be prevented from doing so, because it is wasteful and counterproductive, in the world of urban neo-liberalism, cities should not com-pete but are forced to, and do so with greater or lesser degrees of enthusiasm.

Discussion

This chapter has discussed various theoretical approaches to the notion of urban competitiveness. It has shown how a number of conceptual frameworks have been used to understand the relationship between economic restructuring and urbanisation during a period of profound technological change and an intensi-fication of globalising processes. Whilst accounts that dealt with urban decline, urban obsolescence and urban renaissance certainly do not follow sequentially, there is no doubt that, overall, there has been a remarkable transformation in the way that urban prospects in the developed world have been viewed.

Whilst a number of the approaches examined draw upon rich case study mate-rial, most operate at high levels of abstraction and deal relatively little with the extent to which agents within cities or acting on their behalf affect urban com-petiveness in either sense in which that term has been used. In the next chapter, we turn our attention to theories that attempt to understand how cities act.

Questions for discussion

- The idea that cities act has changed over time. What processes have cast doubt on the idea that cities can act? To what extent do you agree that the politics of globalisation has made cities less important as actors?
- Whilst urban competitiveness usually refers to economic performance, cities are also said to compete politically. Do you think economic and political competitiveness can be separated, or are they related? What consequences follow for the quality of urban life?
- Global interdependence underlies the literature on 'world cities' and 'global cities'. In what way do accounts that use these labels converge and diverge? What strengths and shortcomings do these perspectives share?

Further reading

Post-Fordism

Amin's *Post-Fordism: A Reader* (1994) remains the best general introduction to debates on post-Fordism. Storper's *Regional World* (1997) provides a good discussion of 'flexible accumulation'.

Global and world cities

Sassen's *The Global City* (1991) remains the landmark contribution in this field. Hall's *The World Cities* (1984) provides an interesting contrast. Gugler's *World Cities Beyond the West* (2004), dealing with Global South cities, provides an interesting counterpoint. Brenner and Keil's *The Global City Reader* (2006) provides useful commentary

The LA School

Dear's *From Chicago to LA* (2002) presents a varied selection of writings on LA, each of which provides some contrast with Chicago School approaches. His *Postmodern Urban Condition* (2000) is not an easy read but sets out the strongest claim for considering LA as an emblematic case of postmodern urbanism.

New economic geography

Non-specialists should start with Glaeser's *Triumph of the City* (2011) which captures the spirit of new economic geography arguments without the equations.

Urban neo-liberalism

Brenner's *New State Spaces* (2004) is the key source. Peck's *Constructions of Neoliberal Reason* (2010) is a good guide to the intellectual history of neo-liberal thought.

4

Can cities act? Urban political economy and the question of agency

Learning objectives

- To see how inter-urban spikiness can be studied through the lens of a perspective that takes cities as agents seriously
- To learn about the urban growth machine and urban regime theory as two important approaches that attempt to bring agency into the picture
- To gain an understanding of the differences and similarities between the two perspectives
- To develop an idea of the difficulties of applying these theories to empirical research

The rediscovery of agency within urban theory

The previous chapter assessed theories which help us understand recent changes in the importance of urban areas as centres of economic and political activity and decision-making and the factors that are argued to have affected those changes. Primarily, they address the power *of* places, and explanations as to why places acquire the size, status and characteristics they do, rather than examine the way in which power within or over places is or has been *exercised*. This is not to argue that the theories dealt with in Chapter 3 make no assumptions about the importance of choices made and actions taken by a range of decision-making 'units' – urban residents, commuters, migrants, visitors, governments, firms, investors and so on – or that they make no reference to these 'agents'. Indeed, many of the literatures considered in that chapter rely, to some degree, on empirical case studies that purport to exemplify the processes that the commentator in question considers important. It is nonetheless the case that such theories, because they tend to operate at a high level of abstraction, do not attach a great deal of conceptual importance to the notion of 'agency', other than in the aggregate. Hence, for example, it is far from unusual for case studies of 'urban neo-liberalism' not to pose questions about who exactly the neo-liberals are and what they do when they (allegedly) neo-liberalise. Equally, case studies of 'global' or 'globalising' cities are not always clear about the mechanisms through which processes that operate across national boundaries come to have impacts upon particular places.

Re-employing the term used in Chapter 2, the theories we have considered thus far are not 'methodologically individualist'; that is to say, they do not see individuals as the basic explanatory unit for all social phenomena in the last instance. The literature considered in this chapter is different in that it entails trying to explain how and why it is that cities can 'act', or fail to act, and with what consequences. In taking on this task, commentators in this field – usually referred to as 'urban political economy' – establish a link back to the community power debate of the 1950s and 1960s and its concern with urban politics and decision-making. As will become clear, however, this more recent literature has a broader conception of urban politics which is less concerned with formal political processes and institutions and more interested in how and why a broad range of organisations that have influence over the development and utilisation of urban assets develop the collective capacity to pursue shared purposes. It will also be shown that this stand in the evolution of urban theory, whilst it also has its origins in the US, has had significantly greater influence over conceptual and empirical work in other parts of the world.

Introducing American urban political economy

Political economy first emerged as a field of study in the seventeenth century, focusing upon 'the art of government concerned with the systematic inquiry into the causes of the wealth of nations' (McLean, 1996: 381). Its development comfortably pre-dates that of the two, ultimately more important, disciplines closely associated with it: economics and political science. Even when those two disciplines gained ascendency, however, the term survived. Many Marxist scholars, in particular, continued to describe their work as political economy because they wished to insist that economics and politics cannot be thought of in isolation but have a fundamental bearing upon one another. Over the last century, the term has become less and less specific to the point where it is used to describe a wide range of work, within any discipline, that concerns itself with the interaction between politics and markets. So, for example, political economists analyse the political aspects of economic policy-making or the way markets and market decisions affect politics and public policies.

Were these more relaxed criteria used to categorise work within urban studies over the years, much of it could reasonably be described as *urban* political economy. Indeed, the phrase was occasionally used to categorise 1970s developments in neo-Marxist urban sociology (Forrest et al., 1982). However, it is in describing the work of key urban sociologists, geographers and political scientists in the US from the 1980s onward that the phrase 'urban political economy' has become popularised. It is stretching the imagination to argue that the authors associated with this 'school' developed a new paradigm in urban studies (Feagin, 1987). Like many loose collectives, US urban political economists appear cohesive when judged by what they are not rather than by what they are. In their case, they define themselves by mutual scepticism about structuralist accounts of urban change and particularly about two highly influential approaches summarised in Chapter 2: the ecological approach associated with the Chicago School of urban sociology and the neo-Marxist approaches of the 1970s (Logan & Molotch, 1987: 4–12; Gottdiener & Feagin, 1988; Smith, 1995).

Against public choice

Most of all, though, US urban political economists take issue with the arguments made in 1981 by Paul Peterson in a book entitled *City Limits* (Peterson, 1981; Logan & Swanstrom, 1990).

Peterson's work lies within the 'public choice' tradition. In terms of urban research, public choice approaches are particularly associated with arguments in favour of the efficacy and efficiency of a highly fragmented system of local government, within which local authorities are highly dependent on locally raised resources, in offering 'choice' to residents and businesses who, at least in principle, are mobile and can gravitate to an area whose local authority offers the particular package of taxes and services that best reflects their wants and needs. In effect, 'urban' public choice provides a local institutional dimension, based on competition between local authorities, to the approach to urban 'sorting' first explored by Chicago School theorists. It is dominated by US authors (e.g. Tiebout, 1956; Bish & Ostrom, 1973), and is often seen as an attempt to legitimise the US division of labour between tiers of government, although there have been some attempts to test its assumptions elsewhere – for example, London (John, Dowding, & Biggs 1995).

Peterson's contribution was to develop public choice arguments in order to understand what forms of service provision US local authorities were and were not likely to prioritise. Essentially, his proposition is that cities effectively 'die' if they are deserted by people and firms in big enough numbers. They therefore have no choice but to try and 'capture' and retain potentially mobile businesses and residents if they are to survive. That means city administrations are compelled by the logic of their circumstances to compete against each other by engaging in what Peterson calls 'developmental politics', that is, devising strategies to improve local circumstances with respect to economic development and employment growth. As a result, they are left with virtually no scope for what he calls 'redistributive politics'. City administrations, Peterson argued, cannot behave like latter-day Robin Hoods, taking from the rich to give to the poor. There are strict limits to their capacity to use resources gathered largely from the more affluent sections of the urban population to provide goods and services which primarily benefit their poorer counterparts.

US urban political economists do not take issue with the idea that city administrations engage in competition for firms and households. Neither do they deny the importance of local developmental politics or the existence of inter- and intra-jurisdictional inequalities. Rather, they object to two features of Peterson's

Figure 4.1   Developmental politics or redistributive politics?

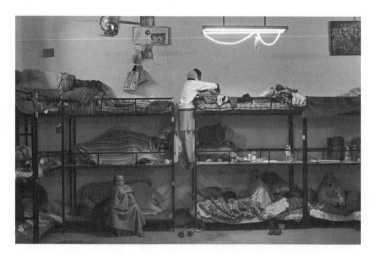

Figure 4.2   Developmental politics or redistributive politics?

analysis. The first is his assertion that local politics hardly matters and that the environment in which city administrations operate determines all their significant choices. The second is his implication that cities have a single set of 'interests' which can be understood without reference to preferences that are actually expressed, by city residents and users, through the political system or other channels. Not all urban political economists disagree violently with Peterson's conclusions, but they do take issue with the way he reached them (Sanders & Stone, 1987a, 1987b; Peterson, 1987). For them, the conditions of urban life are produced and reproduced not by the playing out of some externally imposed 'structural' logic, but by struggles and bargains between different groups and interests within cities. The outcomes of these struggles and bargains, they argue, far from serving 'the good of the city' in any general sense, reward some groups and disadvantage others.

The goal which US critics of Peterson set themselves, then, was to put the politics back into urban political economy. In this chapter, we examine two attempts to do so: the growth machine thesis, developed by Harvey Molotch and John Logan; and urban regime theory, most associated with Clarence Stone and Steven Elkin. Theirs are not the only significant voices within US urban political economy, but they provide the focus here because they offer clear and complementary, but nonetheless different, insights into the 'urban politics of production' and have generated a significant level of interest beyond the US. Neither signify a radical break with the earlier approaches within US urban studies outlined in Chapter 2. Urban regime theory can be seen as an extension of the pluralist approach (Judge, 1995; Stoker, 1995; Harding, 2009), and the growth machine thesis has an affinity with urban elite theory (Harding, 1995; Mossberger, 2009). Together, they nonetheless achieve some important and interesting conceptual advances upon the community power debate.

Urban regimes and growth machines

The original works on growth machines (Molotch, 1976, 1990; Logan & Molotch, 1987) and urban regime theory (Elkin, 1987; Stone & Sanders, 1987; Stone, 1989) combine two of the important developments in urban studies identified in Chapter 2: they are primarily interested in the urban politics of production and they stress the importance of 'human agency' in decision-making within that broad field. Neither approach assumes that the various 'actors' in the urban politics of production are unaffected by forces beyond the immediate locality. That helps distinguish them from the more 'localist' accounts within the community power debate which often ignored external factors, be they the influence of higher levels of government or wider market changes. Both nonetheless insist that, though certain patterns of behaviour may be discernible, there is nothing automatic about the interactions between actors and the effects which flow from them. In contrast to structuralist accounts, they are concerned with the role of human agency in shaping what Logan and Molotch (1987) call 'the political economy of place'.

Refining elite theory

The growth machine (or growth coalition) thesis represents a refinement of early urban elite theory, but the focus of Logan and Molotch's work is subtly different from that of community power theorists. In one sense it is more specific. Logan and Molotch stress the importance of the urban politics of production and make little reference to consumption issues. They do so because they believe decisions concerning the former dominate those relating to the latter. They therefore differ from classical pluralists who tend to assume that one sphere of decision-making has broadly the same weight as another; for example, that education policy is on a par with urban renewal policy (Dahl, 1961). Pluralists had to make assumptions of that kind in order to sustain the argument that groups of influential individuals can dominate decisions made in particular policy areas but that the composition of the influential group differs according to policy area. A rough equality of importance between policy areas was therefore critical to pluralist arguments that no one 'ruled' in an absolute sense. For Logan and Molotch, though, whoever controls the politics of production effectively controls cities.

In another sense, the concerns of the growth machine thesis are broader than those explored by the community power debate. Both pluralist and elite theorists concentrated primarily upon decision-making within local government even if, in the case of elite and neo-elite theory, it was argued that decisions were determined by powerful business leaders rather than by local politicians or officials. For Logan and Molotch, however, local governments are just one of the many players in the urban politics of production. They are interested in how a much wider group of actors relate to each other and do not seek to measure their influence only by tracing their effect on local government decision-making. In other words, the growth machine thesis is concerned with the politics of urban development in a general sense and not just with the local government politics of development.

The growth machine thesis nonetheless provides a firm link back to the community power debate in stressing that it is people, ultimately, who have power. And in the world of Logan and Molotch powerful people exercise real choices; they are not just the 'bearers' of roles somehow determined for them by deep social structures. Events are therefore to be understood as the largely unpredictable outcome of interactions between the powerful. In its approach to power, the growth machine thesis is more voluntaristic than regime theory. Logan and Molotch, like elite theorists before them, essentially view cities as being run by business leaders. They argue that 'the activism of entrepreneurs is, and always has been, a critical force in shaping the urban system' (Logan & Molotch, 1987: 52). One of the reasons why they deliberately adopt this position is that they are more concerned than regime theorists to challenge the structuralist theories that had come to dominate urban studies after the community power debate had ground to a halt.

Use value and exchange value

At the core of the growth machine thesis is a distinction between use values and exchange values, terms that are familiar within economics and have played an important role in the evolution of that discipline. Marx's treatment of them, for example, was crucial to his critique of capitalism. It led him to challenge the labour theory of value propounded by the classical economist Ricardo and to develop his own alternative, drawing upon the concept of surplus value. On the basis of that, Marx developed his understanding of the exploitation of workers under capitalism and the roots of the class struggle that would – he predicted – eventually bring it to an end. Logan and Molotch also use the concepts of use value and exchange value to identify the basis of conflict between different social groups. But they do not use the terms in quite the exacting way that many economists do. Nor is theirs an analysis based on class distinctions (Cox, 1993).

The terms 'use value' and 'exchange value' apply to anything that people use in their day-to-day lives but can also be sold or traded in a market place. In *Urban Fortunes*, though, they are applied primarily to 'property', understood as land and buildings. Logan and Molotch's argument is that most people, at most times, value their property for the day-to-day uses they get from it. For example, even if we own rather than rent our homes, we still tend to value them for the shelter they offer us and the access they provide to things we need rather than for the exchange values we might receive for them if we sold them. There are some property owners, however, whose interest in the use values of their assets is negligible compared to their exchange values and the extent to which these can be used to extract surplus value – financial gain – from others. Logan and Molotch refer to this group as 'rentiers', a term which has traditionally been used pejoratively to describe people who support themselves by charging various forms of rent to those who use their property.

Rentiers, according to *Urban Fortunes*, are at the core of the urban development process. They strive to maximise the value of their land and property holdings by helping to intensify the uses to which they are put or by seeking to replace one set of uses with another, higher-value one. In both cases their concern is to maximise rent. Rentiers, then, are a particularly dynamic and self-serving subset of all property owners, but they cannot achieve their aims alone. Land owners, for example, rarely have the expertise, the resources or the inclination to develop successful office complexes. Instead, they will try to persuade corporations or developers to put together the necessary resources on their 'patch' and take a cut of the profits in the form of rent.

Logan and Molotch consider rentiers to be the most important element of what they call 'parochial capital'. By this they mean that, because the assets rentiers own cannot easily be shifted from place to place, they are parochial in that their material interests are rooted in particular places. They are 'place-bound'; that is, their fortunes are connected to those of 'their' locality in a much more fundamental way than those who own more liquid assets such as money or stocks and shares. If rentiers do not wish to trade in property, to sell up in Blackpool and buy into Santa Barbara, they need to attract what Logan and Moltoch call 'metropolitan capital' – investment that is more mobile. When the assets rentiers own are especially sought after, for example when property markets are particularly buoyant, they may be able to achieve this goal by bargaining directly with non-local investors. Often, though, they will also need to help create the sort of local business climate that will be attractive to inward investors.

It is in trying to secure the conditions in which marriages between parochial and metropolitan capital are most likely to occur that rentiers need allies. They find them in the other 'members' of the growth machine/coalition. Some of these, like property owners, are 'place-bound', whilst others are less geographically constrained. What unites them all is a commitment to economic growth, based on the tangible benefits it will bring them. A growth machine is primarily self-serving. But its members try to legitimise their gains and disarm any critics by espousing an ideology of 'value-free development'. That means subscribing to what is usually called the trickle-down theory of economic development which argues, essentially, that the benefits of economic growth eventually percolate through to all sections of society. People who do not benefit immediately, on this view, need only be patient for the rewards of economic development to reach them. They are also best served, ultimately, by a system which promotes the highest possible level of development rather than one which interferes in it, even when it is ostensibly done in the name of equity and justice for those who derive least from growth.

Rentiers have three sets of allies within the growth machine. One comprises businesses that profit directly from the development process, for example developers, financiers, construction interests and professional practices in areas such as architecture, planning and real estate. These interests may or may not be place-bound. Smaller, locally owned firms will be most dependent on business within a small 'patch'. Locally based branches of larger concerns will be less dependent in the sense that the company has business elsewhere and so has less to fear from local economic fluctuations. But it will still be in the interests of local managements – if only because they wish to prove themselves and move on to more interesting jobs or places – to bring in as much local business as possible. Firms with no local presence at all, on the other hand, are part of 'metropolitan capital'. They are likely to be active growth machine members only if they can see a pay-off from their activity or there are other factors at play – perhaps a personal or emotional commitment to a place by a particular senior executive.

The second set of growth machine allies comprises those who benefit indirectly from economic development projects because they help boost demand for their products and services. Logan and Molotch identify local media and utility companies as particularly good examples here. Both automatically tend to sell more of their products when new residents or firms move into an area. Media companies also benefit from the increased advertising revenues which tend to flow from population growth and business expansion.

A third set of growth machine members, 'auxiliaries' in *Urban Fortunes*, comprises agencies and interests that have local ties and can benefit from some, but not all types of development. Included in this category are universities, cultural institutions such as museums, galleries and concert halls, professional sports clubs, labour unions, the self-employed and small retailers. These institutions and groups may support and involve themselves in the activities of the growth machine when their interests coincide with the core members, but there will be times when they take a more critical stance. Small retailers, for example, may find themselves opposing redevelopment plans which would result in them being displaced from profitable locations by higher-value users.

Challenging growth machines

A growth machine, then, is driven by a self-serving and self-selecting business elite that collectively wields power over the pattern of urban development by virtue of its control over substantial material and intellectual resources and its ability to smooth access to external investment. In Logan and Molotch's view, growth machines need not always embrace all the interests listed above, far less others within the wider urban community. They *can* be challenged by groups who defend the use values of property over their exchange values. Neighbourhood, community and voluntary organisations and environmental groups generally play important parts in such challenges. These and other groups can come together in broader social movements that are anti-growth, or prepared to tolerate only selective growth. Such movements can acquire power, particularly in affluent areas where residents perceive the benefits of growth to be outweighed by the costs, for example in environmental degradation or the loss of their neighbourhood's exclusive feel (Clavel, 1986; Molotch & Logan, 1990; Molotch, 1990; Schneider & Teske, 1993).

When growth machines lose momentum, though, the large corporations that normally remain aloof from local affairs in the US can be pricked into trying to remobilise them. Cleveland is often quoted as a classic case in which lobbying and campaigning by big corporations helped build opposition to and bring down a populist mayor whose policy initiatives selectively threatened the growth interests of the local business community (Swanstrom, 1985). The Cleveland example reminds us that, whatever the relations between the business elite and the wider community at any particular point in time, the success of a growth machine will depend on various forms of support or acquiescence from local politicians and bureaucrats. It is in analysing the relationship between rentiers and their business supporters, on the one hand, and the local government system, on the other hand, that the growth machine thesis becomes a little vague.

Logan and Molotch are unclear whether local governments are actually members of growth machines. But they certainly see them as strong supporters because local governments, they argue, are 'primarily concerned with increasing growth' (Logan & Molotch, 1987: 53). Quite why local governments should be predisposed to support growth strategies is not developed at length. Partly this is because Logan and Molotch expect their readership to be familiar with the US system of politics and administration. But they are also inconsistent, effectively arguing that local governments back growth machines, apart from when they do not. In explaining why they usually do, Logan and Molotch briefly contrast the US with other liberal democracies. It then becomes clear that, not unlike Peterson, they think the various features of the US governmental system predispose local governments towards highly competitive behaviour.

In briefly developing this case, they argue that the US system of local government is fragmented into a large number of units which, because each has a high degree of control over local land use or 'zoning' decisions, encourages inter-authority competition. Those decisions are often 'depoliticised': they are put into the hands of special purpose, professional bodies which operate at arm's length from local government, meaning that local communities and electors find it difficult to hold them to account. US local governments also rely very heavily on taxes raised locally from businesses and residents as opposed to resources transferred from state or national levels and raised through general taxation. As a result of these factors, Logan and Molotch argue, local politicians and officials are particularly receptive to the needs of businesses and there is vigorous competition for investment and development between American cities. They specifically contrast the American picture with the UK where, they argue:

> A strong land-use authority vested in the national government combined with the central funding of local services and the heavy taxing of speculative transactions undermines some of the energy of a growth machine system. Central government, working closely with elites in the production sphere, has relatively greater direct impact on the distribution of development than in the US, where parochial rentiers have a more central role. (Logan & Molotch, 1987: 149)

This contrast between the US and the UK throws up two important considerations. One, explored below, is that we should not assume that growth machine analysis can be transplanted, straightforwardly, into other national contexts. A second is that we need to look carefully at the way different features of local government and different sorts of relation between tiers of government affect the motivations of local public sector decision-makers. On this point, even in the US context, the arguments made within the growth machine thesis are less persuasive than those advanced by urban regime theorists, to whom we now turn.

Urban regime theory

Urban regime theory has many similarities with the growth coalition thesis but is rooted in a different theoretical tradition generally known as neo-pluralism

(Dunleavy & O'Leary, 1987: 271–318). Neo-pluralism was developed by pluralist thinkers – including key contributors to the community power debate – who accepted that their arguments were vulnerable to the critiques of neo-elite theorists and neo-Marxists. The critical issue on which they conceded ground was the relationship between politics and markets, particularly the influence that business interests might theoretically be expected to wield over the choices of governments in liberal democracies. Whereas classical pluralism saw business interests as one pressure group amongst many in the formation of policy, neo-pluralists accept that businesses have an uniquely privileged position.

The clearest neo-pluralist statement on these issues, which also gives urban regime theory much of its conceptual power, was made by Charles Lindblom in *Politics and Markets* (1977). Lindblom argues that liberal democracies have two interdependent systems of authority. One, based on the ballot box, is a system of popular democratic control realised through the various organs of representative government. The other is based on the private ownership of productive assets and is largely controlled by the business community. Business decisions are critical to public welfare since they help provide jobs, incomes and purchasing power. For that reason, public officials cannot be indifferent to business decisions. But since productive assets lie substantially in private hands, officials cannot command businesses to perform their socially 'necessary' functions; they can only provide inducements.

Private businesses as a whole therefore have a degree of 'structural' power from which they benefit automatically. Business leaders do not have to organise themselves within the political system or as an external lobbying force in order that public policy-makers are keen not to damage business performance unduly through their actions. Public officials are also likely to encourage the participation of business representatives – far more than those of other interest groups – in various fora for policy negotiation, bargaining and persuasion. However, business groups do not rest happy in the knowledge that their needs are taken seriously by public officials. They also act instrumentally. They organise themselves in attempts to ensure that the institutional structures for public policy-making, along with the policy choices that flow from them, serve their overall interests. In so doing they can mobilise human and financial resources which far outstrip those of other groups: a business campaign to change legislation, for example, will not struggle for funding in the way that a community campaign for child-care facilities generally will. In short, business interests are structurally and instrumentally *privileged*, but not all-powerful, when it comes to affecting public policy agendas and outcomes.

Urban regime theorists adopt a broadly neo-pluralist position in their analysis of urban decision-making. They see compelling evidence of business privilege at the urban scale. This arises, in substantial part, from the general climate of relations between politics and markets noted by Lindblom. In addition, though, there are a number of institutional features in the US system of government which deepen the dependence of public officials on the business community. Regime theory, especially in Elkin's work, draws these out a little more clearly than Logan and Molotch.

First, local authorities in the US, be they general purpose authorities as in most parts of Europe or special boards established for particular purposes, do not have any constitutional status. They are creatures of state legislatures and are empowered to perform only those functions for which they are given statutory responsibility by a state government. In the economic development field their formal powers are relatively limited. As a result, urban development strategies are heavily dependent on private sector resources.

Second, the way local governments are financed makes them especially sensitive to the buoyancy of the local economy and residents' incomes. The US has no tradition of inter-communal fiscal equalisation; that is, of higher levels of government moving resources between authorities to ensure that the residents of poor areas where there is high demand for local services do not have to pay much higher taxes than those in rich areas where there is low demand. Instead, there is a much more direct relation between local economic circumstances and the financing of local services. This is because grants from federal (national) and state governments have historically accounted for relatively small proportions of local government income compared to that raised from local taxes. Neither does the federal government act as a guarantor against municipal bankruptcy. Local governments must raise the bulk of their capital resources from local bonds. They are therefore reliant on the private credit market – underwriters, buyers and bond-rating agencies – which favour areas perceived to offer a 'good business climate' and tend to reward conservative fiscal discipline (Sbragia, 1983).

Third, the business community plays a strong, direct role in formal urban politics. There is no significant non-business political party in the US equivalent to the social democratic and labour parties found in Europe. As a result, business figures – or others interests acceptable to business – have traditionally tended to be strongly represented in city politics. Where political parties are not particularly important in city politics, business interests still tend to have a crucial say in the selection of political candidates. On the one hand, key politicians, especially mayors, rely heavily on private campaign funds to support their candidatures. On the other hand, business groups often have a significant degree of control over the 'slating' organisations which are responsible for selecting electoral candidates. Business groups have been influential in municipal reform efforts aimed at reducing the role of party politics locally, depoliticising local administration and trimming the powers of patronage available to 'boss' politicians (Erie, 1988).

For regime theorists, a combination of these factors means there is a very strong interdependence between politics and markets at the local level in the US. Local public officials are likely to support business-led development strategies, to enter into agreements with at least some parts of the business community when trying to realise their own development aims, and to consider business views on wider issues such as budgets, taxes and service levels very carefully. As Elkin (1987: 98) argues, '[o]fficials pursue the policies that they do because the structural features within which they work dispose them to certain interpretations'.

If public officials and business leaders are interdependent in a general sense, they have to relate to one another especially closely when it comes to the politics of urban development. Here, more than in policy areas in which the public sector has the power of command, the division of responsibilities between the state and the market means that public–private agreements are necessary to the achievement of major projects. When it comes to urban development projects, Stone suggests, votes count but resources decide. The electoral system, with its strong element of popular control, has little authority over the market decisions which underpin urban economic prosperity. Thus 'successful electoral coalitions do not necessarily govern' (Stone & Sanders, 1987: 286).

The essence of urban regime theory is that a distinction has to be made between holding political power and governing effectively; between local government in a narrow sense and local governance in a wider sense. Its emphasis is on politics before markets. In contrast to Logan and Molotch, whose analysis starts from the needs of businesses and then looks more incidentally at the way public authorities support them, regime theorists concentrate upon the way in which local politicians and bureaucrats deliver the things that will keep them in positions of responsibility and power by forming relations with elements of the business community. Local governments cannot realise all their ambitions alone. They, just like Logan and Molotch's rentiers, must seek allies. They must also adjudicate between proposals emerging from different sections of the business community, a process which encourages them to take sides and to enter into detailed negotiations with parts of the private sector. If the alliances they help to form are to become reasonably predictable and stable over time they need to be turned into robust coalitions characterised by the 'three Cs': commitment, consensus and continuity.

For regime theorists, then, *governing* coalitions must be constructed between those actors who have access to, and the power to deliver, the various resources controlled by key public and private institutions. These include material resources, such as finance, manpower and property, and less tangible ones such as political, regulatory and informational resources. No single organisation or group controls all these resources. Because there is no 'conjoining structure of command' (Stone, 1989: 5) to link the various forces together, a governing regime can only be constructed through informal bargaining and the 'tacit understandings' of regime members.

Urban regimes therefore work through a system of 'civic co-operation' based on mutual self-interest. For Stone, they are 'informal arrangements by which public bodies and private interests function together in order to be able to make and carry out governing decisions' (Stone, 1989: 6). They create order by encouraging important, independent social forces to pull together in a way they would not otherwise do over the range of issues upon which they can agree. As with the growth coalition thesis, regime theorists see a natural alliance between local public officials and place-bound rentiers. They broadly agree, too, on the other important, potential private sector players in urban regimes. Regime theory is a little different from the growth machine literature, however, in that neither Stone nor Elkin argue that all regime members are slaves to the ideology of value-free development. Different members can espouse very different ideological and political agendas. They are nonetheless drawn into regimes by the various factors mentioned above and by the prospect of 'small opportunities' becoming available to realise at least some of their aims.

The business community is once again seen as privileged in that its relatively resource-rich leaders are able to control the flow of opportunities by awarding 'side-payments' to potential opponents. In tracing the evolution of the Atlanta regime over a forty-year period, for example, Stone makes it clear that the ability of a predominantly white group of business leaders to award side-payments to the black middle class in the city was critical in maintaining business influence in an increasingly turbulent political environment. Opposition groups will sometimes feel it would serve their interests better if they refused to support particular schemes rather than accept side-payments or try to influence the way a regime operates from the inside. In such cases opponents can sometimes mobilise to defeat regime-generated development schemes. Unless they can actually put together a stronger counter-regime, though, they will lack the power to transform the structures and challenge the informal agreements which generate a constant flow of such schemes. Opponents win battles but rarely wars.

Growth machine and urban regime theory compared

As outlined so far, urban regime theory is little different from the growth machine thesis. The most important difference between the two, however, is that the former argues there to be different types of regime and not just a single growth machine model. The form a regime takes reflects the wider economic, social and political environment in which it is rooted. Elkin and Stone both identify three ideal types of urban regime which exemplify the range of historical and contemporary variation. Their typologies are a little different but both are based on three broad premises. First, the intensity of urban development issues varies over space and time, meaning that conditions which strongly encourage the growth coalition model are not found everywhere simultaneously. Second, electoral coalitions which are not firmly pro-business can achieve dominance within city politics and construct their own governing regimes. Third, and notwithstanding the previous point, where urban development does become a critical issue, the complex coalitions necessary for regime formation favour some forms of electoral politics over others.

Elkin offers an historical perspective. He distinguishes between pluralist, federalist and entrepreneurial political economies, each of which is associated with a particular sort of regime. Pluralist regimes, he argues, were associated with the physical and economic transformation of downtown business areas in the older metropolitan areas of the US during the 1950s and 1960s. They typically attempted to restore cities' tax bases by stemming the loss of businesses and upper-income residents to the suburbs and beyond. Within pluralist regimes, political leaders were equal or senior partners with 'downtown' (city centre) rentier and other business interests. The 'pluralism' of these regimes lay in the fact that the development regimes were not all-powerful. They coexisted with other, relatively independent coalitions which dominated decision-making in other policy areas.

Elkin's description of the pluralist regime matches those set out in the classic pluralist community power studies. He makes it clear, however, that the pluralism of that system was in many respects illusory. Later experience – particularly the 1970s era of local government financial crises and the fierce federal government expenditure cutbacks of the Reagan years – suggested that the development coalition could become the powerhouse of the regime once external levels of support for cities began to dwindle. In less favourable financial circumstances, he argues, a regime that bears more resemblance to the growth coalition is able to flex its muscles and impose costs – in the form of budget, manpower and service cuts – on other policy areas when the business climate is perceived to be seriously undermined (see also Shefter, 1992).

First, though, came a period dominated by what Elkin calls the federalist political economy. The regimes that typified this period developed in the context of a growing decentralisation of population and economic activity from central cities, a strengthening civil rights movement, greater demands for community services and a backlash against the skewed distribution of costs and benefits which often resulted from the urban land-use changes associated with the pluralist era. The rather narrowly based land-use alliances which formed the backbone of pluralist regimes were ill-equipped to deal with a broader set of non-business demands. On their own, they were likely to struggle to build more inclusive regimes which drew in members from the increasingly confident and demanding ethnic minority and neighbourhood groups.

However, their task was made easier by the federal authorities that developed national programmes to channel significant resources into urban and community development programmes. These federal resources, which can be seen as a form of side-payment, helped absorb the costs of community and neighbourhood politicisation and the pressures they generated for the further development of local services. They managed to head off potential tensions between land-use and development interests and those groups, including local government officials and their various clienteles, who supported growth in services rather than investments which related more directly and immediately to the quest for economic growth. In other words, they forestalled regime failure, and avoided significant change, until the cutbacks of the later 1970s and the Reagan era.

The entrepreneurial political economy and the sort of regime associated with it derives from Elkin's work on Dallas. He implies that circumstances in the US from the 1980s on mean this is the dominant form of contemporary regime, although his historical periodisation breaks down somewhat at this point. Elkin makes it clear that the entrepreneurial political economy is not at all new to Dallas. Indeed, the traditionally strong instrumental business role in city politics had long sustained a set of governing structures (business-dominated slating organisations, a depoliticised city-manager system) which encourage a very strong correlation between the agendas of business figures and public officials and screen out anti-growth protest. Although Elkin saw the Dallas regime as having become more complex in the 1970s and 1980s as corporate identification with the city waned and neighbourhood mobilisation grew, his account suggested that the essentials of the regime remained intact. They could comfortably be maintained through side-payments to opposition groups whose bargaining position was limited by the city's politics and its electoral and administrative arrangements.

Stone's typology suggests variation in space rather than over time. For him, the key questions are not about historical eras and the forces that typified them but the variation in current conditions which encourages different forms of regime. Stone suggests a distinction between caretaker, progressive and corporate (or activist) regimes. The latter, evident in his study of Atlanta, are essentially the land-use-dominated coalitions of Elkin's entrepreneurial political economy and Logan and Molotch's growth machine. Caretaker regimes are the least ambitious, and hence the least complex and inclusive. They are primarily concerned with maintaining the delivery of routine city services rather than helping organise physical and economic transformation. Such regimes provide little threat to business interests – indeed, the electoral coalitions on which they rest are often dominated by small business owners – but neither are they sufficiently broad-based to organise complex development programmes should the need arise.

Progressive regimes, on the other hand, are characterised by strong political and community leaderships who favour anti-growth or controlled growth strategies. They generally aim to ensure a more equitable distribution of benefits, for example by expanding services and maintaining housing choices for a wide range of income groups. Progressive regimes therefore find an accommodation with business interests less easy and tend to be more fragile. External factors have to be propitious for them to maintain ascendency. It helps if the business community is relatively weak and unorganised or has an unusually strong commitment to helping the locality in social as well as economic terms, as was the case, for example, with old style 'company towns'. As Elkin argued, it also helps if support is elicited from higher levels of government, as at the peak of the federalist era. It is interesting that the one example of a progressive regime identified by Stone and Sanders (1987) came from Europe rather than the US. Other commentators nonetheless claim to have found examples of progressive regimes in North America (Clavel, 1986; DeLeon, 1992a).

Power in urban regime theory

It is clear, then, that urban regime theorists have a more complex view of power than that advanced by the growth machine thesis (Stoker, 1995: 64–6). Whilst they see accommodations between powerful individuals as ultimately being decisive, they pay more attention to 'structural' factors. Theirs is effectively a realist analysis (although it is not presented as such), which isolates a number of 'structural' factors, describes how they predispose individuals to particular types of decision, but then leaves the task of tracing out precisely how structures influence actual decisions to empirical analysis. Stone, like Elkin, insists upon the importance of socio-economic and institutional contexts, particularly when it comes to conditioning the behaviour of public sector decision-makers. In his words, 'public officials form their alliances, make their decisions and plan their futures in a context in which strategically important resources are hierarchically arranged' (Stone, 1980: 979). This hierarchical arrangement of resources means a less than equal distribution of power between individuals and groups which cannot be overcome, as classical pluralists suggest, by the sheer force of an interest group's preferences or the extent of its mobilisation. For Stone, those who derive most advantage from this skewed pattern of control over resources have 'systemic power'.

Systemic power is concentrated within key public and private institutions which control substantial resources. It affords certain individuals more *potential* to achieve things than their fellow citizens, whether or not they use it or even appreciate they have it. As a result, other actors will take their interests into account whether or not they are required or asked to do so. But other forms of power need to be used if potential is to be tapped. One of these is *command power*. Belonging to an organisation which controls significant resources is not enough unless powerful individuals can commit those resources, against the wishes of others if necessary. Command power is used to achieve compliance from other individuals or groups in the wider community over whom the organisation has formal authority. It is also deployed within particular organisations by individuals who occupy high positions in the organisational hierarchy; in other words, by those who can tell their colleagues what to do.

Systemic and command power are a formidable combination. They provide the basis for domination – a form of control that does not rely upon the consent of the controlled. Because power is diffused across a wide range of institutions, though, domination over a limited number of 'subjects' is not always enough. Systemic and command power are inadequate for ensuring the successful realisation of more complex strategies and projects involving co-operation between bodies which cannot require compliance from one another. In these cases, the capacities of relatively independent institutions and organisations need to be fused together on the basis of mutual interest and consensus. Two further forms of power therefore become relevant. One is *coalition power*. This is used when decision-makers in institution A use the independence and strength that comes from the resources they control to form an alliance with another independent institution, B, to achieve something that neither A nor B could achieve alone. Coalition power is necessary to all partnerships between independent institutions and groups, no matter how short-lived are their alliances. But it is a fourth form of power that gives them stability and continuity.

Pre-emptive power (Stone, 1988) is the most individualistic form referred to by regime theorists and is best understood as a capacity for leadership. Whilst individuals might have privileged access to the other three forms of power, they will be unable to take part in the building of a governing regime and to help sustain it over time unless they are able to pre-empt the use of power by others. To give a simple illustration of how pre-emptive power works, assume A, B, C and D are independent institutions, that x and y are two potential courses of action and that the co-operation of at least three institutions is needed to follow either course successfully. If A takes the initiative and persuades B to support course x, they automatically pre-empt the future. At the very least, they prevent course y because even if C and D decide they prefer it they will not be able to override A and B. A and B also strengthen their bargaining power *vis-à-vis* C and D considerably because they know that they only need the agreement of one of them to ensure course x is followed.

Pre-emption works in both positive and negative ways. It strengthens and extends relationships between the various parties to a regime whilst at the same time making it harder for alternative regimes to form. The more cohesive a regime becomes and the greater the level of resources controlled by its individual components, the more its critics will be tempted to work alongside it and reap some of the benefits it can bring rather than oppose it outright.

The normative dimension

Neither regime theory nor the growth machine thesis – nor, indeed, the bulk of US urban political economy – seeks only to describe the nature of decision-making for urban development. These theories are descriptive-empirical (Stoker, 1995: 17) in that they explain certain 'facts' by referring to a range of variables which 'cause' them. But they are also normative; that is, they show a concern not just for the way things are but also for the way they should or might be. There are two strands to normative argument. One entails establishing why the way things currently are can be adjudged deficient in some important senses. The growth coalition thesis, along with Elkin's variant of regime theory, is particularly assertive in this respect. The other means specifying how things might be improved. Neither regime theory nor the growth coalition thesis is remotely as strong in this regard. Their nod towards normative concerns nonetheless provides yet another link back to the community power debate. Pluralists and elite theorists asked 'who, if anyone, rules?' not just because they had an academic interest in the answer but because they wished to go on to suggest 'who benefits' and to judge the society they described accordingly. Urban political economy does the same.

For Logan and Molotch (1987: 88), the systematic favouring of exchange values over use values in urban decision-making means that '[i]n many cases, probably in most, additional local growth under current arrangements is a transfer of wealth and life chances from the general public to the rentier groups and their associates'. They argue that the socio-economic burdens of 'urban' decision-making tend to fall disproportionately on low-income communities and marginal local businesses. It is these groups that tend to suffer most from the physical displacement caused by redevelopment strategies. Residents who rely on welfare payments or poorly paid, unskilled jobs also tend to find that they are unable to compete with new residents or commuters for access to many of the better employment opportunities that result from development projects and strategies.

Neither does economic growth necessarily generate genuinely additional economic activity. It can simply shift it around, meaning that local administrations effectively poach from one another by bidding for different forms of economic activity without adding to aggregate wealth. The intense inter-urban competition for development that growth machine or activist regime politics encourages, in the opinion of Logan and Molotch, provides questionable net benefits. For the 'losers' in the competition, the costs of playing the game can be very high. Local administrations commit growing resources to competitive growth strategies but if their efforts are unsuccessful their financial health, and hence their ability to provide other services, invariably suffers.

Urban regime theory, at least in Elkin's variant, takes the higher moral ground in this debate. The systematic bias towards business interests which invariably results from urban regime formation, for Elkin, represents a failure of popular control and places severe limits on 'social intelligence', that is, the extent to which 'problems that city residents face collectively are dealt with' (Elkin, 1987: 5). He argues that urban regimes, as constituted in the periods he wrote about, represent a corruption of the commercial republic envisaged by America's Founding Fathers. Their hope was for a society in which economic buoyancy, based on private ownership, was not an end in itself but provided the platform upon which a democratic society could practise a deliberative, political way of life.

Elkin argues that the historical development of urban political institutions does not encourage communities to engage in measured deliberation about how to reconcile private property rights with a system of representative government for the good of all. Instead, citizens are encouraged to behave in one of two self-interested ways. Either they are reduced to acting as clients to local service-delivering

Figure 4.3 Shrinking cities are paying the price for rising inter-urban inequalities

© Shrinking Cities

bureaucracies which compete for limited resources with others, ostensibly on behalf of their clientele. Or they become active within a governing regime, in which case they are likely to engage in bargaining designed to make sure that decisions favour as far as possible the particular groups or organisations they represent. In both cases, the roles of citizens are substantially created by an institutional system which does not function in their wider interests.

Critiques and applications

Both the growth machine thesis and urban regime theory make valuable contributions to debates about the urban politics of production. They build upon understandings first developed within the community power debate in a way more attuned with later times. Neither are particularly radical. They are 'middle-range' theories which take for granted the essential features of a liberal democratic, capitalist system and the particular relations between politics and markets which exist in the US. Many of the critiques and commentaries on the two theories, similarly, are middle-range ones which come, in the main, from broadly sympathetic US colleagues, including some who have been involved in trying to apply a growth coalition or regime framework to further US case studies (Feagin, 1987; Clark, 1988; Cox & Mair, 1988, 1989; DeLeon, 1992b; Clarke, 1990b; Rosentraub & Helmke, 1996; Beauregard, 1996; Cox, 1996; Horan, 1996; Sites, 1997; Leo, 1998; Lauria, 1996; Stone, 2001a, 2006; Austin & McCaffrey, 2002; Burns, 2002; Imbroscio, 2003; Domhoff, 2006; Mossberger, 2009).

Evaluating US urban political economy

The most common, relatively prosaic criticisms of *Urban Fortunes* are that its authors have a 'limited conceptualisation of the local state' (Clarke, 1990a: 191) and a narrow view of the economic development process (Clarke, 1990a). As noted above, Logan and Molotch are unrepentant about the US-centric nature of their analysis and clearly acknowledge the impact that different forms of intergovernmental relations and resource transfers have on the 'energy' and nature of urban growth politics. That said, they see US federal and state governments as having influence upon growth machines mainly through programmes that support urban property development. This position is rather less sophisticated than Elkin's which demonstrates the more profound effects that constitutional arrangements and the actions of higher levels of government can have on the nature and direction of local policies and the coalitions of interests that support them.

On the issue of economic development, it is said that Logan and Molotch focus disproportionately on property development which is only one facet of the local economy and therefore does not – or should not – always form the centre-piece of local growth strategies. Another charge is that they assume, too readily, that distinctions can be made between rentier and non-rentier business interests and between parochial and metropolitan capital. Together, these two features of Logan and Molotch's analysis allow them to boil down the quest for economic innovation and growth to a simple process in which rentier-led coalitions in different localities compete with each other to offer lowest-cost sites to footloose corporate investors. For many critics, however, the world is more complicated. The rentiers of the growth machine thesis, for one thing, are a dying breed. Growing property speculation and corporate rationalisation, often on an inter-national scale, mean fewer and fewer assets are locally owned. Such property that does remain locally owned often lies in the hands of corporations which operate in a number of different economic sectors. For them, property owner-ship and speculation help spread business risk but are not the sole source of their profitability (Feagin, 1987: 519).

The gist of both arguments is that capital is neither as parochial nor as dom-inated by property dealing as the growth coalition thesis suggests. The level of 'local dependence' which is exclusively related to property ownership is not likely to be as significant as that experienced by Logan and Molotch's rentiers. As a result, those somewhat one-dimensional rentiers will not necessarily per-form the driving role that *Urban Fortunes* anticipates. This set of criticisms underestimates the subtlety of the growth machine thesis a little. In actual fact Logan and Molotch do recognise that more complex and less localised patterns of control over property, one obvious product of globalisation, can reduce the energy of growth machines. However, critics are still entitled to question the importance they attach to parochial rentiers rather than to property owners *per se*. It is not altogether self-evident that rentiers will always necessarily lie at the centre of growth coalitions nor that the desire and search for growth is any less profound in those instances when they do not.

A further criticism is that capital is not as footloose as Logan and Molotch suggest (Cox, 1993). Two potentially important implications for the growth coalition thesis follow. First, inter-city competition may not be quite as fierce as *Urban Fortunes* suggests. Second, even if it is, local attempts to capture metro-politan capital through property measures may not be decisive; there are other policy tools for local economic development that can help 'anchor' mobile eco-nomic activities. Few would argue that the secret of business success begins and ends with taking care of property needs. Locational choices are affected by many other factors such as the availability of local skills and good residential and cultural environments, relations between employers and workforces, the density of local networks of suppliers and business services, availability of risk capital, access to modern communications technologies, the proximity of supportive higher education institutions and so on. These factors, which give rise to huge variation in the 'local social relations of production' (Eisenschitz & Gough, 1993: 120–71), invariably outweigh property considerations when it comes to underpinning economic innovation and growth.

A number of implications follow for the growth machine thesis. One is that companies cannot necessarily play local administrations off against each other for subsidies and incentives as decisively as Logan and Molotch imply. This suggests, in turn, that local economic strategies to lure external capital – or to retain and build local businesses, usually an equally important policy goal – need to extend well beyond a concern with property development. This seems self-evident from the fact that local administrations in the US, as elsewhere, involve themselves in a wide range of economic development initiatives, for example in relation to research and development, capital formation, enterprise and skills training, technology transfer, company product and process innovations, and developments in transport and communications infrastructures. As Cox (1991) argues, policy development in these fields can be just as powerful a basis for inter-city competition as the preparation of competitively-priced sites. Indeed, the success of various academic 'gurus' such as Porter (1996), Etzkowitz (Etzkowitz & Leydesdorff, 2000) and Florida (2005b) in providing commercial analysis and advice to policy-makers is founded on a variety of 'soft' factors that enable economic innovation and growth. The obvious corollary is that the interests involved in growth machines must not only extend well beyond property interests, as Logan and Molotch themselves accept, but also ignore and sometimes contradict them if their efforts are to be effective (see A. Harding, 1991, on the UK experience).

The most fundamental charges levelled against the growth coalition thesis, as well as urban regime theory, however, raise the thorny issue of structure and agency in urban analysis. Logan, Molotch, Elkin and Stone are seen by some as insufficiently critical purveyors of the 'new' urban politics of development. According to this line of argument (Cox, 1993, 1995; Peck, 1995; Jessop, 1996; Ward, 1996; Hall & Hubbard, 1996), US urban political economy, in trying to escape the problems of structural analysis, became too voluntaristic and routinely overemphasised the role of human agency. Notwithstanding the arguments made by Stone in particular about the importance of 'systemic power', its exponents are said to 'assign causal power to local political networks and thereby suggest, unintentionally perhaps, that spatial variations in urban fortunes are merely a by-product of the geography of charismatic leadership' (Jessop, 1996: 6). In other words, they assert that people make their own history but pay insufficient attention to the constrained circumstances in which they do so.

This problem does not mean regime theory and the growth coalition thesis have no merit, but neither can it be resolved easily within the parameters they adopt. The solution, it is argued, is to put urban political economy approaches into a broader analytical framework which can help identify the broad economic and political constraints within which regimes and coalitions operate. In other words, the 'micro-diversity' of regimes and coalitions has to be seen in the context of 'macro-necessities' originating beyond the city (Jessop, 1996: 7).

It should be noted, however, that this particular structure–agency debate relies upon the assumption that the purpose of regime theory and the growth coalition thesis is to explain variations in urban fortunes. As is made clear below, this is a somewhat controversial assumption. Logan, reflecting on the response to his work with Molotch (Logan, Whaley, & Crowder, 1997: 624), conceded that 'after two decades of research we are still unsure whether growth machines make a difference to urban development' and added that they 'did not argue that growth machines *actually* affect growth, but only that they *attempt* to do so' (Logan et al., 1997: 625; emphasis in original). Keating (1991: 189) went further in arguing that 'the main effects of the commitment to growth are on the urban political structure and the priorities of local governments rather than on local economic performance'.

Turning to urban regime theory, it is clear that this form of analysis has slipped into mainstream urban studies even more smoothly than the notion of growth machines. Indeed, it is argued that, in the US especially, it became the 'dominant paradigm' and was seized upon so avidly that 'there is a great danger that [its] very popularity has created a new descriptive catchword – a regime – in place of an explanation of the phenomenon under question' (Stoker, 1995: 62). One paradoxical criticism, therefore, is that regime theory has been absorbed into US urban debates too uncritically. Partly as a consequence, many of the more notable critiques have come from non-American commentators. Their concerns usually stem from attempts to test the relevance of regime analysis in other national contexts (Harding, 1994; Le Galès, 1995; Stoker & Mossberger, 1994; John & Cole, 1998). But other concerns relate to the internal consistency and general value of the theory and its concepts.

Much of the debate about the strengths and weaknesses of urban regime theory arises from different interpretations of its scope and ambitions. At the core of the controversy is what regime theory is really intended to do. That question has three main aspects. One is whether the theory is supposed to be universal; that is, will we find a regime operating in all places at all times so long as we look hard enough? The second is whether the theory is dynamic; that is, can it explain why a regime might develop organically, crumble or give way to another? The third is the ever-powerful 'so what' question; what follows from regime analysis and does it do any more than describe?

On the first of these questions the clear implication of Elkin's work, and Stone's earlier writings, is that regimes are highly specific, not universal. Whilst all the cities which they and their co-authors examined empirically were argued to contain regimes, they were deliberately chosen to illustrate different regime types. Their choice of cities apart, there is nothing in the bulk of Stone and Elkin's analyses to suggest regimes are characteristic of all cities at all times. It is therefore somewhat surprising that Stone subsequently advocated that regimes be defined, very broadly, as 'the arrangements through which urban communities are governed' (Stone, 1997: 7). Whilst this is consistent with critics' suggestion that 'governance' should be the main focus of urban political economy, particularly for the purposes of comparative study (Pierre, 2005), it contradicts Stone's earlier claims that regimes have to be characterised by the use of pre-emptive as well as coalition, command and systemic power. John and Cole (1996) note how the distinctiveness and strengths of urban regime theory are easily lost if a regime is understood as *any* arrangement by which local government co-operates with the business community and other interests. They, like others who have used urban regime theory most productively, suggest one should only speak of a regime when there is stability, predictability and longevity to a specific set of informal governing arrangements, to the institutions, agencies and interests that take part in them, and to the strategic objectives and policies they develop and promote.

Thus regime theory, at least when strictly defined, offers researchers a set of analytic tools with which to understand differences between cities in space and over time. The theory, in and of itself, does not answer the 'so what?' question. Regime theory is primarily analytic rather than predictive. Neither it nor the growth machine approach claims that success in coalition-building leads inevitably to urban economic success, however measured. Indeed, the critical positions taken by Elkin, Logan and Molotch with respect to the *effects* of regimes/coalitions make it clear that they think growth strategies can fail or, even when successful, result in highly uneven patterns of costs and benefits for different groups. Neither argue that cities characterised by regimes and growth machines hold their destinies in their own hands, only that those destinies can be affected more by coalitions of the powerful than they would be in their absence.

The one general characteristic regime theory anticipates is the tension between public and private systems of authority and the need for some form of resolution through public–private relationships, whether that entails co-operation, antagonism or simple non-communication. In using regime concepts, researchers can assess why, and to what effect, 'regime-driven' cities react decisively to certain conditions when the same cannot be said of other places in similar situations.

'Decisive' reactions are not necessarily 'better' or 'more progressive' ones. It is seen as axiomatic that regimes will act in ways which do not benefit all citizens. It is even possible, in the short term, that the strategies they adopt will be detrimental to the majority. Urban regime theory, in contrast to Peterson, simply emphasises the capacity for choice. It insists that decisions taken freely by powerful individuals matter, are not predictable, and that the development trajectories of cities can change as a result.

So, as Orr and Stoker (1994) argue, there are not only variations in regimes but also cities without regimes. Even a city run by an unambitious caretaker regime will differ from a regimeless city. In the former there will be stability and continuity within the political and executive leadership and in the limited collection of allies it needs to ensure the continuation of its policy priorities and the programmes that support them. Regimeless cities, by contrast, will more likely be characterised by political instability, discontinuity in institutional relations, crises and crisis management, and big swings in policy priorities and programme content. It is not the purpose of regime theory, then, to provide a comprehensive typology which accounts for governing arrangements in all places at all times. Stone and Elkin's typologies do not exhaust the possibilities of the real world. They are 'ideal types' of regime intended to illustrate the range of variation that can be expected. The next logical question, therefore, is what causes variation and whether Elkin or Stone's models are dynamic enough to account for change.

Neither Stone nor Elkin describes the transition from one regime to another. Their major empirical studies, of Atlanta and Dallas, deal with evolution rather than revolution in the nature of regimes. Both imply, though, that a more pronounced transition can occur and indeed that regimes can collapse without being replaced (Stone, 2001b). Both see local politics as having an important role in encouraging or preventing such a change, depending upon how local governments respond to pressures from local electorates and business communities. Both acknowledge that instability can arise from wider economic changes and the effect they have locally, for example on the composition of the local business community and its leadership, on the built fabric and environment of the city and on the well-being of city residents and the demands they place on public authorities as a result. Elkin's account, although it is less advanced than others in this regard (Mollenkopf, 1983; Kantor, 1995), also makes it clear that higher levels of government play important roles in predisposing local authorities to certain sorts of decision or cushioning them from the need to make others. In a rough, rule-of-thumb way, then, regime theory is dynamic but there is a need to specify more clearly how transitions between or from regimes take place and in contexts other than that of the US (Stoker & Mossberger, 1995).

Exporting theory

The impact that urban regime theory and the growth machine thesis had within the US proved to be as profound as that which followed from the community power debate. Unlike that earlier literature, however, US urban political economy has also had significant influence beyond the US. It has played at least some role in framing empirical work undertaken in very different parts of the old 'developed' world, including the UK (Cooke, 1988; Lloyd & Newlands, 1988; Bassett & Harloe, 1990; A. Harding, 1991, 2000; Axford & Pinch, 1994; Valler, 1995; Rogerson & Boyle, 2000; Wood, 2004, Tretter, 2008; Harding, Harloe, & Rees, 2010), Denmark (Andersen, 2001), France (Levine, 1994; Le Galès, 1995; Nicholls, 2005; Dormois, 2006; Pinson, 2010), Germany (Strom, 1996; Sellers, 2002; Gissendanner, 2003), the Netherlands (van Ostaaijen, 2010) and Italy (Vicari & Molotch, 1990; Pinson, 2009; Vitellio, 2009), as well as former 'new world' countries such as Canada (Leibovitz, 1999, 2003; Hamel & Jouve, 2008), Australia (Caulfield, 1991), New Zealand (Wetzstein, 2007; Shiba, 2008) and more recently developed and developing counties including Israel (Margalit, 2009), Korea (Bae & Sellers, 2007), Mexico (Cabrero Mendoza, 2005), Russia (Hughes, John, & Sasse, 2002; Brie, 2004; Golubchikov & Phelps, 2011), Turkey (Bezmez, 2008) and even China (Zhu, 1999; Ma, 2002; Zhang, 2002; Yang & Chang, 2007; Zheng & Hui, 2007; Wang & Scott, 2008; Chien & Wu, 2011). There is also a small cross-national comparative literature, including two-country comparisons, for example between the UK with the US (DiGaetano & Klemanski, 1993, 1998) and the UK and France (John & Cole, 1996, 1998), and others drawing upon the experience of three or more countries (Thornley & Newman, 1996; Harding, 1997; Kantor, Savitch, & Haddock, 1997; Molotch, 1990; Molotch & Vicari, 1988).

Difficulties of applying growth machine and urban regime theory

Empirical applications of the two theories, whilst voluminous, vary greatly in their seriousness. The empirical literature has generated a range of insights which would probably not have emerged from previous approaches. Taken together, though, they are characterised by three sets of difficulties. One, related to the previous discussion, concerns the undisciplined way the theories have often been used. A second concerns their ethnocentricity; that is, the extent to which they deal with phenomena that are unique to the US and therefore have limited relevance for cross-national analysis. The third concerns research methodologies and the paucity of guidance urban political economists provide to potential researchers on how to apply their theories.

On the first point, it is clear that the theories are used more sensitively by some empirical researchers than by others. There is an unfortunate tendency for researchers to simply pin a regime or growth machine label to the particular set of governing arrangements they study without demonstrating how or why they came to their conclusions. When empirical realities do not seem to fit the available categories, researchers simply create more. The stock of ideal regime types has therefore grown almost to mirror the complexity of the real world, and the original terms have lost some of their distinctiveness and explanatory power in the process (Ward, 1996). We saw how Stoker (1995) criticised the way the watering down of concepts has generated descriptive typologies rather than conceptual explanation in the US. John and Cole (1996: 5), concentrating upon the European literature, agree, asserting that 'recent case studies seem to count any set of public-private relationships as a regime'.

It is hard to argue with these criticisms. One 'regime' study, for example, describes how one city's political leadership so thoroughly alienated the local business community, the national government and its parent political party at national level that a majority of local politicians were permanently excluded from holding party positions or electoral office. The political leadership in question controlled the city authority for less than 4 years before the electoral coalition was forcibly dismantled. During that time, the local authority failed to develop productive relations with any other significant agencies or interests. And yet that short-lived and ineffectual leadership group is labelled a 'radical regime', one of eight new regime types identified by the authors (Kantor et al., 1997). There are numerous other instances of terms being used imprecisely. Growth machines are identified without any reference being made to rentiers and land owners. Regimes are discovered without any analysis of how civic co-operation was achieved through the selective use of side-payments, the pursuit of small opportunities and so on.

It is difficult to excuse failures to apply a theoretical approach as rigorously as possible. However, there may be reasons why it is not easy to apply. One, an argument constantly made against the cross-national application of both the theories discussed here, is ethnocentricity. So, for example, we might question Bassett and Harloe's (1990) claim to have identified a long-run growth coalition in Swindon. Their account is vulnerable to the criticism that it concentrates entirely upon relations between central and local governments and undertakes no analysis of the actions of the business community and other non-statutory interests or the way they related to the public sector. Strictly speaking, they do not even attempt to operationalise the growth machine thesis. On the other hand, we should see their account in the context of other studies which apply

US concepts more rigorously but still end up identifying a much stronger role for the public sector in the urban politics of production than that predicted by US urban political economists.

Such studies show that in many respects US theories *are* ethnocentric in that they are based on the local institutional structures, the relations between different tiers of government, and the broad division of labour between politics and markets that applies in the US (Harding, 1994). They are therefore blind to the fact that independent businesses and business organisations do not have such a strong political role in other national contexts and do not account easily for differences in intergovernmental financing and systems of financial and land-use regulation. But if the US literature *is* ethnocentric, the question is what, if anything, to do about it. As John and Cole (1996) note, critics of US theories divide into two camps on this issue. Some, having weighed the options, simply deny their utility for analysing non-US experiences (Shaw, 1993; Le Galès, 1995; Davies, 1996; Wood, 1996). Others seek to improve the theories' transferability. On the one hand, this means retaining those aspects that are useful in the analysis of any liberal democracy; primarily the neo-pluralist foundations of regime theory and the notion that coalition-building between levels of government and between public and private sectors is essential to the urban politics of production. On the other hand, it means taking the US out of US urban political economy and replacing those elements of the analysis which are US-specific with others that encourage cross-national comparison. One way this has been attempted is by expanding the range of typologies normally used and placing greater emphasis on bargaining between different levels of government (Keating, 1991; Stoker & Mossberger, 1994). Another, as noted above, is to make links with other theories which can make more sense of cross-national changes and to view US theories more as hypotheses which need empirical testing rather than as truths waiting to be discovered (Jessop, 1996; Harding, 1996).

Whichever option is chosen to place urban political economy approaches in an appropriate cross-national context, a final obstacle to the empirical application of US theories still has to be faced: what methodological tools should be used? On this issue the silence of the main theorists themselves is almost deafening. Given the links which both theories have to the community power debate, in which methodological issues were pored over endlessly, there is surprisingly little discussion of empirical research methods in US urban political economy. Only Stone (1989: 254–60) is explicit about the way he assembled and processed his case study material. He used two sources: the local newspaper plus a series of interviews undertaken, he informs us, not as a record of events but as an 'aid to interpretation'. Beyond that, one searches the literature in vain for any idea of what counts as evidence in the development of theories in urban political economy. It is this gap, more than the problem of ethnocentricity, which prevents more informed debate about the strengths and weaknesses of urban regime theory and the growth coalition thesis in their own terms and as tools for comparative research. We return to these issues in the final chapter.

Questions for discussion

- Urban regime and growth machine theorists have taken issue with the public choice perspective. What are their main objections, where do they differ in their objections, and what do you think about them?
- Urban regime theory challenges the growth coalition thesis. How does the first define power and what does this refinement, in your view, add to the understanding of inter-urban inequalities?
- Inter-urban competition affects urban decisions regarding development versus distribution. Think about examples where intra-urban problems may be reduced or sharpened through development politics.
- This chapter has discussed some of the problems of applying the theories discussed to empirical projects. What strategies can you think of to resolve these issues?

Further reading

The growth machine thesis

The core texts here are Molotch's 'The city as a growth machine' (1976) and Logan and Molotch's *Urban Fortunes* (1987). Logan, Whaley, and Crowder's 'The character and consequences of growth regimes' (1997) offers a very useful review of empirical work on growth machines in the US and reflects thoughtfully on the continued usefulness of Logan and Molotch's original approach.

Urban regime theory

The core texts are Stone and Sanders' *The Politics of Urban Development* (1987), Elkin's *City and Regime in the American Republic* (1987) and Stone's *Regime Politics* (1989). Regime theory is discussed by Stoker in Judge, Stoker and Wolman's *Theories of Urban Politics* (1995), in Lauria's *Reconstructing Urban Regime Theory* (1996), in Imbroscio's *Reconstructing City Politics* (1997) and in DiGaetano and Klemanski's *Urban Governance in Comparative Perspective* (1998).

American urban political economy

For a broader review, see Judd and Kantor's *Enduring Tensions in Urban Politics* (1992) and Mollenkopf's 'Who (or what) runs cities, and how?' (1989). Logan and Swanstrom's *Beyond the City Limits* (1990) puts American urban political economy into a national and international perspective. Harding's 'North American urban political economy, urban theory and British research' (1999) attempts to do the same with specific reference to cross-national work using the growth machine thesis and urban regime theory.

5

Spatial expressions of intra-urban inequalities

Learning objectives

- To understand the difference between the horizontal and vertical paradigm for intra-urban inequalities
- To learn what urban scholars mean by segregation, suburbanisation, gentrification and ghettoisation and what the most important theories on these topics are
- To grasp the meaning of 'neighbourhood effects' and the theory that has brought scholars to think about site effects in this way
- To become familiar with the most important perspectives on urban poverty

Introduction

In the previous two chapters, we have discussed the economic and political perspective on inter-urban inequalities. Anyone who moves through cities, however, not only knows that space organises and strengthens inequalities between urban areas, but also can observe the contrast between the rich and poor within them, perhaps more so than ever before. Due to technological developments, suburbanisation has enabled the affluent to move to the outskirts and find convenient ways to commute to places of work in town. Household staff have been replaced by electrical equipment, from washing machines to security systems, and private daycare centres have replaced individual nannies, segregating the lives of rich and poor, and those serving the rich no longer live in the attics and basements of their houses. The linkages between race/ethnicity, gender and class have taken on new meanings in the postindustrial city. While in cities in the Global South the social mix of service personnel and middle and upper classes is relatively common, the cities in the Global North have become more segregated, a segregation first kicked off by the industrial revolution when quarters for the working classes were purpose-built. Often, such neighbourhoods still had a Gold Coast for teachers, pastors and doctors, but the suburbanisation and decay of inner-city life in the 1960s have left those houses empty or seen them turned into boarding houses or apartments. Since roughly the 1980s, a revival of inner-city living can be seen. This process of hollowing out inner cities has been reversed somewhat, but not with the result, over time, of more social mixing. Upgraded neighbourhoods in those inner cities, products of what urban theorists call gentrification, tend to be homogeneous again. Cities thus show intra-urban inequalities just as much as we see inequalities between cities. This and the next chapter aim to show what urban theory can offer in order to make sense of these inequalities. As Flanagan (2010: 3) has shown in detail, urban sociology especially can be divided into two major strands: those that explore the consequences of urban life on social psychology, culture and organisation, the so-called culturalist approach that is close to but not limited to those we discussed in the context of postmodernism in Chapter 3; and those that are primarily interested in the political economy in cities, the structuralist approach. The first has a sharp eye for actual everyday life in the city and processes of differentiation within cities; the latter may be less close to the life-world and have far less to say about the experience of living the urban but may provide clearer explanatory frameworks for understanding how cities develop as spatial expressions of inequalities. It is such approaches that we start with in this chapter, although we will also see how such lines of demarcation do not really hold up: the most exciting urban studies scholarship aims to include both structure and agency.

We see a spiky urban world within cities, and the differences are big. As has been pointed out by various urban anthropologists (Gupta & Ferguson, 1997), the differentiations between social groups in cities wide apart may actually be smaller than those with their immediate city fellows. Whether or not cities are increasingly polarised – for example, have a sharper contrast between the wealthy and the poor with the middle disappearing, as has been suggested in connection to globalisation (Sassen, 1991) – is subject to discussion (Mollenkopf & Castells, 1992) and varies between cities, depending on their position in the global network of finance, capital and industrial production and on national contexts of the severity of wealth inequality which differs greatly even between OECD countries. While cities are becoming more unequal (Dreier, Mollenkopf, & Swanstrom, 2013), similar to inter-urban inequalities, then, some cities may be spikier than others. In some, due to processes of gentrification, the peaks may be in the city centre while the marginalised are relegated to the fringes of the city. In other cities, a much more diverse pattern may be visible, with gentrified areas bordering deprived inner-city, often immigrant, neighbourhoods, and leafy villa areas on the outskirts. City skylines may at times symbolise their spikiness through the built form (see Figure 5.1) or the sharp contrast of wealth and poverty adjacent to each other (Figure 5.2).

Figure 5.1   São Paulo skyline, with wealthy apartments in skyscrapers of the new downtown in the background and the favela of Paraisopolis in the foreground

© dpa Picture-Alliance GmbH

Figure 5.2   Spikiness and valley adjacent, São Paulo

© Tuca Vieira

In these two chapters, we discuss what urban theory has to say about inequalities and their spatial expressions – segregation – within cities. First, we introduce the vertical and horizontal paradigms for understanding social structure and apply this to cities. A brief discussion of the horizontal and vertical paradigm of European sociology to make sense of the spiky urban world within cities is used here to address various spatial expressions of inequalities and differentiations (segregation, gentrification for the first, identity, subcultures and lifestyles for the second). This chapter then discusses segregation, suburbanisation, gentrification and ghettoisation theories as they aim to explain the spatial expression of stratification in contemporary cities. We show also how these processes have created similarities among social strata across cities in various parts of the world and huge distances between them within cities. As we will see, the vertical paradigm points us to socio-economic status hierarchies, now often expanded to include not just income or assets but also forms of social, economic and political capital, resulting in a perspective of capabilities and resources informed by scholars such as Amatya Sen. He is a social theorist and not an urban scholar, but, as we will see in this chapter, urban scholars can find useful approaches elsewhere, and have indeed done so.

Second, we discuss how diversity as a result of lifestyle differentiations on the basis of ethnicity, race, gender and sexuality has produced urban theory that is primarily concerned with the cultural city. As we discuss these approaches in Chapter 7, we will see that, informed by the perspective of intersectionality, this diversity is not simply a matter of horizontal variations in life styles and life choices, but affect people's capabilities and resources and hence produce the spiky unequal urban world within cities. This discussion demonstrates that it makes little sense to separate the horizontal and the vertical paradigm in understanding inequality and difference when studying the city. Again, these may not all be exactly 'urban theories' but they are social theories that help us understand the urban as the spatial expression of social diversity and inequality. What does make sense, though, is to analytically separate those scholars and sub-themes of the field that are primarily interested in understanding how the urban is linked to inequalities in life chances which may be based on social class as well as, and often in combination with, other ascribed categories of difference, and those primarily interested in describing and understanding the city culturally. The latter ask questions about how the urban as a social space gets produced culturally, that is, how the social and physical fabric of the city becomes meaningful.

This chapter, then, first discusses in a little more detail the vertical and horizontal paradigm for studying social structure. It then moves on to the question how inequality is linked to space through Lefebvre's notion of the production of space and Bourdieu's theory of habitus, habitat and spatial profit. The chapter continues with a discussion of theoretical contributions to understanding some of the spatial expressions of inequality in the city, including segregation, suburbanisation and gentrification. We then turn to a brief discussion of neighbourhood effects. After all, we are not interested only in explaining the urban form as an expression of inequalities, but also in studying how the urban form then helps sharpen or maintain such inequalities. As we will see, ghettoisation can be seen as a form of marginalisation that both creates and reproduces the workings of location, whether or not one prefers to label these workings as neighbourhood effects. After the summary and suggestions for further reading, Chapter 6 then continues with the horizontal paradigm.

Inequalities versus differentiations: vertical and horizontal paradigms

Inequality is what sociologists like to call a relational concept: someone or some social group is always in an unequal position in relation to some individual or group who has more: more money, more access to resources such as good education or health care, and so on. Traditionally, sociologists have viewed inequality in terms of social class: the position of people in relation to the means of production, with an antagonism between the working class and the owners of the means of production. Such a dichotomy is no longer accurate, if indeed it ever was: how can you label the family of a couple who met in a motorbiking club, where he has no academic degree and works in a local hospital cafetaria after working as a garbage collector for years and she operates on women suffering from breast cancer in the same hospital? While this real example may not exactly be the norm, it is no longer possible to ascribe people class positions based on the occupation and income of the head of household. Moreover, the idea of a clear class structure itself has been more and more intensively debated (for an overview, see Devine, 1997; Crompton, 1998). So social scientists have discussed other ways to talk about a stratified society and generally agree that more subtle, less bounded notions of class help make sense of stratification. Perspectives vary widely on what combination of assets or forms of capital should be decisive in ordering social positions in a society, but for urban theory, the importance of this discussion lies in the underlying definition of inequality as unequal life chances based on possession of assets. Scholars who study social stratification and class are said to work with a vertical paradigm: higher and lower social positions are relatively easily differentiated, as economics is the prime determinant of the social structure in this paradigm (Grusky, 1994).

Urban theory is primarily interested in spatial expressions of such inequalities and in the possible ways in which space may organise or even contribute to them.

While social positions explain, to a large extent, where one lives, urban theory is not just about describing social stratification expressed spatially; urban theorists are also interested in how inequalities are reproduced through the spikiness of the urban landscape of unequal resources.

To give a brief example, economic geographers have asked how locations of jobs and residential locations of job seekers are related, and developed the idea of a spatial mismatch (Preston & McLafferty, 1999): changes in both where people live and where low-entry jobs are located make it increasingly hard to find jobs nearby for those who need it most, or getting to work comes with very high transaction costs, so that ethnic segregation can result in occupational segmentation 'as the geographical scope of possible jobs is limited by the need to minimize commuting time on public transport' (Coe, Kelly, & Yeung, 2007: 385). Here, the spatial structure of the city – though by no means natural or given but the effect of state regulations – organises and contributes to income inequality. Does it also reproduce inequality? As we will see, this is one of the hot discussions in the field. Sharkey (2013) provides compelling evidence that neighbourhoods are implicated in the severe stratifications across generations along lines of class and race in American big cities, but, as we will see, the ways in which neighbourhoods function as perpetuating machines of poverty or wealth are not that clear.

In general sociology it has also been acknowledged that inequalities are not just about having money or not. Money alone is an important but not sufficient resource to develop capabilities: to live a life as one desires for oneself (Sen, 1999). It has hence been argued that other factors point to complex dimensions of stratification, such as one's education or the network on which one can draw for support or for information on new opportunities, or the ways in which one manages to earn social status in the eyes of others, build a reputation and achieve or maintain a position. This is why the sociological literature likes to turn to Bourdieu's (1984) notions of positions defined not just by money, but by economic, social, cultural (and, in some corners of the debate, political) capital. Once we start to do this, however, the clear picture of social classes within a vertical social structure becomes blurred.

Beyond either horizontal or vertical

That social stratification models cannot adequately be described by the traditional Marxist model of social classes or Weberian model of status groups has of course gained ground over the years in the sociology of stratification. Stratification theories understood a society's social structure as layered according to a hierarchical principle of vertical rather than horizontal differences. Anthias (2005) discusses the alternatives to this model. First, Weberian approaches focusing on social status have been developed (Crompton, 1998;

Lockwood, 1996). Anthias argues that these are insufficient because they do not take into account the ways in which status may change and is interconnected with race, ethnicity and gender. She then discusses two influential models: the reductionist and intersectionality models. The reductionist model (Hechter, 1987; Phizacklea & Miles, 1980; Myrdal, 1969), of which she is critical, basically incorporates gender and ethnicity in social stratification models by reducing them to a form of class division. The intersectionality model explores the ways in which 'social organization and identification' intersect in specific sites 'to produce forms of social asymmetry' (Anthias, 2005: 32; see Hill Collins, 1999; Anthias & Yuval-Davis, 1992). Anthias sees problems with this perspective too (Anthias, 2005: 36–37) and proposes to speak of narratives of location and positionality as concepts that may help us tell the story of – for us here urban – inequalities: a story about how people place themselves in terms of gender, ethnicity and class at a specific point in time and place (location) and a story about 'being placed'. This reminds us of the notions of location and position that Bourdieu had used. We will thus take away from this discussion, which tends to become highly abstract, that given the problems with seeing stratification as a rather fixed system of classes or status groups, urban inequalities can be understood as the ways in which positionality formed by class, race, ethnicity and gender influences the durable access to resources and assets (or capabilities: Sen, 1999). For urban theory, the two questions then are what mechanisms and processes affect the durable inequalities as they are spatially expressed in the city and how the spikiness of the city affects the durability of these inequalities.

Much of urban studies that engages with divisions, however, does not link these necessarily to inequalities and their reproduction but primarily to living the city and questions of identity. The approach to the city as a site of difference rather than focusing on inequalities in life chances and outcomes, or resources, can be traced back to the very origins of urban sociology. Notwithstanding the neo-Marxist perspectives that looked at the production of space through a Marxist lens and would definitely not prioritise questions of difference and how difference is lived as such, a rather separate strand of urban sociology and urban anthropology has done precisely that. The city, these scholars maintain, is 'more than a backdrop' and 'actively intervenes in the social process. It is created by our collective attitudes and actions and in turn impacts who we are by becoming part of our consciousness and influencing our behaviour' (Flanagan, 2010: 15).

Living in a world of difference

More than in our earlier chapters we see here the connection between city, collective attitudes, consciousness: in short, the city can structure personal experiences, influence personal styles and tastes or make them possible, be a site of fun, desire and entertainment – as in Hannigan's *Fantasy City* (1998) – or be the site of identity politics and other forms of political expression (see Flanagan, 2010: 9–30). With the idea of the city as anonymous, as the expression and site of individualisation and rationalisation, came the concern of urban sociologists with community. For Simmel, the urbanite lived in a world of difference, difference as 'a profound social reality, lived over and over in glancing encounters of the street' (Tonkiss, 2005: 11). For the Chicago School sociologists, too, difference of class and of ethnicity and race structured the city. As Tonkiss (2005: 15) notes, 'identity and community invariably were tied to spatial separation and cultural differentiation. Community gave a social form to these patterns of difference.' Through a natural process of sifting and sorting, groups different in class, ethnicity and race formed a mosaic of social worlds, as Park used to say, where each group found its source for identity, sociability and institutions in particular neighbourhoods in the city. McKenzie assumed that neighbourhoods produced by sifting and sorting were defined by 'peculiar selective and cultural characteristics' (McKenzie, quoted in Tonkiss, 2005: 42), discussions that, similarly to Wirth's work, move to urban culture and to 'an understanding of "personality" as a collective quality' (Tonkiss, 2005: 43). As we will see in Chapter 7, the way in which the recognition of the relevance of culture and social constructivism has been taken on in urban sociology has resulted in a wealth of studies on the symbolic production of space and appropriation of space, especially public space, and to a richness in studies of subcultural diversity of various forms, but has not done that much to treat difference as the organisation of inequalities along categorical lines. Returning to Anthias at the end of Chapter 7, we will show what an approach that does see difference as source of structural inequality, too, can mean.

Cities as sites of resources: space and inequalities

Once urban sociologists started to be critical of the neo-classical economic perspective that had long informed the understanding of cities as the product of market forces that sifted people into places as if they were all equal parties with given preferences in the market, a 'new urban sociology' (Gottdiener & Hutchison, 2011) developed based on political economy perspectives, including the insight that power interests were unequal and that the role of politics and government in urbanisation was a central one. The urban crisis of the 1960s, according to Zukin (1980: 577), forced urban sociologists to rethink their perspectives. Henri Lefebvre, a French scholar, was one of the most important scholars who saw the connection between state power, economics and urban questions critically. We have seen this in earlier chapters, where we discussed the relevance of scholars such as Manuel Castells and David Harvey. For the spatial expression of inequalities within cities, we note that scholars since the late 1960s have started to see these no longer as the result of a natural process of sifting and sorting, as was common in the ecological tradition, but instead as the product of advanced capitalism, including its supportive patriarchy, and government as supporting the capitalist system. Moreover, they have started to think about city neighbourhoods and urban institutions – schools, health care centres and the like – as sites of reproduction of labour.

The production of space

The socio-spatial perspective (Gottdiener & Hutchison, 2011: 2) that developed from here asks what role economic, political and social institutions play in creating and changing settlements, and through what processes they are given meaning by local residents. It includes three elements that Gottdiener and Hutchison (2011: 13) consider distinctive for this new urban sociology: its shift to a global perspective; its attention to political-economic pull factors in urban and suburban development; and its appreciation of the role of culture in urban life and in the construction of the built environment.

Seeing the city as both the product and reproducer of inequalities, then, rests on an understanding of space that leaves behind the idea that space is a container in which stuff happens. Instead, space is thought to *constitute* social relations and meanwhile produced through social relations, and constantly re-created (Gottdiener & Hutchison, 2011: 19). Lefebvre (1991) therefore argued that space was a social product, produced on three interconnected levels. First, space was produced by a spatial practice of production and reproduction. Second, representations of space were produced by government surveyors and planners, by architects and scientists, reflecting their power positions, and creating the rationalised city of maps and plans. Third, representational space included space as it is produced through the way it is lived and experienced: space as produced through experiences, practices of the everyday, and imagined. As Tonkiss (2005: 3) has argued, Lefebvre helped us see that the urban is not just material, but made of 'meanings, language and symbols': 'there is no such a thing as empty space. Space is always and only produced as a complex of relationships and separations, presences and absences.'

While the production of space helps us understand the urban form, the reproduction of inequalities and the role of this urban form in this process cannot be thought through with this perspective alone. Whereas sifting and sorting may not be natural but indeed the product of the mode of production, neither is individual agency irrelevant, as Duncan shows. Duncan (2013: 231) writes:

> There is a belief in our society that the social value of an individual must be roughly commensurate with the social value of the place he frequents. In a society which is socially mobile the objects and settings that one surrounds oneself with are an inseparable part of one's self. This argument logically leads to the notion that if one shares a setting with another then, to a degree, he shares his identity thus allowing stigma to spread by spatial association. A tramp does not have a 'normal', that is propertied, identity but, to put it in Goffman's terms, one that is 'spoiled'. Such people must be separated out for their spoiled identities can spoil the setting and by extension the 'normal' people who are a part of it. Hence the hierarchical division of space according to social value is of critical importance to the host population.

How, then, can agency be connected to the theory of production of space? Prime and marginal space, the concepts that Duncan uses as a scale of relative terms for this hierarchy, imply no inherent value of space itself, but value is assigned to space by how it is viewed and used:

> Thus the tramp must learn the social value that the host group assigns to different types of urban space and to the regular temporal variations in these values: he must then resign himself to spending as much time as possible in marginal space. Marginal space includes alleys, dumps, space under bridges, behind hedgerows, on the roofs of buildings, and in other no man's lands such as around railroad yards which are not considered worth the cost of patrolling.' (Duncan, 2013: 229)

Bourdieu on social space

While this is not the place to do full justice to Bourdieu's complex theory of the reproduction of inequalities as laid down in *Distinction*, we still think it is useful to briefly turn to him here to get a grip on how spatial privileging and marginalising occurs. For Bourdieu, the hierarchy in urban form can be linked directly to inequalities once we see the value assigned to space in terms of reproduction. Social positions, defined by economic, cultural and social capital, constitute the habitus: the 'internalized form of class condition and of the conditionings it entails' (Bourdieu, 1984: 101). Not only the relation to the mode of production defines a class in Bourdieu's eyes, but also a whole set of secondary principles of selection or exclusion, including a certain distribution in geographical space, defines social positions (Bourdieu, 1984: 102). Social space, then, is the set of fields of relations between social positions. Agents are constituted in social space: they are situated in a site of social space defined by their position relative to the positions of others. Reproduction strategies, then, are the various practices that families and individuals, without having to be aware of it, use to 'maintain or increase their assets and consequently to maintain or improve their position in the class structure'. Such strategies depend on the volume and composition of capital (social, economic, cultural) and on the 'instruments' that can be used to reproduce it, such as schools or a legal system; these instruments themselves are in turn a reflection of the power relations between classes (Bourdieu, 1984: 125). From here, it becomes clear why to Bourdieu an important mechanism lies in the connection between the habitus and habitat.

Bourdieu observes that to understand places (the extent of physical space occupied by a group with a social position), we need to analyse the relations between the structures of social space and those of physical space (Bourdieu, 1999: 123). The power over social space is the result of the various forms of capital that agents control. In physical space, the inequality in power takes the form of a relation between the distribution of agents and the distribution of resources (goods, services). In other words, a certain social position is expressed by the occupation of a specific site of physical space. This gives the structure of social space its inertia, as modifying the structure of appropriated physical space is hardly possible and naturalised: social relations are inscribed in physical space in such a long-term, durable way that we understand them as given and not as the result of power. So we end up saying that rich people move to nice neighbourhoods because they can afford it, but do not see how they are constructed socially, and act as if the pattern of the hierarchy of places in the city exists beyond the social. Social space is hence reified as 'the distribution in physical space of different types of goods and services and also of individual agents and of physically situated groups' (Bourdieu, 1999: 127). Spatial distance, then, affirms social distance.

This distance (and proximity) produces *spatial profits* in three ways. First, Bourdieu sees profits of localisation where income (in any form of capital) is derived from the proximity to desirable agents and goods. This is the most important of the three ways for the rest of this chapter, as it points to the differences in quality and quantity of local institutions that urban residents have access to, given their spatial position, and to the capabilities they have to organise those resources, institutionally and otherwise. It is important to note that the exclusions that result from this are produced by an internal focus, not by active attempts to keep other people out; it just means that agents use the capital at their disposal to make the best of their lives for their own, and the 'club effect' of such long-term gatherings is that their strong resources get reinforced, and remain their own. Some of these spatial profits are directly related to the political construction of space: catchment areas of school systems, for example, politically create a spatial profit for those who live in middle-class areas where parents have the habitus that matches the habitus of the school and makes them effective agents in keeping up the performance of schools. Second, profits of position occur when one can derive symbolic profits from the distinction that comes with being in a place. The simplest example here is the positive or negative evaluation one may receive in a job application process based on the address where one lives. Third, profits of occupation are those where physical space can help hold distance and exclude undesirable intrusion (NIMBY movements, where residents collectively act to prevent undesirable land uses in their neighbourhood, such as the building of affordable housing in their area, come to mind).

In short, space and inequality are linked as places in the city are sites inscribed by social space, and symbolise it. In the next sections we will see how specific processes that organise the spatiality of inequalities in the city (e.g. segregation, suburbanisation and gentrification) have been theorised, and aim to show how each of them can be understood as the reification of social space.

Segregation

To say that social space is inscribed in spatial structures means to see physical space as one of the sites were power is asserted and exercised. But inequalities in positions, as we have seen in our discussion of intersectionality above, are being produced at the intersections of people's lives in terms of different positions they hold in relation to class, gender, sexuality and race and ethnicity. Segregation is the term that urban scholars use to refer to the positionality of groups in the city and the extent to which they occupy separate sites in the city. Social theorists like Bourdieu and Anthias have not been extensively used in the debate on segregation. As we will see, the focus of this strand of urban studies, which has produced a huge number of empirical studies, particularly in the United States, is primarily on the measurement of segregation and on theorising and measuring the effects of segregation, a 'cottage industry' (Slater, 2013) that we will discuss in more detail later in our section on neighbourhood effects.

Segregation can refer to ethnic or racial segregation and to social segregation, that is, the segregation by social class. Scholars may want to separate these because of the data they have, the cities they are interested in comparing, or the policy circles they want to address, but they are, of course, not separated in the lived city. As socio-economic status differences manifest themselves spatially, with the affluent living in neighbourhoods with high-status reputation and the poor living in undesirable areas, the city reflects the social stratification of the society at large, another way of saying that social space is inscribed in physical space. Such segregation is not voluntary: contrary to what new economics often assumes, people are not equal market competitors on a free housing market. Not only wealth limits people's housing choices; race, gender and sexuality also affect people's opportunities of where to live. Browne, Lim, and Brown (2009: 6–7), for example, discuss the concentration of gays in American cities as the appropriation of territory as a defensive act in a heterosexist society, out of a need for 'safe' spaces in a society that oppresses gays as men in relation to heterosexual men.

This, then, is linked to a discussion, important to housing studies, of how much choice and constraint there is in the housing choices people make (for an overview, see Clark & Dieleman, 2012). Do people act as free agents on the market, finding ways to consume the type of fixed housing preference that they have, given the economic resources at their disposal? Neo-economists would certainly assume that the market simply does its work. Forced or voluntary segregation has been theorised mostly by saying that segregation either is the result of structure (e.g. agents having different economic capital gives or limits their options to act as free agents on the market), or, given a specific volume of economic capital, is an expression of lifestyle preferences. This discussion has gained particular relevance in recent decades in attempts to explain ethnic concentration, or the phenomenon that people who share ethnicity tend to live in neighbourhoods with others from their own group. Noting that financially they may not need to do so, scholars have looked for other than structural explanations. It is clear from this discussion that the simple division between choice constraints and preference is not very useful, not least because the stories people tell of why they live where they live contain their own rationalisations. In a small study of motives for moving out of a gentrifying neighbourhood in Berlin, for example, Betancourt (2012) found that people referred to the advantages of the neighbourhoods they moved to as motives for their action rather than to the fact that they could no longer afford the rent of where they lived before, or could not meet their housing needs which had changed as a result of their life stage in the neighbourhood in which they grew up due to a lack of affordable housing. And what is a 'preference' in relation to a 'decision' is not the same thing either, so that where the literature treats a move to a new dwelling that matches a 'housing preference' as voluntary, this need not be the case (Floor & van Kempen, 1997; van der Laan Bouma-Doff, 2007b).

Moreover, where people move to is not a free choice either: neighbourhoods have symbolic meaning or aggressively exclude, affecting where people live (Pattillo-McCoy, 1999), and a gap between one's habitus and habitat may affect this choice, as DuBois (2013: 176) signalled more than a hundred years ago:

The Negro who ventures away from the mass of his people and their organized life, finds himself alone, shunned and taunted, stared at and made uncomfortable; he can make few new friends, for his neighbours however well-disposed would shrink to add a Negro to their list of acquaintances. Thus he ... feels in all its bitterness what it means to be a social outcast.

In the United States, a large body of literature has also shown that blacks face racism on the housing market, some institutional, in the location of public housing in inner cities, some more individual, as in cases where real estate agents discourage blacks from moving into certain neighbourhoods or suburbs (Massey & Denton, 1993; Haynes, 2001).

Social segregation

Ethnic or racial segregation is the form of segregation we may be most familiar with. The confusing thing here is that social segregation is also used in contrast to residential or spatial segregation: where the latter refers to the question whether groups different in ethnicity/race or class are living separately from each other in the city, here social segregation refers to the ways in which people who may reside in mixed neighbourhoods have separate social worlds of institutions, networks and the like. Atkinson (2006) has contributed to this line of thought when he discussed how middle-class and upper middle-class residents live in their own enclaves and travel the city through tunnels on their way to socially segregated places of work and leisure, like philharmonic orchestras or expensive restaurants. Butler and colleagues have shown how middle-class residents living in socially and ethnically mixed neighbourhoods in London make school choices that ensure that their children are surrounded by other children with the same habitus, out of fear of social contamination (Butler & Hamnett, 2007). Watt (2009) studied the ways in which middle-class residents in suburban London used their socially mixed neighbourhoods and discusses the social segregation in the facilities they use and avoid in terms of selective belonging.

Such social segregation is more difficult to measure systematically than residential social segregation, as it requires the study of what people do rather than where they live. Unsurprisingly, segregation studies have primarily focused on the measurement of various forms of residential segregation, assuming that the geographical neighbourhood of where we sleep matters most to whom we engage with, and that spatial distance not only expresses social distance but also acts as a basis for distinction in practices that reinforce the habitat, in the formation of social networks and in the generation of forms of capital. The study of segregation has been heavily dominated by American scholarship, where scholars have traditionally been interested in measuring racial segregation and particularly black/white segregation.

Segregation indices

One of the first studies to measure segregation by race in the US was by Taeuber and Taeuber (1965) who developed the 'index of segregation' as the percentage of blacks who would have to move so that all areas in the city would have the same percentage of blacks as the percentage of the overall city. One thus takes the whole racial or ethnic composition of the city, and the degree to which neighbourhoods deviate from this standard of the overall city is the amount of segregation. The now most commonly used measure is the index of dissimilarity that is similar to Taeuber and Taeuber's initial measurement. Their index has since been refined, including for example in the important study of Massey and Denton clustering (black neighbourhoods form an enclave in the city or more like a checkerboard), concentration (black neighbourhoods in one small area in the city or scattered all over the city), and centralisation (whether or not black neighbourhoods are located in the centre or the periphery) and unevenness (overrepresentation or underrepresentation of blacks in neighbourhoods) and isolation (lack of possibilities of interactions with whites based on nearness of a different group).

In the northern European context, it has become increasingly difficult to treat racial/ethnic and class segregation as independent because of the increasingly strong correlation between ethnicity and income. In the US, residential segregation remains extreme even when controlling for socio-economic differences between blacks, whites and Hispanics (Massey & Denton, 2013: 195). Compared to the growth of the black middle class, the indices of residential segregation have hardly changed in America:

> despite the overturning of de jure segregation, de facto segregation continues in America, through practices such as bank and insurance redlining and prejudicial real estate steering ... White flight and continuing segregation have isolated racial minorities in central cities, undermining political coalitions and fragmenting the political landscape and the tax bases between 'white suburbs' and 'chocolate cities'. (Lin & Mele, 2013: 192–3)

Immigration and segregation

Segregation has become an increasing concern within the political context of European countries having to come to accept that they are immigrant countries (Esser, 1986; van Kempen & sule Özüekren, 1998) and studies of segregation have been growing, especially also in the context of the question to what extent the thesis of a polarisation in cities (the idea of a dual city emerging in the context of globalisation discussed earlier in this book) is directly linked to or a precondition for segregation and how much of segregation needs to be theorised as context-specific (Burgers, 1996; Wessel, 2000; Musterd, 2005a; Arbaci, 2007; Maloutas, 2007). Especially in countries like Germany and the Netherlands where immigration was less the result of their colonial pasts and more of the active recruitment of labour migrants in countries such as Turkey and Morocco, the initial general expectation in the 1960s was that these workers would return to their home countries when their labour was no longer needed. But they did not, and 'integration' became part of the national agenda of social problems from the 1970s onwards. With refugees and asylum seekers adding to the urban diversity in the 1980s, neighbourhoods with up to 65 ethnicities can be found in cities such as Rotterdam, where over 85% of the children are now born to parents of immigrant background. Whereas, depending on the geographical level one chooses to study, high concentrations of one dominant ethnic group can also be found, the European immigrant neighbourhoods are typically highly diverse neighbourhoods. Segregation measurements thus tend to compare immigrants to non-immigrants (see van der Laan Bouma-Doff, 2010) and are usually interested in the possible effect of this residential isolation of ethnic minority groups on outcomes in, for example, interethnic friendships (van der Laan Bouma-Doff, 2007a; Drever, 2004; Esser, 1986) and other network ties (van Eijk, 2010; Blokland & van Eijk, 2010) or labour market opportunities (Musterd, 2005b; Musterd & Ostendorf, 1998a; Bolt, Burgers, & van Kempen, 1998; van der Laan Bouma-Doff, 2008). Two theoretical perspectives have been used to explain segregation (Charles, 2003). The spatial assimilation model works with the idea that objective differences in socio-economic status and acculturation explain segregation. Place stratification models maintain that prejudices and discrimination constrain the options for residential mobility of individuals. According to Charles, the two explanatory models are complimentary.

European cities thus also face racialisation of urban space, the process 'by which urban and suburban space is associated with various ethnic and social groups' (Charles, 2003: 382), with extreme segregation as a possible form. Such spaces do not always have to be negative hubs of social problems and exclusions but can also be actively created from within neighbourhoods or groups (Charles, 2003: 383). Indeed, neighbourhood social movements and forms of collective action may rise directly from a shared identity developing around a racialised space, as in the *casitas* that Puerto Rican immigrants erected in the Bronx (Sciorra, 1996: 70–5).

Here it is important to deal with theory carefully: assumptions made about shared identities may work for studying areas where specific castes may concentrate in Hyderabad, Bosniaks and Croats in Mostar (Figure 5.3; see Aceska,

2013), blacks in New York, Mexicans in Los Angeles or Cubans in Miami, or the Pakistanis and Indians in Brick Lane in London (Figure 5.4), but in European cities the segregation of immigrants and non-immigrants is an indicator of ethnic and racial heterogeneity versus homogeneity, so that the assumption of a collective identity can even less easily be made as in the case of ethnically or racially homogeneous areas, even though there too this assumption may reify ethnicity as automatically linked to a social identity, a danger that studies of ethnicity and identity have warned of extensively (Jenkins, 1996; Blokland, 2003b).

Figure 5.3   Mostar, with Muslim Bosniaks and Christian Croats each living on one side of the river

Mostar – Old Town Panorama, Szerkesztő Ramirez, 2007
Source: Wikimedia Commons:
http://commons.wikimedia.org/wiki/File:Mostar_Old_Town_Panorama.jpg.

Figure 5.4   Brick Lane, London, where the ethnic character of the neighbourhood is the basis for the commercialisation of segregation

Segregation and integration

The social problem of integration, which can by way of shorthand be defined as the social and political problem that nation states with substantial numbers of immigrants, whom a deindustrialising economy can no longer absorb easily into its labour market, have to find ways to ensure that they can participate economically, socially, politically (and culturally, though this has been heavily debated) as full members in society to the same extent as non-immigrants. What defines full membership is again heavily contested, a debate primarily concerned with citizenship rights and entitlements (Lebuhn, 2013). For our purposes, what is most interesting is what theories of integration have been developed, and how they are relevant for the urban – how they are linked to the spatial expression of inequalities in the city.

Apart from theories on housing choice and constraints, including discrimination in the housing market, that try to explain the patterns of segregation, much work has been done on understanding the outcomes. Much of the discussion can be seen as asking to what extent ethnic concentration or segregation in urban neighbourhoods stimulates integration or, instead, blocks it (e.g. Dick, 2008). Integration is here generally understood as assimilation: integrated are those immigrants who have socially, economically, politically and culturally become full participants in mainstream society. The idea of assimilation includes the perspective that new immigrants face times of hardship and possibly discrimination upon arrival, but gradually, if not themselves then at least in the generation of their children, adapt to their new country. Assimilation theory holds that they will overcome obstacles and become socio-economically mobile, so that they, as it were, disappear as a visible social group. At most, ethnicity is celebrated, enjoyed through consumption and festivals and implies a choice of when and how to 'play' ethnic roles, so that ethnicity becomes symbolic. It becomes, in Gans' (1996: 436) words, 'a love for or pride in a tradition that can be felt without having to be incorporated into everyday behavior'. For such ethnicity, no functioning groups or networks are a prerequisite, and ethnicity is expressive rather than instrumental (Gans, 1996: 435).

The assimilation thesis has been criticised heavily on various grounds (Rex, 1996). In the European discussion, the debate has primarily focused on the right of immigrants to maintain their cultural identities and the need for mainstream society and cities to define themselves as multicultural (Hannerz, 2004; Keith, 2005; Sandercock, 1998) and culture as fluid and changing rather than as a static 'whole' that one can 'integrate into', in an attempt also to fight forms of new or cultural racism (Hall, 1996; Cohen, 1999). Integration, it has been argued, suggests too much that immigrants are the ones who have to adapt to their new environment and that the social world in which they arrive has to do nothing but absorb them on the basis of sameness (Vertovec & Wessendorf, 2010; Zincone, Penninx, & Borkert, 2011).

In North America, too, alternative theories have been developed that in turn have steered the European discussion. These point, for example, to the subordinate economic position of immigrant groups and the value of ethnic solidarities and ties and of ethnic politics and mobilisation so that resilient ethnic communities may form as a result of disadvantaged economic positions that make smooth assimilation impossible (Portes & Manning, 2013: 204). Portes and Manning, after giving a useful review of the US debate on immigration and the city, argue that the latter brings useful revision to the assimilation thesis, but tends to be as homogenising to the other side of the spectrum: not all migrants are and remain marginalised at the bottom of the labour market. They show that various other models of incorporation are possible, of which the model of the ethnic enclave has gained most attention and has been taken up most strongly by scholars in Europe. Ethnic enclaves, whilst originally defined in economic terms only (Bailey & Waldinger, 1991; Waldinger, 1993) are areas where residence, work, leisure and personal networks within the ethnic group overlap. They may develop when three conditions are met.

First, a substantial number of immigrants must be present with entrepreneurial skills developed in their country of origin so that escape from wage labour is possible. Second, there must be access to capital, whether brought from the home country, pooled within the ethnic group or accumulated personally. Third, labour sources must be given, usually drawn from family members or newly arriving immigrants. Enclave businesses, according to Portes and Manning (2013: 210):

> typically start small and cater exclusively to an ethnic clientele. Their expansion and entry into the broader market requires ... an effective mobilization of community resources. The social mechanism at work here seems to be a strong sense of reciprocity supported by collective solidarity that transcends the purely contractual character of business transactions.

That relations are not purely contractual applies to the sharing of financial resources and to the relationship between employers and employees. Furthermore, ethnic enclaves take spatial forms: there is a need for proximity of an ethnic market which they initially serve, there is a need for proximity to facilitate the exchange of information, and proximity serves the need for ethnic labour supply. This is where concerns about ethnic enclaves have been expressed in urban policy circles, where questions have been asked about the integration of immigrants into mainstream society:

> once an enclave economy has fully developed, it is possible for a newcomer to live his life entirely within the confines of the community. Work,

education, and access to health care, recreation and a variety of other services can be found without leaving the bounds of the ethnic economy. This institutional completeness is what enables new immigrants to move ahead economically, despite very limited knowledge of the host culture and language. (Portes & Manning, 2013: 211)

There is then no longer a necessity of acculturation for social mobility, and diverting from one's ethnic identity is no longer rewarding. It is clear that the ethnic enclave has evoked discussion as to whether its effects are positive or negative: while on the one hand, the enclave may provide networks for new immigrants and economic opportunities, on the other hand the enclave may create negative effects of isolation and concentration. Table 5.1 shows the main arguments that can be found in the broad discussion for or against ethnic concentration. Whereas each can be theorised, it is clear that such theories need empirical testing, and their validity will depend strongly on the particular urban and national context and the migration history of the ethnic group considered as well as the constituent elements of their cultural heritage.

European studies, however, have found that in so far as neighbourhoods produce context effects, for example in so far as there are differences in outcomes along these four dimensions between people living in different neighbourhoods which cannot be explained by their individual characteristics (class, educational level, gender, age, family composition, race/ethnicity), these are due to differences in socio-economic composition of the area. There is no evidence that ethnic or racial residential segregation alone produces any effect, different from the available evidence in the United States. While we may be most familiar with ethnic or racial segregation and read and hear most about how this may 'threaten' society, limit children's life chances and the like, the much more important question is the question of poverty concentration and the possible neighbourhood effects that may follow from living and growing up in a poor neighbourhood, a discussion we will return to later. Let us first look at another

Table 5.1 Overview of arguments for and against 'ethnic neighbourhoods' in European cities

Dimension	For	Against
Social	Network formation, family support	Contacts remain limited to the ethnic group
Economical	Ethnic economy provides jobs	Limited chances for labour market mobility
Political	Communication and organisation of interests	No access to mainstream political domain
Cultural	Conservation of cultural identity	Limited identification, if not withdrawal from dominant culture

process that heavily influences the spatial expression of inequalities in the city and can take a more regional form where cities become contrasted to the surrounding metropolitan area: suburbanisation.

Suburbanisation

Suburbanisation is generally understood residentially, as the process whereby an increasing number of people move out of the city to its outskirts, often to single family houses rather than apartments. Initially and especially in the US this has been written about as a middle-class and white practice with working class families moving much later. In Europe, suburbs include working-class families and do not mean single family housing at all. The Paris *banlieues* and Amsterdam South-east are well-known examples of suburban living that is far remote from the stately house with well-manicured lawns, the gas grill on the deck and the white picket fence that comes to the mind of many Americans when they think about the suburbs. Similarly, large council estates in British cities were often built on the edges. While these can be seen as sub-urban in the sense that they are subordinate to the central city in many ways, it may make more sense to refer to these areas as periphery in relation to the centre, a phrasing common in Latin American urban studies (see Ingram & Carroll, 1981; Gilbert, 1996; Marques et al., 2008) where *favelas* can be found on the edges of the central city. As in European cities, affluent enclaves of suburban character can be found beyond those areas again.

Demand and supply

Gottdiener and Hutchison (2011: 124–8) have pointed to the demand and supply side of suburbanisation and have stressed that the two are intertwined (a discussion not unlike that in the theories of gentrification). Arguments on the demand side maintain that people act as individual market parties with preferences that they like to fulfil. There is a market for it, and that is why new dwellings appear, helped by the technological changes that make commuting to the city and low building costs possible. In a remarkable piece of work, Bruegmann (2011) rejects explanations that see anti-urban sentiment or racism as steering preferences for and thus the development of suburbia. Arguing that the question is not to explain sprawl, but to explain the concerted efforts of urban elites to keep cities from dispersing in earlier times, he identifies privacy, mobility and choice, three factors he sees as depending on affluence and democratic institutions, so that his theory goes beyond a simple assertion about individuals' preferences. When people become more affluent and acquire basic political and economic rights, they can pursue lives previously only available to a small elite. Privacy, then, refers to the ability to take control over one's own living surroundings. Mobility refers to personal and social mobility: being able to travel (by car) and to attain education and employment opportunities. Choice, in Bruegmann's view the most important factor, is the ability of ordinary citizens to choose their living, work and recreational settings (Bruegmann, 2011: 220). The problem with this approach is obvious: it denies the constraints for those who face racism, patriarchy and other forms of power inequalities and discrimination that severely limit all three of these factors. Still, his theory helps explain urban sprawl for those who suburbanised, although it does not explain the limited opportunities for those left behind. As we are interested in the spikiness of cities, suburbanisation should therefore be seen and studied in tandem with the two other processes – segregation and gentrification.

The supply side starts from the idea that capitalists have specific interests in creating a market for suburban living – not just because of the profit to be made on land and buildings, but also, for example, to stimulate the growth of the car industry. It would be wrong to suggest that suburbanisation is simply a question of market supply and demand. Dreier et al. (2013: 151) show that US federal policies have fostered suburbanisation by building highways and stimulating home ownership. This is not unique to the US. After the fall of the Berlin Wall in 1989, a home ownership stimulation programme for former residents of the German Democratic Republic, for whom it was close to impossible to acquire property before the end of communism, resulted in a flight from the city to nearby suburbs, creating a *Speckgürtel* around the city whilst leaving over 30,000 apartments, built in the two decades before, standing empty in the high-rise areas of East Berlin by the mid-1990s. Similarly, there are various reasons for the shrinking of cities in eastern Germany, but the government policy of stimulating home ownership and the suburbanisation that resulted is by no means a small factor in this process (Hannemann, 2004). This shows that it makes little sense for intra-urban inequalities to see the urban as a simple expression of neutral market forces just as it did for inter-urban inequalities: power as it is exercised in the political and social processes in the city is a crucial factor.

Commercial suburbanisation and sprawl

Suburbanisation has not remained residential though. Retailing, in the form of shopping malls, manufacturing in the form of high-tech hubs of production arising in the outskirts, and the relocation of offices and administrative headquarters near convenient highway exits and airports rather than in central cities can all be seen as forms of suburbanisation. They create multi-centred metropolitan regions, of which sprawl can be seen as the most serious outcome (Gottdiener & Hutchison, 2011: 324–5): the unplanned, unregulated regional growth around major cities, claiming farmland for development. Sprawl refers both to such outward development in a metropolitan area and to the forms of such development: highways, strip malls, drive-in fast food stores, multi-storey cinema complexes (Jackson, 2011) and other 'car-centered uses of space' (Williamson, Imbroscio, & Aplerovitz, 2005: 303). For Fishman (2011), the decentralisation of housing, services and office jobs depends on technological innovation of communication, creating what he calls 'technoburbs' or even 'technocities', where the latter still bear the name of the core city but enclose a whole region that is multi-centred sprawl which Fishman (2011: 79) argues, may be unplanned but which is not unstructured, and based on its own logic and efficiency that contrasts with early suburbs:

> The suburb separated [work and residence] into distinct environments, its logic was that of the massive commute, in which workers from the periphery traveled each morning to a single core and then dispersed each evening. The technoburb, however, contains both work and residence within a single decentralized environment.

Williamson et al. point out that while suburbanisation may be excluding and discriminatory and create a lack of tax base (especially in the US where much more of the revenues of the local state depend on local, especially property taxes!) in the central city, planned small town development in a metropolitan area in itself is not the problem. Indeed, the planning of 'New Towns' in British cities, followed also by enlightened urban planners in Dutch and German cities in the 1920s and 1930s, was a social-democratically motivated response of mixed-income communities providing better living conditions than the quickly growing, overcrowded tenement neighbourhoods. Ebezener Howard, probably the best-known name associated with the garden city movement, was convinced that the 'town magnet' with its industrial jobs and its amenities needed to be balanced by the magnets of the country with its features of nature and quiet. He thought it ought to be 'deeply deplored' that human beings should live in the dark overcrowded alleys of the early twentieth-century city (Howard, 2011: 329).

Some of the consequences of sprawl are racial and ethnic segregation, a threat to nature and farm production and therefore a shortage of land for food production (particularly problematic in regions in the US) and high ecological costs, as the distances people have to travel by car in order to go about their daily routines increase. Metropolitan political fragmentation also hampers efficient administration. Intra- and inter-urban inequalities are thus linked. This has led authors such as Dreier et al. to argue that the metropolitan area, not the city as such, may be the adequate scale for studying intra-metro inequalities nowadays.

In short, then, suburbanisation and urban sprawl can be seen as social and political problems. While that may make them relevant, why, then, is suburbanisation of relevance to urban theory, other than as a description of particular empirical patterns?

The relevance of suburbanisation for urban theory

While suburbanisation is to a large extent a class-based process, with the exception of council estates and public housing and of the shanty towns of cities such as São Paulo, it has historically been a process steered by housing choices of the middle classes. However, its theoretical significance for intra-urban inequalities lies in the intersectionality of race, gender and class that is obvious in processes of suburbanisation. First, suburbanisation has been connected to patriarchy and capitalism and discussed within feminist urban theory as an urban development that teaches us that cities 'are not constructed in a gender-neutral way' (Frank, 2008: 127). As we will see later, removing women from the city and the public and making them the queens of the domestic, private sphere in the suburbs, realms of reproduction, outside the city has been critically discussed as a product and expression of capitalism and patriarchy, even though scholars such as Frank have also pointed to the historically changing meaning of suburbia for women's lives.

Second, suburbanisation is a process that helps us understand the formation of racialised spaces. Suburbs within metropolitan areas may try to attract affluent residents because they require less public spending. In the US zoning regulations and in both the US and Europe building codes, prices and straightforward prejudice and discrimination against minorities (see Haynes, 2001) can help some suburbs to remain exclusive. The rise of suburban gated communities may be seen as the extreme form of such suburbanisation. Intersectionality becomes clearest here as those gated communities or common interest developments – areas of housing that do not have to be suburban but also include condominiums in the inner city and are characterised by being run by homeowner associations that provide a range of services privately and set clear regulations on lifestyle – typically are exclusive: their services are exclusive to members, and their practices of selecting who moves in and who is kept out are exclusionary too. To Mike Davis (1990), an urban fear lies behind the development of such fortified enclaves. Caldeira, in her often quoted study of fortified enclaves in São Paulo, points to the class dependency of the middle classes on services delivered by lower-class residents, from providing security to taking care of their children, cleaning the house or, in the case of badly paid 'office boys', to pay their bills and 'standing in all types of lines' (Caldeira, 2013: 407–8). Setha Low (2003) has shown that the trend towards gated communities is taking place in many corners of the world, even though the cultural and social contexts in which it does so are very diverse. Low sees globalisation as leading to increasing hetero-geneity and intra-urban inequalities, which in turn increase crime perceptions and a desire for more safety. Whereas Caldeira and Low hence focus on why people move into such places, Webster (2001) has argued that such communities are produced because services and amenities can be supplied most efficiently and effectively through such small administrations, and the process fits with the neo-liberal turn away from state provisions. It is thus another spatial expression of austerity and inequality with regard to resource access directly related to neo-liberalism and the ideology of the market.

Third, suburbanisation has been discussed within the cultural approaches to urban studies as a residential pattern that induces specific lifestyles and identi-ties. Whereas suburbs are not homogeneous – Schnore (1963) differentiated half a century ago between bedroom suburbs, service suburbs, mixed residential suburbs and workers' suburbs – scholars have asked to what extent living in suburbs creates particular lifestyles, or 'suburbanism as a way of life' that is distinctive from an urban lifestyle (Gans, 1991). Others, such as Douglas Rae (2003), have theorised the consequences of suburbanisation for urban govern-ance. Suburbanisation, Rae argued, geographically disconnects people's social-cultural, economic and political citizenship, affecting the political texture of the city and creating problems of political participation and urban governance. As far as urban theorists are interested in urban culture and the city as producer of meanings, suburbs present important changes to traditional views (Wirth and Simmel) of what living in the city is about, and the cultural practices and mean-ings attached to inner-city and suburban life are also part of the production and consumption of 'spectacles' that link culture to political economic concerns (Lin & Mele, 2013: 347): and culture, Zukin (2013: 350) argues, has become a site for explicit conflicts over social differences and urban fear. Moreover, with dein-dustrialisation and suburbanisation, the central city has become increasingly important as a site of the consumption of culture, with waterfront development, shopping districts and heritage sites as a safe playground for tourists and cul-tural consumers who come, but neither work nor live in the city. The cultural production of symbols and aesthetics is also one of the central aspects of gentri-fication, to which we now turn.

Suburbanisation and gentrification have in common that, as processes, they name two different forms of creating sites in the city where social position and location match: in other words, they are names for the processes of creating habitats that match a habitus, whilst, at the same time, the sites themselves impact the habitus and help its reproduction. As we will see in our discussion of ghettoisation afterwards, these processes of resource generating and hoarding are directly related to the deprivation in locations in the city elsewhere.

Gentrification

Gentrification may well be one of the most studied processes in current urban scholarship, and the case studies, debates and perspectives have become as much a cottage industry as the study of segregation; there is a remarkable absence of explicit links between the two themes, even though scholars do implicitly seem to agree that positions and locations are relational, so that one would expect that the study of middle-class agents, the economic and social processes that contextualise their agency, and the (re)production of inequalities that they bring about could, even should, have a stronger position in the research agenda of urban studies. But gentrification studies have focused more on the middle classes and how they affect the urban than on the interdependence between social groups in the city and the hierarchies that they construct, even though such hierarchies or interdependencies do not go away with gentrification.

With gentrification being such a popular term in urban studies today, the definition of gentrification has been stretched so that it now applies to virtually all forms of neighbourhood upgrading. In its original use by Ruth Glass (1964), however, displacement was a crucial part of the definition. Although scholars have amused themselves with discussions over the issue of definition (see Lees, Slater, & Wyly, 2008), it is useful to reserve the term 'gentrification' for those processes of urban change that actually include displacement, as this brings some conceptual clarity to a highly politicised theme. Eric Clark is among those scholars who have argued that gentrification could benefit from a broader definition and stimulated discussion (1987; see also Butler & Smith, 2007), but the definition above has achieved textbook status. Like other themes discussed in this chapter, gentrification is a visible expression of economic and socio-political processes that shape contemporary cities. Like other phenomena some-times also included as gentrification, such as touristification or the redevelopment of brownfield sites, economic processes or economic restructuring and the shift to the service economy and the political processes connected to neo-liberalism as discussed in Chapter 3 can underlie such changes (Smith & Williams, 2010: 10). Defining gentrification in its simple form should not, however, suggest that explaining gentrification is straightforward, as there is no single theory of a homogeneous gentrification process. Put bluntly, gentrification is not 'simply a facet of capital accumulation' (Beauregard, 2010: 11). That may be so, but Clark makes quite a strong argument for saying that if gentrification is the change in the population of land users so that the new users have a higher socio-economic status in combination with a changing built environment through the investment of fixed capital (Clark, 2010: 25) then how exactly the process of gentrification changes the urban landscape, at what cost and for whom – and perhaps sometimes at no cost for anyone? – is case-based and we may find additional precision in theory; according to Clark, social polarisation and surrounding property rights may, for example, be the keys to the question why sometimes gentrification generates strong protest and in other cases does not, one of the remarkable features of gentrification. Clark's important contribution to the discussion on defining gentrification comes, however, after years in which many scholars have tried, first, to describe gentrification as a process – not exactly theorising it in terms of seeking to explain it but rather trying to classify the stages, the characteristics, the shapes and forms, which shows the strong geographical approach to what is just as much a sociological phenomenon. Second, scholars have theorised explanations of gentrification in various ways. Third, scholars have studied, and to some extent theorised, the consequences of gentrification. There also is a broad spectrum of scholars studying gentrification in primarily descriptive ways; those studies that have explicitly looked at gender and gentrification will be briefly returned to in Chapter 7. For understanding urban inequalities within cities, such descriptive studies have not made much of a theoretical contribution.

Gentrification as a process

Gentrification as a process was modelled influentially and early in the debate by Clay (1979) who distinguished four steps. First the pioneers come – artists, bohemians, people willing to take risks and in search of cheap housing. They are then followed by developers and investors. When the media pick up that an area is becoming 'hip', more established middle classes take an interest in the place and prices rise. Finally, these middle-class professionals are outpriced by managers and business elites. While this notion of stages has gained textbook status, it is now widely felt that this model was too rigid, insufficiently context-dependent and sincerely limits gentrification as usable as a concept only if artists and bohemians move into an area first – as if no gentrification is possible without artists which is, as many smaller Dutch and German cities can testify, definitely not the case. Berry (1985) tried to develop a more inclusive model including the stages in which the role of the various actors involved, not just the gentrifiers themselves, was made clearer and demand and supply sides combined. Bourne's (1993) approach was similar, but his modelling was more a matter of defining conditions for gentrification rather than the stages that the process would follow, and, especially, a plea to see gentrification as one of many of the processes that change cities. Two decades later, many may argue that Bourne was 'wrong' to expect gentrification to become less important when the pool of gentrifiers simply shrank, and more cities may have witnessed some variation of gentrification – whether or not this is the case of course depends on how one defines the process in the first place! – but that does not make the remark with which he concluded his contribution less important: 'the challenge for the future will not be the emergence of the elite inner city, but the instability, vulnerability, and in some instances rapid decline of a host of other neighbourhoods' (Bourne, 1993: 105). Within our metaphor of spikiness, the valleys are valleys because there are peaks, and gentrification can be seen as a spatial expression of more severe inequalities, making the urban landscape spikier. To understand processes of marginalisation, however, requires also the study of gentrification, as both relationally produce sites that structure resource opportunities for their users.

Production versus consumption

Since the 1980s, two perspectives have dominated explanations of gentrification: perspectives that focus on production and those that focus on consumption. The most famous author to explain gentrification through the lens of the mode of production was Neil Smith, a geographer and student of David Harvey, who initially wrote against the 1960s and 1970s explanations that, similar to those we have seen for suburbanisation, assumed consumer sovereignty, and heavily influenced subsequent debate (Smith, 1983). Smith argued that understanding investments and land values was essential to understanding gentrification as a capitalist process. Land and buildings are commodities under capitalism, he argued, and gentrification occurs within the context of the value of land and buildings. The ground rent, that is, the return on the investment given the current land use, may not be optimal, the amount that could be generated by the best use (Smith, 2010: 90) so that a rent gap may exist: the disparity between the potential ground rent level and the actual ground rent capitalised under the present land use (Smith, 2010: 93). He summarises the gentrification process as follows:

> Only when this gap emerges can redevelopment be expected since if the present use succeeded in capitalizing all or most of the ground rent, little economic benefit could be derived from redevelopment. As filtering and neighborhood decline proceed, the rent gap widens. Gentrification occurs when the gap is wide enough that developers can purchase shells cheaply, can pay the builders' costs and profit for rehabilitation, can pay interest on mortgage and construction loans, and can then sell the end product for a sale price that leaves a satisfactory return to the developer. The entire ground rent … is now capitalized; the neighborhood has been 'recycled' and begins a new cycle of use. (Smith, 2010: 93)

Smith later weakened his own position somewhat, acknowledging that gentrification may be explained not only by the actions of advanced capitalists. His rent gap theory has also been heavily debated and criticised, for example by Hamnett (1991), Beauregard (1986), and Ley (1986), and turned out to be difficult to test empirically (Bourassa, 1993). A strong point of criticism by Bourassa (1993) was that the idea of land value or potential rent is explained by a Marxist approach just as little as it is by a neo-economical approach: 'it does not explain how it historically becomes profitable to rehabilitate or redevelop inner-city neighbourhoods'.

Here, then, it becomes clear that explanations of production cannot do without explanations of consumption. Gentrifiers may not do gentrification alone, but without relatively affluent, professional households the whole process cannot take place (Beauregard, 2010: 14). To say they have a preference for urban life means nothing – just as this was not an explanation for the suburban way of life: why do they have such a preference? Various important elements have been discussed here, including the relevance of the changing role of gender relations (women deciding if and when to have children, participating in the labour market and purchasing careers, are important actors in producing new gendered urban spaces and gentrification can be partly seen in this light: Bondi, 2010), or the role of aesthetics and distinction in class practices (Jager, 2010). Ley (1980, 1994) has linked gentrification to left liberal politics of the new middle class of professionals in social and cultural fields for whom living in the central city is a collective identity. For Caulfield (1989), gentrification is (partly) explained by the fact that culture of everyday life is not simply a consumer preference or a demand created by capital, but also active cultural practices that serve the establishment of identities and identifications. As Rose (2010: 209) has discussed, though, some of the spatial solutions people, such as employed women with children, seek to solve their social problems are indications of how people use the city as a site of resources and generate resources in the city. Lifestyle as such is not something they pick up the way you pick clothes or shoes when shopping.

Realising that gentrification hence is also about the gentrifying residents themselves and not just a matter of broad processes, whether accorded a neo-economic or Marxist explanation, does not mean one only needs to think of the demand side as individual people having lifestyle-based preferences, but needs to include the idea that cultural consumption can also be an investment (Zukin, 2010: 225), and can be studied in terms of strategies to ensure resources to reproduce social status and, indeed, create spatial profit in Bourdieu's terms, which is obviously a very different understanding of profit on a different scale than the Marxist perspectives of economic profit and land use.

Displacement

Gentrification, then, comes with the displacement of lower-status users of the space. Displacement, 'the forced disenfranchisement of poor and working class people from the spaces and the places to which they have legitimate social and historical claims' (Lees, Slater, & Wyly, 2010: 317), directly affects the spatiality of inequalities. As displacement alters the access to resources directly, the analyses of displacement seem to be even more politically divided than the debate on the definition of gentrification as such. Here again a definitional issue is at stake. What do we mean by disenfranchisement? When is it forced and when do people voluntarily leave an area? If residents voluntarily leave because they are socially mobile and aspire to a suburban lifestyle, or to suburban schools for their children, is there still displacement? Peter Marcuse has tried to bring some structure to this discussion by distinguishing between direct and indirect displacement. Direct displacement comes in two forms: people can no longer afford the rent and therefore have to move; or repairs are no longer being done, the property is no longer managed and so on so that the quality of life deteriorates so much that people would rather move, the so-called last-resident displacement or chain displacement where prior households occupying the same unit also become displaced. Indirect displacement occurs symbolically as 'pressure of displacement' when changes in the commercial infrastructure, the culture of the neighbourhood and the ways of behaving that dominate public spaces are experienced as exclusionary. As Centner (2008) has pointed out more generally, spatial capital can be used as an exclusionary tool: exclusionary claims on public space that are socially legitimate may, through privileged consumption, create space perceived as exclusionary. Exclusionary displacement, then, is the form of indirect displacement where gentrification comes with new limitations on who is and who is not entitled to move into a dwelling, by a change in condition which affects that dwelling or its immediate surroundings (Marcuse, 1986: 185).

Displacement is an important theme in theories of intra-urban inequalities because it immediately touched on the capabilities to access and create resources to get by and get ahead. Indeed, as Newman and Wyly (2010: 566) have said, those who are forced to leave neighbourhoods may be torn from rich local social networks of information and co-operation. Whether such neighbourhood communities of support and solidarity indeed exist everywhere is doubtful (Blokland 2003a). The extent to which displacement hampers or creates opportunities for the poor is therefore primarily an empirical question and one that is dependent on the context. Clearly, where homelessness and overcrowding are the consequences of capital investment and market speculation, there are no 'advantages'. On the other hand, the strong politicisation of the gentrification debate blurs the view on the consequences. When Curley (2008) found that residents who were relocated through government programmes dispersing the poor (Hope IV) in the US were not suffering but instead were more likely to have a job and more likely to have their children doing better in school after being relocated, she argued that the end of 'draining' their social capital to other members of a poor neighbourhood made these households stronger. It may well be that in terms of feeling at home and belonging they may not have liked their new places that much. It would be odd, however, to be concerned with the life chances and severe structural inequalities of people but then to argue that their right to stay put for cultural and identity reasons is so important that their right to move up is ignored. We do not argue that displacement is not a problem, normatively and politically. Of course it is. However, the idea that, before the evil practices start, gentrifying neighbourhoods are nice, close-knit, positive places for poor residents is a nostalgic image that serves a political debate, but is in strong need of empirical back-up. It is not at all clear that the neighbourhoods undergoing gentrification always match this 'urban village' image that seems to inform the debate. Indeed, it is remarkable that the part of urban sociology that studies poor inner-city areas for their problems and apparent *lack* of cohesion and community is so remote from the part that engages with gentrification. Scholars have become very critical about the idea of a 'social mix' of people differing in race, class and ethnicity. According to Slater's provocative article, academic writers and policy makers debating social mix form 'an excellent example of how the rhetoric and reality of gentrification have been replaced by a different discursive, theoretical and policy language that consistently deflects criticism and resistance' (Slater 2006: 751).

The very idea of gentrification as a 'disruption of community' (Slater, 2006: 752) is based on the assumption that a locally bounded, well-functioning community is there in the first place. The debate on ghettoisation, however, shows that not only reinvestment in inner cities, investment in suburbs, but also economic, political and social deinvestment in poor areas (ghettoisation or spatial marginalisation) is part of the picture of the spiky urban landscape.

Ghettoisation as a spatial process of marginalisation

While segregation and suburbanisation have been discussed as the terms urban theorists have used to make sense of the segregating forces of middle classes and whites and their behaviour on the housing market, including the political economy steering these actions, the twin to these processes is the marginalisation or ghettoisation of other neighbourhoods. One needs to be a little careful with suggesting that gentrification and suburbanisation are responsible for areas of concentrated disadvantage. Poor neighbourhoods, or even 'ghettos' where poverty and ethnic minority or racial status coincide, are the spatial expressions of processes in which local labour market situations, the state and other 'institutional assemblages' entrench poverty (Theodore, 2010: 170). They are spatial expressions of processes of marginalisation. Marginalisation is the opposite process of the advancement of the clustering of forms of capital elsewhere in the city, and the processes that make locations where strong positions can be maintained take place in a double bind with processes in the other direction. As we will see below, these include economic restructuring under conditions of technological development and globalisation, the articulation of racism and discrimination, spatial stereotyping, the ideological construction of 'blaming the poor', if not punishing them, based on behavioural understandings of poverty, and neoliberal policy-making in times of austerity. In this section we trace the linkage between poverty and place back in the development of social sciences, discuss the notion of ghetto and then discuss these four processes of marginalisation.

Ever since the onset of industrialisation and the intense urbanisation that came with it, social critics have been concerned with the living conditions of the lower and working classes, who are the majority in the city: 'temporarily endurable existence for hard work' is how Friedrich Engels described their lives after visiting London and Manchester at the end of the nineteenth century, and their segregated lives seemed to matter to no one: 'society, composed wholly of atoms, does not trouble itself about them; leaves them to take care of themselves and their families, yet supplies them no means of doing this in an efficient and permanent matter' (Engels, 2011: 54). It is not the slum or the poor neighbourhood as such that is new. What is different about poor neighbourhoods in the cities of the Global North now, and since roughly the 1950s, is, first, the way in which they are affected by economic restructuring and, second, the way in which they are affected by neo-liberal policy and austerity measures. Moreover, neighbourhoods may be homogeneous in class and race because society involuntarily segregates some of its members (Gans, 2008: 356) based on racism and discrimination.

'Ghetto' as a term in urban studies

The use of the term 'ghetto' in urban sociology goes back to Wirth's (1928) early work with the same title. Wirth aimed to show how the Jewish European ghetto was reproduced in Chicago at the time, tried to classify the Jews living there according to their lifestyle characteristics and noted that the ghetto was the product of the historical exclusion of Jews from mainstream society. It was strictly used to refer to Jewish neighbourhoods, and Wirth did not see them as much different from other ethnic neighbourhoods where first-generation migrants embarked on their way to assimilation (Haynes & Hutchison, 2008: 349–50). Robert Weaver's (1940) first study of racial segregation then linked the term to black residents, whilst Kenneth Clark discussed in *Dark Ghetto* (1965) the problems that came with racial segregation, referring to both its 'pervasive pathology' and its 'surprising human resilience' (quoted in Haynes & Hutchison, 2008: 351). Two points about this early work are of particular importance. First, notwithstanding his ecological approach, Wirth did note that the ghetto 'is not so much a physical fact as it is a state of mind' (Wirth, 1928: 287, quoted in Tonkiss, 2005: 54). Second, as Tonkiss (2005: 45–6) writes,

> 'thinkers such as ... Wirth wanted to highlight the changing nature of social space in modern cities, and the mutually determining effects of culture and space, but their accounts could not always avoid lapsing into gestures of spatial and cultural fixity. The hangover from [this kind] of thinking is felt in the way that different parts of the city come to be identified with particular cultural, ethnic or racial 'types'. Bounded spaces, that is, are defined, understood and often pathologized in terms of distinct groups.

Public opinion and discourse has come to refer to such areas as ghettos, increasingly also in European media. The tendency is a 'dilution of the notion of ghetto simply to designate an urban area of widespread and intense poverty, which obfuscates the racial basis and character of this poverty and divests the term of both historical meaning and sociological content' (Wacquant, 1997: 342)

While in the US such neighbourhoods have long been called 'ghettos' and European media have hyped this moral panic (Slater, 2010), European scholars have been hesitating to use the term, or have argued that it analytically makes no sense to do so, often claiming that Europe does not have 'American conditions' (Wacquant, 1997, 2008; Agnew, 2010; Nobles, 2010; Slater, 2010; Peach, 1996; Simpson, 2007). More than in the US, it seemed in welfare states such as France, the Netherlands, the Nordic countries, Germany and even Great Britain as if poverty, unemployment and their political and social consequences had disappeared in the booming years of welfare growth and welfare state development after the Second World War. From the 1970s, however, new forms of polarisation began to characterise European cities (Häussermann, Kronauer, & Siebel, 2004: 7) so that European scholars started to note the emergence of new poverty, often linked to migration ('ethnicising' poverty – see Häussermann et al., 2004: 9) and to find spatial expression in neighbourhoods where poor, migrants and the unemployed concentrated, although such concentration could by no means be compared to the concentration known from the US (Musterd & Ostendorf, 1998b). Madanipour (2011: 188–91) prefers to speak of social exclusion rather than poverty or marginalisation, as this allows him to stress the cultural, economic and political dimensions rather than just whether one is poor or not. In European countries such as Germany, Sweden, the Netherlands and France, social exclusion has also been the core concept in policies aimed at combating disadvantage, whereby the 'spatiality of exclusion' has often, as in Britain, resulted in 'attempts to dismantle pockets of deprivation without necessarily dismantling the causes of deprivation or the forces bringing them together in particular enclaves' (2011: 191). Madanipour does see a relevance of spatial practices for exclusion. Exclusion, he writes (2011: 191), is a matter of resource access of various sorts; and such resources have 'clear spatial manifestations'.

Apart from poverty not being as extreme or as extremely concentrated, it has been pointed out that the scale, the exclusive black demography of the impoverished US tracts, and the ubiquity and lethalness of crime in the American ghetto are all unlike the characteristics of very poor European areas (Western, 2010; see also Wacquant 1993: 366–7). Ghettos as neighbourhoods of the unemployed have been analysed by Americans, as O'Connor (2004: 69–70) has warned her European audience, within the tradition of 'analyzing the deviance of the poor in the ghetto without questioning the role of the free economic market as such'. While this may be a little too strong and not do full justice to Wilson and other American scholars, O'Connor of course correctly points out that taking American frames of references as 'theories' to understand empirical patterns of concentrated poverty and the processes of marginalisation that bring them about and make them durable must be done with caution (Wacquant, 1996). Various scholars have pointed to the metaphorical meaning of 'ghetto' in international scholarship nowadays (Monteiro, 2008: 378), with its strong behavioural connotations (Blokland, 2008b). We return to this below, as this ideology of blaming the poor for their own poverty is one of the important processes of marginalisation, a process of symbolic violence.

Economic restructuring and marginalisation

Most urban scholars, whether they reject the 'ghetto' label or not, agree that the economic restructuring in the context of globalisation is one of the main processes of marginalisation. The displacement of manufacturing by service industries and the geographical relocation of industries as part of globalisation have been facilitated by the presence of docile, cheap workforces in the peripheries of the world. Outsourcing has made further fragmentation of the production process possible (Wacquant, 1995: 424). The new urban poverty that we now witness in the increasingly spiky city is not, however, just a matter of the disappearance of work. The workforce is split between highly skilled professional and technical jobs and, where jobs have not disappeared, the deskilling of the labour force. Low-skilled jobs have not gone altogether, but are more often part-time, require flexible working and carry less security and fewer benefits, with social goods such as health care coverage becoming privatised (Wacquant, 1999: 1641–2). One of the current debates focuses on the question whether this precariousness actually constitutes a new social class of 'precariat' (Frase, 2013). It is clear at least that models of the spatial mismatch – the jobs are located where the poor people do not live and bad transportation makes them inaccessible – are too simple. Even when people living in poverty do find jobs, these tend to be poorly paid, part-time, temporary jobs with few if any benefits and no long-term prospects.

While poverty is not new and unemployment is not new either, the type of work available, if any, to the poor has transformed in character, reducing the chance that getting a job is the way out of poverty. Those who grow up in neighbourhoods of extreme poverty, then, are even more disadvantaged in the competition for such low-skilled jobs than poor living in less poor areas. The first reason for this is that, according to some scholars, the habitus needed for being successful in job applications is learnt through socialisation processes of others who work: the absence of such role models makes it difficult to learn the right dress code, manners and body language to get into jobs even as simple as flipping burgers in a fast-food restaurant.

Moreover, since Granovetter's (1973) seminal study on how people find work it has been well known in the social sciences that the few jobs that are available can often be accessed through others in their social networks (see also van Eijk, 2010, for how this is related to neighbourhood). These two factors and spatial mismatch make the situation of poverty more severe and durable for those living in high-poverty areas. In addition, they may be subjected to residential discrimination as a result of spatial stigmatisation.

Stigmatisation was developed theoretically by Ervin Goffman (1990), who discussed how negative group characteristics were ascribed to individuals who then found strategies to cope with stigma, of which distancing was an important one (Blokland, 2008a). The negative stereotyping of high-poverty neighbourhoods as dangerous no-go areas influences the mental maps of many urbanites and becomes a self-fulfilling prophecy once people outside these areas start to avoid going there altogether and treat residents of such areas with fear and disrespect. While there is ample discussion of the supposed consequences of stigmatisation and, as Hastings (2004) shows in her overview of recent literature, various studies discuss the causes of stigmatisation, the actual process remains a black box, as does the question whether applying the under-theorised notion of stigma means the same and works the same ways in each of the very different city and national contexts. Although the evidence is not very systematic, it is often and quickly argued that the media stigmatise by reporting selectively and negatively about specific areas (Cole & Smith, 1996; Damer, 1974; Häussermann & Kapphan, 2002: 230). As in all labelling (Gans, 1995), those who decide what is news (Gans, 1979) have a powerful position to label disadvantaged neighbourhoods as dangerous and immoral urban areas that one should avoid. Such a 'blemish of place' may be superimposed on the already existing stigmata traditionally associated with poverty and ethnic origin or postcolonial immigrant status, to which it is closely linked but not reducible' (Wacquant, 2007: 67).

Wacquant points to the impossibility of being home in a stigmatised neighbourhood: such spaces are no longer places with which one can identify, cannot function as a site for resource mobilisation and become a 'battlefield' (Wacquant, 2007: 70). Residential discrimination occurs when people are ascribed negative attributes based on where they live, affecting chances of finding jobs, interactions with the police and street-level bureaucrats (Wacquant, 1996). One may suspect that institutions deal differently with different people depending on where they live or where the particular institution is located: a boy acting up in school in a deprived area may be ascribed a mentality that is the product of his habitat, while the same behaviour in a boy in an advantaged neighbourhood may be seen as an individual psychological problem in need of remedial support. No one knows to what extent this really happens, as few have studied such internal logics of institutions empirically.

Stigma, discrimination and racism

Residential discrimination and stigma become complex and especially harsh when combined with ethnic or racial discrimination. Discrimination and violence against immigrants occur in all major urban areas in Europe (Wrench & Solomos, 1993; Bjørgo & Witte, 1993). But not all high-poverty areas need to be linked to racism and discrimination. In cities like Helsinki, Warsaw or Budapest this may, given the low ethnic and racial diversity, not make sense, whereas these cities too have their stigmatised areas. In many European cities and in all North American cities, however, a strong connection between extreme poverty and ethnic minority status exists, and high-poverty areas are also the areas where ethnic minorities concentrate, so that then racism and discrimination as marginalising practices do have to be taken into account. Wacquant (1995, 1997) identifies four elementary forms of racial domination, summarised as categorisation, discrimination, segregation and exclusionary violence, and shows how these apply to the Chicago ghetto.

Typically, spatial expressions of racism and ethnic discrimination categorise one group with ascribed characteristics as homogeneous. Scholars have long tried to challenge such actions. Du Bois in *The Philedelphia Negro* had made an effort to counter the tendency to consider African-Americans as a homogeneous mass, arguing that there was a 'class of criminals and prostitutes', a 'class of honest poor with no touch of gross immorality or crime', a respectable working class and a class of 'families of undoubted respectability'. Du Bois stated that 'coloured people are seldom judged by their best classes and often the very existence of classes among them is ignored' (Du Bois, 2013: 179). His work resonates, however, with the connection between poverty and culture that was later found in the culture of poverty thesis and the underclass debate, and also shows similarity to the later distinction, as in the work of Elijah Anderson (1990, between 'the decent' and 'the street'. In a way, the attempt to show that there are morally good people too – and that deviance is a sign of immoral character – does not escape the categorisation of inferiority as such. It is to the culture of poverty through the lens of the ideological construction of blaming the poor as a process of marginalisation that we now turn.

The conceptualisation of the ghetto in terms of space as container is crucial to the underclass concept (Gilbert, 1997, 2000, 2010). This pathologising of specific areas of the city as containing a culture of poverty resonated with the more general debate on urban poverty that has throughout its history carried implicit notions about spatial proximity. From the time social reformists and others starting portraying poverty in the days of Engels quoted above, the poor were seen as 'suffering from individual pathology or from social disorganization' (Gans, 1991: 300). With far less attention to neighbourhood poverty and pathology in the years to follow, the 1960s showed a return to the idea of poor people being deviant and pathological, and what is more, to the notion that they collectively constituted a group that deviated from mainstream society with different morals and norms.

The culture of poverty

Oscar Lewis (1961, 1966a, 1966b) is credited with having coined the 'culture of poverty thesis'. Describing the lives of families living in severe poverty in Mexico and Puerto Rico, Lewis argued that some of the poor developed a culture of poverty as both an adaptation and a reaction to their marginal position in a stratified, individualised society. Their ways of life presented coping strategies in the face of knowing they were unable to escape the despair of their lives in poverty. This, then, is what came to distinguish in the discussions that followed – and there were many – those just being poor from 'the underclass': although initially defined just economically, the concept of the underclass came to be adapted to make similar arguments about the importance of culture for understanding the coping of specific sections of the poor, partly psychological and partly behavioural, not so much to explain poverty as to explain how poverty became durable and inherited over generations. Katz (1990) and Gans (1991) are among those who have traced the development of the concept and shown how it developed in the American debate into a racialised term used for blacks (and Hispanics) and a term pointing to harmful behaviour, so that the concept 'in essence proposes that some very poor people are somehow to be selected for separation from the rest of society' (Gans, 1991: 333) and links the underclass to poor *areas*, which has one way or the other always been the case in the discussion about poverty.

Homogenising people living in high-poverty areas, the culture that they develop internally within their neighbourhood, even though initially their plight may have economic causes, perpetuates the poverty they are in, with its pathologies, because of what in the neighbourhood effects literature has been discussed as lack of cohesion or social control (known as the social disorganisation thesis), the absence of role models or presence of the inappropriate role models (the epidemic or contamination thesis), or deviance as a form of resistance against the mainstream (the subaltern thesis). Katz (1990) has summarised the major issues in the debate around the underclass, where whether individuals are responsible for their own poverty, whether culture plays a role in perpetuating poverty and dependence, whether family structures reproduce social pathologies, whether the ecological context influences behaviour, what the capacity of institutions is (and why they fail) and why poverty persists despite public policy are the questions steering these discussions.

Gans points out that those who have argued that the poor are not suffering from some deviant culture but instead economically deprived take what he has described as a situational view. People respond to situations available to them and change their behaviour accordingly; those taking the cultural view assume that people react to situations out of prior values and modes of behaviour:

> When a behavior pattern is identified as part of a larger and interrelated cultural system, and when the causes of that pattern are ascribed to 'the culture', there is a tendency to see the behavior pattern and its supporting norms as resistant to change and as persisting simply because they are cultural, although there is no real evidence that culture is as unchanging as assumed.

Hence if one is to use a term like 'underclass' in urban theory, it must be a precise, analytical use:

> if the concept of underclass is used, it must be a structural concept: it must denote a new sociospatial patterning of class and racial domination, recognizable by the unprecedented concentration of the most socially excluded and economically marginal members of the dominated racial and

economic group. It should not be used as a label to designate a new breed of individuals molded by a mythical and all-powerful culture of poverty. (Wacquant & Wilson, 2013: 191)

Whilst scholars became critical of the idea of a culture of poverty as an explanation of disadvantage and heavily debated the use or misuse of the term 'underclass', the social disorganisation thesis continued to be important in discussions on poverty concentration and the idea of the ghetto. 'New urban poverty' is the term that scholars like William Julius Wilson (1996: 123) have used for poor, segregated neighbourhoods where a substantial majority of the adult residents are unemployed. It is the absence of work, not poverty as such, that Wilson holds responsible for the severe lack of basic opportunities and resources and inadequate social controls in the 'jobless ghettos' which are different from impoverished neighbourhoods that were 'institutional ghettos' in that their structure and activities paralleled those of the wider society from which its residents were excluded.

Indeed, Loïc Wacquant speaks of the *hyperghetto* in comparison to what he sees as the more traditional ghetto. Ghettos were areas of severe segregation dominated by poverty, but not all were poor and the poor included working-class poor families. Only with deindustrialisation and the mobility of anyone who could move out of these areas (also due to desegregation laws in the US context) did the social infrastructure of these areas collapse, positive role models disappear, and networks to get ahead and get by deteriorate. 'The relatively cohesive black community of the 1950s', says Wacquant (1995: 418), 'has given way to a deepening division between relatively secure middle and working classes and an increasingly vulnerable and isolated segment of minority poor.' The hyperghetto, then, may not be a 'container' in which we can found one 'culture of poverty'. Yet at the same time scholars such as Wacquant have pointed out that socio-economic marginality there does translate, in his view, into 'the corrosion of the self', into 'collective demoralization' (Wacquant, 2010b: 216), mutual distancing and retreat into the private sphere (Wacquant, 2010b: 217). The hyperghetto may have its own social logic; it is also socially disorganised. Social organisation can be defined as

> the extent to which the residents of a neighbourhood are able to maintain effective social control and realize their common goals. There are three major dimensions of neighbourhood social organization: 1) the prevalence, strength and interdependence of social networks; 2) the extent of collective supervision that the residents exercise and the degree of personal responsibility they assume in addressing neighbourhood problems and 3) the rate of resident participation in voluntary and formal organizations. (Wilson, 1996: 124)

Wacquant has maintained that the ghetto is not disorganised but organised on different principles, that it is in fact 'patterned' and has a 'distinctive, if unstable, social logic' (Wacquant, 1997: 347).

Gans (1991: 88) has pointed critically to the sharp reading that this theorising about ghettoisation requires. The writings of Wilson, Wacquant and others on the advanced marginalisation of the hyperghetto are based on the disappearance of jobs (see also Wilson, 1996) *in combination* with the social despair that developed in (not just poor but) high-poverty areas where the working class and lower middle class were living. Gans warns that economic and racial inequalities explain the contrast between the poor inner-city neighbourhoods and richer suburbs. No housing policy could have realistically ended the class and racial inequality: 'the suburban exodus may not have ameliorated these patterns, but it did not cause them'. Gilbert (2010: 149) too has argued that using labels like 'ghetto' or 'hyperghetto' may negate the ways in which the ghetto is created and maintained through wider social, economic and political processes, even though this is exactly what scholars like Wacquant aim to do.

Ghetto and urban policy

Ghettoisation has, finally, been linked to the changing urban policies under conditions of austerity and the neo-liberal turn. Neo-liberalism rests on the assumption that the market is the preferred mechanism for the distribution of goods and resources, and that individuals themselves have the task of acting as actors on that market. This approach fits nicely with the culture of poverty thesis, albeit in a slightly different form: influenced by the work of Charles Murray (1984), poor people are no longer understood as either the passive victims of a deviant culture that reproduces their position or as the passive victims of structural forces that keep them poor as they are marginalised as an unnecessary underclass in the labour market, but instead as rational actors. Murray's favourite group, black young single mothers in the United States, is presented to his readers as active rational actors that weigh up the costs and benefits of finding a low-paid job against relying on welfare payments, welfare payments that become available to them when they have a child without a partner. What have derogatively been called 'welfare queens' are thus in his view no longer people with the wrong morals, but women making choices on the rationality of the welfare state: it is easy to see that in such a stick-and-carrot understanding of poverty, cutting welfare benefits and punishing the poor for not working becomes, and in the United States has become, the next logical step. The retrenchment of the welfare state means that rights to public aid have been replaced by the obligation to work (Wacquant, 1999: 1643). Policy has moved in a similar direction in Europe too, albeit less sharply. Other policy areas have been affected by neo-liberal changes as well. It is not difficult to see how a bigger role of the private market in housing and a retreat of the state from the housing sector add to marginalisation by further relegating poor people to those areas they can still afford when other neighbourhoods are gentrifying, resulting in an increased concentration of poverty in parts of the city, a city that becomes spikier in the process. Disinvestment in public services such as infrastructure and parks, education and social and health services affect those areas disproportionally, because poor people rely on such public services more than those who can afford the alternative of meeting their needs in the private market. Various authors have pointed to the state intervention in poverty areas that have remained (or become) strong, namely where the state acts to control. Body-Gendrot (2000) has argued that cities in the US have turned to repressive policing and crime fighting in ghettos where the French have developed integration policies of various kinds to exert social control over the poor and ethnic minorities, and explains these policies as the state reaction to an increasing insecurity among its constituents: economic crises, globalisation and the flexibilisation of the labour market have heightened an anxiety to which the state has no proper answer as the causes lie elsewhere. Controlling the poor comes with stigmatising them and the places where they live as a project to conceal the impotence of the state to take away such anxieties.

Wacquant goes even further and maintains that the ghetto and the prison belong to the same 'organizational genus': they are 'institutions of forced confinement' (Wacquant, 2010a: 81). The incarceration of black men in the US, for example, is in Wacquant's analysis not a matter of a crime–punishment connection, but a 'core state capacity devoted to managing dispossessed and dishonoured populations' (Wacquant, 2010a: 80).

Segregation, suburbanisation, gentrification and ghettoisation are thus the main processes that create spatial profits for some and spatial disadvantage for others, increasing intra-urban inequalities. The question that arises of course is why this matters. Theories of neighbourhood effects have tried to measure the consequences of the segregated city and to theorise how they come about. The next section discusses these theories.

Neighbourhood effects: spatial profit and disadvantage

Neighbourhoods matter. They may not be communities, they may not define people's entire life-world, but urban scholars generally agree that some provide spatial profit while others do not. How much explanatory power the neighbourhood has is subject to discussion. The most important factors that explain poverty concentration in the US, as Jargowsky (1997: 185) has shown, are metropolitan economic growth and general processes that create sustained segregation by race and class: other factors, such as neighbourhood culture or location, are 'secondary to income generation and neighbourhood sorting, which together explain most of the variations in ghetto poverty'. Yet neighbourhood still matters as a factor, too. In their study of US segregation, Massey and Denton (2013: 197) conclude:

> Where one lives – especially where one grows up – exerts a profound effect on one's life chances. Identical individuals with similar family backgrounds and personal characteristics will lead very different lives and achieve different rates of socioeconomic success depending on where they reside.

Where you live matters more 'as one moves down the economic ladder' (Dreier et al., 2013: 149):

> on the wrong side of the 'digital divide', poor and working-class families are less likely to own a computer, have internet access, or send and receive email. They rely more on local networks to find out about jobs and other opportunities. Often lacking a car (and adequate mass transit) they must live close to where they work. Unable to send their children to private schools, they must rely on local public schools. Unable to afford day care, lower-income families must rely on informal day care provided by nearby relatives and friends.

As Bauder (2002) has argued, it is *because* institutional and political actors assume that neighbourhood effects occur that they become so socially relevant.

Neighbourhood effect studies start with the theoretical assumption that different neighbourhood contexts can influence people's life chances beyond their individual characteristics. These studies ask to what extent the concentration of socially disadvantaged residents has additional disadvantaging effects on people living and growing up in such neighbourhoods – for example, infant mortality, teenage childbearing, dropping out of high school, child maltreatment, adolescent delinquency, and health-related indicators such as homicide or suicide and even smoking behaviour (Brooks-Gunn, Duncan, & Aber, 1997; Sampson, Morenoff, & Earls, 1999; Sampson, Morenoff, & Gannon-Rowley, 2002; Briggs, 1997; Ellen & Turner, 2003; Galster, 2002; Galster & Killen, 1995; Gephart, 1997; Johnson, Helen, & Jens, 2002; Leventhal & Brooks-Gunn, 2000; Buck, 2001; Pickett & Pearl, 2001, Duncan, Jones, & Moon, 1999), as well as labour market chances (Buck, 2001; Musterd, Ostendorf, & de Vos, 2003) . Europe and the US have seen separate paths of development of the literature, discussed in detail by Friedrichs, Galster, and Musterd (2003; see also Galster, 2002, 2012b). These are theories that aim to link macro and micro levels, and so need to address the rather complicated question of how the neighbourhood might develop contextual effects that affect individual outcomes. Several theoretical propositions have been put forward, while the empirical research on the concrete mechanisms is still sparse (Small & Newman, 2001: 30; Jencks & Mayer, 1990). They have been criticised for unclear definitions of 'neighbourhood' (Small & Newman, 2001) and recently even for looking at the wrong variables altogether – Slater (2013) has provocatively argued that social position explains all, and neighbourhoods themselves 'do' nothing – but nevertheless have produced a huge amount of empirical studies, case-based analyses as well as attempts to theorise the 'why' of neighbourhood effects.

The 'why' of neighbourhood effects

Attempts to answer the 'why' have had a major focus on residents' interpersonal interactions producing a 'deviant' culture not unlike the culture of poverty discussed above, as such interactions are thought to be based on 'wrong' norms or deficit private relations within the neighbourhood. The broad literature can be divided between theoretical approaches that conceptualise the effect of interpersonal interactions within the neighbourhood for life chances and upward social mobility, and perspectives from a criminology tradition that focus on the connection between such neighbourhood relations and crime.

The most recent wave of neighbourhood effect research has brought social capital and social networks to the forefront of academic research and policy discussions (Curley, 2010). Very generally, social capital can be defined as 'the ability of actors to secure benefits by virtue of membership in social networks or other social structures' (Portes, 1998: 6). Scholars focusing on neighbourhood social capital argue that neighbourhood effects are (at least partly) produced by the social capital available to residents within their neighbourhoods (Curley, 2010). Wilson (1987) argued that residents in high-poverty neighbourhoods are isolated from the networks of the middle class (Small, 2006: 275; Wilson, 1996; Morgen & Maskovsky, 2003: 318; Small & Newman, 2001). It has been assumed that mixed neighbourhoods – instead of socially and sometimes ethnically segregated ones – will provide low-income residents with greater opportunities to connect with 'better off' people who are following 'mainstream' norms of work and family and to profit from their better job networks (Wilson, 1987; Curley, 2010). This approach points to two distinct aspects linked to the isolation of networks in deprived neighbourhoods.

Firstly, the network isolation model focuses on the fact that living in a poor neighbourhood with many unemployed residents will disconnect individuals from social networks of employed people, making it difficult to obtain information about job opportunities (Wilson, 1996; Small & Newman, 2001). The second aspect relates to norms, values and 'mainstream' culture, seen as particularly important for children growing up in deprived neighbourhoods. One way of conceptualising the effect of neighbourhood norms on children is the *collective socialisation model* (Jencks & Mayer, 1990). Here, it is argued that children are socialised collectively through the behaviour of adults they observe in their neighbourhood (see also Wilson, 1987). If nobody they know is successful and can act as role model, children are assumed to learn that success is impossible and do not envision success for themselves (Jencks & Mayer, 1990: 114ff.; Small & Newman, 2001: 33). Instead of internalising the importance of working hard and behaving prudently, children observe behaviours that are then described as 'ghetto-specific', such as crime, hustling, or dropping out of school, and are encouraged to emulate these lifestyles later in life (Jencks & Mayer, 1990; Wilson, 1987; Jarrett, 1997: 277). In this perspective poor neighbourhoods lack middle-class residents who provide conventional role models for poorer residents and their children.

The so-called *epidemic model* conceptualises similar processes at the peer level. It assumes that 'bad' behaviour is contagious: when many children in a neighbourhood engage in certain behaviours, other children will also be socialised to do so (Small & Newman, 2001: 33). Poor residents and their children thus affect each other's attitudes, values and behaviours in negative ways (Jencks & Mayer, 1990: 114ff.). A similar approach is the *oppositional culture model* (Jencks & Mayer, 1990) that living in segregated poor neighbourhoods causes residents to develop a culture actively opposed to mainstream norms and values (Small & Newman, 2001: 33). Whereas the collective socialisation model sees residents as passive recipients of a deviant 'ghetto culture', this approach highlights the agency of (young) residents in these processes.

The focus of these models on norms and values has been harshly criticised as such approaches seem to 'blame the victims' for their problems, as they imply that people could avoid being poor if they changed their culture, similar to what we have seen as criticism of the idea of a culture of poverty above. They thus often ignore structural forces and the discrimination against such 'deviant' cultures, whether real or imagined, that are effectively hindering access to mainstream society (see also Small, Harding, & Lamont, 2010: 7).

Moreover, such approaches often apply a somewhat simplifying conceptualisation of culture. The literature on inner-city culture thus would have to address more specifically in what ways these cultures differ from mainstream or middle-class culture(s). A strict dichotomy between middle-class and inner-city culture not only runs the danger of doing little more than stereotyping. Empirical accounts have also shown that this dichotomy is too simple: there are heterogeneous, contradictory and unsystematic (inner-city as well as middle-class) cultures to be found in deprived neighbourhoods (see also Newman, 1999; Duneier, 1992; Small & Newman, 2001). Moreover, deviant culture approaches often imply unrealistic assumptions about how much time people spend in their neighbourhoods and with their neighbours and how values are developed (Small & Newman, 2001: 34; Wellman, 1999). Recently, more sophisticated accounts of combining culture with neighbourhood poverty have been developed (see Small et al., 2010). However, several studies have indicated that linking place and networks is empirically weak. Having resource-rich and resource-poor people living side by side seems to be insufficient for building social networks that overcome class divides (van Eijk, 2010; Blokland 2003a; Blokland, 2008c; Butler, 2003; Lees, 2008; Brophy & Smith, 1997; Cummings, DiPasquale, & Kahn, 2002).

Neighbourhood effects and collective efficacy

Another stream within neighbourhood effect studies has focused on questions of social control, safety and crime prevention. The linkage to inequality and spatial profit here is the basic thought that productive, healthy neighbourhoods are those where people care for each other, engage in participation and community activities, and take care of social control that keeps deviance within limits and socialises children in the 'right' norms and values. Social disorganisation means that the ties between residents that enable all these things are missing, so that the neighbourhood as a collective is less able to 'fight' crime and to socially organise to change for the better; and a better neighbourhood in terms of safety and community is expected to have spin-off effects in other spheres of life.

The concept of social capital refers here to the density of ties between residents (Rountree & Warner, 1999; Elliott et al., 1996; Veysey & Messner, 1999; Morenoff, Sampson, & Raudenbush, 2001; Sampson et al., 2002: 457) or the frequency of social interactions and various ways in which people relate to their neighbours (Bellair, 1997, 2000; Warner & Rountree, 1997; Sampson et al., 2002: 457). This kind of social capital is then conceptualised as a precondition for 'collective efficacy': the trustworthiness of neighbours and their willingness to intervene as informal social control agents on behalf of others and the community, a concept that has recently informed a broad range of empirical studies (Browning, 2002; Browning & Cagney, 2002; Browning, Dietz, & Feinberg, 2004; Odgers et al., 2009; Cohen, Finch, Bower, & Sastry, 2006). It is usually measured through scales of the capacity for informal social control (Elliott et al., 1996; Steptoe & Feldman, 2001) and indicators of social cohesion (Rountree & Land, 1996; Markowitz, Bellair, Liska, & Liu, 2001; Sampson et al., 2002: 457ff.).

Mutual trust and shared expectations among residents are crucial here. Sampson et al. (1999) have focused, for example, on the effect that such trust has on residents' willingness to intervene on behalf of children in the neighbourhood. They show that neighbourhoods vary in collective child-related mechanisms of social control. Concentrated disadvantage is, however, not the most important factor in explaining collective efficacy for children. The most profound predictors are concentrated affluence, (low) population density, and residential stability. Yet, the shared expectations for informal social control of children (one of the dimensions of collective efficacy) are significantly lower in disadvantaged neighbourhoods, even when controlled for perceived violence and homicide. The authors conclude: 'Apparently, the concentration of multiple forms of disadvantage depresses shared expectations for collective action regarding children' (Sampson et al., 1999: 656). In neighbourhoods in which rules are unclear and people do not trust each other, it is argued, residents will be less likely to intervene for the public good, or have less collective efficacy (Sampson, Raudenbush, & Earls, 1997).

Qualitative studies shed doubts on such ideas, highlighting that who is to be controlled and by whom is more complicated. Patillo-McCoy (1998) finds that internal networks within neighbourhoods do not always lead to lower crime as crime and drug dealing do not enter the community 'from outside': under conditions of structural economic exclusion, drug dealers in such neighbourhoods are often not simply criminals but also nephews, cousins, and grandchildren. Reluctant to see them in jail, residents often do not seek police interventions (Small & Newman, 2001: 34).

While these approaches are trying to conceptualise the ways in which neighbourhoods impact residents, they generally miss out on important aspects of the agency of residents. It is not the neighbourhood as such that impacts residents or children, but residents themselves or families that play a major role in determining *how* urban environments might do so (Burton & Jarrett, 2000: 1116). Several studies have highlighted how families can employ strategies to counter negative influences of the neighbourhood on their children. These include strategies to manage crime and safety issues as well as questions of cultural and value orientation. Family protection strategies may include the avoidance of dangerous areas, the temporal use of the neighbourhood, restrictions on neighbour relations, and ideological support of mainstream orientations (Anderson, 1990; Furstenberg, 1999; Hannerz, 2004; Jeffers, 1967; Williams, 1981). By these strategies, some residents or families are able to construct social worlds isolated from the neighbourhoods in which they or their children live (Jarrett, 1997: 278).

The need for attention to institutions

In the discussion on ghettoisation we have seen that another factor was said to be important, namely the disappearance or deterioration of institutions in such areas. Curiously, neighbourhood effect studies have done little with the question of the relevance of institutions. It is clear, however, that if spatial profit includes the way in which habitus productively matches habitat and exclusionary mechanisms enable those in suburban, gentrified and other wealthy neighbourhoods to hoard opportunities by keeping others out, the question of the role of institutions as vehicles for resource access, both in terms of their function as meeting points (Blokland & Nast, 2014) and as distributors of services that may differ in quality in different neighbourhoods, is a central one to the understanding of intra-urban inequalities and especially of how they are reproduced. This perspective is only slowly developing (e.g. Small et al., 2010).

Summary and conclusion

This chapter started with a discussion of intra-urban inequality as a set of differential access to resources that can be studied along a vertical axis of stratification and a horizontal one of differentiation. We have seen that while useful as a way to organise the study of the complex world of urban inequalities, the idea that vertical classes or status groups produce inequalities whereas horizontal categories merely produce difference is questionable, and we have used Anthias' summary of the search for an alternative frame of interpretations by sociologists to introduce the idea of the intersectionality of the various categorical inequalities organised along lines of class, race/ethnicity, gender and sexuality. We then discussed those processes that spatially organise inequalities in the city that start primarily from a structural perspective of the economic positions of agents. We did so from the perspective of spatial profit as developed by Pierre Bourdieu. Where habitus and habitat match, Bourdieu argued, sites reproduce and reify the social space, a set of fields of relations between positions based on economic, cultural and social capital. Spatial profit may then consist of profits of position, profits of localisation and profits of occupation.

Segregation, the process whereby people of various categories live distributed unequally over the city, can be understood socially (e.g. in terms of the segregation of economic groups) or racially and ethnically (where people of specific racial or ethnic groups live separated from each other). The intersectionality became obvious there: whereas in postmodern urban theory ethnicity may be one of the identity markers that can find or can be hindered from finding representation in the production of space, that poverty and ethnic minority status or race correlate means that separating class from race/ethnicity becomes difficult. This is not to say that lower class positions are always those of ethnic minority groups and hence that ethnicity can, as in the reductionist model, be reduced to class. On the contrary, to be white and poor and living on a British council estate in a deindustrialised city is a position that cannot simply be hierarchically ranked in comparison to being a small Turkish grocer in a lively but poor Berlin quarter. At the other end of the spectrum, middle-class Turkish families still face exclusionary practices even when they have assimilated strongly into German ways of life and moved to areas where they no longer live in segregation (Barwick, 2013). Our discussion of segregation also included the question of the pros and cons of ethnic segregation in European cities where we have seen that from a perspective of the ethnic enclave of ethnic-specific economic activity as well as from a perspective of intra-ethnic solidarity the jury is out as to whether such ethnic segregation is necessarily harmful for people's access to resources. Whilst here, too, as in the discussion of ghettoisation and of neighbourhood effects later in the chapter, the question of the quality of institutions and the possibility of guaranteeing equality in institutions across areas in the city is a central one, in each of the sub-themes of the field of urban studies such more organisational-sociological questions have not been asked extensively.

We see here two mechanisms of spatial profit at work. Those who live in segregated areas of the dominant ethnic or racial group and the middle and upper classes derive profit of position from the symbolic capital that comes with where they live: their residential location supports and symbolises their social weight as well as their moral status as coming from 'good' parts of the city. In contrast, those living in badly reputed areas of segregated minorities and the poor cannot derive profits of position, but instead have to fight the stigma attached to their place of residence. The second mechanism is the creation of profits of localisation, where the presence of others brings benefits, as in the case of the ethnic entrepreneurs in segregated neighbourhoods and the formation of other forms of ethnically based social capital.

We have discussed suburbanisation as the process through which, helped by technological and economic development, middle classes – or at least initially only middle classes – have moved to the outskirts of cities, creating metropolitan areas with severe inequalities between the parts. We have seen that after being initially just a residential development, economic activities and consumption and leisure are undergoing suburbanisation. The second process that we have discussed as a process of how middle classes construct the city spatially is gentrification; the process whereby previously lower-class areas transform due to an influx of middle-class residents, an upgrading of the area that displaces previous residents. We have seen that the literature offers various explanations for gentrification and that scholars have discussed its consequences in a number of ways. What suburbanisation and gentrification have in common is the creation of relatively homogeneous middle-class enclaves – of which gated communities are the most extreme form. Recalling that Bourdieu identified not only the – obviously present – mechanism of profits of position but also that of profits of occupation, various examples show how this works. Suburban communities may ensure zoning regulations do not allow for the construction of low-income housing. Or gentrifiers may work to historically preserve a park in their area, including the instalment of old park benches but with an armrest in the middle to make sleeping on the bench impossible. Residents moving into gated communities may exclude themselves from public services, thereby effectively creating profits of localisation and occupation by screening anyone who moves in and hence can share such services. Spatial profits created in these parts of the city of course show us how marginalisation is disinvestment and loss of capital by absence of spatial profit in high-poverty neighbourhoods or ghettos.

Neighbourhood effects, then, or the consequences for maintaining and improving one's social position by the structure of physical space and the way in which spatial distance affirms social distance, are generally studied on the 'negative' side of things – for example, deprived neighbourhoods are studied for their effects, and theories, as discussed above, are developed to explain why location affirms social position and reproduces it. We have touched upon the relevance of culture throughout this chapter, finding that a simple split between structural and cultural approaches makes little sense, and that actually cultural notions and symbolic meanings are used to legitimise current urban hierarchies and stratifications of neighbourhoods. Culture is central to those theories that have primarily occupied themselves with understanding the representation of space (one of the three conceptualisations of space from Lefebvre's triad that we introduced in the beginning of this chapter) and the urban landscape as a landscape of diversity. It is to this, traditionally studied within the horizontal paradigm of difference, that we will turn to in the next chapter.

Questions for discussion

- Urban policy-makers express concern about segregation and argue for more social mix. What risks do you think segregation can pose and do you think desegregation will overcome these possible problems?
- Gentrification includes the displacement of working-class residents from areas undergoing upgrading. What forms of displacement have you learnt about in this chapter and how do you think could urban policy mediate these?
- How do gentrification and suburbanisation affect the spikiness of cities and how do they contribute to sharper inequalities beyond the mere morphology of cities?
- Suburbanisation has effects in the social, political and ecological sense. What effects can you think of, and to what extent can suburbanisation also be evaluated positively?
- The processes of segregation, gentrification, suburbanisation and ghettoisation have been discussed here within the horizontal paradigm that pays limited attention to culture. Which cultural factors do you think are overlooked by this paradigm?

Further reading

Segregation

Most of the common textbooks that are organised thematically have sections on subur-banisation, segregation and gentrification. These processes have been particularly strongly developed with case study illustrations and linkage to urban policy development in US textbooks such as Gottdiener and Hutchison (2011). The most widely quoted study on segregation is Massey and Denton's *American Apartheid* (1993). van der Laan Bouma-Doff (2010), in her collection of papers published on segregation, includes a quite extensive overview of the relevant theoretical approaches in Europe and the US and is particularly good for reading more on ethnic segregation in Europe.

Suburbanisation

Kenneth Jackson's *Crabgrass Frontier* (1985) offers a historical account of suburbanisation in America. In Kazepov's *Cities of Europe* (2005) suburbanisation is a sub-theme of various chapters. Mark Clapson and Ray Hutchison have recently edited a volume in the 'Research in Urban Sociology' series that treats suburbanisation in a global context, including schol-ars and cases from Global North and Global South (Clapson & Hutchison, 2010).

Gentrification

The available literature on gentrification is massive. Most starting students learn first about the difference between the production and consumption explanations of gentrification, starting with essays by Neil Smith (1979, 1982) and David Ley (1983, 1986, 2003), respectively. A good introduction to the various themes that matter to the academic discussion on gentrification is Lees, Slater and Wyly's (2010) collection of excerpts of important authors in the debate. They also wrote a good introduction to the whole theme (Lees, Slater, & Wyly, 2008).

Ghettoisation

From our discussion it has become clear that Loïc Wacquant is the most important scholar on marginalisation (1993, 1995, 1996, 2009, 2010a). Other excellent relational perspec-tives on marginalisation are offered by Philippe Bourgois' *In Search of Respect* (1995), and MacLeod's *Ain't No Making It* (1987). The latter is a little older but an excellent example of the way in which a very implicit intersectional understanding of race and class can inform an empirical research project.

Notwithstanding the criticism on the culture of poverty thesis, Oscar Lewis' original thick descriptions like *La Vida* (1968) and *The Children of Sánchez* (1961) are still very good reads today. Working from a cultural perspective whilst attempting to not make a fully cultural argument is Hannerz's *Soulside* (1969). The choice of ethnographic studies discussing poor people's life and culture is extensive, including classics like Whyte's *Street Corner Society* (1981) and Gans' *The Urban Villagers* (1962). Many overview studies trace the origins of the cultural approaches of poverty; Small and Newman (2001) overview may be a good point to start. Katz traces both the development of the underclass debate (in *The 'Underclass' Debate* (1993)) as well as the stigmatisation of the poor over time (in *The Undeserving Poor* (1990)). How exactly negative labelling and stigmatising of the poor occurs is discussed in a very accessible little book by Herbert Gans, *The War against the Poor* (1995).

6

Spatial expressions of differentiation

Learning objectives

- To understand the city as a place of diversity from the perspective of the horizontal paradigm
- To learn about urban spaces as gendered and sexualised spaces and gain insight into the major theoretical perspectives on gender, sexuality and the city
- To get to know the various ways in which urban scholars have defined and used the concept of public space
- To develop insight into the relevance of race and ethnicity and of age and generations as relevant dimensions of the city of diversity
- To learn about the ways in which lifestyles and subcultures have become important within a culturalist perspective on the city
- To see the shortcomings of the horizontal paradigm and the relevance of intersectionality to understand intra-urban inequalities

Introduction

In Chapter 5 we discussed the vertical paradigm that is usually applied to understand inequalities. In this chapter we turn to the horizontal paradigm where attention is drawn to understanding differences. Differentiation – the term sociologists used initially to refer to a more functional division of labour, resulting in an organic solidarity (Durkheim, 1984) of dependency of all on all others because, when all our jobs consist of only parts of the tasks that need to be done, we cannot do without others – has been stretched to refer to difference in the social and cultural sense. The city, the American public intellectual Lewis Mumford (2011: 93) wrote, is characterised by its social division of labour, which serves 'not merely economic life but the cultural processes'. Differentiation refers to the ways in which groups form and draw boundaries on the basis of race, ethnicity, gender or sexuality, and it is often studied in terms of lifestyle and identity. This is in line with the individualisation thesis that minimal institutions, in the sense of patterns of activity reproduced over time and space (Giddens, 1986: 12), provide individual freedom to determine our own conduct in practice (Elias, 1991).

Indeed, individualisation of thought and conduct has typically been linked to the industrial and postindustrial society as one of the crucial processes of modernity (Kumar, 1978: 55). And the city seen socially provides a special framework for such differentiation with the aid of signs and symbols: 'the personalities of the citizens themselves become many-faceted: they reflect their specialized interests, their more intensively trained aptitudes, their finer discriminations and selections: the personality no longer presents a more or less unbroken traditional face to reality as a whole' (Mumford, 2011: 93). Obviously, individualisation includes the possibility of forming social identifications on the basis of choice rather than tradition: plurality of lifestyles, especially visible in the density of cities, and systems of meanings supply few compulsory frameworks for identifications; and yet such identifications do not become mental events of the individual either. Social differences are constructed in tandem with subjectivities and identities, and the city becomes 'pivotal as a location' (Eade & Mele, 2002b: 11) where this takes place and through which, at the same time, the city is made: 'partially through representation and discourse and as a site of interlocking and conflicting meanings of cultural, political and economic relations' (ibid.). Instead, social identities in a differentiated world are relationally produced, in interaction with others, and group boundaries are actively drawn in the process (Jenkins, 1996). For cities and neighbourhoods, this means that the symbolic use we make of urban places (or, to put it in more fashionable language, our engagement in place-making) makes such sites important for doing community, but urban places do not determine either meaning or form of community. We will discuss the spatial expression of differentiation in relation to neighbourhood and community later in this chapter.

The horizontal paradigm

Such processes of identification and boundary work are usually discussed within the horizontal paradigm of social structural analyses. We have pointed in Chapter 5 to the fact that the analytical separation of horizontal and vertical differentiations has limited value as the intersection of race/ethnicity, class, gender and sexuality makes it difficult to separate them. Here we explicitly discuss gender and queer studies with an urban focus and ethnicity and race, as well as the currently increasingly important division of generations, expressed in the actions of urban youth. As we will see in this chapter, the approach to difference comes with a nod to the structural mechanisms of exclusion to resources and resulting inequalities, but generally tends to be informed by a rather flat understanding of the urban. Some scholars who have worked within the horizontal paradigm have done so from a perspective that asks how diverse identities can be granted recognition (Fincher & Iveson, 2011: 129) in the multicultural city (Amin, 2002), especially within urban planning. In this discussion, scholars have engaged with questions of what recognition can mean, how essentialising difference can be avoided, what inclusive planning based on recognition may entail and what risks come with it (for an overview, see Fincher & Iveson, 2011; see also Benhabib, 2002; Calhoun, 1994; Fincher & Jacobs, 1998; Young, 1990, 2000). 'Diversity represents the new guiding principle for city planners', wrote Fainstein (2010: 115), following the plea for stimulating physical and social heterogeneity since the 1960s, inspired by Jane Jacobs. Diversity, it is believed, and as Fainstein shows in her overview, stimulates creativity and encourages tolerance, an argument effectively communicated to city planners by Richard Florida's (2005b) work on the creative class. Fainstein points out that the connection between diversity and tolerance is not clear though: it can also give rise to conflicts over identities (see also Fincher & Iveson, 2011: 133). Moreover, it may lose sight of the structural factors of inequalities and ignore social exclusions (Fincher & Iveson, 2011: 123–4) so that 'developing an appropriate physical setting for a heterogeneous urbanity ... can only go so far in the generation of a just city' (Fincher & Iveson, 2011: 126). Diversity is a coexistence of differences, differences that challenge the idea of a mass society, but meanwhile suggests a coexistence in which power and resource access seems to play a very limited role indeed and, where they do, primarily a role in claims on public space; for this reason, this chapter includes a section on the various ways public space has been written about in urban studies.

Exceptions here are those scholars who, though not necessarily within urban studies, have attempted to link horizontal differences and vertical stratifications through the notion of intersectionality introduced in Chapter 5. We hope to show that whilst we find this conceptual turn fruitful, it runs the risk of not bringing us much further than registering intersectionality and narratives of identity through qualitative case studies of subcultural groups and how they make sense of the urban around them, without linking this explicitly to their livelihood and life chances so that a flat image of a city of subcultures claiming space and doing identity emerges, an image from which the question how symbolic boundary work arrives at durable social boundaries (Tilly, 1998) has disappeared. In the final part of the chapter, we argue that what in gender and race/ethnic studies has often been described as the 'matrix of oppression' can, especially when we include recent urban theory from the Global South perspective, be combined in a fruitful way with thinking of sites and resources as a 'matrix of resources', bringing the dimensions of power and politics together with the sociological and cultural geography perspectives discussed here, and making the first step in the direction of the final chapter.

The cultural turn

The cultural turn can be summarised as 'theory and research based on the overall notion that the key to understanding contemporary society and transforming it lies in the ways that culture orients our behaviour and shapes what we are able to know about the world' (Storper, 2001: 161). This is a relativistic position, as it implies that knowledge and practices are always culturally determined, and hence disavows metanarratives. In its radical forms, culturalist perspectives celebrate difference for its own good, and are therefore fundamentally depoliticising, as Storper (2001) argued: there are various narratives and they are all equal, so much of the research done under this flag simply documents difference.

The challenge from culturalist perspectives came relatively late to urban studies (Eade & Mele, 2002a: 5) under the influence of feminist and postcolonial perspectives that theorised difference, and scholars began to read the city 'not in terms of explanatory processes but in terms of surface effects' (Eade & Mele, 2002a: 5) , turning the city into a 'text' (King, 1996: 4). They saw the city as 'a semiotic space shaped by struggles over meaning and signification' (Fincher, Jacobs, & Anderson, 2002: 27) out of an uneasiness with 'totalizing' theory (Beauregard & Body-Gendrot, 1999: 3). They have come to believe that seeing the city as representation is the only way of knowing the city's reality. The city, in other words, itself *is* a representation (Shields, 1996: 227), an approach that goes back to the postmodern thought of Derrida's theory of deconstruction. Discourses about the city are thought to produce the city (Eade & Mele, 2002a: 6), which hence cannot be seen as a thing in itself (Lees, 2002: 101), and authors have more and more concentrated on the subjective experience of the city (Donald, 1999). Discourse analysis, or the study of how language is used within discursive events (why is a particular vocabulary strategy applied, how should it be interpreted, what is accomplished by the strategy, how is it situated in context?), has become the dominant method of scholars adhering to this view. The idea that representations are visual has also resulted in a growth of visual methods in urban studies (see Shields, 1996: 235).

The cultural turn and postmodernism

There is a direct connection here between the cultural turn and postmodernism, including its poststructuralist strand. Short (2006: 42–3) points out that 'post' suggests something has changed from modernism. He rightly points out that postmodernism is directly related to the postindustrial city; this is the understanding of postmodernism of the LA school that we discussed in Chapter 3. Postmodern culture, Short (2006: 47) summarises, contrasts with modernism:

> The dominant rendering of culture in the modernist tradition emerges from the importance of class-determined modes of life in the class-dominated cities, or from the decline of community in the rural to urban reorientation, or from the gaze of the *flâneur* as the archetypical modern urban commentator. In the postmodern rendering, the emphasis on urban culture highlights the varieties of experience above, beyond and below these three traditional discourses.

This attitude towards the city fits with an overall belief that we experience the world through processes and practices by which we represent the world: meanings are not given, but made, shared and negotiated through language and discourse (Hastings, 1999: 7). Savage, Warde, and Ward (2003: 73) summarise the key elements of postmodern urban studies:

> a new radical skepticism about the role of scientific knowledge; a new concern with aesthetics rather than morality; enhanced reflexivity on the part of individuals about their identity and the grounds for their conduct; a magnified importance for mass media in the framing of everyday life; an intensification of consumerism, the demise of socialist politics and its replacement by the local and personal politics of new social movements.

This has consequences for understanding cultural differentiation, as meanings, then, do not depend on class, but gender, sexuality, ethnicity and race are now seen to reflect and shape urban culture (Short, 2006: 47). This approach was taken up by cultural geographers, who put meaning and interpretation centre-stage and started to seek answers to the question how spatial phenomena were represented in literature such as novels and poems, often referred to as the study of the iconography of the city.

Power may not be as explicit a focus as, for example, in the study of the city along the lines of the political economy that we discussed in earlier chapters, but plays a role more implicitly as how city spaces act symbolically is seen as including or excluding, and the organisation of space is seen as contributing to identities and behaviour. Primarily, though, the city becomes a space of performance, theatre and spectacle (not of inequalities, a criticism we will return to later). This shows the heritage of poststructuralism. Poststructuralists maintain that language produces concepts and categories to make sense of the world, and is not a transparent medium that merely transmits, a point of view inspired by Foucault, who argued that discourses produce social knowledge and practice through a connection with power, and that language reflects power.

Lefebvre, de Certeau and the production of space

This attention to representation is, as Short (2006: 50–3) points out, leading to renewed attention to the work of Henri Lefebvre (1995), a French philosopher who is generally associated with new Marxism. His theory of space included three elements: space as perceived (representation of space), as conceived (representational space) and as lived (as phenomenological representations). The latter resonates with Michel de Certeau's understanding of the urban practice of everyday life, which he contrasts with the elevated view of the urban planner, who sees the city from above, metaphorically caught by seeing New York from the top of the former World Trade Center:

> To be lifted to the summit of the World Trade Center is to be lifted out of the city's grasp. One's body is no longer clasped by the streets that turn and return it according to an anonymous law; nor it is possessed, whether as player or played, by the rumble of so many differences and by the nervousness of New York traffic. When one goes up there, he leaves behind the mass that carries off and mixes up in itself any identity of authors or spectators. (de Certeau, 2010: 111)

The ordinary practices of life on the street do not allow for the totalising rationality of the urban planner. Instead, these 'microbe-like, singular and plural practices which an urbanistic system was supposed to administer or surpress' (de Certeau, 2010: 113) are spatial practices that create a discreteness, a discreteness that according to de Certeau (2010: 116) can best be understood through the rhetoric of walking:

> To walk is to lack a place. It is the indefinite process of being absent and in search of a proper. The moving about that the city multiplies and concentrates makes the city itself an immense social experience of lacking

a place – an experience that is, to be sure, broken up into countless tiny deportations (displacements and walks), compensated for by the relationships and intersections of these exoduses that intertwine and create an urban fabric, and placed under the sign of what ought to be, ultimately the place but it is only a name, the City. (de Certeau, 2010: 117)

A similar approach can be found in Walter Benjamin's work. As Savage (1995: 207) has pointed out, Benjamin's interest in the *flâneur* was not an interest in the social type as such. To him, the *flâneur* was a theoretical, critical counter to the idea of a mass; 'the *flâneur* can reveal things through aimless wandering hidden to those intent on purposive linear goals' (Savage, 1995: 207). Benjamin hence stressed, similar to the third art of production of space of Lefebvre and to de Certeau's practices of everyday life, the urban fabric as it is perceived.

A fourth author in whose work a somewhat similar approach can be found and who has also (next to, obviously, Simmel's work on the metropolis and the mental life) has regained popularity since the cultural turn is Lewis Mumford. Borer discusses his approach in his discussion of the cultural turn as a scholar who saw the city as a stage to enact and re-enact cultural drama, listing six ways in which this could be done: images and representations; communities and civic cultures; place-based myths, narratives and collective memories; sentiments and meanings of and for places; urban identities and lifestyles; and social interactions and practices. Advocates of the culturalist perspective do not see culture as the by-product of political economy (Borer, 2006) and stress the importance of the relationship between culture and places, where cities are seen as places where identities are built, community is constructed and local sentiments develop. Later in this chapter we will especially return to lifestyles, communities and social interactions; as these all find their expressions in public space, we also discuss the concept of public space below. The awareness that people use places as part of their cultural repertoires and that these can affect a city's social and physical environment has brought Gieryn (2000, 2002), among others, to argue for a spatial turn in sociology: places, he argued, are not just contexts in which other things take place, a topic on which German scholars, especially such as Martina Löw, have developed spatial sociology (Löw, 2009). Instead, the ways in which people make sense of the world are tied to the places (understood as unique geographical locations of a material form invested with meanings and values) where they practice culture. The cultural turn in urban geography and the spatial turn in urban sociology have thus created a bridge between geography and sociology that is unique to the development of both disciplines and one of the reasons why many have moved to speak of urban studies. Community studies have been at the forefront of taking this bridge further.

The city as a realm of community and lifestyles

As discussed in Chapter 2, the Chicago School sociologists thought of the city as a mosaic of social worlds, sorted into specific neighbourhoods in the city, each with its own cultural traits. To Wirth, urbanism was a way of life, influenced by density, heterogeneity and size, a way of life that stood in contrast to life in the village and that tended to anonymity and pathology, as the city did not provide the community with a set of norms and a basis for belonging in the way the rural village and small town could do. Criticism came from scholars such as Herbert Gans (1967) who, in contrast, argued that the city itself did not determine a way of life, and that village-like communities could be found in the city just as urban lifestyles could be found beyond the city borders. This then resulted in a debate on community (see Wellman & Leighton 1979), where the main concern was to sort out what had happened to 'community'. Was it lost in the sense that cities could no longer provide a sense of community and brought alienation to their residents? Or was community saved so that it could still be found in neighbourhoods, especially immigrant neighbourhoods, where they continued to exist as urban villages, as in Gans' (1962) famous study with the same title? Or had community been liberated, i.e. had the city freed people from the pressure of small town social control, so that community could now more voluntarily be created by people, and no longer have to be bound to a specific geographical location?

Most importantly in this debate, the field of urban studies, especially urban sociology, has moved away gradually from the assumption that neighbourhood equals community (and in urban policy terms that if it does not, something is wrong that needs to be repaired).

Community and neighbourhood

This meant a departure from a tradition of community studies that began with work such as Willmott and Young's study of East London (Young & Willmott, 1979; also Willmott & Young, 1967) and Elizabeth Bott's (1957) study of family and kinship ties in the city. Bell and Newby (1974) provided an extensive overview of community studies, differentiating between those using an ecological approach and those approaching the topic from a social networks perspective, the stream of community studies that over time has proven to be the most fruitful, as it does not assume a straightforward link between place and community (for a full discussion of the question of place and community, see Blokland, 2003a).

Within the context of globalisation, the local has been seen as either 'the cultural space of embedded communities' or 'an inexorable space of collective resistance to disruptive processes of globalization' (Smith, 2002: 109), which has brought Smith (2002: 110) to argue for a more dynamic conception of locality that enables their transnational relations to be included. The network theorist Barry Wellman argued that one should study people's personal networks to find out what constituted their community rather than simply take where they lived (or rather, slept at night) as the point of departure (Wellman & Leighton, 1979). He maintained that the neighbourhood may but does not have to be significant: urbanites are involved in a variety of ties, and these are organised in a variety of networks, so that we must think about community and neighbourhood. Blokland (2003a) has argued, however, that the role of neighbourhood for people's sense of community, their identifications and categorisations of themselves and others through the lens of the imagined community and the role of the place of residence in these, still needs to be theorised. Recent work on elective belonging (Savage et al., 2005) and selective belonging (Watt, 2009) asks how people make use of their locality to enhance, symbolise and distinguish themselves with regard to their social position.

It is clear that in urban planning and urban policy the quest for community in the neighbourhood continues to be of importance. This is motivated by a belief that liveable neighbourhoods cannot be anonymous, and that therefore planning should be done in such a way that everyday interaction is possible, that people can form coalitions when they want to, and that if neighbourhoods are not communities they should at least be able to develop some degree of collective efficacy (Sampson & Raudenbush, 2004). Mobility and sprawl are thought to prevent people from developing community ties and getting involved: getting involved in community affairs is more inviting – or abstention less attractive – when the scale of everyday life is smaller and more intimate (Putnam, 2000: 205). Putnam's plea for neighbourhoods rich in social capital, to be achieved through neighbours' interactions, resonates the thesis of Jane Jacobs (1961) that modernist, functional city planning destroys the neighbourhood community, whereas such community is a precondition for neighbourhood safety.

Coming from Greenwich Village in New York, which she feared would be subjected to modernist urban planning interventions, Jane Jacobs was concerned with defining a viable city; as an architect and social activist, she reflected on the role of urban design for liveable cities. In her famous book *The Death and Life of Great American Cities*, originally published in 1961, she advocated a form of urban policy and planning that would take social interactions and the city as it is lived on the street more seriously. She was especially interested in showing how specific forms of urban design, including a functional mixture of residential and other uses, short blocks and abundant squares and parks, would provide the space to socialise children, exercise informal social control and build social ties among neighbourhood residents. Her study was not based on extensive empirical research. The easy criticism of Jacobs' work was that it leaves steps in the causal chain she sees unexplained: while, for example, people having their eyes on the street may mean that they develop public familiarity (e.g. are able to recognise others as familiar faces without knowing their names), it remains to be seen how eyes on the street lead to social control (see Blokland, 2009). The media report regularly, for example, how bystanders of assaults in public spaces fail to intervene. What Jacobs has done, however, is point to the relevance of spatial arrangements, including built environment, the mixture of functions, and the design of streets, squares and other public spaces for the social interactions of people in the city. Lofland (1989, 1998), too, has shown how the urban is neither anonymous nor village-like, but includes public, parochial and private spheres at various sites and times, and argues that the study of urban life needs to include the study of the various forms of everyday interaction. Through such interactions urban areas become meaningful, culturally and socially. Amin and Thrift (2002) have pointed to the significance of the 'banality of everyday life in the city'. This goes back to the work of Henri Lefebvre that we noted before: space is produced in various ways, and the everyday practices produce space on one of Lefebvre's three levels.

Neighbourhoods as socially and culturally produced sites of symbols thus seem to have drawn increasing attention from urban scholars now that the question whether neighbourhoods are the sites for interactional communities is no longer of great interest. Because place continues to matter and does so through the production of symbolic capital, the question of the consequences of the reputation of place becomes all the more salient for understanding urban inequalities. Take, for example, the problem of neighbourhood reputation and school quality. In many countries in Europe, this is an increasingly important topic. With multiculturalism becoming the situational norm, parents with non-immigrant backgrounds (but not only them – see Zhou, 1997) are increasingly worried about the 'quality' of education of their children; this worry is linked to an anxiety about the reproduction of social class and social mobility in times in which formal educational credentials have increased tremendously to ensure a relatively secure life – in contrast to the high days of industrialisation when a 13-year-old leaving school was not seen as a drop-out, but would go on to learn skills in carpentry, welding or other industrial semi-skilled trades on the job. Such anxiety makes finding the 'right' education a bigger theme than ever, and interestingly, even in countries where public schools dominate the educational landscape and private schools are still the exception or (as in the Netherlands) virtually non-existent, and where schools are equally funded over an urban area, parents have strong views on 'good' and 'bad' schools, views often based, if anything, on school performance in reading and mathematics as measured at the end of elementary school. However, such measures do not reflect the gain in education of the children and say much about the school population, but little about the quality of education as such. Schools scoring badly tend to be located in deprived inner-city immigrant neighbourhoods, so that in turn stereotypical generalisations are easily made that schools with many immigrants are 'bad', that segregated areas have segregated schools, and that these schools need to be avoided at all costs. Whereas the location of a school in a deprived area says nothing about its quality, the decision of well-educated parents to avoid such areas homogenises the school population. And as well-educated parents have more social and cultural capital to ensure school quality by making demands on the school and by providing the school with additional resources, schools in deprived areas may well end up being worse than those in neighbourhoods with better reputations. As Fincher and Iveson (2008: 132) have argued, such reputations of places may mark people as different because of their association with a particular place, and stereotypes may affect them negatively (see also Body-Gendrot, 2000)

Lifestyles

As neighbourhood reputation is symbolic – albeit with real consequences once defined as real, as the example above suggests – lifestyles become crucial, and neighbourhoods can be seen as lifestyle enclaves or milieux. Some, like Paquot (1999: 87), have argued that lifestyles have been urbanised, for which television, 'with its daily production of stereotypes, ready-made phrases, and attitudes', especially in commercials, is responsible. Others, like Stout (2011: 150–3), have pointed to the technological changes that (as was the case with photography) have enhanced the role of visual representations in the symbolic production of cities and neighbourhoods.

Indeed, as we have seen in our discussion of the postmodern city in Chapter 2, consumer culture and the aestheticisation of everyday life in the city have become crucial. From the idea that in the city a lifestyle no longer is a relatively fixed habitus but consists of practices and tastes that are 'more actively formed' (Featherstone, 1991: 95), it follows that they are no longer linked to vertical inequalities, but expressions of diversity. And whereas such symbolic meanings may have real consequences, such consequences are not necessarily the focus of urban studies within the cultural perspective.

In a somewhat different direction, the debate has developed around the question not so much what community may mean in contemporary society and whether it ought to be celebrated or lamented in contrast to (an often undefined and rather crudely used) 'past' of traditional times. As Elias (1974) has pointed out, lamenting or celebrating the loss of the traditional makes little sense. Thinking in tradition versus modernity grossly ignores the question when exactly tradition stopped and something else ('the modern') started and is based on a view of history as having breaking points rather than as a continuum of gradual change. This view of history seems to inform dichotomous understandings of community. Acknowledging this, scholars have more and more tried to ask what urbanism may mean if one is to be non-deterministic about it and believes, theoretically as well as empirically, that the question what are the essentials of urbanism as a way of life is perhaps not the right one to ask. Claude Fisher can be said to be the most important theorist here, and his subcultural thesis is our main concern in the next section.

Both of these discussions have in common that instead of asking questions about the economic patterns and processes that produce the city form, their focus is on the city as a cultural construct, socially constructed through people's actual lifestyles and the way in which their daily practices produce the urban space. This harks back to the early discussion of Wirth and Simmel, who tried to pin down what it was about the city that produced a way of life that was distinctively urban. As we will see in the next section, urban sociology has since moved beyond this question, but is still interested in how heterogeneous, dense settlements may matter, as enabling rather than determining, for ways of life.

The subcultural thesis

As mentioned above, the subcultural thesis has heavily informed the theorising on the culture of cities. Subcultural theory has developed most strongly in the strand of the sociology of youth and of deviance (see Brake, 2002; see also Clarke, 1974; Gordon, 1947) and became particularly popular from the 1960s onwards, becoming part of common parlance so that now '"subculture" with its mysterious underground associations is … a term in use by many people who have never studied its legacy in depth in the seminar room' (Huq, 2004: 3). Culture, as Peterson (1979) has laid out in detail, can be seen as including norms, values, beliefs and expressive symbols. The assertion of subcultural theory, then, is that groups that regularly deviate from societal norms are subcultural conformists (Peterson, 1979: 147), and often develop around expressive symbols, forming lifestyle groups or, in Weber's terminology, status cultures. Peterson notes that in the industrial society status cultures fitted neatly with class cultures, but that increased overall wealth and the expansion of consumer-oriented industries have created a wider range of tastes that are more independent of class: people choose from a wide range of definitions of situations or fabricate new ones themselves to fit their needs and desires (Peterson, 1979: 160).

The origin of the term 'subculture' can be traced back to Trasher, a member of the Chicago School in the 1920s, who used the term in his study of Chicago delinquent gangs (Trasher, 1927). Since then, subculture has often been used as a membership category or network rather than as a system of beliefs and practices or group normative system (Yinger, 1960: 626); while membership can apply to a substructure (say, 'youth') and hence can be purely structurally defined, this is not the same as being able to assume that such members of a category also adopt one set of values (not all youth share one youth culture, after all). In such usage, 'subculture' does not refer to a clearly defined population that shares cultural knowledge, a problem with this use of the term pointed out by Fine and Kleinman (1979: 9).

Of the subcultures that developed, youth cultures have been the most extensively studied. The connection to inequality and resources lies in the idea that various subcultures include stocks of cultural capital, cultural capital that can be transferred into economic capital and power – even though, as Peterson (1979: 150) points out, it is unclear how this transfer happens. As to the development of subcultures, Yinger (1960: 627) proposes to reserve 'subculture' for the values and norms developed in in-groups as status groups which do not necessarily actively oppose mainstream values. He speaks of counter-cultures where in-groups contain norms that arise specifically from frustrating situations or conflicts and which values are counter-values opposing the mainstream.

Subcultural theory has become important to urban studies in two ways. First, it has been used in attempts to theorise the relationship between urbanism and what living in the city means to the social psychology of the individual, an approach of which Claude Fischer became the most prominent scholar and which goes back to questions asked by classic scholars such as Simmel and Wirth at the beginning of the development of the discipline. Second, subcultural theory informs various perspectives on identity and the city and the ways in which urban space can serve the production of expressive symbols that subcultures engage in.

Fischer compares the two standard approaches to the social-psychological consequences of urbanism, summarised as the deterministic theory and the compositional theory (Fischer, 2013: 44). The first is most commonly associated with Louis Wirth whom we met in the second chapter, and draws heavily on Georg Simmel's idea that the metropolitan environment overstimulates the senses so that a blasé attitude must be adapted to deal with this stress. Wirth took this further by arguing that the city caused relationships to be impersonal, people to be estranged from each other and the social structure to be disorganised. Herbert Gans (1991) can be seen as one of the main critics of this approach. In his view, people continue to live in primary groups with strong ties, but what they look like depends on class, race and ethnicity and stage in the life cycle, so that the social fabric of the city is the result of the composition of its residents and their characteristics. Fischer (1975) attempted to bring elements of both approaches together. He maintained that, in contrast to the compositional theorists, urbanism did have an independent effect on social life that could not be explained by other characteristics of the urbanites. Intimate social groups do persist, and size and density, two central characteristics of the city in Wirth's theory, do not produce anomie and estrangement but instead foster social groups and strengthen them.

Subcultures, or a mosaic of social worlds, become possible in the city, for two reasons. First, large communities attract migrants with various cultural backgrounds and create a critical mass of diversity. Second, a large city generates structural differentiation that gives rise to specialised institutions that are linked to subcultures. The critical mass makes subcultures stronger: sufficient numbers allow the founding of a storefront church, the opening of a gay bar or the creation of a self-help group for teenage single mothers. In sum, then:

> like the compositional approach [subcultural theory] argues that urbanism does not produce mental collapse, anomie, or personal estrangement; that urbanites at least as much as ruralites are integrated into viable social worlds. However, like the determinist approach, it also argues that cities *do* have effects on social groups and individuals – that the differences between rural and urban persons have other causes than the economic, ethnic or life-style circumstances of those persons. Urbanism does have *direct* consequences. (Fischer, 2013: 49; emphasis in original)

Criticisms of the subcultural thesis include that it treats subcultures as static and ahistoric entities with clearly demarcated borders. But subcultures may die or evolve into the mainstream (Peterson, 1979: 156). Moreover, as culture always changes, subcultures cannot be thought of as closed, homogeneous social entities isolated from the 'larger' society (Fine & Kleinman, 1979). In addition, it can be argued that the subcultural thesis holds a rather optimistic picture of the city when it comes to the tolerance of cities towards subcultures: it has been pointed out that cities vary widely in this respect and can be repressive towards the presence of gays, Muslims, homeless or poor minorities (Smith, 1997). For Fischer, the city may not automatically sift and sort people into specific areas in the way the ecologists of the Chicago School saw this happening, but the city he presents us with is still a rather conflict-free, emancipating space where each of us can adopt the lifestyle of the subculture of our liking. He pays little attention to the ways in which discrimination, patriarchy and racism make certain lifestyles through the production of space available to some but not to others.

The subcultural thesis does, however, help us to move away from seeing the divided city primarily along the lines of who lives where, with the risk of reifying neighbourhoods as geographical containers, and points to the relevance of social differentiations and segregation patterns that are not primarily residential. The ways in which people use spatial references and occupy spaces in the city to 'make places' that help them form and strengthen identities are not limited to their neighbourhoods, but take place everywhere in the metropolitan region. To understand such place-making practices where positions are used to create locations that in turn strengthen positions of groups in the city again, it is important to realise that identities are not labels that we can simply glue to people based on some characteristics. As we noted briefly in the discussion of ethnicity in relation to ethnic enclaves above, such characteristics are socially produced through boundary work, and like ethnicity, other identities too can best be seen as identifications, as this term reveals the processual and agent-driven character of adopting understandable, coherent positions in our everyday life through comparing ourselves with others with whom we perceive differences and similarities, rather than suggesting something static (Lemert, 1995; de Swaan, 1995; for an overview, see Blokland, 2003a).

This, then, is the focus of a body of literature concerned with place-making, in particular with place-making in public space, as identity and community emerge primarily through social practices, such as 'saying this or that, participating in rituals, mounting political protest, fishing together or whatever. It is in and out of what people do that a shared sense of things and a shared symbolic universe emerge. It is in talking together about community – which is, after all, a public doing – that its symbolic value is produced and reproduced' (Jenkins, 1996: 106). The cultural turn and the subcultural perspective thus both point to the importance of public space, a concept that has been subject to considerable debate in urban studies and beyond. The next section looks at some of the main perspectives.

The representational city: public space

Urban scholars have been increasingly preoccupied with the study of public space for at least two reasons. First, the cultural, often postmodern turn has increased attention to the ways in which diversity is expressed, creates conflicts, is governed and controlled and negotiated in public space. Second, in the neo-liberal city, privatisation in times of austerity is not just the transfer of public service provision to the market and public–private partnerships, but also an increasing privatisation of sites that we used to think of as public spaces: shopping streets are less and less important than privately owned, managed and secured shopping malls and arcades; business district organisations can raise taxes for their businesses in their section and set their own rules of control and surveillance, where public–private partnerships create a private city beyond democratic control (Squires, 2011: 207–12); public parks disappear when condominium developments with private yards are built there instead; and gated communities include the almost full retreat from public space and public services while creating a world of their own behind the gates; and tourism infrastructure squeezes out more every day in attempts to compete for consumers between cities where the diversity of urban areas is turned into 'diversion districts' in which diversity can be safely consumed (Judd, 2011: 266).

Celebration, an actual town built by the Disney Corporation, is of course the ultimate example of this *disneyfication*, a term now widely used by authors who seek to show how downtown areas, shopping streets or ethnic neighbourhoods are turned into theme parks for consumption (Sorkin, 1992; Zukin, 1991; Fainstein & Stokes, 1998; Eeckhout, 2001; Souther, 2007). Crawford (2011: 343) warns about the nostalgia creeping into such arguments:

> the existence and popularity of these commercial public spaces is used to frame a pervasive narrative of loss that contrasts the current debasement of public space with golden ages and golden sites – the Greek agora, the coffeehouses of early modern Paris and London, the Italian piazza, the town square.

Defining public space

Low and Smith (2006a: 3) point to the problem of coming up with a clear definition of public space; as is common in quite a few strands of urban theory, such definitional questions have led to much debate. Others have noted that the demarcation of public and private does not really hold up that well (Watson, 2002: 52); indeed, we suggest below that a continuum may be as good as it gets. For political economists, it was a space of collective consumption in opposition to capital (Watson, 2002: 49). With the cultural turn, urbanists have moved to an understanding of public space as symbolic and imaginary (Watson, 2002: 55). Richard Sennett (1973, 1992a, 1992b, 1994) can certainly be seen as one of the most important urban scholars writing on the public realm and public space, two notions that he, unlike Lofland (1998), does not systematically separate. His definition sounds deceptively simple: a place where strangers meet, so that public differs from private in the amount of knowledge one has about others and vice versa. This definition can be called an *interactionist* as it primarily focuses on what happens in encounters between people, whether strangers or not, in their everyday lives.

This understanding of public space is relevant to theorising the city within the horizontal paradigm in two ways. First, the city streets and squares and public transport routes are the connectors between the nodes of our every-day routines. As Byrne (1978) has argued, these in-between spaces may not be experienced as places but are conducive to our understandings of the social around us: everyday brief encounters matter for how we define our-selves socially and how we identify others. As Crawford (2011: 345) put it, 'everyday space is the connective tissue that binds daily lives together, amor-phous and so persuasive that it is difficult even to perceive'. Second, public spaces such as streets and squares and transport routes are subjected to unwritten rules of interaction, and as Lofland (1998) has shown, the ways in which urbanites obey or do not obey such rules influence the social texture of the city and how we experience it. This is not always an easy matter and may evoke conflicts. 'The everyday spaces of the street, the subway or the square are sites for a micro-politics of urban life in which individuals exer-cise their spatial rights while negotiating the spatial claims of others' (Tonkiss, 2005: 59).

Privacy, in this interactionist approach, is the control over information about ourselves (Bulmer, 1986: 91–2): the extent to which we can determine when, how and what information we give others about ourselves. It is questionable whether this is the most useful conceptualisation, although it is broadly used and fits with lay people's definition of 'making something public' or 'keeping some-thing private'. It is a confusing approach because the term refers to a character-istic of social relationships or interactions, but can easily get mixed up with a spatial definition, which is not correct: 'the friendly greeter on the streets may have very few friends, while the reserved subway rider may have a thriving social life' (Fischer, 1982: 61–2).

Public space along two axes

We may instead want to think of this sharing or withholding of information as a grid with two dimensions (see Blokland, 2003a). On one axis is the continuum of privacy, of control over information about ourselves. At one end of the con-tinuum is anonymity, representing those social interactions which may be brief and superficial or repeated and frequent but are not personal relations in the strict sense in which people act without supplying more than the minimally necessary information about themselves. At the other end of the continuum, intimacy characterises social interactions in personal relations in which large amounts of personal information are shared. This is not the same as a 'good' or positively affective relationship (think of abusive relationships between partners or between parents and children).

Private and public may be reserved as terms to denote the other axis. Public spaces are those accessible to everyone who conforms somewhat to the very generally expected patterns of action. Who is allowed in is not completely open but regulated. This can be done by rules and regulations and their enforcement, by symbolic practices of exclusion or, as in the case of park benches with an armrest in the middle to make lying down and sleeping impossible, by design (Whyte, 2004). It is also defined by how behaviour gets sanctioned, explicitly or subtly, which is closely related to symbolic access. 'Whereas private space is demarcated', Low and Smith (2006b: 4) explain, 'and protected by state-regulated rules of private property use, public space, while far from free of regulation, is generally conceived as open to greater or lesser public participation.' That a man waving a gun is not tolerated in a square does not stop it from being a public space; that a shopping mall that forbids smoking or skateboarding cannot be accessed by those smoking or skateboarding does not either, because what is rejected is not their presence as individuals but the specific acts that they are performing. Of course there is an element of social control in this that can to various degrees make people conform to behavioural norms that further their acts as consumers and nothing else; it can said to be exclusionary to some, as when a homeless person is said to be allowed in a park but not to sleep on the bench, or a drug user to be allowed in an underground station to travel but not to shoot up drugs.

Contestation over space and appropriation of space concern themselves with addressing these dilemmas and their oppressive dimensions, and certainly pose a challenge to urban planning when recognition of diversity is what motivates the planners. Mitchell and Staeheli (2006: 144) go even further and maintain that public space as a space of sociality is limited by 'politics of power' (also Low, 2003; Staeheli & Mitchell, 2004; Hopkins, 1990; Goss, 1993). Our perceptions of space are regulated through codes and signs 'preventing us from entering some spaces through outright warning or more subtle deterrents' (Madanipour, 2011: 191). Such scholars fear the end of public space, inspired by the question of who has the right to the city:

> As cities have redeveloped, public space has become a key battleground – a battleground over the homeless and the poor and over the rights of developers, corporations, and those who seek to make over the city in an image attractive to tourists, middle- and upper-class residents, and suburbanites. (Mitchell & Staeheli, 2006: 144)

Quite a few authors are concerned with the increased surveillance and privatisation of public space, where tactics such as forbidding napping or sitting on walls or street vending support corporate control of public goods through public–private partnerships of various sorts (Low, 2013: 402–3). But to refer to all restrictions on the use (as distinct from the property) of public space as exclusion is also slightly problematic. Goffman (1959) and other symbolic interactionists have, however, convincingly shown that the everyday interactions of social life in public spaces do need some unwritten rules to be possible at all. While the radical scholar may be quick to judge that it is social control, repression or revanchism to evict heroin users from a park, the poor mother with five children whose kids have nowhere to play but the little park can do little with this apparent 'radical' criticism of attempts to regenerate a park. Regeneration is not always about the profit for developers. Sometimes, regeneration is about quality of life of the weak.

The other pole of the continuum of access, then, is private space, where agents are able to exclude others unless they have deliberately decided to let them in. Violations here are possible and do happen, of course, as with razzias and police raids. This space is, however, least governed by rules of conduct generally held in society, making it free but not safe, as domestic violence is typically possible within the privacy of a home.

A small but interesting literature on third places identifies a more or less middle point on this continuum (Oldenburg, 1999): bars, coffee shops and corner stores such as Tally's Corner (Liebow, 1967) where one goes for the 'joys of association' (Oldenburg, 1999: 26). In one of the very first issues of the *American Journal of Sociology*, Moore (1897) argued that the distinctive characteristic of saloons was the freedom to come and be oneself, or pretend to be someone else for that matter, in control over information one provides about oneself, but above all the low cost of exit: leaving the saloon never to return, even though the bar may be the place 'where everybody knows your name', as the American sitcom *Cheers* had it in its lead tune, comes at no loss of reputation, credit or other forms of social capital usually related to investments in social ties. Home territories, as discussed by Lyman and Scott (1967) and Cavan (1963), may be seen as special cases of such third places.

Public, parochial and private realm

Lofland (1998: 9) adds another set of concepts to the public and private space. First, she describes the city as the site where, as soon as one has left one's private space, 'one moves into a world of many unknown or only categorically known others (biographical strangers), many of whom may not share one's values, history, or perspective (cultural strangers)'. Lofland then proceeds to develop three 'realms' within the city that are social, not physical, territories. The *public realm* is the world just described; the *private realm* is 'characterised by ties of intimacy among primary group members who are located within households and personal networks'; the *parochial realm* by a sense of commonality among acquaintances and neighbours in personal networks. Although she says these realms do not match specific places, the prototypes she gives suggest otherwise, so that in the use of her concepts for empirical work, realm and space often do become one. The sharp point of Lofland's framework for analysing urban life is, however, that her conceptual tools enable us to see process rather than fixed state: as Blokland and Soenen (2004) have shown, the ways specific groups of people position themselves and talk with each other on public transport, for example, can be a temporary parochialisation of a public space.

Public space as arena of deliberation

Notwithstanding his simple definition, Sennett was after a rather different understanding of public space and has, like some urban geographers, connected the discussion on public space with that on the public sphere as the arena of public deliberation and participation and the democratic ideal (Harvey, 2006: 17; see also Amin & Thrift, 2002). He aligns himself with Goffman, and says he is interested in the theatre of public life. Whilst maintaining that public space is a place, he argues that what is more important is what happens there when strangers gather. He presents two additional schools of thought on the public realm to what we have called the interactionists. Hannah Arendt is the leading scholar in thinking about public realm in terms of broad politics:

> she imagines an ideal realm in which people can discuss and debate freely and equally; to do so they need to cut loose from their particular, private circumstances in order to discuss and debate … whatever people's origins, gender, style of life, class, they should have an equal voice as citizens. (Sennett, 2010: 261)

The second approach draws on Jürgen Habermas who has a slightly broader approach and defines public space as 'any medium, occasion or event which prompts open communication between strangers' (Sennett, 2010) and stresses the communicative process in which they engage, based on the idea that free communication will make people move beyond their self-interest. Bridge and Watson convincingly present Sennet's work as in line with these more politically oriented understandings of an ideal public space characterised by 'an idea … of the richer types of relationships that are possible among strangers who are different from one another. It is a self-constituting political sphere' (Bridge & Watson, 2010).

Sennett engages with architecture and urban design especially in *The Fall of Public Man* (1992b): he sees the city, due to its physical form, as prompting people to think of it as meaningless – note that this was before the cultural turn! – and the enormousness of modern architecture as creating emptiness or 'dead public space', inhibiting 'any relationship to the milieu in which the

(built) structure is set' (Sennett, 1992b: 12–14). Sennett then traces the development of the psychological (felt) need for intimacy above all and of a desire
for community as warm and personal and embracing as a dismissal of urban
life with strangers as cold and impersonal, thereby destroying the potential of
a community of civility – and here he does get close to Goffman's (1963)
work on civility and Elias's (1987) work on involvement and detachment.

Public space and representation

After the cultural turn, few would still dare to speak of any materiality as devoid
of meaning. Public space is meaningful, represents, and is representation: from
de Certeau's (1984) claims about the way in which the city is made meaningful
and appropriated through walking, to critical assessments by scholars such as
Mitchell and Staeheli (2006), Blackmar (2006), Herbert (2010) and Smith
(2001) of policies of zero tolerance and other active acts of exclusion, power is
expressed and reinforced in and through public space, and public space is always
immersed with meanings, and can therefore become a site of contestation. As
space of representation, monumental buildings, Hausmannian boulevards in
Paris and the like are of course clear examples of how public space is produced
as a system of meaning that conveys power and hierarchy.

As Body-Gendrot and Beauregard (1999: 5) have pointed out, much of urban
theory 'representation' is centred on urban form, rather than on how social life
in cities is representational. In our next section, we turn to the ways in which
public space, political in the broad everyday sense, is a site for the display and
celebration of cultural identities, as well as a site for contestation over such identities and the claims people make on the basis of them. This, then, connects our
discussion on subcultures and diversity of lifestyles and lifestyle communities –
rather than neighbourhood-based ones – to public space understood empirically
in terms of the ways in which it is constituted and in flux due to processes of
parochialisation and privatisation, on the one hand, and of the political ideal of
recognition of difference and openness of deliberation among equal citizens, on
the other.

Cultural diversity: identities in public space

Within the horizontal paradigm, with its focus on diversity, the question must
be asked how such differences are made, transformed, defended or challenged
and what is 'urban' about such processes. This section discusses gender and
sexuality or sexual orientation, race/ethnicity and age, with a particular focus
on youth and their subcultures, as not exclusive but important main boundaries

along which difference is produced, experienced and negotiated. This is not to say that social class in our view does not also carry symbolic and representational meanings and can be analysed through a lens of culture and difference. It can. We still believe, however, that for social class the analysis starts with structural inequalities of which cultural differentiations are not the cause, but the outcome, whereas, as will become clear, for differences of these other identities, inequality results from a hierarchy imposed on such differences for which neither neo-economic nor neo-Marixst explanations suffice. When Tilly (1998) argued that durable inequalities (e.g. the continued difference in pay for men and women with the same jobs, or the systematic underperformance of students of migration background independent of social class) are still in a Pandora's box when it comes to understanding the processes and mechanisms that cause them, in our view it was such inequalities based on difference that he had in mind.

Sexualities

Especially in geography, scholars have developed in recent years, under the continuing influence of 'queer theories' (Knopp, 2009: 21), a focus on the geography of sexualities, starting with the highly influential collection *Mapping Desire* (Bell & Valentine, 1995), where the central theme is the investigation of the relationship between space, place and sexualities: how are sexualities geographical and how are spaces and places sexualised (Browne et al., 2009: 2)? They start from the assumption that just as an individual does not have a pre-given sexual identity, spaces do not either (Oswin, 2008: 90). There are norms and expectations regarding acceptable sexual practices, which may differ in various contexts and may lead to contestation and resistance (as with the 'kissing protests' in Turkish cities), but space is always sexualised in one way or another.

That we may often not realise this is the consequence of what the literature has called 'heteronormativity' which is hegemonic: not questioned, but unremarkable (Hubbard, 2008; this notion has also been criticised for homogenising heterosexuality, see Binnie, 2009). Sexuality as a social relation, these authors maintain, is spatial just like all relations are, as various geographers have argued (Bell & Valentine, 1995; Aldrich, 2004; Adler & Brenner, 1992; Armstrong, 2002). Browne et al. (2009) provide an overview of the major strands of thought compromising the field of geographies of sexualities, and what is most striking is that in terms of its theoretical relevance, the field is small. They rightly pose that sexualities, with all their regulations, norms, institutions and desires, are to be understood through the spaces in which they are constituted and practised (Browne et al., 2009: 4), as is true for all social action – as Gans (2002) put it, we are all bound to the ground by gravity so social action is always taking place somewhere and place is being produced through such actions.

Heterosexualised spaces are dominant, because mainstream society acts on the principle that heterosexuality is the norm and queer the departure from the norm. Gay spaces where gay men appropriated urban space (more so than lesbians – see Casey, 2009: 122–23; Rothenberg, 1995) became for a while the focus of geographies of sexuality, but scholars such as Podmore (2001) criticised such scholarship for understanding urban space as narrowly territorial, as only focusing on gay and no other identities and as stressing visibility too much (Browne et al., 2009: 7). Initial queer geographies then studied how gendered and sexed performances produced space, following Judith Butler's (1990, 1993, 1997) approach to performativity.

Sexualities have been associated with the city ever since the times of ancient Athens (Aldrich, 2004), and Aldrich traces historically how a 'vernacular linkage' between homosexuality and the city can be illustrated in novels and travellers' accounts. Browne and Brown (2009) have also pointed out that from the eighteenth century onwards vital homosexual subcultures existed in major cities; they became the subject of academic attention with the gay liberation movement of the 1970s. Referred to as gay spaces, the sites of concentrations of gay lifestyles stressed the uneven gendering of these spaces. Feminists have claimed that such analyses overlook women's use of the city, advocating more attention for the spatiality of lesbian and bisexual lives. Sociologists and historians have also done so, leading Bech (1997) to go so far as to say that homosexual existence is a phenomenon of the city, not just in the city. In his introductory text on cities and sexualities, Hubbard (2012) lists how the city can reflect and reproduce dominant moral orders; how sexuality, monogamy and 'the family' are reflected in the form of residential landscapes (2012: 63–90); how the binary of public and private of urban space structures ideas about sex and sexuality; how urban consumption and leisure are always sexualised (2012: 129–47), including the city as marketplace for sexual images and materials (2012: 148–76; see also Agustín, 2005; Lasker, 2001; Sanchez, 2004); and how world cities organise the network of sexualised flows (Hubbard, 2012: 176–203). This association is not surprising, given what we have learnt earlier in this chapter about public space and about subcultures.

Public spaces of cities are, first, so important to the study of sexualities and gender in the city because much of the discussion revolves around the question of the liberty to be in public, to construct and live out identities there without threat or fear. Some themes addressed here include Herman's (2009) 'bondage, discipline and sadomasochistic sexual practices' as a practice that can severely harm one's social position and possibly lead to prosecution, the complicated issue of visibility and anonymity for 'drag queens' (Browne, 2009), the panoptical qualities of spaces for commercial sex and sex work (Prior, Boydell, & Hubbard, 2012; Ryder, 2004; Cameron, 2004) and red light districts as 'moral regions' (Ryder, 2004; Ward, 1975; and, very early on, McCabe, 1882; Becker, 1899), and the dangers of street prostitution for women who face punitive policing policies and conservative heterosexual discourses (Sanders, 2004; Hubbard, 2004).

Second, the city provides, according to Karp (1973) and in line with the subcultural thesis above, the anonymity where impression management can be applied to hide from outsiders when one is up to something considered 'deviant' by mainstream society, in his case the visiting of pornographic bookstores. He also notes, however, that this anonymity is not a given: it is produced by interactions, and constitutes a norm that is maintained when persons are collectively 'hiding certain identities from one another' where thus 'each participant is aware of and feels constrained to respect the façade of anonymity that each other participant is producing' (Karp, 1973: 447), as was the case among the visitors of the bookstore that Karp studied. But beyond this anonymity, the city also provides, as in the subcultural thesis, the density that makes it possible to form collective lifestyles with like-minded people. Harry (1974: 246), for example, pointed to the possibility of interpersonal ties in the big city that the small town could not provide; Simon and Gagnon (1967) and Achilles (1967) are examples of scholars who have studied specific gay institutions, bars in their case, and the space for identity that they provide, whereas Nash and Bain (2007) write about the violations of this right of (largely invisible) recognition in a lesbian bathhouse. Qualitative in their research methods, often inspired by postmodern or poststructuralist perspectives, and descriptive rather than directed towards answering a very explicit research question, these and other studies have provided a broad range of fascinating insights in the marginalised spaces of gays and lesbians in the city.

Third, the public space of the city is also the stage for visibility, a visibility that can be seen as identity politics to claim the right of recognition and that finds its expression through consumption (Jayne, 2006: 141). Large-scale gay festivals or publicly displayed same-sex affection potentially challenge the heteronormativity and transgress social norms (Browne et al., 2009; Kates & Belk, 2001). Queer visibility is used by Tucker (2009: 3) as a geographical concept to examine how queer groups are 'able to overcome the heteronormativity of particular urban spaces; the options that are available for them to do so'. Urban life depends on regulative power, which in turn depends on other structures in society. Tucker studied queer visbilities in Cape Town, South Africa, and his study shows powerfully that there is no such thing as one regulative heteronormativity, but that heteronormativity is context-dependent and that relations of gender and sexuality are negotiated at the very local level in the urban environment. His and other studies have shown that there are different ways in which urban communities appreciate sexual diversity and define differences, ways structured also by inequalities of race and class (see also Binnie & Skeggs, 2004). Such approaches have been especially strongly developed with regard to the ways in which, as early noted by Castells (1983), gay men have claimed space through social movements and residential concentration, creating gay villages in the world – see Andersson (2009) and Collins (2004) on London; Binnie and Skeggs (2004) on Manchester; Nash (2006) and Bouthilette (1994) on Toronto; Beemyn (1997) on Chicago, Philadelphia, Detroit and Washington; Sibalis (2004) on Paris; and Castells and Murphy (1982) on San Fransisco. Such locations then also become subject to representations elsewhere, as in the case of the Gay Village of Manchester that became the setting for a television series *Queer as Folk* (Skeggs, Moran, Tyrer, & Binnie, 2004), and are increasingly discussed as sexual spaces of a particular kind, fitting into the tournament of urban entrepreneurialism (Bell & Binnie, 2004) and hence excluding other kinds.

Scholars writing about sexualities and the city ask similar questions to those writing on gender and the city, where the issue how space 'matters to the construction of gender in material and symbolic ways' (Watson, 2010: 237) also takes centre-stage. We now turn to those studying the city as gendered space.

Gender

The spatial structure of the city is directly linked to gender relations, or 'the beliefs, expectations and behaviour that characterize interactions between men and women' (Spain, 2011: 178). Although scholars from the early Chicago School to the LA School have not thought adequately about gender relations, feminist scholars have argued that urban space is gendered space. As urban theory has been a predominantly male paradigm, too little attention has been paid to gender (DeSena, 2008: 2; Sewell, 2011; Bondi & Rose, 2003). Recent collections such as *Gender in an Urban World* (DeSena, 2008), *Gender in Urban Research* (Garber & Turner, 1995) and *Gendering the City* (Miranne & Young, 2000) are attempts to overcome the male dominance in urban theory from a feminist perspective.

The search for 'a feminist approach' within urban theory is not straightforward for two reasons. First, it has become axiomatic in general debates about feminism not only that there is no single feminist approach or feminist theory but also that the conceptual and empirical interests of feminists have become increasingly fragmented, even mutually incompatible, over time. Feminist scholars have established, drawn upon, developed, and taken issue with many different theoretical approaches within the social sciences. Within the last three decades, claims have been made for a wide range of distinctive 'feminisms'. Liberal, radical, Marxist, socialist, dual systems, anarchist, separatist, materialist, postmodern, and eco-feminism each draw upon different, if sometimes overlapping, conceptual frameworks (Tong, 1998; Bryson, 1992; Humm, 1992). Feminists are also active within a wide range of academic disciplines, from those like geography, sociology, and politics, which have established 'urban' dimensions, through to psychology, anthropology, cultural studies, and linguistics which focus overtly upon cities and urban environments much more rarely.

Second, there is considerable dispute as to whether the urban scale of analysis is particularly appropriate to feminists. Certainly many feminists are uncomfortable with the idea that they *should* be particularly attracted to local/urban research because it is often concerned with what are patronisingly seen as 'women's issues', for example local social and welfare provision or the notion of community (Phillips, 1996). Such claims are often dismissed on the basis that they entail precisely the sort of pigeon-holing of women which feminists seek to overcome. More importantly, the analysis, understanding and critique of gender inequality which lies at the heart of feminism is often taken to imply that the appropriate level of analysis is the whole society, if not the world as a whole. Whilst there has been much debate within feminism about the feasibility and desirability of universal sisterhood – particularly whether the concerns of 'Western', white and often middle-class women can be generalised to others who are less privileged, not white and/or from the less developed world – there has been less concern to distinguish between women or women's experiences on the basis of locality. In the building of houses, for example, women's needs have not been taken into account in traditional architecture, but scholars have discussed whether a 'feminist architecture' is possible at all, given that a 'single feminist ideal cannot meet all [women's] needs' (Wright, 2011: 148) Yet most feminist writing tends to deal with universal or society-wide aspects of female disadvantage, for example with respect to male violence, the representation of sexuality, the operation of the labour market, the division of domestic labour, reproductive technologies, political representation and activism, and so on.

On the face of it, then, one might expect to find that urban theory and research is not an especially powerful current within feminism and that issues of gender are not especially well developed, conceptually or empirically, in urban studies of the sort covered in this book so far. This is not an inaccurate prediction. As Vaiou (1992: 247) argues, even '[a]fter two decades of feminist writing on "the urban question", the urban scholar is struck, in particular, by the absence of gender from the analysis and understanding of urban development'. But that is not to say feminist approaches to cities and urban issues have not grown considerably in strength and number in recent years. Indeed, each of the major concerns of the feminist project have found some expression within urban theory and research. Feminist critiques are ranged against many of the theoretical approaches covered in previous chapters. Thus, for example, Staeheli and Clarke

(1995: 20) argue that '[t]he failure to incorporate gender relations into theories has led to partial analyses of urban development', particularly within American urban political economy. These theories focus too heavily upon the interaction of *male* elites and do not ask why there are male elites. Before examining how this has been achieved, however, we need to remind ourselves what those major concerns are.

Feminism is essentially a radical project the goal of which is to transform gender relations by challenging, and ultimately eradicating, patriarchy – the social, economic, political, cultural and ideological domination of women by men. This fundamental radicalism means that feminism as a whole shares the level of ambition, but also many of the dilemmas and problems, of other radical approaches within the social sciences. Just as we found with respect to radical theories developed by neo-Marxists and neo-Weberians in Chapter 2, for example, there is a tension between analytical work that seeks to understand the patriarchal world and more prescriptive and normative work that might help to change it. Although most feminists stress the need to unify theory and praxis, the links between them are not always that strong (Little, 1994: 1; Foord & Gregson, 1986). Similarly, feminists, like neo-Marxists, are relatively united upon and expansive about what they are against, but less clear when it comes to what they are for.

Feminist social scientists nonetheless share a core concern with the importance of gender as opposed to sex. Whilst a minority of feminists adopts the 'essentialist' position that attributes of gender are directly related to sex (Firestone, 1979) – that is, that they stem from biological differences between women and men – there is a broad consensus that gender is socially constructed and not 'natural'. In other words, gender roles are acquired through socialisation. Women and men are treated differently, have different experiences and acquire different knowledges and skills as a result of the way gender roles are defined and reinforced within patriarchal societies. There is also consensus that the 'gendering' of social science cannot be achieved merely by 'adding women' to established approaches – for example, by studying the role of women in public life and academic production or researching women's experiences of disadvantage. But the implications of this consensual starting point for feminist analysis have been followed through, conceptually and empirically, in a number of ways.

At a broad, philosophical level, feminism poses two key questions. First, why are issues of gender left out of dominant theoretical approaches within the social sciences? And second, how can gender be made more central to social scientific theory? In addressing the first question, feminist critiques of the way gender is understood in patriarchal societies have set out to demonstrate that social science, in all its established forms, has been overwhelmingly *androcentric* or male-centred. The main argument here is that whilst most theoretical positions in the social sciences are ostensibly 'gender blind' – that is, they are not overtly sexist – in practice they are characterised by a gender bias. They concentrate upon and take most seriously qualities, properties, and activities commonly associated with the male gender and relegate those associated with the female gender to the category of 'other'. In this way, maleness becomes the norm and women effectively disappear from view.

Central to this argument is the idea that dominant views of gender stem from a number of dualisms in social science, the most important of which are the public versus the private sphere, culture versus nature, the rational versus the emotional, and objectivity versus subjectivity. These dichotomies underpin dominant perceptions of what constitutes 'good theory' (i.e. that based on the first part of each dualism) and what can safely be ignored for the purposes of social science theory building (the second part). At the same time, they provide categories which distinguish the concerns and qualities of archetypal men (the first part) from those of archetypal women (the second part). These dualisms therefore provide the basis upon which women are effectively excluded from scientific enterprises.

Feminists have responded to the problem of dualisms in rather different ways. The more common responses have disputed the relevance of dualisms as the basis for social scientific practice. Thus, for example, it has been argued that social science theory which ignores the supposedly 'inferior' part of each dualism is inevitably partial and incomplete. Similarly, some feminists have sought to demonstrate that the knowledge and behaviour of women are not adequately captured by only one half of each dualism. Others have taken a different tack and sought to reinforce the importance of dualisms but in ways which emphasise the positive virtues of stereotypically female ways of perceiving and behaving. Some radical feminists, for example, advocate 'anti-rationalism' (McDowell, 1992: 410–11) which involves inverting each of the dualisms and insisting that the supposedly 'inferior' parts actually form a superior basis for conceptual work.

Whichever approach is adopted, one central issue that exercises most feminists concerns the way in which the notion of objectivity is treated within the social sciences. S. G. Harding (1991), for example, casts doubt upon the idea that theory-building and research, in practice, are as value-free, impartial, and dispassionate as those who defend the idea of objectivity suggest.

> If the community of 'qualified' researchers and critics systematically excludes ... women of all races, and if the larger culture is stratified by ... gender and lacks powerful critiques of this stratification, it is not plausible to imagine that ... sexist interests and values would be identified within a community of scientists composed entirely of

people who benefit – intentionally or not – from institutional ... sexism.
(S. G. Harding, 1991: 143)

The second question sets feminists the more complex philosophical task of
exploring whether there are forms of theory and research that can provide an
alternative to androcentric ways of perceiving and gaining knowledge. This task
has caused controversy within feminism. One camp, sometimes described as
'feminist empiricists' (S. G. Harding, 1991: 111–18), argues that androcentricity
results not from established social scientific concepts and methods in themselves
but from the way these are applied, by men or women who ignore issues of gender, to 'gender-blind' issues and objects of study. In other words, current social
science is androcentric in practice rather than in principle. Gender bias occurs at
the point at which it is decided what research should focus upon, which hypotheses should be tested, and how the results of research should be evaluated.

Feminist standpoint theorists (Haraway, 1988; S. G. Harding, 1991: 119–37),
on the other hand, argue that social science can be androcentric in principle; that
is, particular concepts can be more or less supportive of or antagonistic to
enlightened gender analysis. In this view all knowledge, and the concepts that
are developed to express it, is socially situated; that is, it is shaped by the particular experiences of individuals and social groups. Since virtually all known
societies are fundamentally stratified by gender, it follows that women have
particular knowledge which is different from that of men. Hence women's – and,
less frequently, men's – attempts to make sense of women's knowledge and concerns, through the development of concepts and theories, generate 'truths' which
could not be discovered through conventional, androcentric theories and methods. Indeed, standpoint theorists go further than this and claim that theories and
concepts which are rooted in women's experiences and struggles, because they
take account of the invisible world of the oppressed as well as the highly visible
world of the oppressor, are inherently more critical, less partial and perverse,
and more objective.

These alternative methodological approaches within feminism do not limit the
choice of research methods. Feminist empiricists can – and do – adopt a variety
of approaches based upon positivism, hermeneutics and realism. The arguments
of feminist standpoint theorists in particular, however, suggest a special affinity
between feminism and hermeneutics (Mackenzie, 1989: 57). This is particularly
clear in the way objectivity and subjectivity are treated. Feminist scepticism with
traditional notions of objectivity affects the way in which the relation between
researcher and researched is perceived. The feminist argument that all knowledge
is socially situated means many feminists take issue with the idea that the academic 'author' is an authoritative, informed and impartial observer who can
make sense of the experience of less informed and partial research subjects. As

Gross (1986: 199) argues: 'the conventional assumption that the researcher is a disembodied, rational, sexually indifferent subject – a mind unlocated in space, time, or constitutive inter-relationships with others – is a status normally attributed only to angels'. As a result, most feminist authors/researchers are concerned to make their own standpoints clear and to have a more 'democratic' relationship with those they research. At the same time, the commitment to base feminist analysis on the actual, rather than assumed, experiences of women means a great deal of credibility is attached to the subjective views of the researched in defining what is analysed and how.

In practice, this means that particular emphasis is placed upon qualitative research methods – especially participant observation – and more open-ended and less structured interaction between researcher and researched, which enables the latter to perform a fuller role in the research process. There is a great deal of debate within feminism as to whether this approach fully addresses the issue of power relationships between researchers and their subjects (McDowell, 1992: 407–9). It also raises difficult issues about how feminists deal with men – especially powerful men – in qualitative research. However, it remains the case that feminists, in general, are encouraged to 'study up', in a spirit of critical curiosity, rather than 'study down', from a position of assumed authority.

Feminist methodologies do not point to particular themes or subjects of research, either. Certainly they do not imply an exclusive focus upon women and women's experiences. Men and masculinity are just as important a focus for feminist analysis. The one essential requirement of feminist research is that it should be not so much *about* women as *for* women. Whilst concepts such as patriarchy and gender inequality are particularly useful to, and monopolised by, feminists, there is in principle no reason why they cannot be used by non-feminists. What distinguishes feminist use of such concepts is a commitment to contribute to the liberation of women. In practice, this aim has been pursued in a variety of ways. The broader conceptual tasks have been to provide critiques of androcentric theories and to use feminist theory to define alternative research themes and agendas which better contribute to the study of gender and gender inequality. Empirical studies, on the other hand, have concentrated upon understanding how patriarchy works in practice and upon 'foregrounding women', particularly in assessing how gender inequality is challenged and with what effect. All of these approaches have been adopted in feminist work within urban studies.

Feminist interest in 'places' – and by extension in urban studies – is a function of two overarching concerns, both of which derive from feminism's insistence upon the 'situatedness' of knowledge. One concerns differences in the way men and women experience places in a general sense. The other concerns the way in which gender relations vary between places. Thus, on one hand, it is argued that because women's use of time and space is invariably different from that of men, so is their experience of all places (McDowell, 1983, 1992). In other words, men and women tend to inhabit different worlds, even when they live in the same city, the same neighbourhood, or even the same household (see also Doan, 2010). Feminist urban analysis has the task of understanding how and why this is the case, and of making the implications for women's lives clear. Little, Peake, and Richardson (1988: 2) summarise this area of concern when they argue that feminist urban studies must seek to understand 'how [women's] use of space and time ... affect[s], and [is] affected by, spatial structure and environmental change' which primarily reflect the needs of men.

On the other hand, feminists are also concerned with the way gender relations vary from place to place. As Vaiou (1992: 260) argues, 'women's experiences are partially constituted by and through their location in the web of social relations that make up any society'. Since social relations are not uniform but vary geographically it follows that, even if we assume patriarchy in a general sense is universal, place matters. For example, the gender relations associated with mining communities are not the same as those associated with the stockbroker belt, even though both operate within a wider patriarchal system. Appleton (1995: 44) summarises this theme within feminist urban studies succinctly when she points out that '[a]ll cities are patriarchal, but neither all cities nor all patriarchies are the same'.

These particular 'urban' interests combine with the more general concerns of the feminist project to set feminist urban studies four key challenges. The first is to provide a critique of androcentric urban theory. The second is to insist upon and conceptualise the way gender roles operate within 'patriarchal cities'. The third is to understand and assess the degree to which gender roles vary in space and over time. The fourth is to establish how patriarchy in cities is, or can be, challenged or modified, for example by general socio-economic change, the mobilisation of women, or the reform of public policies. The focus in this discussion is upon the more conceptual tasks, but the empirical concerns of feminists are touched upon in order to give an indication of the range of work to which conceptual development has given rise.

Much feminist writing on cities begins with a critique of established urban theories as androcentric and stresses the damage that is, or should be, caused to the credibility of mainstream urban studies as a result. It is argued that androcentric theories are of little relevance to women *as women*, rather than as undifferentiated, seemingly genderless members of other groups such as households or social classes. Too often, it is argued, established theories see the division of labour between genders as 'natural' and unproblematic and therefore do not appreciate, or focus inquiry upon, central features of women's experiences. This argument is often linked to the issue of dualisms within social science. In particular, feminist urban analysis takes issue with the distinction between public and private spheres and related dichotomies such as politics versus home life, waged employment versus domestic labour, and production versus reproduction. Androcentric theorists, it is argued, focus a disproportionate amount of attention upon the 'public' realm of production, waged work, and formal political activity, and concentrate very little upon the 'private' realm of the household, unwaged domestic work, and reproduction; that is, providing for the material and emotional needs of partners and/or dependents.

There are two slightly different arguments as to why a reliance upon these particular dualisms results in gender bias. One suggests that androcentricity produces a bias toward men; that is, theories based upon dualist dichotomies, even when produced by people sympathetic to feminism, lead inevitably to an overemphasis on spheres of activity traditionally dominated by men whilst underemphasising those more associated with women. The other argues that a bias towards men underlies androcentric theory; that is, certain conceptual foci remain dominant precisely because theorists prioritise the interests and activities of men. Whichever argument is used, most feminists agree that the dualist approach must be confronted by insisting that the theorist/researcher, when analysing women's experiences, cannot retain hard-and-fast distinctions between the public and private spheres, and production and reproduction.

Feminist approaches have clearly established a foothold within urban studies in recent years. As this brief discussion indicates, this work has not led to the development of a unified feminist urban theory comparable to those in previous chapters. Nonetheless there are signs of the emergence of distinctive feminist urban theor*ies* which, like other theoretical approaches examined in this book, share the characteristics of the weaker definition of urban theory outlined in Chapter 1; that is, they consciously apply a distinctive body of knowledge and concepts to urban phenomena. Feminists' critiques of androcentric urban theories have encouraged a focus upon some key concepts – patriarchy, gender and gender relations, reproduction, the dual role of women – which differentiate feminist approaches from others.

Let us look at some of these in more detail. There are two aspects to consider: the movement from seeing women as victims to women as agents in shaping their environments and creating women's spaces; and the arguments that women suffer from specific spatial constraints as a consequence of male-dominated planning and city building, directly connected to the problems created by a division between the women's sphere as private/home/reproduction/apolitical and the male's sphere as public (work, politics)/production/political.

First, feminists have been writing about women, the city and social control and safety (e.g. Wilson, 1991), taking a critical stance towards the idea that women are passive victims of the wrong moral character of the city, that both threatens them and makes them a threat, inviting promiscuity from men by their mere presence in the public space of cities. There was the mainstream understanding that rapidly industrialising cities were unsafe places for women, which lasted until the first half of the twentieth century. Hayden, for example, has shown how the male-dominated field of architecture enabled the sexist nature of urban spaces as the physical form of cities was controlled by men: houses were built to provide tranquillity for men and further isolated women (Hayden, 1984; Doan, 2010; Wilson, 1991: 112). Visible and invisible boundaries provided mechanisms that enabled the dichotomy of gendered space, for example where women who entered male-dominated spaces would experience violence or harassment (Stansell, 1986). Feminist scholars have hence all but denied that in cities, gender-based violence, increased poverty and deteriorating infrastructures have impacted women's lives (Andrew, 1995; Whitzman, 2004; Sweet, 2010) and pleaded for planning for non-sexist cities (Greed, 1994; Reeves & Greed, 2003; Uteng & Cresswell, 2008). In dominant discourses and practices, though, women were seen less as subject to danger and more as dangerous; from the Roman Empire onwards, the control and surveillance of the city have always been directed at women (Wilson, 1991: 14), especially working-class women, resulting in strong anti-urbanism with clear roles for women depending on class and ideas for planned new towns and suburban neighbourhoods:

> while working-class women were to be regulated in the model towns envisaged by industrialists and politicians, the role of the middle-class women was to preside over a semi-rural retreat, which was the opposite in all particulars of the noisy, bustling city which her husband had to negotiate every day. Rest, peace and comfort were the ideals. (Wilson, 1991: 45)

Women were seen as uncontrolled and not rational; the development of department stores in the nineteenth century gave them a legitimate place in the city as consumers, but the lore of the products that would enhance their homes also stressed their role as homemakers and stressed the emotional, not instrumental nature of their shopping behaviour. Feminist scholars have argued that such understandings of women are typically patriarchal, and urged urban scholars to think of women as agents in the production of space, rather than simply presuming their 'thereness' (DeSena, 2008: 2). Vacchelli (2008), for example, has made this concrete in her study of the creation and participation in visual landscapes of women differing in class and race/ethnicity in the city of Milan, and Patch (2008) has done something similar in exploring the ways in which women entrepreneurs in Brooklyn are 'faces on the street' who contribute to gentrification.

The relegation of women to a position of passive subject goes together with the understanding of private and public as bipolar (i.e. either/or), linking both to other gendered concepts. Such dichotomies, then, are the second aspect at which feminist scholars have directed their criticism. For Daphne Spain, one of the scholars who have given a feminist critique on, for example, gentrification studies, the city includes gendered spaces, both masculine and feminine, where her interest is in the spaces that women collectively occupy. Following the critical theorist Nancy Fraser, she argues that gender constructs generally marginalise women and family issues as 'private' while legitimising men's issues as public; yet gendered spaces, in her concrete examples the medieval béguinage, late nineteenth-century American settlement houses and Mother Centres in Germany, are women's institutionalised efforts to find identities outside the home, and provide contexts in which 'subaltern counterpublics' can prosper (Spain, 2008: 11). These gendered spaces, she concludes, 'gave women voluntary spatial identities associated with a place outside the home. The places were typically liminal, partly private and partly public, serving as a meeting ground for community' (Spain, 2008: 24). The béguinage communities of Catholic women who lived in small groups occupied a unique place in the city, creating exclusively women's spaces (Simone, 2010).

Women are dominant homemakers but also breadwinners, often in invisible, poorly rewarded ways structured around the needs of dependents. Caring tasks are shared with other female members of the extended family, not men. More affluent households generally buy the services of other women, as caretakers or cleaners, to free the time of women to work. Women remain thus less visible in the public realm, as consumers (city-centre leisure services), public figures (e.g. politicians), and workers.

Due to the confinement of women to the sphere of social reproduction, and hence to the private sphere, urban space is patriarchal structured, Markusen (2013: 250) argues: 'the dominance of the single-family detached dwelling, its separation from the workplace, and its decentralized urban location are as much the products of patriarchal organization of households as of the capitalist organization of wage work'. Frank (2008: 127) points out that because suburbanisation rested on the realisation of the traditional nuclear middle-class family it has come to stand as the patriarchal space *per se* for urban scholars studying gender. Indeed, as Frank (2008: 130–1) describes, male reformers did think they could change the moral decay caused by the industrial city with women and family as their subject by the strict separation of the private and the public sphere: 'in the male model of suburbanisation the eliminating of women from the world of the city and from gainful occupation' was a price they paid – a price for absolute power in the domestic realm, and suburbs became a place where gender roles were experimented with (Frank, 2008: 133): 'thus the gender trouble', Frank continues (2008: 134), 'typical for both the city and the suburb at the time, did not stop at suburbia. Initially believed to solve the urban gender crisis, the new way of life turned out to be its continuation with different features.' Spain, like Frank, discusses the post-World War II changes that made it possible for women to decide about childbearing, raise their educational attainment, enter the labour force in larger numbers and more often become heads of household. This has affected urban life, for example as neighbourhood surveillance is less self-evident when women are no longer at home, and it is in the suburbs that labour market participation is highest (Frank, 2008: 143). More importantly, it shifts the realm of public and private: services performed by women in their private homes before, such as child care, care for the elderly and food preparation, have been transformed to the public space – and contributed to urban sprawl as well (Spain, 2011: 182–3). Mackenzie (1989) also argued that women's use of time and space within cities has been changed by their efforts to extend control over fertility and childbirth, and extend resources available for child care. This, in turn, has meant more interaction between the home/community and the public sphere and altered the nature of the community, created new spaces and networks in cities (e.g. socialisation of child care through co-operative, informal or state arrangements) and altered the relations between allegedly public and private environments (the private becoming more public or politicised, and the public becoming more concerned with the private or domestic sphere).

The literature on gender and the city is broad, and our review here cannot do justice to the entire debate. What we see in the context of our discussion of diversity as a horizontal paradigm, however, is that much attention is paid to the role of patriarchy and what this means for women's presence and their role in the production of space in the city, where they are dominated by men, although recent accounts also show how this may be shifting. It is remarkable, however, that there is in the literature on gender and the city relatively little attention to the consequences of such gendered spaces. Frank (2008: 143) worries about the 'flat feminist verdict' of suburbanisation as the ultimate expression of patriarchy and exclusion of women as well as the more optimistic thesis 'which accredits the socio-spatial patterns of postindustrial landscapes with intrinsic emancipatory effects': she points out that the mere fact that more women in suburbia work does not address questions of just distribution and payment or of a fair division of labour within the family. She also argues that within workplaces gender inequalities continue. And she makes a sharp connection between gender, class and race/ethnicity when she writes:

> most notable, the blossoming of the suburbs has produced direct and indirect effects on the socio-spatial and socio-structural development of the inner cities, from which the middle classes continue to flee. Women are

especially affected by this migration of jobs out to the suburbs. Increasing social and spatial polarization are the consequences. It is no coincidence that the feminization of poverty has its central place in the inner cities. (Frank, 2008: 144)

We will return to this in the conclusion.

Ethnicity/race

While we have discussed segregation and its consequences in terms of neighbourhood effects, and hence in relation to a hierarchy of resource access, in Chapter 5, a large body of literature takes a rather different approach to ethnicity and is primarily interested in the question of the multicultural city. Moving away from a natural ordering of a mosaic of social worlds along ethnic lines as Park had outlined within the Chicago School, scholars have studied ethnicity as an identity and asked questions about how ethnic difference is negotiated within cities on a daily basis. Elias and Scotson (1965) discuss how an established community develops prejudices against a group of newcomers moving into a nearby new housing development, and although they do not frame the tensions and practices of discrimination and exclusion that result in terms of ethnicity, this is a good starting point for learning about the social mechanisms that people apply to establish in-group virtues and out-group vices (Merton, 1968).

This is another large field of research, but we will focus in this chapter on two sub-themes of the field. First, we look at the ways in which the multicultural city is conceptualised and what concepts scholars have used to do so. We then present the two most dominant theories of interethnic contact in the multicultural city that have guided much of the empirical research ever since their introduction: the contact hypothesis and the conflict hypothesis. While neither is limited to urban studies, they have both given rise to a large number of empirical studies which, interestingly, put culture at centre-stage but do not, as culturalist perspectives, do so from a postmodern angle, and they often are based on quantitative data collections and analyses.

In the study of segregation, racial and ethnic groups as statistical categories are assumed to be measurable as static bounded units. Yet many social scientists agree that ethnicities are not simply available categories but are socially constructed (Hall, 1996). They also agree that such social categories have multiple meanings (Verkuyten, 1997: 44 –5). Ethnicity is a widely contested concept, albeit less so in everyday life. 'In societies with large immigrant populations', Milton Yinger (1986: 22) writes, 'there is a tendency to use the term "ethnic group" to refer to people who share a common former citizenship and who refer to but need not have the same heritage and cultural background'. Ethnicities are understood by sociologists as 'the cultural practices and outlooks that distinguish a given community of people' (Giddens, 1989: 243), and this term is much more commonly used in Europe than the term 'race'; naturally race is not primordial either, but differs from ethnicity in that it can be understood as 'physical variations singled out by the members of a community or society as ethnically significant' (Giddens, 1989: 246). Clearly, ethnicity has an element of ascription or categorisation (Jenkins, 1996): others classify a person as having a specific ethnicity or race. But it can also be a matter of identification: people may feel they belong to an ethnic group and feel comfortable with its cultural practices because of their heritage and socialisation, and/or also because of the discriminatory practices they face outside of this group.

In the city of diversity, people from various ethnic groups interact increasingly with each other, in so far as ethnic segregation does not confine their contacts. Given that ethnic differences are linked to prejudices and discrimination, it may come as no surprise that they have gained a lot of attention from scholars studying the city. Cities are, especially under conditions of globalisation, diverse places of ethnicities that owe their growth to migration by people who often come from afar. That said, the level of exclusion or discrimination may of course be at least as high or even higher in smaller settlements where those with different practices stand out, as there is, following the subcultural thesis, no mass to absorb them and not enough mass to find others to form a community with. The city therefore may not sort people by a natural process in a mosaic of social worlds, but the formation of ethnic communities which may also have an institutional dimension, with dedicated religious buildings, shops, language schools and other services, is possible in the multicultural city. We discussed this in Chapter 5 under the rubric of ethnic enclaves. We saw there, too, following Herbert Gans' approach to ethnicity as symbolic, that over generations, migrants may come to think of their ethnicity as primarily a practice of consumption that they choose to engage with at certain events and not as entirely constituting their identity. However, such symbolic ethnicity can obviously only be practised to the extent that others do not ascribe ethnicity and attach prejudices and practices of discrimination to this ethnic classification. Prejudice refers to 'opinions and attitudes held by members of one group about another' (Giddens, 1989: 247); discrimination refers to the 'activities which serve to disqualify the members of one grouping from opportunities open to others' (Giddens, 1989: 247). In cities, for example, housing market discrimination is a much researched theme, ever since the classic study of Rex and Moore (1967). Prejudices of course influence people's attitudes towards people whom they have defined as different from themselves and therefore play an important role in interethnic relations.

Sociologists have studied interethnic relationships from the 'contact hypothesis' (Homans, 1950; Allport, 1979; Pettigrew, 1980). While the initial idea was that contact would result in liking, the debate and research that followed have qualified this general idea. Positive experiences of contact are supported by a fairly equal social status among the people involved, common interests and the presence of people or institutions (such as neighbourhood workers or teachers) that encourage understanding. Indeed, Wagner and his colleagues find for Germany that prejudices are less severe when there are friendships and intensive contacts between people of diverse ethnic backgrounds in schools and neighbourhoods (Wagner, van Dick, Pettigrew, & Christ, 2003). An important perspective on interethnic contact that has resulted in much discussion is Putnam's approach to diversity and trust. According to Putnam, in ethnically diverse neighbourhoods residents tend to 'hunker down': 'trust (even of one's own race) is lower, altruism and community cooperation rarer, friends fewer'. While he sees this effect of ethnic diversity, a diversity that is, as he notes, on the rise in many European cities, in the long term societies that have dealt with immigration successfully have managed to counter such fragmentation. Here, new forms of solidarity across ethnic and racial boundaries have developed and more encompassing identities have flourished. Putnam has remarkably little to say about how such success can be achieved. This rather bleak idea of interethnic contacts in multicultural neighbourhoods is confirmed in empirical studies that show that even residents who consciously opt for a diverse neighbourhood because it is the diversity they appreciate have limited ethnic diversity in their personal networks (Blokland & van Eijk, 2010).

As we have argued elsewhere (Blokland, 2003b) the problem with the contact hypothesis is that it aims to present an all-encompassing thesis with a broad generalisability. However, in one neighbourhood the contact hypothesis may be valid for some, while others have more conflictual ties to people of diverse ethnic groups. In cities, of course, the range of possible ties between ethnic groups is even wider. The conflict hypothesis diverts from the contact hypothesis: these scholars build on the early work by Simmel (1964) and Coser (1956) who thought about how groups develop antagonistic, or even conflict-ridden, relationships. Groups seek conflicts, in their perspective, in order to maintain in-group cohesion:

> Hostilities not only prevent boundaries within the group from gradually disappearing, so that these hostilities are often consciously cultivated to guarantee existing conditions. Beyond this, they also are of direct sociological fertility: often they provide classes and individuals with reciprocal positions which they would not find or not find in the same way, if the causes of hostility were not accompanied by the *feeling* and the expression of hostility – even if the same objective causes of hostility were in operation. (Simmel, 1964: 18)

Simmel did not differentiate between hostilities and the actions they may generate. As Coser observed, hostilities do not necessarily give rise to conflicts. Such feelings usually arise from an unequal distribution of privileges and rights (Coser, 1956: 35, 37). According to Coser, the occurrence of conflict depends in part on whether this distribution is considered legitimate. The sociologist Merton (1968: 475–90) has stated that the definition of legitimacy is contingent on the distribution of power between the parties concerned. Coser distinguishes realistic conflicts from non-realistic conflicts to focus on actions. Realistic conflicts are means towards achieving a certain end. Non-realistic conflicts do not concern parties pursuing antagonistic objectives. Rather, they enable one of the parties to release tension. Competition is an indirect conflict in which the victory over the opponent is not an intrinsic objective in its own right. The idea of a struggle for scarce resources as a form of conflict underlies the competition hypotheses, which is a counterpart to the contact hypothesis (Portes & Manning, 2013; Banton, 1983; Olzak, 1992; Hannan, 1994). Both the question whether members of ethnic groups actually compete over, for example, jobs, housing, neighbourhood facilities or public space (Vermeulen, 1990: 230) and the question whether they experience such competition are relevant (van Niekerk, Sunier, & Vermeulen, 1989).

For all conflicts, it is not relevant whether there is an objective basis to them, Coser argues, drawing on what is called the Thomas theorem in sociology (see Merton, 1968: 475–90): 'if men define a threat as real, although there may be little or nothing in reality to justify this belief, the threat is real in its consequences – and among these consequences is the increase of group cohesion' (Coser, 1956: 107). Prejudices are important to people affected by 'degrouping', which is the loss of cohesion in a city to which they belong. These prejudices provide them, Coser argues from a rather functionalist perspective, with the possibility of drawing boundaries and creating group assets from which others can be excluded. How does this then play out in urban neighbourhoods? First, researchers have investigated how fear of unemployment under economic restructuring and housing scarcity have created competition, or at least the experience of competition, among the established and the outsiders. By turning virtue into vice, prejudices could be developed and a sense of relative deprivation or entitlement based on a notion of superiority could develop. A second field where competition can be seen to lead to conflict is where multiple users compete over scarce public space. Claims on public space, often the result of group-specific behaviour, produce spaces which represent the identities of some but not of others and therefore exclude them from symbolic ownership. This, however, is a theme not restricted to ethnic groups. Due to the history of migration in European cities there is diversity in ethnicity that coincides with diversity in age cohorts. Due to economic restructuring and its consequences for the labour market, young people with immigrant backgrounds tend, in many cities, to have a lot of leisure time that is often spent in public space, where they encounter others who may, being non-immigrant and older, take offence at the claims they make on public spaces in their neighbourhoods. By doing so, urban youth has gained a presence that is increasingly noted politically. It is to the theme of age and generations that we now turn.

Age and generations

It seems to us that the youth in the first decades of the twenty-first century are becoming an increasingly visible political presence. The contrast between the securities of older generations and the precariousness of the younger ones is rising; as discussed in Chapter 3, neo-liberalism has taken away some of the securities that came with the high days of the industrial era. Job security is no longer a given; finding a job at all is no longer a given, and in times of austerity the provision of existential security by the welfare state is no longer guaranteed. In many urban places, we see youth taking to the street to address their need for income, housing and job security. That generations are important for understanding social change was first pointed out by Mannheim. He insisted that we need to clearly define what we mean by generations: 'The unity of a generation does not consist primarily in a social bond of the kind that leads to the formation of a concrete group, although it may sometimes happen that a feeling for the unity of a generation is consciously developed into a basis for the formation of concrete groups' (Mannheim, 1952: 165). As he continues later in his essay:

> Generation location is based on the existence of biological rhythm in human existence – the factors of life and death, a limited span of life, and aging. Individuals who belong to the same generation, who share the same year of birth, are endowed, to that extent, with a common location in the historical dimension of the social processes. (Mannheim 1952: 167)

Meanwhile, the position of older generations is also shifting. Think, for example, of condominiums or assisted living for the elderly and retirees, empty-nesters returning to gentrified areas of the city and a changing mortgage and housing market that makes buying property increasingly risky for young newcomers on the housing market while the older generations cash in on the increased value of their properties. We expect that over the years, age cohort divisions in the city, already visible to some extent in immigrant settlements in cities such as Jakarta (Simone, 2010), will provide another spatial expression for an inequality that is taking on new forms and strongly related to the forms of inequalities commonly accepted as relevant, such as race, ethnicity, class and gender. So far, however, it makes sense to discuss age and generations within the horizontal paradigm of diversity as the consequences for inequalities have been scrutinised little in urban studies. The 'problem' of generational diversity seems to have been studied primarily by looking at youth. Broadly speaking, there are two bodies of literature in urban studies that do so.

First, there is the approach that connects closely to the subcultural theory we have discussed above. Even stronger, it seems that some of the literature understands subculture to be primarily a matter of youth culture and the terms are then used interchangeably. This approach also fits neatly with ideas about the city as a landscape of pleasure and entertainment. For Miles (2007) youth are full members of consumer society, and with the city becoming the playground of consumption, their subcultures can be interpreted as significantly shaping the city (see also Chatterton & Hollands, 2002).

At the same time, youth can use the city as a playground as long as they remain in their roles as consumers, which actually gives them very few places to go in the city (Jayne, 2006: 148). Various studies have reported on nightlife in the city (Hollands, 2002; Skelton & Valentine, 1997; Ocejo, 2009; Farrer, 2004) and the transformation of space by urban youth, graffiti (Figure 6.3) and skateboarding (Figure 6.4) as forms of the production of space for youth (Atencio, Beal, & Wilson, 2009; Karsten & Pel, 2000; Chiu, 2009), or the claims on space through criminality and drug-dealing (Bourgois, 1995;

Figure 6.1   Youth culture defined as urban subculture: punks in Berlin

Figure 6.2 Youth culture defined as urban subculture: young clubbers in Manchester

© Wolfram Latschar

Williams, 1990). Tonkiss (2005: 140) argued that young people make their presence felt through graffiti and sees graffiti as a tactic in establishing competing claims on space. They take the surface of the city to make demands: 'Outside a formal public sphere of political exchange and reportage, graffiti deals in an economy of slogans and signs' (Tonkiss, 2005: 140). Skateboarders (Tonkiss, 2005: 144) also are involved in a tactical use of space, appropriating the urban built environment, questioning function and ownership, creating an 'other space' (Tonkiss, 2005: 145) 'in which subcultural identities are declared and enacted'.

Many ethnographers have studied urban youth and their subcultures, the classic study being that of Whyte (1981 [1943]). Much more recently, Winlow (2001) has written a particularly enlightening study on the street life of a group of young men in a now decayed mining town in Britain. Whereas his study is very ethnographic, his study goes far beyond empirical description. It makes the theoretical claim that the young men, sons of miners, were prepared for life in the pits with all the masculine identity that came with that. However, when the mines closed, they lost the perspective of a working life in the mines and the scope for developing their male identities. Winlow claims that their production of urban space, with violent crime-related behaviour, can be seen within the context of deindustrialisation as a styling of masculinity for which there was no other frame. Many studies that take youth as an object of study treat them sympathetically. However, Winlow's study, like others on drugs and youth violence, also links to fear for the city, especially to fear for what is often euphemistically called 'inner-city youth'.

Figure 6.3   Graffiti as a practice of producing space

U Bahn Rom Graffiti Basilika St Paolo, Clemensfranz, 2012
Source: Wikimedia Commons:
http://commons.wikimedia.org/wiki/File:U_Bahn_Rom_Graffiti_Basilika_St_Paolo.jpg.

Figure 6.4   Skateboarding as a practice of producing space

© iStock/caracter design
http://www.istockphoto.com/stock-photo-4578449-risky-business.php?st=4e99b53

Historically, fear of the urban has been strong. Even in the past, when the
knowledge of crime would go no further than a horseback ride, people in cities
were constantly involved in a dialogue with fear. 'Fear everywhere, fear always',
Henri Lefebvre, a French historian, once remarked' (Body-Gendrot, 2000: xix).
Similarly, the triad of fear, urban space and youth has been present for a long

time, most pronounced at times of rapid societal change. As Austin and Willard (1998: 2) argue, since the 'scientific' invention of adolescence, reformers have claimed that young people need special policy consideration, as they go through a particularly unstable period of life. Getis (1998) shows that while it has long been recognised that the teenage years are different from childhood and adulthood, the beginning of the twentieth century saw a concerted attempt to define adolescence, making youth more dependent and regulated. The growing interest of scholars in studying juvenile delinquency at the time underscores the linkage between urban space, crime and youth. With rapid urbanisation a public attention to gangs 'was a signal that most middle class Americans were alarmed by the increasing evidence of unruly boys in the streets' (Mechling, 1998: 38). The fear of the urban and the fear of the working-class masses in the urban public space have changed little over time. According to Austin and Willard (1998: 1):

> The public debates surrounding 'youth' are important forums where new understandings about the past, present and future of public life are encoded, articulated and contested. 'Youth' becomes a metaphor for perceived social change and its projected consequences, and as such is an enduring locus for displaced social anxieties. Pronouncements such as 'the problems of youth today', used as a scapegoat for larger social concerns, objectify and reify young people *as the problem in itself*.

In Holland, the problem of youth in urban areas has also become a racial issue, where the Moroccan youths have become the 'folk devils' (Cohen, 1972) of the contemporary social-political situation. Globalisation and its insecurities can be said to be experienced heavily, thus demarcating these times as times of change similar in scale and tempo to those of a century ago.

In studies that take youth as a problem of urban space, much attention has been paid to how to insert social control. A famous theory here is the broken window theory (Wilson & Kelling, 1982) which maintains that an environment that is not well kept gives off a sign that violation of the law is acceptable there; another important theory is the theory of defensible space which draws a connection between the possibilities and impossibilities of social control (Newman, 1973). Many studies have addressed the feelings of lack of safety that the presence of youth evokes. Little attention has been paid to the experience of safety of the youth themselves (but see Binken & Blokland, 2012).

Conclusion: cities as a matrix of resources

In this chapter we have discussed gender and sexuality, ethnicity and generations as expressions of diversity within the context of lifestyle and subcultures. We have approached these themes from the horizontal paradigm that presents diversity as non-hierarchical and different from the vertical paradigm of inequalities. With our brief discussion of intersectionality in Chapter 5, we have already prepared the ground for the idea that the two paradigms should perhaps be brought together. Recall that the model of intersectionality explores the ways in which 'social organisation and identification intersect in specific sites 'to produce forms of social asymmetry' (Anthias, 2005: 32; see also Collins, 1990; Anthias & Yuval-Davis, 1992). Thinking of the city as a matrix of gender, race/ethnicity, age, sexuality and social class layered over each other, we can see people's structural and cultural positioning and theorise what the city means to them: this matrix can provide them with a field for practices to create and access resources, or can show how these practices are exclusionary and oppress the possibilities of creating and accessing resources of others. For example, a woman in a suburb who drives her children to their after-school activities, sits on the board of the parent–teacher association and volunteers at cake sales and school parties, helps the children with their homework and cooks them healthy food every day reproduces the position of her children in terms of class and ethnicity. As for gender, she may be said by feminists to be oppressed by patriarchal norms but, with her husband being out all day at work, she is the most important agent in reproducing the structural position of her children and does so from a powerful position, as what her social capital (connections with women like her) and her cultural capital (the right habitus and educational credentials) cannot buy her, her money can buy: the refusal of a place at the school she prefers for her children can be contested in court as she can afford a lawyer, her son's behaviour at school can be medicalised by therapies covered by private insurance, and his under-performance at school can be addressed by private tutors. She may use the city as if she is moving through a tunnel, removed from the daily realities of the urban poor (Atkinson, 2006). Neighbourhood effects may strengthen this, as we have learnt from our discussion of site effects introduced by Bourdieu (see Chapter 5).

Take, in contrast, a poor immigrant family living in the inner city. The gender roles may be very different here: even though the mother may be staying at home as well, this may be due to labour market and skills but also to cultural aspects of gender expectations within subcultures. However, her scope for creating and accessing resources to reproduce or improve the social positions of her children is much more limited. This is where thinking in terms of intersections becomes crucial: her attempts to, for example, get a school teacher to take problems of her child seriously are hampered by her cultural and social capital (e.g. her sources of information) but also by a possible difference between her position, including her habitus, and the normative structure or climate of the school. This may also be severed by site effects if and when teachers and school officials act on the basis of what they know to be or think they know to be the representation of the neighbourhood.

To elaborate this approach, intra-urban inequalities need to be thought of as multi-dimensional, which greatly complicates doing research. One approach that is developing slowly in urban studies is to address questions of inequality from a relational perspective. Rather than taking individuals as bound units with fixed attributes, it focuses on the relations between individuals and groups. Relational sociologists study how relations produce exclusions and exploitations as well as opportunity-hoarding practices. Such practices are strengthened by adaptations of people to their positions and by what Charles Tilly (1998) has called emulation, or the transfer of experiences with and interpretations of realities from one context to the other. There is a spatial dimension to this too that links directly to our previous discussion of neighbourhood effect and spatial capital. From an attempt to hoard opportunities, albeit not consciously so, exclusionary practices make take spatial forms.

We can think of the city, then, as a matrix of resources where positions and locations coincide, and where intersectionality means that different constellations of class, race/ethnicity, gender and age as well as residential location combined influence, yet never determine, the abilities of urban residents to make a life of their own liking. This means leaving behind the discussion whether the spikiness, the spatially visible expression of the matrix of resources in the urban infrastructure, built environment and web of affiliations, is only vertically unequal or horizontally differentiated, but promises to bring the two paradigms together.

Questions for discussion

- Public space has been defined in various ways by urban scholars. Compare the various definitions and discuss their analytical value: what definition would you prefer, and why?
- Urban space is said to be sexualised and gendered. Can you think of examples from your own experience where this is the case, and to what extend does this experiences reflect inequalities between genders and/or sexualities?
- As we have seen in earlier chapters, authors have suggested that the differentiation between city and hinterland no longer makes much sense. From the perspective of the subcultural thesis, do you think subcultural scholars agree with this, and what is your own view?
- The culturalist perspective focuses on the production of space in daily practices. Discuss the methodological consequences of this approach. Does it exclude statistical methods?
- Scholars of urban interethnic relationships have argued from either the conflict thesis or the contact hypothesis. Do you think they are mutually exclusive? If not, how could one combine them?
- Students of urban youth in the city argue that graffiti, skateboarding and the like are typical contemporary claims on urban space by a specific age group. Can you think of other groups making claims on space? And does this focus mean that place-making by urban youth is a new phenomenon?

Further reading

The cultural turn

Postmodernism is now discussed in most introductory textbooks in social theory, but a good introduction with a chapter on the city is Mike Featherstone's *Consumer Culture and Postmdernism* (1991). More specifically on consumer culture and the city, a decent introduction has been written in Malcolm Miles' *Cities and Cultures* (2007). King's edited book *Re-presenting the City* (1996) is a good example of a collection of both theoretical and empirical papers from a more or less postmodern and culturalist perspective. Flanagan (2010) provides an introduction to urban sociology that relies more than most on the cultural perspective and includes various of the sub-themes of our previous and present chapters. Mark Jayne's *Cities and Consumption* (2006) is of a similar introductory level to Miles' book, but with an explicit focus on postmodernism and consumption. The collection *Urban Life*, edited by Gmelch and Zenner (2002), gives an interesting insight into the way a culturalist approach can be put into empirical practice.

Public space

Accessible excerpts on public space can be found in *The New Blackwell Companion to the City*, edited by Gary Bridge and Sophie Watson (2011), which also includes various empirically oriented chapters on public culture. Lofland's *Public Realm* (1998) is excellent both as a further discussion of the various realms we have discussed and a source that gives an overview of many of the important dimensions of the debate on public space. A good overview of the various theoretical perspectives that draw on or take issue with Habermas' notion of the public sphere can be found in Calhoun's *Habermas and the Public Sphere* (1992). An interesting study of the construction of public space by migrant women, one example of many empirical studies on public space, is Yücesoy's *Everyday Urban Public Space* (2006). Seitha Low is a well-known scholar who has published various empirical studies on the use of public parks and beaches and provides her readers with methodological tools for such studies (Low, Taplin, & Scheld, 2005; Low & Smith, 2006b).

Gender and sexuality

The collection of essays *Gender in an Urban World* (DeSena, 2008) is an accessible introduction to the field, with a good combination of theory and empirical chapters. Another collection is Garber and Turner's *Gender in Urban Research* (1995). General introductions to feminist sociology include Abbott and Wallace (1997). Our text has noted the most influential books on gender and sexuality in the city.

Race and ethnicity

Rex and Moore's (1967) book on housing and racism remains a classic in the field, and Elias and Scotson's *The Established and the Outsiders* (1965) remains an exciting study for those wanting to read more on the practices of drawing group boundaries. Richard Jenkins' (2008) text on ethnicity helps understand the idea of ethnicity as a social construct – but not just a construct. An extensive but not urban-focused collection of essays on ethnicity can be found in Sollors (1996).

Intersectionality

Further readings can be found in McCall (2005), Valentine (2007) and Shields (2008), all writing from a feminist perspective. bell hooks (2000) and Patricia Cohen (1999) are very important early contributors. A wonderful example of a qualitative empirical study on intersectionality is Vargas and Alves' 'Geographies of death' (2010).

7

Urban theory reconsidered

The 'crisis' in urban theory revisited

In both the Foreword and Chapter 1, mention was made of a perception, not uncommon but far from widespread, that there was something of a crisis in urban theory and that urban studies had increasingly become a 'theory-free zone'. Disappointment with the analytical and predictive power or the practical impact of social scientific inquiry is not, of course, confined to urban studies. There will always be social scientists who, to paraphrase Marx and Engels (1965)[1], believe that the primary purpose of analytical work and conceptual inquiry is to change the world rather than simply interpret it and who variously express concern that their colleagues' work is insufficiently theoretical or that their own conceptual insights are ignored. Some occasionally go so far as to admit that their own attempts at theory-building have been misplaced and that they have been blindsided by a particular course of events.

Similarly, there are policy-makers and policy-watchers, searching for simple answers to complex questions, along with research commissioners, keen to maximise the 'impact' and 'relevance' of the work they support, who can and do occasionally express disappointment that theory does not inform practice as much as they believe it could or should. All such criticisms tend to be made most forcibly at times of rapid change and upheaval. During the last 30 years of the twentieth century and the early part of the twenty-first, for example, a sense of disenchantment and introspection with respect to urban theory, along with calls for its reinvigoration, was variously triggered by the widespread protests against the materialism and social conservatism of relatively affluent Western societies

---

1 'The philosophers have only *interpreted* the world, in various ways; the point is to *change it.*'

in the late 1960s, the onset of fiscal retrenchment provoked by oil price rises in the mid- to late 1970s and the impact of the global financial crisis of 2008.

It is to be hoped that the last four chapters have gone some way towards dispelling concerns about the vitality of urban theory and provided some evidence to suggest that reports of its death have been somewhat exaggerated. It is nonetheless worth dwelling a little on the nature of the perceived crisis as a first step towards drawing the key themes of the book together. Let us start by recognising that the two aspects of 'crisis' noted above are not the same thing; that is, a turning point with respect to theory-building might well be triggered by its ostensible absence from a particular body of work, but it cannot necessarily be equated with that absence. The second allegation is easier to refute. Urban studies clearly are not, nor have they ever been, a theory-free zone. The easiest way to counter such a claim is to repeat the observation, made in Chapter 1, that the idea of knowledge without theory is an absurdity. In order to 'know' the urban world, or any aspect of it, we must all make use of some sort of theoretical understanding, no matter how subliminal, confused, contradictory or simply wrong it is. But this is a rather glib response to a more serious point that is implicit within the charge: that there is insufficient evidence of the overt development and application of theory within urban studies.

That more specific allegation, as noted earlier, has some force when it is applied to much of the literature on urban policies. Urban policy analysts for the most part have rarely demonstrated themselves to be on more than nodding terms with major theorists who are interested in explaining processes of urban change. Once we move away from the policy literature, however, the charge loses much of its resonance. Urban theory in the relaxed sense of the term, as outlined in Chapter 1, has, if anything, been shown to have undergone something of a renaissance as social scientists of all stripes have rediscovered an interest in the relationship between subnational places and social and economic processes in an unstable, globalising world. Chapters 3–6, whilst necessarily selective, provided numerous examples of the two sorts of relaxed urban theory outlined in Chapter 1: those that derive theoretical propositions from consciously chosen 'urban' observations, and those that apply more general theoretical propositions to 'urban' subject matter or at least inspire others to do so. Is it still possible, then, to refer to a crisis in urban theory?

The answer to that question could be 'yes', but only if one has certain expectations about the nature, role and status of theory. Three arguments might be made as to why urban theory, although it is being produced in more copious amounts, is nonetheless in crisis. First, returning to the observation first made in Chapter 2, it is clear that the period since the early 1980s has not witnessed the further development of urban theory in the strict sense of that term. In other words, we have not seen any serious attempts to provide insights into towns and cities or urban life *as a whole* on the basis of theories which claim to provide a single, unifying theoretical object for urban studies. No one appears to assume any more, in an increasingly urbanised and interconnected world, that cities can be seen as self-contained social systems or that there are essential features of urbanism which mark urban areas out from other sorts of place. The proponents of this argument might therefore contend that the body of literature which might loosely be defined as such is not really 'proper' urban theory.

Second, one might see the sheer range and eclecticism of contemporary urban theory as a weakness rather than a strength. A diversity of theoretical viewpoints and approaches, on this argument, should be taken as evidence that urban theory as a whole is confused, lacks a sense of direction, and has no unifying theme, subject matter or methodology. Such arguments may appear to gain more force once it is acknowledged, as it was in Chapter 1, that this book is far from comprehensive and has not covered – indeed, could not cover – all the conceptual literatures that might lay claim to being urban theory in the relaxed sense. It could rightly be argued, for example, that previous chapters have not dealt in sufficient depth with conceptual issues relating to urban environmental sustainability, urbanisation in the Global South, international labour mobility, security and vulnerability, and so on. More important, though, is the fact that theoretical diversity can be seen as a sign of crisis only if one takes the view that 'progress' in the social sciences can only happen through the rise and fall of dominant 'paradigms'; that is, bodies of analysis and knowledge which are popularly acknowledged to command the intellectual centre-stage at any particular point in time. If one agrees with commentators who advance that argument most forcefully (e.g. Kuhn, 1962), then urban theory could be said to be in crisis. But if one sides with its critics (e.g. Mulkay, 1979), then diverse theoretical positions can just as easily be interpreted as a sign of growing conceptual energy and innovation.

It should be evident from the very existence of this book that we do not see these two criticisms as unduly damaging. On the one hand, the 'decline' of urban theory in the strict sense is all but inevitable in an increasingly urbanised world. In an age when a constantly growing majority of human beings live in urban areas, and the demand for resources associated with urbanisation is the single most powerful factor shaping change in areas that have conventionally been labelled 'rural' or 'remote' – even 'extra-terrestrial' – urban theory knows no geographical boundaries. On the other hand, although it makes writing books like this something of a challenge, the proliferation of 'relaxed' urban theories is not generally seen as a problem, certainly within the community of urban scholars.

We must consider a third charge, however, which is that urban theory is in crisis not because it has no single object of study or is not unified and coherent, but because even in its diversity it does not provide many useful or powerful insights into the nature and form of contemporary cities and urban life. In crude terms, it does not amount to much. The remaining question, then, is one which Harvey posed long ago when he suggested, with particular reference to urban geography, that there was 'a clear disparity between the sophisticated theoretical and methodological framework which we are using and our ability to say anything really meaningful about events as they unfold around us' (Harvey, 1973: 128).

The remainder of this chapter briefly examines various aspects of this question by way of concluding this investigation into the history and current state of urban theory. It does so in four further sections. The next section asks, very broadly, how theories perform: what are their respective strengths and weaknesses, what are they good at and what are they good for? The section that follows tackles one of the underlying concerns with theoretical diversity in asking whether theories are commensurable; in other words, whether there is anything to be gained from an attempt to combine the insights and approaches associated with different theoretical positions or whether we must accept that theorists simply talk past each other, effectively forcing us to choose one approach over all others.

We then consider the possibility that urban theories have limited resonance not because they are deficient in their own terms or cannot be made commensurable with one another, but because they are not articulated effectively to 'non-theorists'. This begs some questions about the relationship between theory and political debate and practice. The section therefore asks whether contemporary theories engage effectively in critiques of – or, indeed, justifications for – current urban social, economic, and political conditions and the way they are reproduced or changed and, if so, how theorists perform these roles in practice. A final section then turns to the question of whether the approaches examined in Chapters 3–6, for all their diversity, suggest the development of a new urban agenda. It asks whether theories help us anticipate the future functions, forms and experiences of cities and the major issues and conflicts that will arise from current development paths or, alternatively, whether the nature of 'the urban agenda' differs depending upon which theory we consider.

The performance of theories

During the broad period covered by the literatures examined in Chapters 3–6, the world became more urbanised and its urban areas became more interrelated and more differentiated. To reuse the word we borrowed in Chapter 2, it became spikier. It would be difficult to argue that the material examined in the last four chapters does not enable readers to understand key aspects of that spikiness, the way it is produced and reproduced, at both inter- and intra-urban scales, why variations occur, and the implications that are seen to flow from various theory-driven interpretations of change. In that sense, a growing volume of relaxed urban theories has done a reasonable job of grappling with what we see as a key feature of the emerging urbanised world. At the same time, however, it would be hard to claim that recent developments in urban theory have produced much in the way of overarching, synthetic accounts of urban 'spikiness'. Rather, they have used a variety of methodologies to present more or less empirically evidenced accounts of its causes and/or consequences for or within particular types of urban settlement, in certain respects, over various time periods.

As was the case during the longer-run evolution of urban theory traced in Chapter 2, no one set of concepts or methods dominated this later period. Whilst there was a notable revival in positivist approaches, as evidenced most clearly by the (re)discovery of the importance of agglomeration by a new generation of neo-classical economists and the reinvigoration of spatial economics, it is also possible to trace the continued influence of other traditions over later work. Thus, for example, the urban political economy literature examined in Chapter 4 was clearly rooted in the pluralist and elite theory approaches that dominated the earlier community power debate. Similarly, the concern with culture and 'difference' that pervades much of the ostensibly postmodern urban research covered in Chapters 3 and 6 links back, in many ways, to humanistic geography, and the ethnographic tradition established by the Chicago School. Just as clearly, the literature on urban neo-liberalism that was examined in Chapter 3 can be traced back to the radical approaches of the 1970s and extends the realist approach favoured, in particular, by neo-Marxist work.

In throwing light upon myriad aspects of urban change, many of the theoretical approaches we examined effectively attempted to resolve perennial structure–agency and place–process dilemmas largely by privileging one particular understanding of what drives (or, indeed, prevents) change over all others. Thus, for example, new economic geographers were found to accord primacy to 'new' agglomeration forces in a purportedly knowledge-driven economy, whilst a new generation of critical political economists accorded analytical priority to the notion of neo-liberalism and processes of ostensible neo-liberalisation. Feminist urban theory, meanwhile, gave its customary primary emphasis to the notion of patriarchy and the ways in which it is given tangible form within urban life. In the best examples of work along these lines, theoretical propositions have been developed around a core concept – agglomeration, neo-liberalism, patriarchy – and empirical work has been employed to test the explanatory power of related hypotheses. Critiques of such approaches then tend to focus upon whether the core concept is as important as the theorist claims, whether empirical inquiry is genuinely based upon open, refutable hypotheses, as opposed to the selective use of evidence to support preordained positions, and the robustness of the method-ologies employed to generate and analyse results. The main focus of theoretical dispute therefore tends to be whether the underlying structures or key processes that are considered to be critical by particular theorists possess adequate explan-atory power. Concerns with the importance of agency and places are generally seen as second-order issues.

Postmodern theory, at least in its strong form, is the main exception to this rule in so far as its adherents refuse to accept that any one set of structures or processes can claim analytical superiority or precedence when it comes to understanding contemporary urbanisation and urban experiences. In that sense, postmodern approaches effectively accord greater explanatory power to agency and place. Whereas the 'grand narratives' they criticise involved the destruction of space by time – that is, they assumed all places to be involved in a single developmental journey, irrespective of the stage they might have reached at any one time – postmodern theory involves the destruction of time by space. In other words, it emphasises difference and discontinuity and rejects any assumption that experiences of, or within, cities necessarily converge over time.

It is understandable that many theorists found the notion of postmodernity attractive, precisely because it questioned the privileging of certain dominant 'ways of seeing' and created space for alternative viewpoints, including those that are, or can be argued to be, associated with the urban life experiences of non-powerful groups. As noted in Chapters 3 and 6, however, a case for theo-retical pluralism is difficult to establish unless it simultaneously de-privileges *all* viewpoints. The postmodern rejection of 'grand narratives' is therefore inescap-ably bound up with the tendency to lapse into a relativism that is ultimately no more supportive of previously ignored ways of seeing than was the case within modernity.

The commensurability of theories

Given its radical scepticism about grand narratives, postmodern theory is also associated with the strongest, albeit negative, position in relation to the com-mensurability of different theoretical approaches. At least in its stronger version, it effectively argues that theories are inherently incommensurable and that it is not possible to weigh the truth claims of theories against one another. Alternative positions are eminently possible on the basis of the review we undertook in Chapters 3–6, but it is hard to deny that the possibility of using theories *in com-bination* in order to achieve greater analytical purchase remains a significant challenge that urban theorists find difficult to face.

It is easier to contemplate when theorists are prepared to concede that they find it hard to make claims for the universality of their analyses. We saw in Chapter 3, for example, how certain North American urban political economists accepted, explicitly or at least tacitly, that their understanding about the formation of urban regimes and growth coalitions was, in certain key respects, ethnocentric, and how this had led to comparative work that effectively tried to take the US out of US urban political economy. Even in this case, though, it was rare that comparative work was deliberately situated within a broader, more universal, conceptual approach that could enable cross-national variation in framework conditions to be accounted for more effectively.

If this apparent reluctance to combine theories that operate at different levels of abstraction holds true even in the case of approaches that have generated significant cross-national interest, it is easy to see how the challenge of making theories commensurable would be harder still when theorists make some sort of claim for universality. To give a further example from Chapter 3, one of the conclusions that might be drawn from the discussion about the growth, cross-nationally, of inter-urban disparities is that a more penetrating analysis of its causes, consequences and implications might fruitfully draw upon a better fusion of new economic geography literatures and insights from accounts based upon the notion of urban neo-liberalism. No such fusion has been attempted, however, largely because the theories in question exist in parallel conceptual universes and are guarded jealously by warring tribes. The question how a theoretical hybrid might be constructed that could test the truth claims of both has therefore not been posed.

Were the prospects for combining theoretical perspectives ever to be explored in a more determined way, they would generate some challenging questions for methodology and the benefits that might be derived from utilising mixed methods. We saw in Chapter 6, for example, how the impact of 'the cultural turn' on certain themes within urban studies resulted in an almost exclusive reliance upon qualitative methods, leading to detailed descriptions of 'exotic' urban practices, ranging from S&M parties to graffiti tagging, the behaviour of men seeking paid sex and community gardening festivals. Whilst such studies certainly provided insight into everyday lives and show how urban space is made or claimed, they were found to provide few insights into the way vertical dimensions of inequality intersect with horizontal dimensions of difference. In this case, it seems clear that fetishism with respect to qualitative methods is based on a misunderstanding of systematic quantitative methods, which tend to be dismissed as positivist (and therefore inherently conservative). What remains largely unexplored, as a result, is how quantitative and qualitative methods could be combined more effectively to give theories of intra-urban inequality and the way they are expressed spatially a significantly stronger empirical base.

Theory, politics and practice

When dealing with the question of what urban theory is good for, we might have added that theorists themselves rarely feel the need to answer. Neither do they always strive to set out their view of 'what should be done' in respect of the particular issues in which they are interested. It is perfectly adequate, for some, to throw useful conceptual light on those issues, to clarify and explain, and to leave others to grapple with – and even to take on the task of providing practical interpretations of – the implications of their observations. As we have already noted, this can be the source of some frustration to politicians, policy-makers and practitioners, for whom 'what is to be done' is invariably the starting point for analysis rather than an optional extra that might follow upon conceptual work.

It is not necessarily a weakness of urban theory that it often leaves decision-makers with some work to do before they can think about using theoretical insights to practical effect. At best, this is a misunderstanding about what theory is for. At worst, it can reflect laziness or dismissiveness on the part of decision-makers who would ideally prefer to receive – or at least buy – neatly packaged and simple answers to what are invariably complex questions and to absolve themselves of responsibility for generating and interpreting evidence. Given the breadth of interests and approaches we have found even in a selective review of the field, it would also be unrealistic to expect that the body of urban theory associated with a particular period in time could point unambiguously to particular forms of political analysis, discreet party programmes or specific policy prescriptions.

This last observation does not apply, though, to individual theorists whose work, by its very nature, tends to be relatively deep and specialised and hence, in principle, to be a potentially fruitful source of inspiration and ideas for politicians, policy-makers and practitioners. Notwithstanding that claims by academics that their work is 'value-free' and hence effectively 'above politics' are taken less seriously than ever, there are important reasons why theorists, even if they are tempted, often avoid becoming overly associated with particular parties and political programmes or the policy approaches they favour. The first reflects the mundane fact that parties in power change and policy positions shift in ways that can leave the practical prescriptions of theorists isolated and out of favour. Given the way that funding for urban research tends to gravitate to academics who are seen, at any point in time, as independent and authoritative by funding bodies, the appearance of political non-alignment and objectivity is a precious commodity to theorists who wish to engage with political and policy processes and retain their reputation for integrity and their commitment to a spirit of critical inquiry.

For these reasons, and because a genuinely open-ended approach to ideas and the implications of research is not easily made compatible with the inevitably crude 'bundling' of ideas and approaches within party programmes, very close and overt relationships between theorists – as opposed to academic 'policy advisers' – and practitioners of various stripes are comparatively rare. At the same time, though, theoretical developments continue to inform the perceptions and choices of practitioners. The question, therefore, is how. And the answer, unsurprisingly, is 'in various ways', depending upon the preferences and choices of theorists and the contexts within which they work.

Three alternative ways in which theorists might influence or try to influence political debate and policy agendas can be illustrated by theorists whose work is covered in our review. In none of these examples is it the case that academics sacrifice their objectivity and independence in order to influence policy debate and practice. Nonetheless the models they provide challenge some of the more simplistic assumptions that are sometimes made about the need to 'make theory relevant'. The most traditional way in which theory is expected to inform prac-tice is through influencing the climate of opinion such that politicians' and practitioners' views of reality, and of cause and effect, are changed. Sassen's work on global cities is one case in point, although there is reason to suspect that the level of exposure it achieved in non-academic circles is based at least as much on misunderstanding – and on an interest, by decision-makers, in how cities can 'become global' – as on an appreciation of her key messages, none of which suggest that becoming a global city can be achieved by acts of will or that global city status is an unalloyed good. A more interesting, and probably more typical, example of this mode of academic operation can be found in the work of Manuel Castells.

The evolution of Castells' thinking, covered in Chapters 2 and 3, is interesting in this respect because it illustrates that theorists, as distinct from the theories with which they are associated at any one time, are not necessarily consistent but implicitly make judgements about what forms of analysis 'fit' most effec-tively the times in which they write. Castells' perspective on the urban world, along with the methods he adopted and the evidence he utilised to support his arguments, changed radically over the course of his career. Although what caused these conceptual transitions to occur is not always made explicit in his writings, it is nonetheless evident that what appear, on the surface, to be substan-tially different, and mutually incompatible, certainties about the urban world reflect a steady evolution in his approach to how theory should be produced, what role it plays in empirical research, and what are the major factors underly-ing urban change.

In his earliest work, Castells was an unrepentant structuralist who rejected empirical inquiry in favour of an approach that claimed to distinguish science from ideology and implicitly put faith, in terms of 'real world' change, in a revolutionary, vanguardist politics, armed with the 'right' analysis, that could prosecute the class struggle, and achieve an extension of socialised consumption, by bringing together 'struggles' based on the workplace and the home. Castells Mk II, by contrast (see Chapter 2), having developed an appreciation of the limits of structuralist arguments to process of social change and turned to empirical work on the development of urban social movements, adopted a more pluralistic understanding of what supports 'progressive' urban change and came out in favour of cultural movements, rather than right-thinking political parties, as the mechanism through which 'urban meaning' might be transformed in the longer term. Castells Mark III, by further contrast, was far more pessimistic about the prospects for radical transformation in the conditions of capitalist urbanisation and developed arguments about urban change that bordered on technological determinism.

In each of his evolutionary guises, Castells maintained a keen interest in the mechanisms of urban change but largely limited himself to scholarly analysis – albeit of very different sorts – and academic commentary. This approach is subtly different from that of, for example, Ed Glaeser, whose scholarly work has been central to the reinvigoration of spatial economics but who has supplemented his academic output with a range of work intended to reach non-academic audiences more directly. His *Triumph of the City* (2011), for example, whilst clearly drawing upon the insights generated by his scholarly articles, is an impressionistic work of urban economic history that attempts to reach out to a general audience. He has also been a prodigious columnist for a variety of popular and lay publications in the US on topical urban issues and has used his columns to rehearse conclusions formed on the basis of his scholarly work in ways that contribute directly to contemporary policy debate.

A third, archetypal model of popular engagement is exemplified by Richard Florida, whose work on the 'geography of talent' is the subject of significant academic controversy but is seen by many policy-makers and practitioners as a potentially authoritative source of evidence for decision-making that can support economic growth. Whether they are right to see this potential in Florida's work or not, policy-makers and/or their sponsors, should they be able to mobilise the necessary resources, have the option of securing commercial advice from the Creative Class Group, the company created by Florida to provide practical support for those who find his arguments persuasive.

Our purpose in drawing attention to these rather different models of how urban theory informs practice is not to favour one over another. Neither is it to suggest that they are typical of the way in which those urban theorists who are interested in informing 'real world' debate and choices realise such an aspiration. Indeed, the reality for those who do not achieve the level of exposure that

Castells, Glaeser and Florida have, in very different ways, is rather more mundane: a seminar or conference appearance here, a research commission or policy briefing there. The key point we wish to make is that in none of these examples is there a suggestion, as critics sometimes suggest, of theoretical work being compromised by the search for, or achievement of, societal influence. But neither is there much support for the increasingly fashionable view, outside academia, that there is, or should be, an unbroken line that connects social scientific scholarship to publication, through dissemination activity and onto societal impact.

A new urban agenda?

We introduced our review of contemporary urban theory in Chapter 2 by expressing scepticism about whether the age of modernity was at an end. We did so because we find it hard to believe that the spread of industrialisation and urbanisation that has been triggered by the intensification of globalising processes represents a clean break with the faith in freedom, progress, rationality and science that are taken to characterise modernity. Modernity, it seems to us, is ultimately a teleological project that affirms the perfectability of human life and anticipates an end point to which the course of history is tending. That this end point is neither clearly specified nor agreed is rather less important than the notion, embedded within the idea of modernity, that barriers to 'progress', however they are understood, can be surmounted. Such faith appears to be as important a part of contemporary industrialisation and urbanisation as it was at the time of the original industrial revolution. It also appears to inform the vast majority of new urban theory.

This is not to argue that the future of the project of modernity is clearly laid out or will necessarily follow historical precedent. Seen in the broadest terms, the model of development that has been associated with the globalisation of capitalism has proven remarkably consistent over time. Industrialisation and urbanisation have tended to be associated with growing material wealth, an increasingly sophisticated division of labour, the development of an educated, assertive middle class and self-organisation within the workforce, both of which have found political expression and led to pressures for the socialisation of the costs of human reproduction. It may be that this model is beginning to break down and that the development models of China and India, in particular, will take a different form that will have serious implications for the old developed as well as the newly developed world. It may be, too, that 'ways of seeing' that give analytical priority to human life will prove to be unsustainable in the face of threats of environmental catastrophe and that less human-centred approaches, or at least ones that reframe the way that 'development' is valued, will be essential.

We do not pretend to have a crystal ball that gives us privileged insights into the future of a bewilderingly complex urbanised world or enables us to map out a path that future urban theories should take. Neither, we suspect, does anyone else who is or has been active within the field of urban theory. Rather than speak of a new urban agenda as if there were some obvious template that could be set out and followed, then, we prefer to conclude this review with a number of more modest observations about how some of the limitations we have identified within contemporary urban theory might be addressed. The key to this, we feel, is the development of a more relational approach to the understanding of urban phenomena that encompasses four key strands: the choice of units of analysis, comparitivism, interdisciplinarity and falsifiability.

With respect to the first of these, we have seen that the development of complex, extended urban forms – whether we refer to city-regions, mega-regions, megalopolises or some other descriptor – has meant that administrative boundaries have less and less relevance either to the way urban life is lived or to understandings of the connectedness between urban phenomena. Whilst there have been a number of efforts to produce statistics for spatial areas within which one or more cities have an important influence, there is still much evidence that 'boundaryism' bedevils many forms of urban analysis. It has contributed, for example, to distinctions between 'cities' and 'suburbs' continuing to play a central role in urban theory in the US even though the implicit contrast these terms suggest between a 'core' and a 'periphery' has long since ceased to apply.

Better comparisons and contrasts between urban areas depend upon a better resolution to the 'units of analysis' problem than have been developed thus far. Such a resolution is not, however, entirely dependent upon better statistics. It is also a conceptual challenge which requires theorists, whatever the 'boundaries' of the spatial areas they concentrate upon, to think about how the 'inside' is produced through interaction with the 'outside'. As Scott and Storper (2014) rightly observe:

> the city is to the space-economy as a mountain is to the wider topography in which it is contained. In neither the case of the city nor the mountain can a definite line be drawn that separates it from its wider context, but in both instances, certain differences of intensity and form make it reasonable and pragmatically meaningful to treat each of them as separable entities.

The analogy is imperfect in the sense that what happens in any one mountain range does not affect another which may be thousands of miles away. Nonetheless an urban theory that recognises the existence of mountains, the way in which they interact with one another, and the fact that they each have an internal topography, is crucial to making sense of the spiky world in which we now live. Such an understanding is as important to avoiding some of the pitfalls of area fetishism that has limited the analysis of neighbourhood effects, at a micro scale, as it is to understanding interactions between the local and the global in producing hybrid forms of urbanism at the macro scale.

Improvements in comparative methods are also critical to understanding hybrid forms of global urbanism. The focus of this book has largely been upon theories produced within, and observations drawn from studies of, what has generally been referred to latterly as the Global North. It is clear, however, that the processes of economic modernisation and urbanisation that are shaping the emerging urban world are dominated by changes in the Global South. Traditional ways of framing this broad distinction between different areas of the globe, based upon notions of 'exploitation' and 'dependence', offered one route into understanding interrelationships between processes of urban change and the mechanisms that connect Global North and Global South development patterns. Any regularities in these patterns that might have existed are rapidly breaking down, however, to the extent that it is increasingly difficult to make such stark distinctions. In a world where at least some Global South cities have Global North characteristics, and vice versa, it will become increasingly important that urban theory develops the means to conduct more structured comparative inquiry. This, in turn, is likely to mean that greater account will need to be taken of ways in which urban change happens in what is now called the Global South in such a way that it feeds into genuinely global urban theories rather than gets categorised as an exotic exception to 'Global North theories'.

A more thoroughgoing interdisciplinarity needs to be part of the enterprise of constructing better conceptual platforms for comparative work. There is something of a paradox, here, that whilst the field of urban studies is inherently cross-disciplinary, in the sense that is nurtured by work in the urban sub-fields of all the major social sciences, there is still a tendency for debates on urban theory to take place largely within, rather than across, disciplines. We do not underestimate the challenges involved in creating better dialogue between urban subdisciplines and arriving at some sort of consensus about how mixed-methods approaches could improve the analytical and prescriptive power of urban theory. What seems clear from our review, however, is that conceptual innovation tends to occur at the boundaries between disciplines, rather than at their 'cores', and that a willingness on the part of urban theorists to expose themselves to different ways of seeing is more likely to generate the challenges that can extend interdisciplinary endeavour than remaining within the confines of single-disciplinary approaches to understanding urban change.

The final plea we would make is that urban theories should be empirically testable and falsifiable. We have little sympathy with the antagonism of postmodernists to synthetic theory and 'grand narratives'. However, we do detect a tendency amongst theorists who are brave enough to attempt universalistic explanations of urban phenomena to create conceptual boxes into which empirical material can be filed rather than to develop hypotheses that can be confirmed or falsified through careful methodological design and good, forensic empirical testing. If only for the reason that non-falsifiable propositions generate more heat than light and are largely unpersuasive to non-believers, we feel that the potential of urban theory to have an impact upon real world decision-making would be improved if non-specialists could be convinced that theorists are prepared to be proven wrong.

Greater clarity about units of urban analysis and a commitment to more comparative, interdisciplinary work that tests falsifiable hypotheses appear to us to hold out greater potential for future urban theory than the pessimism, in the face of the bewildering complexity and differentiation, that we detect in postmodern approaches. In and of themselves they would, of course, do little to guarantee that urban theory is seen, outside academia, as vital and worthwhile. For that to happen, there needs to be a more realistic understanding, on the part of decision-makers, about what theory does and what theorists can provide. There is also a challenge to theorists, however, which would appear to be partly about humility and partly about ambition. Our review suggests urban theory has had, and continues to wield, significant influence over the way urban change has been understood in a variety of direct and indirect ways. Urban theorists, in effect, have a constantly evolving toolbox, unavailable to politicians, policy-makers or practitioners, which rarely fixes the particular problems that decision-makers face at any one point in time but enables them to think more carefully about the nature of the questions they ask and whether they are the right ones. The tools exist. All that is needed is the will to use them.

References

Abbott, P., & Wallace, C. (Eds.) (1997). *An Introduction to Sociology: Feminist perspectives* (2nd ed.). London: Routledge.

Abrams, P. (1982). *Historical Sociology*. Ithaca, NY: Cornell University Press.

Abu-Lughod, J. L. (1991). *Changing Cities: Urban sociology*. New York: HarperCollins.

Abu-Lughod, J. L. (1999). *New York, Chicago, Los Angeles: America's global cities*. Minneapolis: University of Minnesota Press

Aceska, A. (2013). *'We' and 'They' in a Divided City: Boundary-work and identity-formation in post-war Mostar, Bosnia-Herzegovina* (dissertation). Humboldt-Universität zu Berlin, Berlin.

Achilles, N. (1967). The development of the homosexual bar as an institution. In J. H. Gagnon & W. Simon (Eds.), *Sexual Deviance* (pp. 228–44). New York: Harper & Row.

Adler, S., & Brenner, J. (1992). Gender and space: Lesbians and gay men in the city. *International Journal of Urban and Regional Research*, 16, 24–34.

Agnew, J. A. (2010). Slums, ghettos, and urban marginality. *Urban Geography*, 31(2), 144–147.

Agustín, L. M. (2005). New research directions: The cultural study of commercial sex. *Sexualities*, 8(5), 618–31.

Albrow, M. (1996). *The Global Age: State and society beyond modernity*. Cambridge: Polity Press.

Aldrich, R. (2004). Homosexuality and the city: An historical overview. *Urban Studies*, 41(9), 1719–37.

Allport, G. W. (1979). *The Nature of Prejudice: The classic study of the roots of discrimination*. New York: Basic Books.

Alonso, W. (1960). The theory of urban land market. *Papers in Regional Science*, 6(1), 149–57.

Althusser, L. (1969). *For Marx*. London: Allen & Unwin.

Althusser, L., & Balibar, E. (1970). *Reading 'Capital'*. London: New Left Books.

Amin, A. (1989) Flexible specialisation and small firms in Italy: myths and realities, *Antipode*, 21(1), 13–34.

Amin, A. (Ed.) (1994) *Post-Fordism: A reader*, Oxford: Blackwell.

Amin, A. (2002). Spatialities of globalisation. *Environment and Planning A, 34*(3), 385–400.

Amin, A., & Malmberg, A. (1992). Competing structural and institutional influences on the geography of production in Europe. *Environment and Planning A, 24*, 401–16.

Amin, A., & Robins, K. (1990). The re-emergence of regional economies? The mythical geography of flexible accumulation. *Environment and Planning D: Society and Space, 8*(1), 7–34.

Amin, A., & Thrift, N. (Eds.) (1994). *Globalization, Institutions, and Regional Development in Europe*. Oxford: Oxford University Press.

Amin, A., & Thrift, N. (2002). *Cities: Reimagining the urban*. Cambridge: Polity Press.

Andersen, J. (2001). The politics of gambling and ambivalence: Struggles over urban policy in Copenhagen. *Geographische Zeitschrift, 89*(2/3), 135–44.

Anderson, E. (1990). *Streetwise: Race, class, and change in an urban community*. Chicago: University of Chicago Press.

Anderson, E. (2000). *Code of the Street: Decency, violence, and the moral life of the inner city*. London: Norton.

Anderson, N. (1923). *The Hobo: The sociology of the homeless man*. Chicago: University of Chicago Press.

Andersson, J. (2009). East End localism and urban decay: Shoreditch's re-emerging gay scene. *London Journal, 34*(1), 55–71.

Andrew, C. (1995). Getting women's issues on the municipal agenda: Violence against women. In J. A. Garber & R. S. Turner (Eds.), *Gender in Urban Research* (pp. 99–118). Thousand Oaks, CA: Sage.

Anthias, F. (2005). Social stratification and social inequality: Models of intersectionality and identity. In F. Devine, M. Savage, J. Scott, & R. Crompton (Eds.), *Rethinking Class: Cultures, identities & lifestyle* (pp. 24–45). Basingstoke: Palgrave Macmillan.

Anthias, F., & Yuval-Davis, N. (1992). *Racialised Boundaries: Race, nation, gender, colour and class and the anti-racist struggle*. London: Routledge.

Appadurai, A. (1996a). *Modernity at Large: Cultural dimensions of globalization*. Minneapolis: University of Minnesota Press.

Appadurai, A. (1996b [1990]). Disjuncture and difference in the global cultural economy. In A. Appadurai, *Modernity at Large*. Minneapolis: University of Minnesota Press.

Appleton, L. M. (1995). The gender regimes of American cities. In J. A. Garber & R. S. Turner (Eds.), *Gender in Urban Research* (pp. 44–59). Thousand Oaks, CA: Sage.

Arbaci, S. (2007). Ethnic segregation, housing systems and welfare regimes in Europe. *European Journal of Housing Policy, 7*(4), 401–33.

Armstrong, E. A. (2002). *Forging Gay Identities: Organizing sexuality in San Francisco, 1950–1994*. Chicago: University of Chicago Press.

Arnott, R., & McMillen, D. P. (2006). *A Companion to Urban Economics*. Oxford: Blackwell.

Ashton, J. (1992). *Healthy Cities*. Milton Keynes: Open University Press.

Ashworth, G., & Tunbridge, J. (1999). Old cities, new pasts: Heritage planning in selected cities of Central Europe. *GeoJournal, 49*(1), 105–16.

Atencio, M., Beal, B., & Wilson, C. (2009). The distinction of risk: Urban skateboarding, street habitus and the construction of hierarchical gender relations. *Qualitative Research in Sport and Exercise, 1*(1), 3–20.

Atkinson, R. (2006). Padding the bunker: Strategies of middle-class disaffiliation and colonisation in the city. *Urban Studies, 43*(4), 819–32.

Austin, J., & McCaffrey, A. (2002). Business leadership coalitions and public-private partnerships in American cities: A business perspective on regime theory. *Journal of Urban Affairs, 24*(1), 35–54.

Austin, J., & Willard, M. (Eds.) (1998). *Generations of Youth: Youth cultures and history in twentieth century America*. New York: New York University Press.

Axford, N., & Pinch, S. (1994). Growth coalitions and local economic development strategy in southern England: A case study of the Hampshire Development Association. *Political Geography, 13*(4), 344–60.

Aydalot, P., & Keeble, D. (Eds.) (1988). *High Technology Industry and Innovative Environments*. London: Routledge.

Bachrach, P., & Baratz, M. (1962). Two faces of power. *American Political Science Review, 56*, 947–52.

Bachrach, P., & Baratz, M. (1970). *Power and Poverty: Theory and practice*. Oxford: Oxford University Press.

Badcock, B. (1984). *Unfairly Structured Cities*. Oxford: Blackwell.

Bae, Y., & Sellers, J. M. (2007). Globalization, the developmental state and the politics of urban growth in Korea: A multilevel analysis. *International Journal of Urban and Regional Research, 31*(3), 543–60.

Bagguley, P., Mark-Lawson, J. & Shapiro, D. (1990). *Restructuring: Place, class and gender*. London: Sage.

Bahrdt, H. P. (1998). *Die moderne Großstadt: Soziologische Überlegungen zum Städtebau*. Opladen: Leske & Budrich.

Bailey, T., & Waldinger, R. (1991). Primary, secondary and enclave labour markets: A training systems approach. *American Sociological Review, 56*(4), 432–45.

Bailly, A., Jensen-Butler, C., & Leontidou, L. (1996). Changing cities: Restructuring, marginality and policies in urban Europe. *European Urban and Regional Studies, 2*(3), 161–76.

Banfield, E. C. (1966). *City Politics*. New York: Vintage.

Banfield, E. C. (1970). *The Unheavenly City: The nature and future of our urban crisis*. Boston: Little, Brown.

Banton, M. (1983). *Racial and Ethnic Competition*. Cambridge: Cambridge University Press.

Barwick, C. (2013). "'It is only because of the school. If it was not for the kids, we would have stayed here": Residential choice in the light of educational aspirations of the Turkish-German middle classes in Berlin. Paper presented at the RC21 Conference, Berlin, 31 August–2 September 2013.

Bassett, K., & Harloe, M. (1990). Swindon: The rise and decline of a growth coalition. In M. Harloe, C. G. Pickvance, & J. Urry (Eds.), *Place, Policy, and Politics: Do localities matter?* (pp. 42–61). London: Unwin Hyman.

Bauder, H. (2002). Neighbourhood effects and cultural exclusion. *Urban Studies, 39*(1), 85–93.

Bauman, Z. (1978). *Hermeneutics and Social Science: Approaches to understanding*. London: Hutchinson.

Beauregard, R. A. (1986). The chaos and complexity of gentrification. In N. Smith & P. Williams (Eds.), *Gentrification of the City* (pp. 11–23). Boston: Allen & Unwin.

Beauregard, R. A. (1996). City planning and the postwar regime in Philadelphia. In M. Lauria (Ed.), *Reconstructing Urban Regime Theory: Regulating urban politics in a global economy* (pp. 171–18). London: Sage.

Beauregard, R. A. (2010). The chaos and complexity of gentrification. In L. Lees, T. Slater, & E. K. Wyly (Eds.), *The Gentrification Reader* (pp. 11–23). London and New York: Routledge.

Beauregard, R. A., & Body-Gendrot, S. (Eds.) (1999). *The Urban Moment: Cosmopolitan essays on the late-20th-century city*. Thousand Oaks, CA: Sage.

Beavon, K. (1977). *Central Place Theory: A reinterpretation*. London: Longman.

Bech, H. (1997). *When Men Meet: Homosexuality and modernity*. Chicago: University of Chicago Press.

Beck, U. (2002). The cosmopolitan society and its enemies. *Theory, Culture & Society, 19*(1–2), 17–44.

Becker, J. E. de (1899). *The Nightless City or the History of the Yoshiwara Yūkwaku*. Yokohama: Z. P. Maruya.

Beemyn, B. (Ed.) (1997). *Creating a Place for Ourselves: Lesbian, gay, and bisexual community histories*. London: Routledge.

Bell, C., & Newby, H. (1971). *Community Studies*. London: Allen & Unwin.

Bell, C., & Newby, H. (Eds.) (1974). *The Sociology of Community: A selection of readings*. London: Frank Cass.

Bell, D. (1973). *The Coming of Post-industrial Society: A venture in social forecasting*. New York: Basic Books.

Bell, D., & Binnie, J. (2004). Authenticating queer space: Citizenship, urbanism and governance. *Urban Studies, 41*(9), 1807–20.

Bell, D., & Valentine, G. (Eds.) (1995). *Mapping Desire: Geographies of sexualities*. London: Routledge.

Bellair, P. E. (1997). Social interaction and community crime: Examining the importance of neighbor networks. *Criminology, 35*(4), 677–704.

Bellair, P. E. (2000). Informal surveillance and street crime: A complex relationship. *Criminology, 38*(1), 137–70.

Benhabib, S. (2002). *The Claims of Culture: Equality and diversity in the global era*. Princeton, NJ: Princeton University Press.

Benko, G., & Strohmayer, U. (1997). *Space and Social Theory: Interpreting modernity and postmodernity*. Oxford: Blackwell.

Berger, P. L., & Luckmann, T. (1966). *The Social Construction of Reality: A treatise in the sociology of knowledge*. New York: Anchor Books.

Berry, B. J. L. (1976). *Urbanization and Counterurbanization*. Beverly Hills, CA: Sage.

Berry, B. J. L. (1985). Islands of renewal in seas of decay. In P. E. Peterson (Ed.), *The new urban reality* (pp. 69–96). Washington, DC: Brookings Institution.

Betancourt, C. (2012). *Wieso – weshalb – wohin? Wohnbiographien als Instrument der sozialräumlichen Verdrängungsanalyse* (Bachelor's thesis. Humboldt-Universität zu Berlin, Berlin.

Betts, R. F., Ross, R., & Telkamp, G. J. (1985). *Colonial Cities: Essays on urbanism in a colonial context*. Dordrecht: Kluwer Academic.

Bezmez, D. (2008). The politics of urban waterfront regeneration: The case of Haliç (the Golden Horn), Istanbul. *International Journal of Urban and Regional Research, 32*(4), 815–40.

Bhaskar, R. (1993). Philosophy of social science. In W. Outhwaite & T. B. Bottomore (Eds.), *The Blackwell Dictionary of Twentieth-century Social Thought* (pp. 469–71). Oxford: Blackwell.

Binken, S. and Blokland, T. (2012). Why repressive politics towards urban youths do not make streets safe: four hypotheses. *The Sociological Review. 60*(2): 292–311.

Binnie, J. (2009). Sexuality, the erotic and geography: Epistemology, methodology and pedagogy. In K. Browne, J. Lim, & G. Brown (Eds.), *Geographies of Sexualities. Theory, practices, and politics* (pp. 29–38). Aldershot: Ashgate.

Binnie, J., & Skeggs, B. (2004). Cosmopolitan knowledge and the production and consumption of sexualized space: Manchester's gay village. *Sociological Review, 52*(1), 39–61.

BIS (UK Department of Business, Innovation and Skills) (2010). Understanding local growth. *BIS Economics Paper No. 7*. London: BIS.

Bish, R. L., & Ostrom, V. (1973). *Understanding Urban Government: Metropolitan reform reconsidered*. Washington, DC: American Enterprise Institute for Public Policy Research.

Bjørgo, T., & Witte, R. (1993). *Racist Violence in Europe*. Basingstoke: Macmillan.

Blackmar, E. (2006). Appropriating 'the commons': The tragedy of property rights discourse. In S. Low & N. Smith (Eds.), *The Politics of Public Space* (pp. 49–80). London: Routledge.

Blaikie, N. W. H. (1993). *Approaches to Social Enquiry*. Oxford: Polity.

Blair, T. L. (1974). *The International Urban Crisis*. St. Albans: Paladin.

Blokland, T. (2003a). *Urban Bonds*. Cambridge: Polity Press.

Blokland, T. (2003b). Ethnic complexity: Routes to discriminatory repertoires in an inner-city neighbourhood. *Ethnic and Racial Studies, 26*(1), 1–24.

Blokland, T. (2008a). 'You got to remember you live in public housing': Place-making in an American housing project. *Housing, Theory and Society, 25*(1), 31–46.

Blokland, T. (2008b). From the outside looking in: A 'European' perspective on the ghetto. *City & Community, 7*(4), 372–7.

Blokland, T. (2008c). Gardening with a little help from your (middle class) friends: Bridging social capital across race and class in a mixed neighbourhood. In T. Blokland & M. Savage (Eds.), *Networked Urbanism. Social capital in the city* (pp. 147–70). Aldershot: Ashgate.

Blokland, T. (2009). *Oog voor elkaar: Veiligheidsbeleving en sociale controle in de grote stad*. Amsterdam: Amsterdam University Press.

Blokland, T.V. & Nast, J. (2014). From public familiarity to comfort zone: The relevance of absent ties for belonging in mixed neighbourhoods. Forthcoming in: *International Journal of Urban and Regional Research*.

Blokland, T. V., & Soenen, R. (2004). Veilig met de tram: Een etnografisch perspectief op veiligheid in het openbaar vervoer. *B&M: Tijdschrift voor beleid, politiek en maatschappij, 31*(3), 173–84.

Blokland, T., & van Eijk, G. (2010). Do people who like diversity practice diversity in neighbourhood life? Neighbourhood use and the social networks of 'diversity-seekers' in a mixed neighbourhood in the Netherlands. *Journal of Ethnic and Migration Studies, 36*(2), 313–32.

Bluestone, B. & Harrison, B. (1982). *The Deindustrialisation of America*. New York: Basic Books.

Blumer, M. (1984). *The Chicago School of Sociology: Institutionalization, diversity, and the rise of sociological research*. Chicago: University of Chicago Press.

Body-Gendrot, S. (2000). *The Social Control of Cities? A comparative perspective*. Oxford: Blackwell.

Body-Gendrot, S., & Beauregard, R. A. (1999). Imagined cities, engaged citizens. In R. A. Beauregard & S. Body-Gendrot (Eds.), *The Urban Moment. Cosmopolitan essays on the late-20th-century city* (pp. 3–24). Thousand Oaks, CA: Sage.

Boland, P. (2007). Unpacking the theory-policy interface of local economic development: An analysis of Cardiff and Liverpool. *Urban Studies*, 44(5), 1019–39.

Bolay, J.-C., & Rabinovich, A. (2004). Intermediate cities in Latin America: Risks and opportunities of coherent urban development. *Cities*, 21(5), 407–21.

Bolt, G., Burgers, J., & van Kempen, R. (1998). On the social significance of spatial location: Spatial segregation and social inclusion. *Netherlands Journal of Housing and the Built Environment*, 13(1), 83–95.

Bondi, L. (2010). Gender divisions and gentrification: A critique. In L. Lees, T. Slater, & E. K. Wyly (Eds.), *The Gentrification Reader* (pp. 263–71). London: Routledge.

Bondi, L., & Rose, D. (2003). Constructing gender, constructing the urban: A review of Anglo-American feminist urban geography. *Gender, Place & Culture: A Journal of Feminist Geography*, 10(3), 229–45.

Borer, M. I. (2006). The location of culture: The urban culturalist perspective. *City & Community*, 5(2), 173–97.

Bott, E. (1957). *Family and Social Networks: Roles, norms, and external relationships in ordinary urban families*. London: Tavistock.

Bourassa, S. C. (1993). The rent gap debunked. *Urban Studies*, 30(10), 1731–44.

Bourdieu, P. (1977). *Outline of a Theory of Practice*. Cambridge: Cambridge University Press.

Bourdieu, P. (1984). *Distinction: A social critique of the judgement of taste*. Cambridge, MA: Harvard University Press.

Bourdieu, P. (1999). Site effects. In P. Bourdieu (Ed.), *The Weight of the World: Social suffering in contemporary society* (pp. 123–9). Stanford, CA: Stanford University Press.

Bourgois, P. (1995). *In Search of Respect: Selling crack in El Barrio*. Cambridge: Cambridge University Press.

Bourne, L. (1993). The demise of gentrification? A commentary and prospective view. *Urban Geography*, 13(1), 95–107.

Bouthilette, A. M. (1994). Gentrification by gay male communities: A case study of Toronto's Cabbagetown. In S. Whittle (Ed.), *The Margins of the City. Gay men's urban lives* (pp. 65–83). Aldershot: Arena.

Brake, M. (2002). *Comparative Youth Culture: The sociology of youth cultures and youth subcultures in America, Britain and Canada* (reprint). London: Routledge.

Braudel, F. (1986). *L'identité de la France*. Paris: Arthaud-Flammarion.

Brenner, N. (2004). *New State Spaces: Urban governance and the rescaling of statehood*. Oxford: Oxford University Press.

Brenner, N. & Keil, R. (Eds.) (2006). *The Global City Reader*. London: Routledge.

Bridge, G., & Watson, S. (Eds.) (2010). *The Blackwell City Reader* (2nd ed.). Oxford: Wiley-Blackwell.

Bridge, G., & Watson, S. (Eds.) (2011). *The New Blackwell Companion to the City*. Oxford: Wiley-Blackwell.

Brie, M. (2004). The Moscow political regime: The emergence of a new urban political machine. In A. B. Evans & V. Gel'man (Eds.), *The Politics of Local Government in Russia* (pp. 203–34). Lanham, MD: Rowman & Littlefield.

Briggs, X. de S. (1997). Moving up versus moving out: Neighbourhood effects in housing mobility programs. *Housing Policy Debate*, 8(1), 195–234.

Brooks-Gunn, J., Duncan, G. J., & Aber, J. L. (Eds.) (1997). *Neighborhood Poverty: Context and consequences for children*. New York: Russell Sage Foundation.

Brophy, P. C., & Smith, R. (1997). Mixed-income housing. Factors for success. *CityScape. A Journal of Policy Development and Research*, 3(2), 3–31.

Brotchie, J. (Ed.) (1995). *Cities in Competition: Productive and sustainable cities for the 21st century*. Melbourne: Longman Australia.

Browne, K. (2009). Drag queens and drab dykes: Deploying and deploring femininities. In K. Browne, J. Lim, & G. Brown (Eds.), *Geographies of Sexualities. Theory, practices, and politics* (pp. 113–24). Aldershot: Ashgate.

Browne, K., Lim, J., & Brown, G. (Eds.) (2009). *Geographies of Sexualities: Theory, practices, and politics*. Aldershot: Ashgate.

Browning, C. R. (2002). The span of collective efficacy: Extending social disorganization theory to partner violence. *Journal of Marriage and Family*, 64(4), 833–50.

Browning, C. R., & Cagney, K. (2002). Neighborhood structural disadvantage, collective efficacy, and self-rated physical health in an urban setting. *Journal of Health and Social Behavior*, 43(4), 383–99.

Browning, C. R., Dietz, R. D., & Feinberg, S. L. (2004). The paradox of social organization: Networks, collective efficacy, and violent crime in urban neighborhoods. *Social Forces*, 83, 503–34.

Bruegmann, R. (2011). The causes of sprawl. In R. T. LeGates & F. Stout (Eds.), *The City Reader* (5th ed., pp. 211–21). London: Routledge.

Bryant, C. G. A. (1985). *Positivism in Social Theory and Research. Theoretical traditions in the social sciences*. New York: St. Martin's Press.

Bryson, V. (1992). *Feminist Political Theory: An introduction*. Basingstoke: Macmillan.

Buck, N. (2001). Identifying neighbourhood effects on social exclusion. *Urban Studies, 38*(12), 2251–75.

Bulmer, M. (1986). *The Chicago School of Sociology: Institutionalization, diversity, and the rise of sociological research.* Chicago: University of Chicago Press.

Bunge, W. (1962). *Theoretical Geography.* Lund: CWK Gleerup.

Burgers, J. (1996). No polarization in Dutch cities? Inequality in a corporatist country. *Urban Studies, 33*(1), 99–110.

Burgess, E. W. (1924). The growth of the city: An introduction to a research project. *Publications of the American Sociological Society, 18,* 85–97.

Burgess, E. W. (1925). The growth of the city. In R. E. Park, E. W. Burgess, & R. D. McKenzie (Eds.), *The City.* Chicago: University of Chicago Press.

Burgess, E. W. (1927). The determination of gradients in the growth of the city. *Publications of the American Sociological Society, 21,* 178–84.

Burns, P. F. (2002). The intergovernmental regime and public policy in Hartford, Connecticut. *Journal of Urban Affairs, 24*(1), 55–73.

Burton, L. M., & Jarrett, R. L. (2000). In the mix, yet on the margins: The place of families in urban neighborhood and child development research. *Journal of Marriage and Family, 62*(4), 1114–35.

Butler, J. (1990). *Gender Trouble: Feminism and the subversion of identity.* London: Routledge.

Butler, J. (1993). *Bodies That Matter: On the discursive limits of 'sex'.* New York: Routledge.

Butler, J. (1997). *The Psychic Life of Power: Theories in subjection.* Stanford, CA: Stanford University Press.

Butler, T. (2003). Living in the bubble: Gentrification and its 'others' in North London. *Urban Studies, 40*(12), 2469–86.

Butler, T., & Hamnett, C. (2007). The geography of education: Introduction. *Urban Studies, 44*(7), 1161–74.

Butler, T., & Smith, D. (2007). Conceptualising the sociospatial diversity of gentrification: 'To boldly go' into contemporary gentrified spaces, the 'final frontier'? *Environment and Planning A, 39*(1), 2–9.

Byrne, N. T. (1978). Sociotemporal considerations of everyday life suggested by an empirical study of the bar milieu. *Urban Life, 6*(4), 417–38.

Cabrero Mendoza, E. (2005). *Acción municipal y desarrollo local: ¿cuáles son las claves del éxito?* Mexico City: Centro de Investigación y Docencia Económicas.

Caldeira, T. P. R. (2013). Fortified enclaves: The new urban segregation. In J. Lin & C. Mele (Eds.), *The Urban Sociology Reader* (2nd ed., pp. 405–13). London: Routledge.

Calhoun, C. J. (Ed.) (1992). *Habermas and the Public Sphere.* Cambridge, MA: MIT Press.

Calhoun, C. J. (Ed.) (1994). *Social Theory and the Politics of Identity*. Oxford: Blackwell.

Calthorpe, P., & Fulton, W. B. (2001). *The Regional City: Planning for the end of sprawl*. Washington, DC: Island Press.

Cameron, S. (2004). Space, risk and opportunity: The evolution of paid sex markets. *Urban Studies, 41*(9), 1643–57.

Cannato, V. J. (2001). *The Ungovernable City: John Lindsay and his struggle to save New York*. New York: Basic Books.

Carter, H. (1995). *The Study of Urban Geography* (4th ed.). London: Arnold.

Casey, M. E. (2009). The queer unwanted and their undesirable 'otherness'. In K. Browne, J. Lim, & G. Brown (Eds.), *Geographies of Sexualities: Theory, practices, and politics* (pp. 125–36). Aldershot: Ashgate.

Castells, M. (1972). *La question urbaine. Textes à l'appui*. Paris: Maspero.

Castells, M. (1974). *La questione urbana*. Biblioteca Marsilio. le scienze della nuova società architettura e urbanistica: Vol. 24. Venice: Marsilio.

Castells, M. (1977). *The Urban Question: A Marxist approach. Social structure and social change: Vol. 1*. Cambridge, MA: MIT Press.

Castells, M. (1978). *City, Class, and Power. Sociology, politics, and cities*. London: Macmillan.

Castells, M. (1983). *The City and the Grassroots*. London: Edward Arnold.

Castells, M. (1989). *The Informational City: Information technology, economic restructuring, and the urban-regional process*. Oxford: Blackwell.

Castells, M. (1996). *The Rise of the Network Society*. Oxford: Blackwell.

Castells, M. (1997). *The Power of Identity*. Oxford: Blackwell.

Castells, M. (1998). *End of Millennium*. Oxford: Blackwell.

Castells, M., Godard, F., & Balanowski, V. (1974). *Monopolville. Analyse des rapports entre l'entreprise, l'état et l'urbain à partir d'une enquête sur la croissance industrielle et urbaine de la région de Dunkerque*. Paris and The Hague: Mouton.

Castells, M., & Hall, P. (1994). *Technopoles of the World: The making of twenty-first-century industrial complexes*. London: Routledge.

Castells, M., & Murphy, K. (1982). Cultural identity and urban structure: The spatial organization of San Francisco's gay community. In N. I. Fainstein (Ed.), *Urban Policy Under Capitalism* (pp. 237–59). Thousand Oaks, CA: Sage.

Caulfield, J. (1989). Gentrification'and desire. *Canadian Review of Sociology/ Revue canadienne de sociologie, 26*(4), 617–32.

Caulfield, J. (1991). Community power, public policy initiatives and the management of growth in Brisbane. *Urban Policy and Research, 9*(4), 209–19.

Cavan, S. (1963). Interactions in home territories. *Berkeley Journal of Sociology, 8*(1), 17–32.

Centner, R. (2008). Places of privileged consumption practices: Spatial capital, the dot-com habitus, and San Francisco's internet boom. *City & Community, 7*(3), 193–223.

Champion, A. G. (1991). *Counterurbanization*. London: Edward Arnold.

Champion, A. G. (2001). Urbanization, suburbanization, deurbanization and reurbanization. In R. Paddison (Ed.), *Handbook of Urban Studies* (pp. 143–61). London: Sage.

Charles, C. Z. (2003). The dynamics of racial residential segregation. *Annual Review of Sociology, 29*, 167–207.

Chatterton, P., & Hollands, R. (2002). Theorising urban playscapes: Producing, regulating and consuming youthful nightlife city spaces. *Urban Studies, 39*(1), 95–116.

Chien, S.-S., & Wu, F. (2011). The transformation of China's urban entrepreneurialism: The case study of the city of Kunshan. *Cross Current: East Asian History and Culture Review (online), 1*, 1–28.

Chiu, C. (2009). Contestation and conformity: Street and park skateboarding in New York City public space. *Space and Culture, 12*(1), 25–42.

Christaller, W., & Baskin, C. W. (1966). *Central Places in Southern Germany*. Englewood Cliffs, NJ: Prentice Hall.

Ciccone, A. (2002). Agglomeration effects in Europe, *European Economic Review, 46*(2), 213–27.

Clapson, M., & Hutchison, R. (2010). *Suburbanization in Global Society*. Bingley: Emerald.

Clark, E. (1987). *The Rent Gap and Urban Change: Case studies in Malmö 1860-1985*. Lund: Lund University Press.

Clark, E. (2010). The order and simplicity of gentrification – a political challenge. In L. Lees, T. Slater, & E. K. Wyly (Eds.), *The Gentrification Reader* (pp. 24–30). London: Routledge.

Clark, G. L. (1988). Review of the book *Urban Fortunes: The political economy of place*, by J. R. Logan & H. L. Molotch. *Political Geography Quarterly, 7*(4), 374–5.

Clark, T. N. (1994). *Urban Innovation: Creative strategies for turbulent times*. London: Sage.

Clark, W. A. V., & Dieleman, F. M. (2012). *Households and Housing: Choice and outcomes in the housing market*. New Brunswick, NJ: Transaction Publishers.

Clarke, M. (1974). On the concept of 'sub-culture'. *British Journal of Sociology, 25*(4), 428–441.

Clarke, S. E. (1990a). 'Precious' place: The local growth machine in an era of global restructuring. *Urban Geography, 11*(2), 185–93.

Clarke, S. E. (1990b). Review: The competitive city: The political economy of suburbia. By Mark Schneider The ecology of city policymaking. By Robert J. Waste. *Journal of Politics, 52*(3), 981–4.

Clavel, P. (1986). *The Progressive City: Planning and participation, 1969-1984*. New Brunswick, NJ: Rutgers University Press.

Clay, P. L. (1979). *Neighborhood Renewal*. Lexington, MA: Lexington Books.

Cloke, P., Philo, C., & Sadler, D. (1991). *Approaching Human Geography: An introduction to contemporary theoretical debates*. London: Paul Chapman.

Cloward, R. A., & Piven, F. F. (1975). *The Politics of Turmoil: Essays on poverty, race and the urban crisis*. New York: Vintage Books.

Coe, N. M., Kelly, P. F., & Yeung, H. W.-C. (2007). *Economic Geography: A contemporary introduction*. Oxford: Blackwell.

Cohen, D. A., Finch, B. K., Bower, A., & Sastry, N. (2006). Collective efficacy and obesity: The potential influence of social factors on health. *Social Science & Medicine, 62*(3), 769–78.

Cohen, P. (1999). *New Ethnicities, Old Racisms?* London: Zed Books.

Cohen, R. B. (1981). The new international division of labour, multinational corporations and urban hierarchy. In M. Dear & A. Scott (Eds.), *Urbanisation and Urban Planning in Capitalist Society* (pp. 287–315). London: Methuen.

Cohen, S. (1972). *Folk Devils and Moral Panics*. London: MacGibbon and Kee.

Cole, I., & Smith, Y. (1996). *From Estate Action to Estate Agreement: Regeneration and change on the Bell Farm Estate, York*. Bristol: Policy Press.

Collins, A. (2004). Sexual dissidence, enterprise and assimilation: Bedfellows in urban regeneration. *Urban Studies, 41*(9), 1789–1806.

Collins, P. H. (1990). *Black Feminist Thought: Knowledge, consciousness and the politics of empowerment*. London: Harper Collins.

Collins, R. (1985). *Three Sociological Traditions: Selected readings*. Oxford: Oxford University Press.

Cooke, P. (1988). Flexible integration, scope economies and strategic alliances: Social and spatial mediations. *Society and Space, 6*(3), 281–300.

Cooke, P. (Ed.) (1995). *The Rise of the Rustbelt*. London: UCL Press.

Cooke, P., & Lazzeretti, L. (Eds.) (2008). *Creative Cities, Cultural Clusters and Local Economic Development*. Cheltenham: Edward Elgar.

Cooke, P. & Morgan, K. (1998). *The Associational Economy: Firms, regions and innovation*. Oxford: Oxford University Press.

Corden, C. (1977). *Planned Cities: New towns in Britain and America*. London: Sage.

Coser, L. A. (1956). *Functions of Social Conflict*. New York: Free Press.

Cox, K. R. (1991). The abstract, the concrete and the argument in the new urban politics. *Journal of Urban Affairs, 13*(3), 299–306.

Cox, K. R. (1993). The local and the global in the new urban politics: A critical view. *Environment and Planning D: Society and Space, 11*(4), 434–48.

Cox, K. R. (1995). Globalization, competition and the politics of local economic development. *Urban Studies, 32*(2), 213–24.

Cox, K. R. (1996). Governance, urban regime analysis, and the politics of local economic development. In M. Lauria (Ed.), *Reconstructing Urban Regime*

Theory: Regulating urban politics in a global economy (pp. 99–121). London: Sage.

Cox, K. R., & Mair, A. (1988). Locality and community in the politics of local economic development. *Annals of the Association of American Geographers*, 78(2), 307–25.

Cox, K. R., & Mair, A. (1989). Review of the book *Urban Growth Machines and the Politics of Local Economic Development*, by J. R. Logan & H. L. Molotch. *International Journal of Urban and Regional Research*, 13(1), 137–46.

Crawford, M. (2011). Blurring the boundaries: Public space and private life. In S. S. Fainstein & S. Campbell (Eds.), *Readings in Urban Theory* (3rd ed., pp. 342–51). Oxford: Wiley-Blackwell.

Cressey, P. G. (1932). *The Taxi-dance Hall: A sociological study in commercialized recreation and city life*. Chicago: University of Chicago Press.

Crompton, R. (1998). *Class and Stratification: An introduction to current debates* (2nd ed.). Cambridge: Polity Press.

Cummings, J. L., DiPasquale, D., & Kahn, M. E. (2002). Measuring the consequences of promoting inner city homeownership. *Journal of Housing Economics*, 11(4), 330–59.

Curley, A. M. (2008). A new place, a new network? Social capital effects of residential relocation for poor women. In T. Blokland & M. Savage (Eds.), *Networked Urbanism. Social capital in the city* (pp. 85–104). Aldershot: Ashgate.

Curley, A. M. (2010). Relocating the poor: Social capital and neighbourhood resources. *Journal of Urban Affairs*, 32(1), 79–103.

Curry, J. & Kenny, M. (1999). The paradigmatic city: Postindustrial illusion and the Los Angeles School, *Antipode*, 31(1), 1–28.

Czempiel, E. O., & Rosenau, J. N. (Eds.) (1989). *Issues in World Politics. Global changes and theoretical challenges: Approaches to world politics for the 1990s*. Lexington, MA: Lexington Books.

Dahl, R. A. (1961). *Who Governs?* New Haven, CT: Yale University Press.

Damer, S. (1974). Wine alley: The sociology of a dreadful enclosure. *Sociological Review*, 22(2), 221–48.

Darwin, C. (1859). *On the Origin of the Species by Means of Natural Selection or the Preservation of Favoured Races in the Struggle for Life*. London: John Murray.

Davies, J. S. (1996). *Urban Regime Theory in Critical Perspective: A study of regeneration policy in the London Borough of Merton*. York Papers in Politics and Policy, Vol. 3. York: Department of Politics, University of York.

Davies, J. S., & Imbroscio, D. L. (Eds.) (2009). *Theories of Urban Politics* (2nd ed.). London: Sage.

Davies, W. K. (1984). *Factorial Ecology*. Aldershot: Gower.

Davis, M. (1990). *City of Quartz: Excavating the future in Los Angeles*. New York: Vintage.

Davis, M. (2001). *Magical Urbanism: Latinos reinvent the US city* (rev. and expanded ed.). London: Verso.

de Certeau, M. (1984). *The Practice of Everyday Life*. Berkeley: University of California Press.

de Certeau, M. (2010). The practice of everyday life. In G. Bridge & S. Watson (Eds.), *The Blackwell City Reader* (2nd ed., pp. 111–18). Oxford: Wiley-Blackwell.

de Swaan, A. (1995). Widening circles of identification: Emotional concerns in sociogenetic perspective. *Theory, Culture & Society*, 12(2), 25–39.

Dear, M. J. (2000). *The Postmodern Urban Condition*. Oxford: Blackwell.

Dear, M. J. (2002). *From Chicago to LA: Making sense of urban theory*. Thousand Oaks, CA: Sage.

Dear, M. J. (2003). The Los Angeles school of urbanism: An intellectual history. *Urban Geography*, 24(6), 493–509.

Dear, M. J. & Dahmann, N. (2008). Urban politics and the Los Angeles school of urbanism. *Urban Affairs Review*, 44(2), 266–79.

Dear, M. J. and Flusty, S. (2002). The resistible rise of the L.A. school, in M. J. Dear (Ed.) *From Chicago to LA: Making sense of urban theory*. Thousand Oaks, CA: Sage.

Dear, M. J., & Scott, A. (1981). *Urbanisation and Urban Planning in Capitalist Society*. London: Methuen.

Delanty, G. (1997). *Social Science: Beyond constructivism and realism*. Minneapolis: University of Minnesota Press.

DeLeon, R. E. (1992a). *Left Coast City: Progressive politics in San Francisco, 1975–1991*. Lawrence: University Press of Kansas.

DeLeon, R. E. (1992b). The urban antiregime: Progressive politics in San Francisco. *Urban Affairs Review*, 27(4), 555–79.

DeSena, J. N. (Ed.) (2008). *Gender in an Urban World*. Bingley: Emerald.

Devine, F. (1997). *Social Class in America and Britain*. Edinburgh: Edinburgh University Press.

Dick, E. (2008). *Residential Segregation – Stumbling Block or Stepping Stone? A case study on the Mexican population of the West Side of St. Paul, Minnesota*. Vienna: Lit.

Dicken, P. (2010). *Global Shift: Mapping the changing contours of the world economy*. London: Sage.

DiGaetano, A., & Klemanski, J. S. (1993). Urban regime capacity: A comparison of Birmingham, England and Detroit, Michigan. *Journal of Urban Affairs*, 15(4), 367–84.

DiGaetano, A., & Klemanski, J. S. (1998). *Urban Governance in Comparative Perspective: The politics of urban development in the UK and US.* Minneapolis: University of Minnesota Press.

Doan, P. L. (2010). Gendered space. In R. Hutchison (Ed.), *Encyclopedia of Urban Studies* (pp. 298–302). Thousand Oaks, CA: Sage.

Dollinger, P. (1999). *The German Hansa.* London: Routledge.

Domhoff, G. W. (2006). The limitations of regime theory. *City & Community,* 5(1), 47–51.

Donald, J. (1992). The city as text. In R. Bocock & K. Thompson (Eds.), *Social and Cultural Forms of Modernity* (pp. 417–61). Oxford: Polity.

Donald, J. (1999). *Imagining the Modern City.* Minneapolis: University of Minnesota Press.

Dormois, R. (2006). Structurer une capacité politique à l'échelle urbaine. Les dynamiques de planification à Nantes et à Rennes (1977-2001). *Revue Française de Science Politique,* 56(5), 837–67.

Dowding, K. (1996). *Power.* Buckingham: Open University Press.

Dreier, P., Mollenkopf, J., & Swanstrom, T. (2013). Metropolitics for the twenty-first century. In J. Lin & C. Mele (Eds.), *The Urban Sociology Reader* (2nd ed., pp. 148–56). London: Routledge.

Drever, A. I. (2004). Separate spaces, separate outcomes? Neighbourhood impacts on minorities in Germany. *Urban Studies,* 41(8), 1423–39.

Driver, F., & Gilbert, D. (Eds.) (1999). *Imperial Cities: Landscape, display and identity.* Manchester: Manchester University Press.

Du Bois, W. E. B. (1996 (1899)). *The Philadelphia Negro: A Social Study.* Philadelphia: University of Pennsylvania Press.

Du Bois, W. E. B. (2013). The environment of the Negro. In J. Lin & C. Mele (Eds.), *The Urban Sociology Reader* (2nd ed., pp. 174–81). New York: Routledge.

Duncan, C., Jones, K., & Moon, G. (1999). Smoking and deprivation: Are there neighbourhood effects? *Social Science & Medicine,* 48(4), 497–505.

Duncan, J. S. (2013). Men without property: The tramp's classification of the use of urban space. In J. Lin & C. Mele (Eds.), *The Urban Sociology Reader* (2nd ed., pp. 225–33). New York: Routledge.

Duneier, M. (1992). *Slim's Table: Race, respectability, and masculinity.* Chicago: University of Chicago Press.

Duneier, M. (1999). *Sidewalk.* New York: Straus and Giroux.

Dunford, M. and Kafkalas, G. (Eds.) (1992). *Cities and Regional Development in the New Europe: The global-local interplay and spatial development strategies.* London: Belhaven Press.

Dunleavy, P. (1980). *Urban Political Analysis: The politics of collective consumption.* London: Macmillan.

Dunleavy, P., & O'Leary, B. (1987). *Theories of the State: The politics of liberal democracy*. Basingstoke: Macmillan.

Durkheim, É. (1984). *The Division of Labour in Society* (2nd ed.). Basingstoke: Macmillan.

Eade, J., & Mele, C. (Eds.) (2002a). *Understanding the City: Contemporary and future perspectives*. Oxford: Blackwell.

Eade, J., & Mele, C. (2002b). Understanding the city. In J. Eade & C. Mele (Eds.), *Understanding the City: Contemporary and future perspectives* (pp. 3–24). Oxford: Blackwell.

Eaton, R. (2001). *Ideal Cities: Utopianism and the (un)built environment*. Antwerp: Mercatorfonds.

Eeckhout, B. (2001). The 'disneyfication' of Times Square: Back to the future? *Critical Perspectives on Urban Redevelopment*, 6, 379–428.

Eisenschitz, A., & Gough, J. (1993). *The Politics of Local Economic Policy: The problems and possibilities of local initiative*. Basingstoke: Macmillan.

Elias, N. (1974). Towards a theory of community. In C. Bell & H. Newby (Eds.), *The Sociology of Community. A selection of readings* (pp. iv–xi). London: Frank Cass.

Elias, N. (1987). *Involvement and Detachment*. Oxford: Blackwell.

Elias, N. (1991). *Society of Individuals*. Oxford: Blackwell.

Elias, N., & Scotson, J. L. (1965). *The Established and the Outsiders: A sociological enquiry into community problems*. London: Frank Cass.

Elkin, S. L. (1987). *City and Regime in the American Republic*. Chicago: University of Chicago Press.

Ellen, I. G., & Turner, M. A. (2003). Do neighborhoods matter and why? In J. M. Goering & J. D. Feins (Eds.), *Choosing a Better Life? Evaluating the Moving to Opportunity social experiment* (pp. 313–38). Washington, DC: Urban Institute Press.

Elliott, B., & McCrone, D. (1982). *The City: Patterns of domination and conflict*. London: Macmillan.

Elliott, D. S., Wilson, W. J., Huizinga, D., Sampson, R. J., Elliott, A., & Rankin, B. (1996). The effects of neighborhood disadvantage on adolescent development. *Journal of Research in Crime and Delinquency*, 33(4), 389–426.

Engels, F. (2011). The great towns. In R. T. LeGates & F. Stout (Eds.), *The City Reader* (5th ed., pp. 46–54). London: Routledge.

Entrikin, J. N. (1976). Contemporary humanism in geography. *Annals of the Association of American Geographers*, 66(4), 615–32.

Erickcek, G. A., & McKinney, H. (2006). 'Small cities blues': Looking for growth factors in small and medium-sized cities. *Economic Development Quarterly*, 20(3), 232–58.

Erie, S. P. (1988). *Rainbow's End: Irish-Americans and the dilemmas of urban machine politics, 1840–1985*. Berkeley: University of California Press.

Esser, H. (1986). Social context and inter-ethnic relations: The case of migrant workers in West German urban areas. *European Sociological Review*, 2(1), 30–51.

Etzkowitz, H., & Leydesdorff, L. (2000). The dynamics of innovation: From national systems and 'Mode 2' to a triple helix of university–industry–government relations. *Research Policy*, 29(2), 109–23.

Evans, A., & Eversley, D. (Eds.) (1980). *The Inner City*. London: Heinemann.

Fainstein, S. S. (2010). *The Just City*. Ithaca, NY: Cornell University Press.

Fainstein, S. S., & Campbell, S. (Eds.) (2011). *Readings in Urban Theory* (3rd ed.). Oxford: Wiley-Blackwell.

Fainstein, S. S., & Stokes, R. J. (1998). Spaces for play: The impacts of entertainment development on New York City. *Economic Development Quarterly*, 12(2), 150–65.

Fainstein, S. S., Gordon, I., & Harloe, M. (1992). *Divided Cities: New York and London in the contemporary world*. Oxford: Blackwell.

Farrer, J. (2004). Making urban nightscapes: Youth cultures, pleasure spaces and corporate power by Paul Chatterton, Robert Hollands, Chrystalla Ellina. *Contemporary Sociology*, 33(6), 693–4.

Feagin, J. R. (1987). Urban political economy: The new paradigm matures. *Contemporary Sociology*, 16(4), 517–19.

Featherstone, M. (Ed.) (1990). *Theory, Culture & Society. Global culture, nationalism, globalization and modernity*. London: Sage.

Featherstone, M. (1991). *Consumer Culture and Postmodernism*. London: Sage.

Featherstone, M. (1993). Global and local cultures. In J. Bird, C. Barry, T. Putnam, G. Robertson, & L. Tickner (Eds.), *Mapping the Future: Local cultures, global change* (pp. 169–87). London: Routledge.

Fincher, R., & Iveson, K. (2008). *Planning and Diversity in the City: Redistribution, recognition and encounter*. Basingstoke: Palgrave Macmillan.

Fincher, R., & Iveson, K. (2011). Cities and diversity: Should we want it? Can we plan for it? In S. S. Fainstein & S. Campbell (Eds.), *Readings in Urban Theory* (3rd ed., pp. 129–46). Oxford: Wiley-Blackwell.

Fincher, R., & Jacobs, J. M. (1998). *Cities of Difference*. New York: Guilford Press.

Fincher, R., Jacobs, J. M., & Anderson, K. (2002). Rescripting cities with difference. In J. Eade & C. Mele (Eds.), *Understanding the city. Contemporary and future perspectives* (pp. 27–48). Oxford: Blackwell.

Fine, G. A., & Kleinman, S. (1979). Rethinking subculture: An interactionist analysis. *American Journal of Sociology*, 85(1), 1–20.

Firestone, S. (1979). *The Dialectic of Sex: The case for feminist revolution*. London: Women's Press.

Fischer, C. S. (1975). Toward a subcultural theory of urbanism. *American Journal of Sociology*, 80(6), 1319–41.

Fischer, C. S. (1982). *To Dwell Among Friends: Personal networks in town and city*. Chicago: University of Chicago Press.

Fischer, C. S. (2013). Theories of urbanism. In J. Lin & C. Mele (Eds.), *The Urban Sociology Reader* (2nd ed., pp. 42–9). London: Routledge.

Fishman, R. (2011). Beyond suburbia: The rise of the technoburb. In R. T. LeGates & F. Stout (Eds.), *The City Reader* (5th ed., pp. 75–84). London: Routledge.

Flanagan, W. G. (2010). *Urban Sociology: Images and structure* (5th ed.). Lanham, MD: Rowman & Littlefield.

Floor, H., & van Kempen, R. (1997). Analysing housing preferences with decision plan nets. *Scandinavian Housing & Planning research*, 14(1), 27–42.

Florida, R. (2005a). The world is spiky: Globalization has changed the economic playing field, but hasn't leveled it. *The Atlantic*, October, 48–51.

Florida, R. (2005b). *Cities and the Creative Class*. London: Routledge.

Foord, J., & Gregson, N. (1986). Patriarchy: Towards a reconceptualisation. *Antipode*, 18(2), 186–211.

Forrest, R., Henderson, J. W., & Williams, P. (1982). The nature of urban studies. In R. Forrest, J. W. Henderson, & P. Williams (Eds.), *Urban Political Economy and Social Theory. Critical essays in urban studies* (pp. 1–14). Aldershot: Gower.

Fothergill, S., & Gudgin, G. (1982). *Unequal Growth: Urban and regional employment change in the UK*. London: Heinemann Educational Books.

Foucault, M. (1980). *Power/Knowledge*. New York: Pantheon Books.

Frank, S. (2008). Gender trouble in paradise: Suburbia reconsidered. In J. N. DeSena (Ed.), *Gender in an Urban World* (pp. 127–48). Bingley: Emerald.

Frase, P. (2013). The precariat: A class or a condition? *New Labor Forum*, 22(2), 11–14.

Frazier, J. (1981). Pragmatism: geography and the real world. In M. Harvey & B. Holly (Eds.), *Themes in Geographic Thought*. London: Croom Helm.

Frêche, G., & Lapousterle, P. (1990). *La France ligotée. Les idées, les faits et les hommes*. Paris: P. Belfond.

Friedmann, J. (1986). The world city hypothesis. *Development and Change*, 17(1), 69–83.

Friedmann, J. & Wolff, G. (1982). World city formation: An agenda for research and action, *International Journal of Regional and Urban Research*, 3, 309–44.

Friedman, T. (2005). *The World is Flat: A brief history of the twenty-first century*. New York: Farrar, Straus & Giroux.

Friedrichs, J., Galster, G. C., & Musterd, S. (2003). Neighbourhood effects on social opportunities: The European and American research and policy context. *Housing Studies*, 18(6), 797–806.

Frobel, F., Heinrichs, J. & Kreye, O. (1980). *The New International Division of Labour: Structural unemployment in industrialised countries and industrialisation in developing countries*. Cambridge: Cambridge University Press.

Fujita, M., Krugman, P. & Venables, A. (1999). *The Spatial Economy: Cities, regions and international trade*. Cambridge, MA: MIT Press.

Fujita, M. & Thisse, J. (2002). *The Economics of Agglomeration*. Cambridge: Cambridge University Press.

Furstenberg, F. F. (1999). *Managing to Make It: Urban families and adolescent success*. Chicago: University of Chicago Press.

Galster, G. C. (2002). Investigating behavioural impacts of poor neighbourhoods: Towards new data and analytic strategies. *Housing Studies*, 18(6), 877–92.

Galster, G. C. (2012a). *Driving Detroit: The quest for respect in the motor city*. Philadelphia: University of Pennsylvania Press.

Galster, G. (2012b). The mechanisms of neighbourhood effects: Theory, evidence and policy implications. In M. van Ham, D. Manley, N. Bailey, L. Simpson, & D. Maclennan (Eds.), *Neighbourhood Effects Research: New perspectives* (pp. 23–56). Amsterdam: Springer.

Galster, G. C., & Killen, S. P. (1995). The geography of metropolitan opportunity: A reconnaissance and conceptual framework. *Housing Policy Debate*, 6(1), 7–43.

Gans, H. J. (1962). *The Urban Villagers: Group and class in the life of Italian-Americans*. New York: Free Press.

Gans, H. J. (1967). *The Levittowners: Ways of life and politics in a new suburban community*. New York: Pantheon Books.

Gans, H. J. (1968). *People and Plans: Essays on urban problems and solutions*. New York: Basic Books.

Gans, H. J. (1979). *Deciding What's News: A study of CBS evening news, NBC nightly news, Newsweek, and Time*. New York: Pantheon Books.

Gans, H. J. (1991). *People, Plans, and Policies: Essays on poverty, racism, and other national urban problems*. New York: Columbia University Press and Russell Sage Foundation.

Gans, H. J. (1995). *The War Against the Poor: The underclass and antipoverty policy*. New York: Basic Books.

Gans, H. J. (1996). Symbolic ethnicity: The future of ethnic groups and cultures in America (1979). In W. Sollors (Ed.), *Theories of Ethnicity: A classical reader* (pp. 425–59). London: Macmillan.

Gans, H. J. (2002). The sociology of space: A use-centered view. *City & Community*, 1(4), 329–339.

Gans, H. J. (2008). *Imagining America in 2033: How the country put itself together after Bush*. Ann Arbor: University of Michigan Press.

Garber, J. A., & Turner, R. S. (Eds.) (1995). *Gender in Urban Research*. Thousand Oaks, CA: Sage.

Garreau, J. (1991). *Edge City: Life on the new frontier*. New York: Doubleday Anchor.

Geddes, P. (1915). *Cities in Evolution*. London: Williams & Norgate.

Geddes, K. (2009). Marxism and urban politics. In J. S. Davies & D. L. Imbroscio (Eds.), *Theories of Urban Politics* (2nd ed., pp. 55–72). London: Sage.

Geertz, C. (1993). *The Interpretation of Cultures: Selected essays*. London: Fontana Press.

Gephart, M. A. (1997). Neighbourhood and communities as contexts for development. In J. Brooks-Gunn, G. J. Duncan, & J. L. Aber (Eds.), *Neighborhood Poverty: Vol. 1. Context and consequences for children* (pp. 99–146). New York: Russell Sage Foundation.

Getis, V. (1998). Experts and juvenile delinquency, 1900–1935. In J. Austin & M. Willard (Eds.), *Generations of Youth: Youth cultures and history in twentieth century America* (pp. 21–36). New York: New York University Press.

Giddens, A. (1979). *Central Problems in Social Theory*. Basingstoke: Macmillan.

Giddens, A. (1981). *A Contemporary Critique of Historical Materialism*. Basingstoke: Macmillan.

Giddens, A. (1984). *The Constitution of Society*. Cambridge: Polity Press.

Giddens, A. (1986). *Sociology: A brief but critical introduction* (2nd ed.). London: Macmillan.

Giddens, A. (1989). *Sociology*. Cambridge: Polity Press.

Giddens, A. (1990). *The Consequences of Modernity*. Cambridge: Polity Press

Gieryn, T. F. (2000). A space for place in sociology. *Annual Review of Sociology*, 26, 463–96.

Gieryn, T. F. (2002). Give place a chance: Reply to Gans. *City & Community*, 1(4), 341–3.

Gilbert, A. (1996). *The Mega-city in Latin America*. Tokyo: United Nations University Press.

Gilbert, J. B. (1991). *Perfect Cities: Chicago's utopias of 1893*. Chicago: University of Chicago Press.

Gilbert, M. R. (1997). Identity, space and politics: A critique of the poverty debates. In J. P. Jones, H. J. Nast, & S. M. Roberts (Eds.), *Thresholds in Feminist Geography: Difference, methodology, and representation* (pp. 29–45). Lanham, MD: Rowman & Littlefield.

Gilbert, M. R. (2000). Identity, difference and the geographies of working poor women's survival strategies. In K. B. Miranne & A. H. Young (Eds.), *Gendering the City: Women, boundaries, and visions or urban life* (pp. 65–87). Lanham, MD: Rowman & Littlefield.

Gilbert, M. R. (2010). Place, space, and agency: Moving beyond the homogenous 'ghetto'. *Urban Geography*, 31(2), 148–52.

Gissendanner, S. (2003). Methodology problems in urban governance studies. *Environment and Planning C: Government and Policy*, 21(5), 663–86.

Glaeser, E. (2011). *The Triumph of the City*. New York: Penguin.

Glass, R. (1964). *London: Aspects of change*. London: MacGibbon & Kee.

Glock, B. (2006). *Stadtpolitik in schrumpfenden Städten*. Frankfurt: VS Verlag für Sozialwissenschaften.

Gmelch, G., & Zenner, W. P. (Eds.) (2002). *Urban Life: Readings in urban anthropology* (4th ed.). Prospect Heights, NY: Waveland Press.

Goffman, E. (1959). *The Presentation of Self in Everyday Life*. New York: Doubleday Anchor.

Goffman, E. (Ed.) (1963). *Behavior in Public Places: Notes on the social organization of gatherings*. New York: Free Press.

Goffman, E. (1990). *Stigma: Notes on the management of spoiled identity*. London: Penguin.

Golledge, R., & Couclelis, H. (1984). Positivist philosophy and research on human spatial behaviour. In T. Saarinen, D. Seamon, & J. Sell (Eds.), *Environmental Perception and Behaviour*. Chicago: University of Chicago Press.

Golubchikov, O., & Phelps, N. A. (2011). The political economy of place at the post-socialist urban periphery: Governing growth on the edge of Moscow. *Transactions of the Institute of British Geographers, 36*(3), 425–40.

Gordon, I. R. & McCann, P. (2000). Industrial clusters: Complexes, agglomeration and/or social networks? *Urban Studies, 37*(3), 513–32

Gordon, M. M. (1947). The concept of the sub-culture and its application. *Social Forces, 26*(1), 40–2.

Goss, J. (1993). The 'magic of the mall': An analysis of form, function, and meaning in the contemporary retail built environment. *Annals of the Association of American Geographers, 83*(1), 18–47.

Gottdiener, M. (1985). *The Social Production of Urban Space*. Austin: University of Texas Press.

Gottdiener, M. (1986). *Cities in Stress: A new look at the urban crisis*. London: Sage.

Gottdiener, M., & Feagin, J. R. (1988). The paradigm shift in urban sociology. *Urban Affairs Quarterly, 42*(2), 163–87.

Gottdiener, M., & Hutchison, R. (2011). *The New Urban Sociology* (4th ed.). Boulder, CO: Westview Press.

Graham, S. (2011). *Cities under Siege: The new military urbanism*. London: Verso.

Granovetter M. (1973). The strength of weak ties. *American Journal of Sociology, 78*, 1360–1380.

Gramsci, A. (1982). Americanism and Fordism. In Q. Hoare and G. Nowell Smith (Eds.), *Selections from the Prison Notebooks of Antonio Gramsci* (pp. 277–320). London: Lawrence and Wishart.

Greed, C. (1994). *Women and Planning: Creating gendered realities*. London: Routledge.

Gregory, D. (1978). *Ideology, Science and Human Geography*. London: Hutchinson.

Gregory, D., & Urry, J. (Eds.) (1985). *Social Relations and Spatial Structures*. Basingstoke: Macmillan.

Gregson, N. (1989). On the (ir)relevance of structuration theory to empirical research. In D. Held & J. B. Thompson (Eds.), *Social Theory of the Modern Societies. Anthony Giddens and his critics* (pp. 235–48). Cambridge: Cambridge University Press.

Gross, E. (1986). Conclusion: What is feminist theory? In C. Pateman & E. Gross (Eds.), *Feminist Challenges. Social and political theory* (pp. 190–204). Boston: Northeastern University Press.

Guelke, L. (1974). An idealist alternative in human geography. *Annals of the Association of American Geographers*, 64(2), 193–202.

Grusky, D. B. (1994). The contours of social stratification. In D. B. Grusky (Ed.), *Social Inequality Series. Social stratification. Class, race, and gender in sociological perspective* (pp. 3–38). Boulder, CO: Westview Press.

Gugler, J. (2004). *World Cities Beyond the West: Globalization, development and inequality*. Cambridge: Cambridge University Press.

Gupta, A., & Ferguson, J. (1997). Beyond 'culture': Space, identity, and the politics of difference. In A. Gupta & J. Ferguson (Eds.), *Culture, Power, Place. Explorations in critical anthropology* (pp. 33–51). Durham, NC: Duke University Press.

Haggett, P. (1965). *Locational Analysis in Human Geography*. London: Edward Arnold.

Hall, P (1966). *The World Cities*. London: Weidenfeld and Nicolson.

Hall, P. (Ed.) (1981). *The Inner City in Context,* London: Heinemann.

Hall, P. (1984). *The World Cities* (3rd ed.). London: Weidenfeld and Nicolson.

Hall, P. (1988). The geography of the fifth Kondratieff. In D. Massey & J. Allen (Eds.), *Uneven Redevelopment: Cities and regions in transition* (pp. 51–67). London: Hodder and Stoughton.

Hall, P. (2002). *Cities of Tomorrow: An intellectual history of urban planning and design in the twentieth century* (3rd ed.). Oxford: Blackwell.

Hall, P. and Markusen, A. R. (Eds.) (1985). *Silicon Landscapes*. Boston: Allen & Unwin.

Hall, P., Thomas, R., Gracey, H. and Drewett, R. (1973). *The Containment of Urban England*. London: Allen & Unwin.

Hall, S. (1996). New ethnicities. In D. Morley & K.-H. Chen (Eds.), *Stuart Hall. Critical dialogues in cultural studies* (pp. 442–51). London: Routledge.

Hall, T. (2007). *Urban Geography* (3rd ed., reprinted). London: Routledge.

Hall, T., & Hubbard, P. (1996). The entrepreneurial city: New urban politics, new urban geographies? *Progress in Human Geography*, 20(2), 153–74.

Hamel, P., & Jouve, B. (2008). In search of a stable urban regime for Montreal: Issues and challenges in metropolitan development. *Urban Research & Practice*, 1(1), 18–35.

Hamnett, C. (1991). The blind men and the elephant: The explanation of gentrification. *Transaction of the Institute of British Geographers*, 16(2), 173–89.

Hamnett, C. (1994). Social polarisation in global cities: Theory and evidence, *Urban Studies*, 31(3), 401–24.

Hamnett, C. (1996). Why Sassen is wrong: A reply to Burgers. *Urban Studies*, 33(1), 107–10.

Hamnett, C. (2003). *Unequal City: London in the global arena*. London: Routledge.

Hannan, M. T. (1994). Dynamics of ethnic boundaries. In D. B. Grusky (Ed.), *Social Stratification. Class, race, and gender in sociological perspective* (pp. 500–508). Boulder, CO: Westview Press.

Hannemann, C. (2003). Schrumpfende Städte in Ostdeutschland: Ursachen und Folgen einer Stadtentwicklung ohne Wirtschaftswachstum. *Aus Politik und Zeitgeschichte, Beilage zur Wochenzeitung Das Parlament*, B28, 16–23.

Hannemann, C. (2004). *Marginalisierte Städte: Probleme, Differenzierungen und Chancen ostdeutscher Kleinstädte im Schrumpfungsprozess*. Berlin: Berliner Wissenschafts-Verlag.

Hannerz, U. (1969). *Soulside: Inquiries into ghetto culture and community*. New York: Columbia University Press.

Hannerz, U. (1980). *Exploring the City: Inquiries toward an urban anthropology*. New York: Columbia University Press.

Hannerz, U. (2004). Cosmopolitanism. In D. Nugent & J. Vincent (Eds.), *A Companion to the Anthropology of Politics* (pp. 69–85). Oxford: Blackwell.

Hannigan, J. (1998). *Fantasy City: Pleasure and profit in the postmodern metropolis*. London: Routledge.

Haraway, D. (1988). Situated knowledges: The science question in feminism and the privilege of partial perspective. *Feminist Studies*, 14(3), 575–99.

Harding, A. (1991). The rise of urban growth coalitions, U.K.-style? *Environment and Planning C: Government and Policy*, 9(3), 295–317.

Harding, A. (1994). Urban regimes and growth machines: Towards a cross-national research agenda. *Urban Affairs Quarterly*, 29(3), 356–82.

Harding, A. (1995). Elite theory and growth machines. In D. Judge, G. Stoker, & H. Wolman (Eds.), *Theories of Urban Politics* (pp. 35–53). London: Sage.

Harding, A. (1996). Is there a new community power and why should we need one? *International Journal of Urban and Regional Research*, 20(4), 637–55.

Harding, A. (1997). Urban regimes in a Europe of the cities? *European Urban and Regional Studies*, 4(4), 291–314.

Harding, A. (1999). North American urban political economy, urban theory and British research. *British Journal of Political Science*, 29(4), 673–98.

Harding, A. (2000). Regime-formation in Manchester and Edinburgh. In G. Stoker (Ed.), *Government Beyond the Centre. The new politics of British local governance* (pp. 54–71). New York: St. Martin's Press.

Harding, A. (2009). The history of community power. In J. S. Davies & D. L. Imbroscio (Eds.), *Theories of Urban Politics* (2nd ed., pp. 27–39). London: Sage.

Harding, A., Harloe, M., & Rees, J. (2010). Manchester's bust regime? *International Journal of Urban and Regional Research*, 34(4), 981–991.

Harding, A. & Le Galès, P. (1997). Globalization, urban change and urban policy. In A. Scott (Ed.), *The Limits of Globalization. Cases and arguments.* London: Routledge.

Harding, S. G. (1991). *Whose Science? Whose knowledge? Thinking from women's lives.* Ithaca, NY: Cornell University Press.

Harloe, M. (1977). *Captive Cities: Studies in political economy of cities and regions.* London: Wiley.

Harloe, M. (Ed.) (1981). *New Perspectives in Urban Change and Conflict.* London: Heinemann.

Harry, J. (1974). Urbanization and the gay life. *Journal of Sex Research*, 10(3), 238–47.

Harvey, D. (1969). *Explanation in Geography.* London: Edward Arnold.

Harvey, D. (1973). *Social Justice and the City.* London: Edward Arnold.

Harvey, D. (1982). *The Limits to Capital.* Oxford: Blackwell.

Harvey, D. (1985a). *Consciousness and the Urban Experience.* Oxford: Blackwell.

Harvey, D. (1985b). *The Urbanization of Capital.* Oxford: Blackwell.

Harvey, D. (1987). Three myths in search of a reality in urban studies. *Environment and Planning D: Society and Space*, 5, 367–76.

Harvey, D. (1989a). *The Condition of Postmodernity: An enquiry into the origins of cultural change.* Oxford: Wiley-Blackwell.

Harvey, D. (1989b). *The Urban Experience.* Oxford: Blackwell.

Harvey, D. (2006). The political economy of public space. In S. Low & N. Smith (Eds.), *The Politics of Public Space* (pp. 17–34). New York: Routledge.

Hasluck, C. (1987). *Urban Unemployment: Local labour markets and employment initiatives.* London: Longman.

Hastings, A. (1999). Discourse and urban change: Introduction to the special issue. *Urban Studies*, 36(1), 7–12.

Hastings, A. (2004). Stigma and social housing estates: Beyond pathological explanations. *Journal of Housing and the Built Environment*, 19(3), 233–54.

Häussermann, H., & Kapphan, A. (2002). *Berlin - von der geteilten zur gespaltenen Stadt? Sozialräumlicher Wandel seit 1990* (2nd ed.). Opladen: Leske + Budrich.

Häussermann, H., Kronauer, M., & Siebel, W. (Eds.) (2004). *An den Rändern der Städte: Armut und Ausgrenzung.* Frankfurt am Main: Suhrkamp.

Haughton, G., & Hunter, C. (2003). *Sustainable Cities.* London: Routledge.

Hawley, A. H. (1950). *Human Ecology: A theory of community structure.* New York: Ronald Press.

Hay, C. (1995). Restating the problem of regulation and re-regulating the local state. *Economy and Society, 24*(3), 387–407.

Hayden, D. (1984). *Redesigning the American Dream: The future of housing, work, and family life.* New York: Norton.

Haynes, B. D. (2001). *Red Lines, Black Spaces: The politics of race and space in a black middle-class suburb.* New Haven, CT: Yale University Press.

Haynes, B. D., & Hutchison, R. (2008). The ghetto: Origins, history, discourse. *City & Community, 7*(4), 347–52.

Hechter, M. (1987). Nationalism as group solidarity. *Ethnic and Racial Studies, 10*(4), 415–26.

Held, D. (1991). Democracy, the nation-state and the global system. *Economy and Society, 20*(2), 139–72.

Held, D. & McGrew, A. (1993). Globalization and the liberal democratic state. *Goverment and Opposition, 28*(2), 261–88.

Herbert, D. T., & Thomas, C. J. (1982). *Urban Geography: A first approach.* Chichester: Wiley.

Herbert, S. (2010). From the south side to Susanville: Tracing the logics and geographies of contemporary segregation. *Urban Geography, 31*(2), 153–7.

Herman, R. (2009). Playing with restraints: Space, citizenship and BDSM. In K. Browne, J. Lim, & G. Brown (Eds.), *Geographies of Sexualities. Theory, practices, and politics* (pp. 89–100). Aldershot: Ashgate.

Hill Collins, P. (1999). *Black Feminist Thought: Knowledge, consciousness, and the politics of empowerment.* New York: Routledge.

Hirst, P. (1994). *Associative Democracy: New forms of economic and social governance.* Cambridge: Polity Press.

Hohenberg, P. M., & Lees, L. H. (1995). *The Making of Urban Europe, 1000–1994* (2nd ed.). Cambridge, MA: Harvard University Press.

Hollands, R. (2002). Divisions in the dark: Youth cultures, transitions and segmented consumption spaces in the night-time economy. *Journal of Youth Studies, 5*(2), 153–71.

Homans, G. C. (1950). *The Human Group.* New York: Harcourt Brace.

hooks, b. (2000). *Feminist Theory: From margin to center.* London: Pluto Press.

Hopkins, J. S. (1990). West Edmonton Mall: Landscape of myths and elsewhereness. *Canadian Geographer/Géographe canadien, 34*(1), 2–17.

Horan, C. (1996). Coalition, market and state. In M. Lauria (Ed.), *Reconstructing Urban Regime Theory. Regulating urban politics in a global economy* (pp. 149–70). London: Sage.

Howard, E. (2011). 'Author's introduction' and 'The town-country magnet'. In R. T. LeGates & F. Stout (Eds.), *The City Reader* (5th ed., pp. 328–35). London: Routledge.

Hubbard, P. (2004). Cleansing the metropolis: Sex work and the politics of zero tolerance. *Urban Studies, 41*(9), 1687–1702.

Hubbard, P. (2008). Here, there, everywhere: The ubiquitous geographies of heteronormativity. *Geography Compass, 2*(3), 640–58.

Hubbard, P. (2012). *Cities and Sexualities* London: Routledge.

Hughes, J., John, P., & Sasse, G. (2002). From plan to network: Urban elites and the post-communist organisational state in Russia. *European Journal of Political Research, 41*(3), 395–420.

Humm, M. (Ed.) (1992). *Feminisms: A reader*. New York: Harvester Wheatsheaf.

Hunter, F. (1953). *Community Power Structure: A study of decision makers*. Chapel Hill: University of North Carolina Press.

Huq, R. (2004). *Beyond Subculture: Pop, youth and identity in a postcolonial world*. London: Routledge.

Imbroscio, D. L. (1997). *Reconstructing City Politics: Alternative economic development and urban regimes*. Thousand Oaks, CA: Sage.

Imbroscio, D. L. (2003). Overcoming the neglect of economics in urban regime theory. *Journal of Urban Affairs, 25*(3), 271–84.

Ingram, G. K., & Carroll, A. (1981). The spatial structure of Latin American cities. *Journal of Urban Economics, 9*(2), 257–73.

Isard, W. (1956). *Location and Space Economy*. London: Chapman & Hall.

Isard, W. (1960). *Methods of Regional Analysis: An introduction to regional science*. Cambridge, MA: MIT Press.

Jackson, K. T. (1985). *Crabgrass Frontier: The suburbanization of the United States*. Oxford: Oxford University Press.

Jackson, K. T. (2011). The drive-in culture of contemporary America. In R. T. LeGates & F. Stout (Eds.), *The City Reader* (5th ed., pp. 65–74). London: Routledge.

Jackson, P. (1985). Urban ethnography. *Progress in Human Geography, 9*(2), 157–176.

Jackson, P., & Smith S. J. (Eds.) (1984). *Exploring Social Geography*. London: Allen & Unwin.

Jacobs, J. (1961). *The Death and Life of Great American Cities*. New York: Vintage.

Jacobs, J. (1969). *The Economy of Cities*. New York: Vintage.

Jacobs, J. (1984). *Cities and the Wealth of Nations*. New York: Vintage.

Jager, M. (2010). Class definition and the esthetics of gentrification: Victoriana in Melbourne. In L. Lees, T. Slater, & E. K. Wyly (Eds.), *The Gentrification Reader* (pp. 153–60). London: Routledge.

Jargowsky, P. A. (1997). *Poverty and Place: Ghettos, barrios, and the American city*. New York: Russell Sage Foundation.

Jarrett, R. L. (1997). African American family and parenting strategies in impoverished neighborhoods. *Qualitative Sociology, 20*(2), 275–88.

Jayne, M. (2006). *Cities and Consumption*. London: Routledge.

Jeffers, C. (1967). *Living Poor: A participant observer study of priorities and choices*. Ann Arbor, MI: Ann Arbor Publishers.

Jencks, C., & Mayer, J. (1990). The social consequences of growing up in a poor neighborhood. In L. E. Lynn & M. G. H. McGeary (Eds.), *Inner-city Poverty in the United States* (pp. 111–86). Washington, DC: National Academy Press.

Jenkins, R. (1996). *Social Identity. Key ideas*. London: Routledge.

Jenkins, R. (2008). *Rethinking Ethnicity* (2nd ed.). Thousand Oaks, CA: Sage.

Jenks, M., & Burgess, R. (Eds.) (2000). *Compact Cities: Sustainable urban forms for developing countries*. New York: E. & F.N. Spon.

Jessop, B. (1996). A neo-Gramscian approach to the regulation of urban regimes: Accumulation strategies, hegemonic projects and governance. In M. Lauria (Ed.), *Reconstructing Urban Regime Theory. Regulating urban politics in a global economy* (pp. 51–74). London: Sage.

John, P. & Cole, A. (1996). *Urban Regimes and Local Governance in Britain and France: Policy adaption and coordination in Leeds and Lille*. Paper presemted to the American Political Science Association conference, Panel 16-9: Growth politics reconsidered. San Francisco, September.

John, P., & Cole, A. (1998). Urban regimes and local governance in Britain and France: Policy adaption and coordination in Leeds and Lille. *Urban Affairs Review, 33*(3), 382–404.

John, P., Dowding, K., & Biggs, S. (1995). Residential mobility in London: A micro-level test of the behavioural assumptions of the Tiebout model. *British Journal of Political Science, 25*(3), 379–97.

Johnson, M. P., Helen, F. L., & Jens, L. (2002). The benefits and costs of residential mobility programmes for the poor. *Housing Studies, 17*(1), 125–38.

Johnston, R. J. (1979). *Geography and Geographers: Anglo-American human geography since 1945*. London: Edward Arnold.

Johnston, R. J. (1980). *City and Society: An outline for urban geography*. Harmondsworth: Penguin.

Johnston, R. J. (1991). *Geography and Geographers: Anglo-American human geography since 1945* (4th ed.). London: Edward Arnold.

Jones, J. B., & Keating, M. (1995). *The European Union and the Regions*. Oxford: Clarendon Press.

Jones, N. (2009). *Between Good and Ghetto: African American girls and inner-city violence*. New Brunswick, NJ: Rutgers University Press.

Judd, D. R. (2011). Promoting tourism in US cities. In S. S. Fainstein & S. Campbell (Eds.), *Readings in Urban Theory* (3rd ed., pp. 247–70). Oxford: Wiley-Blackwell.

Judd, D. R., & Fainstein, S. S. (1999). *The Tourist City*. New Haven, CT: Yale University Press.

Judd, D. R., & Kantor, P. (Eds.) (1992). *Enduring Tensions in Urban Politics*. New York: Macmillan.

Judge, D. (1995). Pluralism. In D. Judge, G. Stoker, & H. Wolman (Eds.), *Theories of Urban Politics* (pp. 13–34). London: Sage.

Judge, D., Stoker, G., & Wolman, H. (Eds.) (1995). *Theories of Urban Politics*. London: Sage.

Kantor, P. (1995). *The Dependent City Revisited: The political economy of urban development and social policy*. Boulder, CO: Westview Press.

Kantor, P., & David, S. M. (1988). *The Dependent City: The changing political economy of urban America*. Glenview, IL: Scott & Foresman.

Kantor, P., Savitch, H. V., & Haddock, S. V. (1997). The political economy of urban regimes: A comparative perspective. *Urban Affairs Review*, *32*(3), 348–77.

Karp, D. A. (1973). Hiding in pornographic bookstores: A reconsideration of the nature of urban anonymity. *Journal of Contemporary Ethnography*, (1), 427–52.

Karsten, L., & Pel, E. (2000). Skateboarders exploring urban public space: Ollies, obstacles and conflicts. *Journal of Housing and the Built Environment*, *15*(4), 327–40.

Kates, S. M., & Belk, R. W. (2001). The meanings of lesbian and gay pride day: Resistance through consumption and resistance to consumption. *Journal of Contemporary Ethnography*, *30*(4), 392–429.

Katz, M. B. (1990). *The Undeserving Poor: From the war on poverty to the war on welfare*. New York: Pantheon Books.

Katz, M. B. (Ed.) (1993). *The 'underclass' debate: Views from history*. Princeton, NJ: Princeton University Press.

Katznelson, I. (1993). *Marxism and the City. Marxist introductions*. Oxford: Clarendon Press.

Kazepov, Y. (2005). *Cities of Europe: Changing contexts, local arrangements, and the challenge to urban cohesion*. Oxford: Blackwell.

Keating, M. (1988). *The City that Refused to Die: Glasgow: the politics of urban regeneration*. Aberdeen: Aberdeen University Press.

Keating, M. (1991). *Comparative Urban Politics: Power and the city in the United States, Canada, Britain, and France*. Aldershot: Edward Elgar.

Keating, M. (1997). The invention of regions: Political restructuring and territorial government in Europe. *Environment and Planning C: Government and Policy*, *15*, 383–98.

Keil, R. (2010). Crisis, what crisis? Towards a global bust regime? *International Journal of Urban and Regional Research*, *34*(4), 941–2.

Keith, M. (2005). *After the Cosmopolitan? Multicultural cities and the future of racism*. London: Routledge.

King, A. D. (Ed.) (1996). *Re-presenting the City: Ethnicity, capital, and culture in the 21st-century metropolis*. New York: New York University Press.

Knopp, L. (2009). From lesbian and gay to queer geographies: Pasts, prospects and possibilities. In K. Browne, J. Lim, & G. Brown (Eds.), *Geographies of sexualities: Theory, Practices, and Politics* (pp. 21–8). Aldershot: Ashgate.

Knox, P. L. (1996). *Urban Social Geography: An introduction* (3rd ed.). Harlow: Longman Scientific & Technical.

Komninos, N. (2012). *Intelligent Cities: Innovation, knowledge systems and digital spaces*. London: Routledge.

Krugman, P. (1991). Increasing returns and economic geography. *Journal of Political Economy*, *99*(3), 483–99.

Kuhn, T. S. (1962). *The Structure of Scientific Revolutions*. Chicago: University of Chicago Press.

Kumar, K. (1978). *Prophecy and Progress: The sociology of industrial and post-industrial society*. Harmondsworth: Penguin.

Kumar, K. (1995). *From Post-industrial to Post-modern Society: New theories of the contemporary world*. Oxford: Blackwell.

Kurtz, L. (1984). *Evaluating Chicago Sociology: A guide to the literature with an annotated bibliography*. Chicago: University of Chicago Press.

Lake, R. W. (Ed.) (1983). *Readings in Urban Analysis: Perspectives on urban form and structure*. New Brunswick, NJ: Center for Urban Policy Research.

Lasker, S. (2001). Sex and the city: Zoning pornography peddlers and live nude shows. *UCLA Law Review*, *49*, 1139–85.

Laughlin, J. (1996). 'Europe of the regions' and the federalization of Europe. *Publius*, *26*(4), 141–62.

Lauria, M. (Ed.) (1996). *Reconstructing Urban Regime Theory: Regulating urban politics in a global economy*. London: Sage.

Le Galès, P. (1995). *Urban Regimes and Comparative Urban Politics*. Paper presented to European Consortium for Political Research joint sessions workshop 'The Changing Local Governance of Europe', Bordeaux, March.

Le Galès, P. (2002). *European Cities: Social conflicts and governance*. Oxford: Oxford University Press.

Le Galès, P., & Harding, A. (1998). Cities and states in Europe. *West European Politics*, *21*(3). 120–45.

Le Galès, P., & Lequesne, C. (1998). *Regions in Europe*. London: Routledge.

Lebuhn, H. (2013). Local border practices and urban citizenship in Europe: Exploring urban borderlands. *CITY. Analysis of Urban Trends, Culture, Theory, Policy, Action*, 17(1), 37–51.

LeGates, R. T., & Stout, F. (Eds.) (2011). *The City Reader* (5th ed.). London: Routledge.

Lees, G., and Lambert, J. (1985). *Cities in Crisis*. London: Arnold.

Lees, L. (2002). Rematerializing geography: The 'new' urban geography. *Progress in Human Geography*, 26(1), 101–12.

Lees, L. (2008). Gentrification and social mixing: Towards an inclusive urban renaissance? *Urban Studies*, 45(12), 2449–70.

Lees, L., Slater, T., & Wyly, E. (2008). *Gentrification*. London: Routledge.

Lees, L., Slater, T., & Wyly, E. K. (Eds.) (2010). *The Gentrification Reader*. London: Routledge.

Lefebvre, H. (1991). *The Production of Space*. Oxford: Blackwell.

Lefebvre, H. (1995). *The Production of Space* (reprint). Oxford: Blackwell.

Leibovitz, J. (1999). New spaces of governance: Re-reading the local state in Ontario. *Space & Polity*, 3(2), 199–216.

Leibovitz, J. (2003). Institutional barriers to associative city-region governance: The politics of institution-building and economic governance in 'Canada's Technology Triangle'. *Urban Studies*, 40(13), 2613–42.

Lemert, C. (1995). *Sociology After the Crisis*. Boulder, CO: Westview Press.

Leo, C. (1998). Regional growth management regime: The case of Portland, Oregon. *Journal of Urban Affairs*, 20(4), 363–94.

Leventhal, T., & Brooks-Gunn, J. (2000). The neighborhoods they live in: The effects of neighborhood residence on child and adolescent outcomes. *Psychological Bulletin*, 126(2), 309–37.

Levine, M. A. (1994). The transformation of urban politics in France: The roots of growth politics and urban regimes. *Urban Affairs Quarterly*, 29(3), 383–410.

Levitt, R. L. (1987). *Cities Reborn*. Washington, DC: Urban Land Institute.

Lewis, O. (1961). *The Children of Sánchez*. New York: Random House.

Lewis, O. (1966a). *La Vida: A Puerto Rican family in the culture of poverty – San Juan and New York*. New York: Random House.

Lewis, O. (1966b). *The Culture of Poverty*. San Francisco: W. H. Freeman.

Lewis, O. (1968). *La Vida*. London: Panther.

Ley, D. (1974). *The Black Inner City as Frontier Outpost: Images and behaviour of a Philadelphia neighbourhood*. Washington, DC: AAG.

Ley, D. (1980). Liberal ideology and the postindustrial city. *Annals of the Association of American Geographers*, 70(2), 238–58.

Ley, D. (1983). *A Social Geography of the City*. New York: Harper & Row.

Ley, D. (1986). Alternative explanations for inner-city gentrification: A Canadian assessment. *Annals of the Association of American Geographers, 76*(4), 521–35.

Ley, D. (1994). Gentrification and the politics of the new middle class. *Environment and Planning D, 12*(1), 53–74.

Ley, D. (2003). Artists, aetheticisation and the field of gentrification. *Urban Studies, 40*(12), 2527–44.

Liebow, E. (1967). *Tally's Corner: A study of Negro streetcorner men.* Boston: Little, Brown.

Lin, J., & Mele, C. (Eds.) (2013). *The Urban Sociology Reader* (2nd ed.). London: Routledge.

Lindblom, C. E. (1977). *Politics and Markets: The world's political economic systems.* New York: Basic Books.

Lipietz, A. (1987). *Mirages and Miracles: The crises of global Fordism.* London: Verso.

Little, J. (1994). *Gender, Planning and the Policy Process. Politics, planning, and critical theory.* Oxford: Pergamon Press.

Little, J., Peake, L., & Richardson, P. (1988). *Women in Cities: Gender and the urban environment.* New York: New York University Press.

Lloyd, M. G., & Newlands, D. A. (1988). The 'growth coalition' and urban economic development. *Local Economy, 3*(1), 31–9.

Lockwood, D. (1996). Civic integration and class formation. *British Journal of Sociology of Education, 43*(3), 531–50.

Lofland, L. H. (1989). Private lifestyles, changing neighborhoods, and public life: A problem in organized complexity. *Tijdschrift voor Economische en Sociale Geografie, 80*(2), 89–96.

Lofland, L. H. (1998). *The Public Realm: Exploring the city's quintessential social territory. Communication and social order.* Hawthorne, NY: Aldine de Gruyter.

Logan, J. R., & Molotch, H. L. (1987). *Urban Fortunes: The political economy of place.* Berkeley: University of California Press.

Logan, J. R., & Swanstrom, T. (Eds.) (1990). *Beyond the City Limits: Urban policy and economic restructuring in comparative perspective.* Philadelphia: Temple University Press.

Logan, J. R., Whaley, R. B., & Crowder, K. (1997). The character and consequences of growth regimes: An assessment of 20 years of research. *Urban Affairs Review, 32*(5), 603–30.

Lösch, A. (1965). *The Economics of Location* (2nd rev. ed.). New Haven, CT: Yale University Press.

Löw, M. (2009). *Raumsoziologie.* Frankfurt am Main: Suhrkamp.

Low, S. M. (2003). *Behind the Gates: The new American dream.* London: Routledge.

Low, S. M. (2013). The erosion of public space and the public realm. In J. Lin & C. Mele (Eds.), *The Urban Sociology Reader* (2nd ed., pp. 401–4). London: Routledge.

Low, S., & Smith, N. (2006a). Introduction: The imperative of public space. In S. Low & N. Smith (Eds.), *The Politics of Public Space* (pp. 1–16). London: Routledge.

Low, S., & Smith, N. (Eds.) (2006b). *The Politics of Public Space*. London: Routledge.

Low, S. M., Taplin, D., & Scheld, S. (2005). *Rethinking Urban Parks: Public space & cultural diversity*. New York: New York University Press.

Loughlin, J. (1997). "Europe of the Regions" and the federalization of Europe. *Publius, 26*(4), 141–62.

Lowe, S. (1986). *Urban Social Movements: The city after Castells*. Basingstoke: Macmillan.

Luard, E. (1990). *The Globalization of Politics: The changed basis of political action in the modern world*. London: Macmillan.

Lukes, S. (1974). *Power: A Radical View*. Basingstoke: Macmillan.

Lyman, S. M., & Scott, M. B. (1967). Territoriality: A neglected sociological dimension. *Social Problems, 15*(2), 236–49.

Ma, L. J. (2002). Urban transformation in China, 1949–2000: A review and research agenda. *Environment and Planning A, 34*(9), 1545–70.

Mackenzie, S. (1989). Women in the city. In R. Peet & N. Thrift (Eds.), *New Models in Geography: Vol.2* (pp. 109–26). London: Routledge.

MacLeod, J. (1987). *Ain't No Makin' It: Leveled aspirations in a low-income neighborhood*. Boulder, CO: Westview Press.

Macmillan, B. (Ed.) (1989). *Remodelling Geography*. Oxford: Blackwell.

Madanipour, A. (2011). Social exclusion and space. In R. T. LeGates & F. Stout (Eds.), *The City Reader* (5th ed., pp. 186–94). London: Routledge.

Maloutas, T. (2007). Segregation, social polarization and immigration in Athens during the 1990s: Theoretical expectations and contextual difference. *International Journal of Urban and Regional Research, 31*(4), 733–58.

Mannheim, K. (1952). The problem of a sociology of knowledge. In P. Kecskemeti (Ed.), *Essays on the Sociology of Knowledge* (pp. 134–90). London: Routledge.

Marcuse, P. (1986). Abandonment, gentrification, and displacement: The linkages in New York City. In N. Smith & P. Williams (Eds.), *Gentrification of the City* (pp. 333–47). Boston: Allen & Unwin.

Marcuse, P., & van Kempen, R. (2000). *Globalizing Cities: A new spatial order?* Oxford: Blackwell.

Margalit, T. (2009). Public assets vs. public interest: Fifty years of high-rise building in Tel Aviv-Jaffa. *Geography Research Forum, 28*, 48–82.

Markowitz, F. E., Bellair, P. E., Liska, A. E., & Liu, J. (2001). Extending social disorganization theory: Modeling the relationships between cohesion, disorder and fear. *Criminology, 39*(2), 293–319.

Markusen, A. (1991). The military industrial divide. *Environment and Planning C: Government and Planning D: Society and Space, 9,* 391–415.

Markusen, A. (1996). Sticky places in slippery space: A typology of industrial districts. *Economic Geography, 72*(3), 293–313.

Markusen, A. (2013). City spatial structure, women's household work and national urban policy. In J. Lin & C. Mele (Eds.), *The Urban Sociology Reader* (2nd ed., pp. 249–59). London: Routledge.

Markusen, A., Glasmeir, A. and Hall, P. (1986). *High Tech America: The what, how, where and why of the sunrise industries.* London: Allen & Unwin.

Marques, E., Bichir, R., Moya, E., Zoppi, M., Pantoja, I., & Pavez, T. (2008). Personal networks and urban poverty: Preliminary findings. *Brazilian Political Science Review, 3.*

Marshall, A. (1890). *Principles of Economics.* London: Macmillan.

Martin, R. & Rowthorn, B. (Eds.) (1986). *The Geography of Deindustrialisation.* London: Macmillan.

Marx, K. (1978). *The Eighteenth Brumaire of Louis Bonaparte.* Peking: Foreign Languages Press.

Marx, K. (1948). *Le Capital: Critique de l'économie politique.* Paris: Éditions sociales.

Massey, D. (1984). *Space, Place and Gender.* Cambridge: Polity Press.

Massey, D., & Denton, N. (Eds.) (1993). *American Apartheid: Segregation and the making of the underclass.* Cambridge, MA: Harvard University Press.

Massey, D., & Denton, N. A. (2013). Segregation and the making of the underclass. In J. Lin & C. Mele (Eds.), *The Urban Sociology Reader* (2nd ed., pp. 192–201). London: Routledge.

Massey, D., & Meegan, R. (1980). Industrial restructuring versus the cities. In A. Evans & D. Eversley (Eds.), *The Inner City* (pp. 78–107). London: Heinemann.

Massey, D. and Meegan, R. (1982). *The Anatomy of Job Loss: The how, why and where of employment decline.* London: Methuen.

Matthews, F. (1977). *Quest for an American Sociology: Robert. E. Park and the Chicago School.* Montreal: McGill-Queen's University Press.

Mazlish, B. (1989). *A New Science: The breakdown of connections and the birth of sociology.* Oxford: Oxford University Press.

McCabe, J. D. (1882). *New York by Sunlight and Gaslight.* Philadelphia: Hubbard Brothers.

McCall, L. (2005). The complexity of intersectionality. *Signs, 30*(3), 1771–1800.

McDowell, L. (1983). Towards an understanding of the gender division of urban space. *Environment and Planning, 1,* 59–72.

McDowell, L. (1992). Doing gender: Feminism, feminists and research methods in human geography. *Transaction of the Institute of British Geographers, 17*(4), 399–416.

McKenzie, R. D. (1924). The ecological approach to the study of the human community. *American Journal of Sociology, 30,* 287–301.

McLean, I. (Ed.) (1996). *The Concise Oxford Dictionary of Politics.* Oxford: Oxford University Press.

Mechling, J. (1998). Heroism and the problem of impulsiveness for early twentieth-century American youth. In J. Austin & M. Willard (Eds.), *Generations of Youth: Youth cultures and history in twentieth century America* (pp. 36–49). New York: New York University Press.

Melo, P. C., Graham, D. J. & Noland, R. B. (2009). A meta-analysis of estimates of urban agglomeration economies. *Regional Science and Urban Economics, 39*(3), 332–42.

Merton, R. K. (1968). *Social Theory and Social Structure.* New York: Free Press.

Miles, M. (2007). *Cities and Cultures.* London: Routledge.

Mills, E. S. (Ed.) (2004). *Handbooks in Economics: Vol. 7. Urban economics.* Amsterdam: North-Holland.

Miranne, K. B., & Young, A. H. (Eds.) (2000). *Gendering the City: Women, boundaries, and visions or urban life.* Lanham, MD: Rowman & Littlefield.

Mitchell, D., & Staeheli, L. A. (2006). Clean and safe? Property redevelopment, public space, and homelessness in downtown San Diego. In S. Low & N. Smith (Eds.), *The Politics of Public Space* (pp. 143–76). London: Routledge.

Mollenkopf, J. H. (1983). *The Contested City.* Princeton, NJ: Princeton University Press.

Mollenkopf, J. H. (1989). Who (or what) runs cities, and how? *Sociological Forum, 4*(1), 119–37.

Mollenkopf, J. H., & Castells, M. (Eds.) (1992). *Dual City: Restructuring New York.* New York: Russell Sage Foundation.

Molotch, H. L. (1976). The city as a growth machine: Toward a political economy of place. *American Journal of Sociology, 82*(2), 309–32.

Molotch, H. L. (1990). Urban deals in comparative perspective. In J. R. Logan & T. Swanstrom (Eds.), *Beyond the City Limits. Urban policy and economic restructuring in comparative perspective* (pp. 175–98). Philadelphia: Temple University Press.

Molotch, H. L., & Logan, J. R. (1990). The space for urban action: Urban fortunes – a rejoinder. *Political Geography Quarterly, 9*(1), 85–92.

Molotch, H. L., & Vicari, S. (1988). Three ways to build: the development process in the United States, Japan and Italy. *Urban Affairs Review, 24*(2), 188–214.

Monteiro, C. (2008). Enclaves, condominiums, and favelas: Where are the ghettos in Brazil? *City & Community*, 7(4), 378–83.

Moore, E. (1897). The social value of the saloon. *American Journal of Sociology*, 3(1), 1–12.

Morenoff, J. D., Sampson, R. J., & Raudenbush, S. W. (2001). Neighborhood inequality, collective efficacy, and the spatial dynamics of urban violence. *Criminology*, 39(3), 517–58.

Morgen, S., & Maskovsky, J. (2003). The anthropology of welfare 'reform': New perspectives on U.S. urban poverty in the post-welfare era. *Annual Review of Anthropology*, 32(1), 315–38.

Morris, R. N. (2007 [1968]). *Urban Sociology*. London: Routledge.

Mossberger, K. (2009). Urban regime analysis. In J. S. Davies & D. L. Imbroscio (Eds.), *Theories of Urban Politics* (2nd ed., pp. 40–54). London: Sage.

Mulkay, M. (1979). *Science and the Sociology of Knowledge*. London: Allen & Unwin.

Mullins, P. (1990). Tourist cities as new cities: Australia's gold coast and sunshine coast. *Australian Planner*, 28(3), 37–41.

Mumford, L. (2011). What is a city? In R. T. LeGates & F. Stout (Eds.), *The City Reader* (5th ed., pp. 96–104). London: Routledge.

Murray, C. (1984). *Losing Ground: American social policy, 1950–1980*. New York: Basic Books.

Musterd, S. (2005a). Housing mix, social mix, and social opportunities. *Urban Affairs Review*, 40(6), 761–90.

Musterd, S. (2005b). Social and ethnic segregation in Europe: Levels, causes, and effects. *Journal of Urban Affairs*, 27(3), 331–48.

Musterd, S., & Ostendorf, W. (1998a). Segregation, polarisation and social exclusion in metropolitan areas. In S. Musterd & W. Ostendorf (Eds.), *Urban Segregation and the Welfare State. Inequality and exclusion in western cities* (pp. 1–14). London: Routledge.

Musterd, S., & Ostendorf, W. (Eds.) (1998b). *Urban Segregation and the Welfare State: Inequality and exclusion in western cities*. London: Routledge.

Musterd, S., Ostendorf, W., & de Vos, S. (2003). Neighbourhood effects and social mobility: A longitudinal analysis. *Housing Studies*, 18(6), 877–92.

Myrdal, G. (1969). *An American Dilemma*. New York: Harper & Row.

Nash, C. J. (2006). Toronto's gay village (1969–1982): Plotting the politics of gay identity. *Canadian Geographer/Géographe canadien*, 50(1), 1–16.

Nash, C. J., & Bain, A. (2007). 'Reclaiming raunch'? Spatializing queer identities at Toronto women's bathhouse events. *Social & Cultural Geography*, 8(1), 47–62.

Newman, K., & Wyly, E. K. (2010). The right to stay put, revisited: Gentrification and resistance to displacement in New York City. In L. Lees, T. Slater, & E. K. Wyly (Eds.), *The Gentrification Reader* (pp. 542–72). London: Routledge.

Newman, K. S. (1999). *No Shame in My Game: The working poor in the inner city*. New York: Knopf and Russell Sage Foundation.

Newman, O. (1973). *Defensible Space: Crime prevention through urban design*. New York: Collier Books.

Nicholls, W. J. (2005). Power and governance: Metropolitan governance in France. *Urban Studies*, 42(4), 783–800.

Nobles, M. (2010). 'Here a ghetto, there a ghetto': The value and peril of comparative study. *Urban Geography*, 31(2), 158–61.

Ocejo, R. E. (2009). As it seems: Producing and consuming nightlife in the postindustrial city. *Sociological Forum*, 24(3), 720–5.

O'Connor, A. (2004). Rasse, Klasse und Ausgrenzung: Das Konzept der Unterklasse in historischer Perspektive. In H. Häussermann, M. Kronauer, & W. Siebel (Eds.), *An den Rändern der Städte. Armut und Ausgrenzung* (pp. 43–70). Frankfurt am Main: Suhrkamp.

Odgers, C., Moffia, T., Tach, L., Sampson, R., Taylor, A., Matthews, C., & Caspi, A. (2009). The paradox of social organization: Networks, collective efficacy, and violent crime in urban neighborhoods. *Developmental Psychology*, 45(4), 942–61.

Ohmae, K. (1993). The rise of the region state. *Foreign Affairs*, 72(2), 78–87.

Oldenburg, R. (1999). *The Great Good Place: Cafés, coffee shop, bookstores, bars, hair salons, and other hangouts at the heart of a community*. Cambridge: Da Capo Press.

Olzak, S. (1992). *The Dynamics of Ethnic Competition and Conflict*. Stanford, CA: Stanford University Press.

Orr, M. E., & Stoker, G. (1994). Urban regimes and leadership in Detroit. *Urban Affairs Review*, 30(1), 48–73.

Oswin, N. (2008). Critical geographies and the uses of sexuality: Deconstructing queer space. *Progress in Human Geography*, 21(1), 89–103.

Outhwaite, W. (1987). *New Philosophies of Social Science: Realism, hermeneutics, and critical theory*. New York: St. Martin's Press.

Pahl, R. E. (1970). *Whose City? And other essays on sociology and planning*. London: Longman.

Pahl, R. E. (1975). *Whose City? And further essays on urban society*. Harmondsworth: Penguin.

Pahl, R. E. (1977). Stratification, the relation between states and urban and regional development. *International Journal of Urban and Regional Research*, 1(1–4), 6–18.

Paquot, T. (1999). The post-city challenge. In R. A. Beauregard & S. Body-Gendrot (Eds.), *The Urban Moment. Cosmopolitan essays on the late-20th-century city* (pp. 79–98). Thousand Oaks, CA: Sage.

Park, R. E. (1950). *Race and Culture*. Glencoe, IL: Free Press.

Park, R. E., Burgess, E. W., & McKenzie, R. D. (Eds.) (1925). *The City*. Chicago: University of Chicago Press.

Parsons, T. (1951). *The Social System*. New York: Free Press.

Pascal, A. (1987). The vanishing city. *Urban Studies*, 24(6), 597–603.

Patch, J. (2008). 'Ladies and gentrification': New stories, residents, and relationships in neighborhood change. In J. N. DeSena (Ed.), *Gender in an Urban World* (pp. 103–26). Bingley: Emerald.

Pattillo-McCoy, M. (1999). *Black Picket Fences: Privilege and peril in the black middle class neighborhood*. Chicago: University of Chicago Press.

Pattillo-McCoy, M. E. (1998). Sweet mothers and gangbangers: Managing crime in a black middle-class neighborhood. *Social Forces*, 76(3), 747–74.

Pawson, R. (2003). Nothing as practical as a good theory. *Evaluation*, 9(4), 471–90.

Peach, C. (1996). Does Britain have ghettos? *Transactions of the Institute of British Geographers*, 21(1), 216–35.

Peck, J. (1995). Moving and shaking: Business elites, state localism and urban privatism. *Progress in Human Geography*, 19(1), 16–46.

Peck, J. (2010). *Constructions of Neoliberal Reason*. Oxford: Oxford University Press.

Peck, J., Theodore, N. & Brenner, N. (2010). After neoliberalization?. *Globalizations*, 7(3), 327–45.

Peck, J. & Tickell, A. (2002). Neoliberalizing space. *Antipode*, 34(3), 380–404.

Peet, R. (1977). *Radical Geography: Alternative viewpoints on contemporary social issues*. Chicago: Maaroufa Press.

Peet, R. & Thrift, N. (Eds.) (1989). *New Models in Geography: Vol.2*. London: Routledge.

Peirce, N. R., with Johnson, C. W. & Hall, J. S. (1993). *Citistates: How urban America can prosper in a competitive world*. Washington, DC: Seven Locks Press.

Perry, D. & Watkins, A. (Eds.) (1977). *The Rise of the Sunbelt Cities*. London: Sage.

Peterson, P. E. (1981). *City Limits*. Chicago: University of Chicago Press.

Peterson, P. E. (1987). Analyzing development politics: A response to Sanders and Stone. *Urban Affairs Review*, 22(4), 540–7.

Peterson, R. A. (1979). Revitalizing the culture concept. *Annual Review of Sociology*, 5, 137–66.

Pettigrew, T. F. (1980). *The Sociology of Race Relations: Reflection and reform*. New York: Free Press.

Phillips, A. (1996). Feminism and the attraction of the local. In D. S. King & G. Stoker (Eds.), *Rethinking Local Democracy* (pp. 111–29). Basingstoke: Macmillan.

Phizacklea, A., & Miles, R. (1980). *Labour and Racism*. London: Routledge & Kegan Paul.

Pickett, K. E., & Pearl, M. (2001). Multilevel analyses of neighbourhood socio-economic context and health outcomes: A critical review. *Journal of Epidemology and Community Health*, 55(2), 111–22.

Pickles, J. (1985). *Phenomenology, Science and Geography: Spatiality and the human sciences*. New York: Cambridge University Press.

Pickvance, C. G. (Ed.) (1976). *Urban Sociology: Critical essays*. London: Tavistock.

Pierre, J. (2005). Comparative urban governance: Uncovering complex causalities. *Urban Affairs Review*, 40(4), 446–62.

Pinson, G. (2009). The new urban leaders: Changing modes of operation and legitimacy amongst local elected officials in Venice and Manchester. In H. Reynaert, P. Delwit, J.-B. Pilet, & K. Steyvers (Eds.), *Local Political Leadership in Europe. Town chief, city boss or loco president?* (pp. 225–46). Brugge: Vanden Broele.

Pinson, G. (2010). The governance of French towns. From the centre-periphery scheme to urban regime. *Análise sociale*, 45(197), 717–37.

Piore, M. and Sabel, C. (1984). *The Second Industrial Divide*. New York: Basic Books.

Podmore, J. A. (2001). Lesbians in the crowd: Gender, sexuality and visibility along Montréal's Boul. St-Laurent. *Gender, Place & Culture: A Journal of Feminist Geography*, 8(4), 333–55.

Polsby, N. (1980). *Community Power and Political Theory* (2nd ed.). New Haven, CT: Yale University Press.

Popper, K. (1934). *The Logic of Scientific Discovery*. London: Hutchinson.

Porter, M. (1990). *The Competitive Advantage of Nations*. New York: Free Press

Porter, M. E. (1996). Competitive advantage, agglomeration economies, and regional policy. *International Regional Science Review*, 19(1/2), 85–90.

Porter, M. (1998). Clusters and the new economics of competition, *Harvard Business Review*, November–December, 77–90.

Portes, A. (1998). Social capital: Its origins and applications in modern sociology. *Annual Review of Sociology*, 24(1), 1–24.

Portes, A., & Manning, R. D. (2013). The immigrant enclave: Theory and empirical examples. In J. Lin & C. Mele (Eds.), *The Urban Sociology Reader* (2nd ed., pp. 202–13). London: Routledge.

Pred, A. (1967). *Behaviour and Location: Foundations for a geographic and dynamic location theory*. Lund: GWK Gleerup.

Preston, V., & McLafferty, S. (1999). Spatial mismatch research in the 1990s: Progress and potential? *Papers in Regional Science*, 78(4), 387–402.

Prior, J., Boydell, S., & Hubbard, P. (2012). Nocturnal rights to the city: Property, propriety and sex premises in inner Sydney. *Urban Studies*, 49(8), 1837–52.

Putnam, R. D. with Leonardi, R. & Nanetti, R. Y. (1993). *Making Democracy Work*. Princeton, NJ: Princeton University Press.

Putnam, R. D. (2000). *Bowling Alone: The collapse and revival of American community*. New York: Simon & Schuster.

Rae, D. W. (2003). *City: Urbanism and its end*. New Haven, CT: Yale University Press.

Redfield, R. (1947). The folk society. *American Journal of Sociology, 52*(4), 293–308.

Reeves, D., & Greed, C. (2003). *Gender Mainstreaming Toolkit*. London: Royal Town Planning Institute.

Relph, E. (1970). An enquiry into the relations between phenomenology and geography. *Canadian Geographer, 14*(3), 193–201.

Rex, J. (1996). National identity in the democratic multi-cultural state. *Sociological Research Online, 1*(2).

Rex, J., & Moore, R. S. (1967). *Race, Community, and Conflict: A study of Sparkbrook*. Oxford: Oxford University Press.

Robertson, R. (1992). *Globalization: Social theory and global culture*. London: Sage.

Robinson, J. (2002). Global and world cities: a view from off the map. *International Journal of Urban and Regional Research 26*(3), 531–54.

Robinson, J. (2006). *Ordinary Cities: Between modernity and development*. London: Routledge.

Rogerson, R., & Boyle, M. (2000). Property, politics and the neo-liberal revolution in urban Scotland. *Progress in Planning, 54*(3), 133–96.

Rose, D. (2010). Rethinking gentrification: Beyond the uneven development of Marxist urban theory. In L. Lees, T. Slater, & E. K. Wyly (Eds.), *The Gentrification Reader* (pp. 195–219). London: Routledge.

Rosentraub, M. S., & Helmke, P. (1996). Location theory, a growth coalition, and a regime in the development of a medium-sized city. *Urban Affairs Review, 31*(4), 482–507.

Rothenberg, T. (1995). 'And she told two friends': Lesbians creating urban social space. In D. Bell & G. Valentine (Eds.), *Mapping Desire. Geographies of sexualities* (pp. 165–81). London: Routledge.

Rountree, P. W., & Land, K. C. (1996). Perceived risk versus fear of crime. Empirical evidence of conceptually distinct reactions in survey data. *Social Forces, 74*(4), 1353–76.

Rountree, P. W., & Warner, B. D. (1999). Social ties and crime: Is the relationship gendered? *Criminology, 37*(4), 789–814.

Rowles, G. D. (1978). *Prisoners of Space?* Boulder, CO: Westview Press.

Ryder, A. (2004). The changing nature of adult entertainment districts: Between a rock and a hard place or going from strength to strength? *Urban Studies, 41*(9), 1659–86.

Sabel, C. F. (1989). Flexible specialisation and the re-emergence of regional economies. In P. Hirst & J. Zeitlin (Eds.), *Reversing Industrial Decline? Industrial structure and policy in Britain and her competitors.* Oxford: Berg.

Sampson, R. J., Morenoff, J. D., & Earls, F. (1999). Beyond social capital: Spatial dynamics of collective efficacy for children. *American Sociological Review*, *64*(5), 633–60.

Sampson, R. J., Morenoff, J. D., & Gannon-Rowley, T. (2002). Assessing 'neighborhood effects': Social processes and new directions in research. *Annual Review of Sociology*, *28*(1), 443–78.

Sampson, R. J., & Raudenbush, S. W. (2004). Seeing disorder: Neighborhood stigma and the social construction of 'broken windows'. *Social Psychology Quarterly*, *67*(4), 319–42.

Sampson, R. J., Raudenbush, S. W., & Earls, F. (1997). Neighborhoods and violent crime: A multilevel study of collective efficacy. *Science*, *277*(5328), 918–24.

Sanchez, L. E. (2004). The global erotic subject, the ban, and the prostitute-free zone. *Environment and Planning D: Society and Space*, *22*(6), 861–83.

Sandercock, L. (1998). *Making the Invisible Visible: A multicultural planning history*. Berkeley: University of California Press.

Sanders, H. T., & Stone, C. N. (1987a). Competing paradigms: a rejoinder to Peterson. *Urban Affairs Review*, *22*(4), 548–51.

Sanders, H. T., & Stone, C. N. (1987b). Developmental politics reconsidered. *Urban Affairs Review*, *22*(4), 521–39.

Sanders, T. (2004). The risks of street prostitution: Punters, police and protesters. *Urban Studies*, *41*(9), 1703–17.

Sassen, S. (1991). *The Global City: New York, London, Tokyo*. Princeton, NJ: University Press.

Sassen, S. (1994). *Cities in a World Economy*. Thousand Oaks, CA: Pine Forge Press.

Sassen, S. (2007). The repositioning of cities and urban regions in a global economy: Pushing policy and governance options. In OECD, *What Policies for Global Cities? Rethinking the urban policy agenda*. Paris: OECD.

Saunders, P. (1979). *Urban Politics: A sociological interpretation*. London: Hutchinson.

Saunders, P. (1985). Space, the city and urban sociology. In D. Gregory & J. Urry (Eds.), *Social Relations and Spatial Structures* (pp. 67–89). Basingstoke: Macmillan.

Saunders, P. (1986). *Social Theory and the Urban Question* (2nd ed.). New York: Holmes & Meir.

Saunders, P. (1990). *A Nation of Homeowners*. London: Unwin Hyman.

Savage, M. (1995). Walter Benjamin's urban thought: A critical analysis. *Environment and Planning D*, *13*, 201–16.

Savage, M., & Warde, A. (2005). Modernity, post-modernity and urban culture. In N. Kleniewski (Ed.), *Cities and Society* (pp. 72–80). Oxford: Blackwell.

Savage, M., Bagnall, G., & Longhurst, B. (2005). *Globalization and Belonging*. London: Sage.

Savage, M., Warde, A., & Ward, K. (2003). *Urban Sociology, Capitalism and Modernity* (2nd ed.). Basingstoke: Palgrave.

Savitch, H. V. (1988). *Post-industrial cities: Politics and planning in New York, Paris, and London*. Princeton, NJ: Princeton University Press.

Saxenian, A. L. (1996). *Regional Advantage: Culture and competition in Silicon Valley and Route 128*. Cambridge, MA: Harvard University Press.

Sayer, R. A. (1992). *Method in Social Science: A realist approach* (2nd ed.). London: Routledge.

Sbragia, A. M. (Ed.) (1983). *The Municipal Money Chase: The politics of local government finance*. Boulder, CO: Westview Press.

Schneider, M., & Teske, P. (1993). The antigrowth entrepreneur: Challenging the 'equilibrium' of the growth machine. *Journal of Politics, 55*(3), 720–736.

Schnore, L. F. (1963). The socio-economic status of cities and suburbs. *American Sociological Review, 28*(1), 76–85.

Schumpeter, J. (1944). *Capitalism, Socialism and Democracy*. London: Allen & Unwin.

Sciorra, J. (1996). Return to the future: Puerto Rican vernacular architecture in New York City. In A. D. King (Ed.), *Re-presenting the City: Ethnicity, capital, and culture in the 21st-century metropolis* (pp. 60–92). Basingstoke: Macmillan.

Scott, A. (Ed.) (1997). *The Limits of Globalization: Cases and arguments*. London: Routledge.

Scott, A. & Storper, M. (2014, forthcoming). The nature of cities: The scope and limits of urban theory, *International Journal for Urban and Regional Research*.

Scott, A. J. (Ed.) (2001). *Global City-regions: Trends, theory, policy*. Oxford: Oxford University Press.

Scott, A. J. and Soja, E. W. (1996) Los Angeles: Capital of the late 20th century. *Society and Space, 4*, 249–54.

Sellers, J. M. (2002). *National political economies and urban regime building*. Paper presented at Urban Affairs Association Annual Meeting, Boston, March.

Sen, A. K. (1999). *Commodities and Capabilities*. Oxford: Oxford University Press.

Sennett, R. (1973). *The Uses of Disorder*. Harmondsworth: Penguin.

Sennett, R. (1992a). *The Conscience of the Eye: The design and social life of cities*. New York: Norton.

Sennett, R. (1992b). *The Fall of Public Man*. New York: Norton.

Sennett, R. (1994). *Flesh and Stone: The body and the city in western civilization*. New York: Norton.

Sennett, R. (2010). The public realm. In G. Bridge & S. Watson (Eds.), *The Blackwell City Reader* (2nd ed., pp. 261–72). Oxford: Wiley Blackwell.

Sewell, J. E. (2011). Gendering urban space. In G. Bridge & S. Watson (Eds.), *The New Blackwell Companion to the City* (pp. 596–605). Oxford: Wiley Blackwell.

Sharkey, P. (2013). *Stuck in Place: Urban neighborhoods and the end of progress toward racial equality*. Chicago: University of Chicago Press.

Shaw, C. R., & McKay, H. D. (1942). *Juvenile Delinquency and Urban Areas*. Chicago: University of Chicago Press.

Shaw, K. (1993). The development of a new urban corporatism: The politics of urban regeneration in the North East of England. *Regional Studies, 27*(3), 251–9.

Shefter, M. (1992). *Political Crisis/Fiscal Crisis: The collapse and revival of New York City*. New York: Columbia University Press.

Shevky, E., & Bell, W. (1955). *Social Area Analysis: Theory, illustrative application, and computational procedures*. Stanford, CA: Stanford University Press.

Shiba, H. (2008). *Comparative Local Governance: Lessons from New Zealand for Japan* (dissertation). Victoria University of Wellington, Wellington.

Shields, R. (1996). A guide to urban representation and what to do about it: Alternative traditions of urban theory. In A. D. King (Ed.), *Re-presenting the City: Ethnicity, capital, and culture in the 21st-century metropolis* (pp. 227–52). Basingstoke: Macmillan.

Shields, S. A. (2008). Gender: An intersectionality perspective. *Sex Roles, 59*(5–6), 301–311.

Short, J. R. (1984). *An Introduction to Urban Geography*. London: Routledge.

Short, J. R. (1989). *The Humane City: Cities as if people matter*. Oxford: Blackwell.

Short, J. R. (1996). *The Urban Order: An introduction to cities, culture and power*. Cambridge, MA: Blackwell.

Short, J. R. (2006). *Urban Theory: A critical assessment*. Basingstoke: Palgrave Macmillan.

Sibalis, M. (2004). Urban space and homosexuality: The example of the Marais, Paris' 'gay ghetto'. *Urban Studies, 41*(9), 1739–58.

Simmel, G. (1950 [1908]). The metropolis and mental life. In K. H. Wolff (Ed.), *The Sociology of Georg Simmel* (pp. 409–24). New York: Free Press.

Simmel, G. (1964). *Conflict: The Web of Group-affiliations*. New York: Free Press.

Simon, H. (1957). *Models of Man*. New York: John Wiley.

Simon, W., & Gagnon, J. H. (1967). Homosexuality: The formulation of a sociological perspective. *Journal of Health and Social Behavior, 8*(3), 177–85.

Simone, A. M. (2010). *City Life from Jakarta to Dakar: Movements at the cross-roads*. London: Routledge.

Simpson, L. (2007). Ghettos of the mind: The empirical behaviour of indices of segregation and diversity. *Journal of the Royal Statistical Society A, 170*(2), 405–24.

Sites, W. (1997). The limits of urban regime theory: New York City under Koch, Deakins, and Giuliani. *Urban Affairs Review, 32*(4), 536–57.

Skeggs, B., Moran, L., Tyrer, P., & Binnie, J. (2004). Queer as folk: Producing the real of urban space. *Urban Studies, 41*(9), 1839–56.

Skeldon, R. (1997). Hong Kong: Colonial city to global city to provincial city? *City, 14*(5), 256–71.

Skelton, T., & Valentine, G. (Eds.) (1997). *Cool Places: Geographies of youth cultures*. London: Routledge.

Sklair, L. (1991). *Sociology of the Global System. Social change in global perspective*. New York: Harvester Wheatsheaf.

Slater, T. (2006). The eviction of critical perspectives from gentrification research. *International Journal of Urban and Regional Research, 30*(4), 737–57.

Slater, T. (2010). Ghetto blasting: On Loïc Wacquant's *Urban Outcasts*. *Urban Geography, 31*(2), 162–8.

Slater, T. (2013). Your life chances affect where you live: A critique of the 'cottage industry' of neighbourhood effects research. *International Journal of Urban and Regional Research, 37*(2), 367–87.

Small, M. L. (2006). Neighborhood institutions as resource brokers: Childcare centers, interorganizational ties, and resource access among the poor. *Social Problems, 53*(2), 274–92.

Small, M. L., Harding, D. J., & Lamont, M. (2010). Reconsidering culture and poverty. *Annals of the American Academy of Political and Social Science, 629*(1), 6–27.

Small, M. L., & Newman, K. (2001). Urban poverty after the truly disadvantaged: The rediscovery of the family, the neighborhood, and culture. *Annual Review of Sociology, 27*(1), 23–45.

Smith, D. (1988). *The Chicago School: A liberal critique of capitalism*. London: Macmillan.

Smith, D. A. (1995). The new urban sociology meets the old: Rereading some classical human ecology. *Urban Affairs Review, 30*(3), 432–57.

Smith, M. P. (1980). *The City and Social Theory*. Oxford: Blackwell.

Smith, M. P. (2002). Power in place: Retheorizing the local and the global. In J. Eade & C. Mele (Eds.), *Understanding the City: Contemporary and future perspectives* (pp. 109–30). Oxford: Blackwell.

Smith, M. P., & Feagin, J. R. (Eds.) (1987). *The Capitalist City: Global restructuring and community politics*. Oxford: Blackwell.

Smith, N. (1979). Toward a theory of gentrification: A back to the city movement by capital, not people. *Journal of the American Planning Association*, *45*(4), 538–48.

Smith, N. (1982). Gentrification and uneven development. *Economic Geography*, *58*(2), 139–55.

Smith, N. (1983). Towards a theory of gentrification. In R. W. Lake (Ed.), *Readings in Urban Analysis. Perspectives on urban form and structure* (pp. 278–98). New Brunswick, NJ: Center for Urban Policy Research.

Smith, N. (1997). The satanic geographies of globalization: Uneven development in the 1990s. *Public Culture*, *10*(1), 169–89.

Smith, N. (2001). Global social cleansing: Postliberal revanchism and the export of zero tolerance. *Social Justice*, *28*(3(85)), 68–74.

Smith, N. (2010). Toward a theory of gentrification: A back to the city movement by capital, not people. In L. Lees, T. Slater, & E. K. Wyly (Eds.), *The Gentrification Reader* (pp. 85–98). London: Routledge.

Smith, N., & Williams, P. (2010). Alternatives to orthodoxy: Invitation to a debate. In L. Lees, T. Slater, & E. K. Wyly (Eds.), *The Gentrification Reader* (pp. 9–10). London: Routledge.

Soja, E. W. (1989). *Post-modern Geographies: The re-assertion of space in critical social theory*. London: Verso.

Soja, E. W. (2000). *Postmetropolis: Critical studies of cities and regions*. Oxford: Blackwell.

Sollors, W. (Ed.) (1996). *Theories of Ethnicity: A classical reader*. London: Macmillan.

Sorkin, M. (1992). *Variations on a Theme Park: The new American city and the end of public space*. New York: Hill and Wang.

Souther, J. M. (2007). The disneyfication of New Orleans: The French Quarter as facade in a divided city. *Journal of American History*, *94*(3), 804–11.

Spain, D. (2008). Gendered spaces and the public realm. In J. N. DeSena (Ed.), *Gender in an Urban World* (pp. 9–28). Bingley: Emerald.

Spain, D. (2011). What happened to gender relations on the way from Chicago to Los Angeles? In R. T. LeGates & F. Stout (Eds.), *The City Reader* (5th ed., pp. 176–85). London: Routledge.

Spencer, H. (1864). *The Principle of Biology*. London: Williams and Norgate.

Squires, G. D. (2011). Partnership and the pursuit of the private city. In S. S. Fainstein & S. Campbell (Eds.), *Readings in Urban Theory* (3rd ed., pp. 207–28). Oxford: Wiley-Blackwell.

Stacey, M. (1969). The myth of community studies. *British Journal of Sociology*, *20*(2), 134–47.

Staeheli, L. A., & Clarke, S. E. (1995). Gender, place, and citizenship. In J. A. Garber & R. S. Turner (Eds.), *Gender in Urban Research* (pp. 3–23). Thousand Oaks, CA: Sage.

Staeheli, L. A., & Mitchell, D. (2004). Spaces of public and private: Locating politics. In C. Barnett & M. Low (Eds.), *Spaces of Democracy: Geographical perspectives on citizenship, participation and representation* (pp. 147–60). London: Sage.

Stansell, C. (1986). *City of Women: Sex and class in New York, 1789–1860.* New York: Knopf.

Steptoe, A., & Feldman, P. J. (2001). Neighborhood problems as sources of chronic stress: Development of a measure of neighborhood problems, and associations with socioeconomic status and health. *Annals of Behavioral Medicine., 23*(3), 177–85.

Sternberg, R. (1996). Reasons for the genesis of high-tech regions – theoretical explanation and empirical evidence. *Geoforum, 27*(2), 205–23.

Stoker, G. (1995). Regime theory and urban politics. In D. Judge, G. Stoker, & H. Wolman (Eds.), *Theories of Urban Politics* (pp. 54–71). London: Sage.

Stoker, G., & Mossberger, K. (1994). Urban regime theory in comparative perspective. *Environment and Planning C: Government and Policy, 12*(2), 195–212.

Stoker, G., & Mossberger, K. (1995). The post-Fordist local state: The dynamics of its development. In J. Stewart & G. Stoker (Eds.), *Local Government in the 1990s.* Basingstoke: Macmillan.

Stone, C. N. (1980). Systemic power in community decision making: A restatement of stratification theory. *American Political Science Review, 74*(4), 978–90.

Stone, C. N. (1988). Preemptive power: Floyd Hunter's 'community power structure' reconsidered. *American Journal of Political Science, 32*(1), 82–104.

Stone, C. N. (1989). *Regime Politics: Governing Atlanta, 1946–1988.* Lawrence: University Press of Kansas.

Stone, C. N. (1997). *Urban Regime Analysis: Theory, service provision, and cross-national considerations.* Paper presented to the ECPR workshop on Local Elites in a Comparative Perspective, Bern, February.

Stone, C. N. (2001a). Civic capacity and urban education. *Urban Affairs Review, 36*(5), 595–619.

Stone, C. N. (2001b). The Atlanta experience re-examined: The link between agenda and regime change. *International Journal of Urban and Regional Research, 25*(1), 20–34.

Stone, C. N. (2006). Power, reform, and urban regime analysis. *City & Community, 5*(1), 23–38.

Stone, C. N., & Sanders, H. T. (Eds.) (1987). *The Politics of Urban Development.* Lawrence: University Press of Kansas.

Storper, M. (1993). Regional 'worlds' of production: Learning and innovation in the technology districts of France, Italy and the USA, *Regional Studies,27*(5), 433–55.

Storper, M. (1997). *The Regional World*. New York: Guilford Press.

Storper, M. (2001). The poverty of radical theory today: From the false promises of Marxism to the mirage of the cultural turn. *International Journal of Urban and Regional Research*, 25(1), 155–79.

Storper, M., Kemeny, T., Makarem, N. & Osman, T. (forthcoming). *The Economies of City-regions: The divergence of Los Angeles and San Francisco, 1970 to the present*. Stanford, CA: Stanford University Press.

Storper, M., & Manville, M. (2006). Behaviour, preferences and cities: Urban theory and urban resurgence. *Urban Studies*, 43(8), 1247–74.

Storper, M. & Scott, A.J. (Eds.) (1992). *Pathways to Industrialization and Regional Development*. London: Routledge.

Stout, F. (2011). Visions of a new reality: The city and the emergence of modern visual culture. In R. T. LeGates & F. Stout (Eds.), *The City Reader* (5th ed., pp. 150–3). London: Routledge.

Strom, E. (1996). In search of the growth coalition: American urban theories and the redevelopment of Berlin. *Urban Affairs Review*, 31(4), 455–81.

Swanstrom, T. (1985). *The Crisis of Growth Politics: Cleveland, Kucinich, and the challenge of urban populism*. Philadelphia: Temple University Press.

Sweet, W. L. (2010). Woman and the city. In R. Hutchison (Ed.), *Encyclopedia of Urban Studies* (pp. 963–66). Thousand Oaks, CA: Sage.

Swyngedouw, E. (2009). The antinomies of the postpolitical city: In search of a democratic politics of environmental production. *International Journal of Urban and Regional Research*, 33(3), 601–20.

Taeuber, K. E., & Taeuber, A. F. (1965). *Negroes in Cities: Residential segregation and neighborhood change*. Population Research and Training Center monographs. Chicago: Aldine.

Taylor, P. J. (2004). *World City Network: A global urban analysis*. London: Routledge,

Taylor, P. J., Derudder, B., Saey, P. & Witlox, F. (Eds.) (2006). *Cities in Globalization*. London: Routledge.

Theodore, N. (2010). Urban underclass: The wayward travels of a chaotic concept. *Urban Geography*, 31(2), 169–74.

Thomas, W. I., & Znaniecki, F. (1918–20). *The Polish Peasant in Europe and America: Monograph of an immigrant group*. Chicago: University of Chicago Press.

Thornley, A., & Newman, P. (1996). *Urban Planning in Europe: International competition, national systems and planning projects*. London: Routledge.

Tiebout, C. M. (1956). A pure theory of local expenditures. *Journal of Political Economy*, 64(5), 416–24.

Tilly, C. (1998). *Durable Inequality*. Berkeley: University of California Press.

Tilly, C., & Blockmans, W. P. (1994). *Cities and the Rise of States in Europe, A.D. 1000 to 1800*. Boulder, CO: Westview Press.

Tong, R. (1998). *Feminist Thought: A more comprehensive introduction* (2nd ed.). Boulder, CO: Westview Press.

Tonkiss, F. (2005). *Space, the City and Social Theory: Social relations and urban forms*. Cambridge: Polity.

Toyne, P. (1974). *Organisation, Location and Behaviour: Decision-making in economic geography*. London: Macmillan.

Trasher, F. M. (1927). *The Gang: A study of 1313 gangs in Chicago*. Chicago: University of Chicago Press.

Tretter, E. M. (2008). Scales, regimes, and the urban governance of Glasgow. *Journal of Urban Affairs, 30*(1), 87–102.

Tucker, A. (2009). *Queer Visibilities: Space, identity and interaction in Cape Town*. Oxford: Wiley-Blackwell.

Turok, I., & Edge, N. (1999). *The Jobs Gap in Britain's Cities*. Bristol: Policy Press.

Uteng, T., & Cresswell, T. (2008). *Gendered Mobilities*. London: Ashgate.

Vacchelli, E. (2008). Milan 1970–1980: Women's place in urban theory. In J. N. DeSena (Ed.), *Gender in an Urban World* (pp. 29–52). Bingley: Emerald.

Vaiou, D. (1992). Gender divisions in urban space: Beyond the rigidity of dualist classifications. *Antipode, 24*(4), 247–62.

Valentine, G. (2007). Theorizing and researching intersectionality: A challenge for feminist geography. *Professional Geographer, 59*(1), 10–21.

Valler, D. (1995). Local economic strategy and local coalition-building. *Local Economy, 10*(1), 33–47.

van der Laan Bouma-Doff, W. (2007a). Confined contact: Residential segregation and ethnic bridges in the Netherlands. *Urban Studies, 44*(5/6), 997–1017.

van der Laan Bouma-Doff, W. (2007b). Involuntary isolation: Ethnic preferences and residential segregation. *Journal of Urban Affairs, 29*(3), 289–309.

van der Laan Bouma-Doff, W. (2008). Concentrating on participation: Ethnic concentration and labour market participation of four ethnic groups. *Zeitschrift für Wirtschafts- und Sozialwissenschaften, 128*(1), 153–73.

van der Laan Bouma-Doff, W. (2010). *Puzzling Neighbourhood Effects: Spatial selection, ethnic concentration and neighbourhood impacts*. Amsterdam:IOS Press.

van Eijk, G. (2010). *Unequal Networks: Spatial segregation, relationships and inequality in the city*. Amsterdam: IOS Press.

van Kempen, R., & Sule Özüekren, A. (1998). Ethnic segregation in cities: New forms and explanations in a dynamic world. *Urban Studies, 35*(10), 1631–56.

van Niekerk, M., Sunier, T., & Vermeulen, H. (1989). *Bekende vreemden: Surinamers, Turken en Nederlanders in een naoorlogse wijk*. Amsterdam: Het Spinhuis.

van Ostaaijen, J. (2010). *Aversion and Accommodation: Political change and urban regime analysis in Dutch local government, Rotterdam 1998–2008*. Delft: Eburon.

Vargas, J. C., & Amparo Alves, J. (2010). Geographies of death: An intersectional analysis of police lethality and the racialized regimes of citizenship in São Paulo. *Ethnic and Racial Studies*, *33*(4), 611–36.

Veltz, P. (1996). *Mondialisation, villes et territories: L'*économie d'archipel. Paris: Presses Universitaires de France.

Venkatesh, S. A. (2000). *American Project: The rise and fall of a modern ghetto.* Cambridge, MA: Harvard University Press.

Verkuyten, M. (1997). *Redelijk racisme: Gesprekken over allochtonen in oude stadswijken.* Amsterdam: Amsterdam University Press.

Vermeulen, H. (1990). De multi-etnische samenleving op buurtniveau. In H. B. Entzinger & P. J. J. Stijnen (Eds.), *Etnische minderheden in Nederland* (pp. 216–43). Meppel: Boom.

Vertovec, S., & Wessendorf, S. (Eds.) (2010). *The Multiculturalism Backlash: European discourses, policies and practices.* London: Routledge.

Veysey, B. M., & Messner, S. F. (1999). Further testing of social disorganization theory: An elaboration of Sampson and Groves's 'Community structure and crime'. *Journal of Research in Crime and Delinquency*, *36*(2), 156–74.

Vicari, S., & Molotch, H. L. (1990). Building Milan: Alternative machines of growth. *International Journal of Urban and Regional Research*, *14*(4), 602–24.

Vitellio, I. (2009). *Regimi urbani e grandi eventi: Napoli, una città sospesa.* Milan: FrancoAngeli.

Wacquant, L. (1993). Urban outcasts: Stigma and division in the black American ghetto and the French urban periphery. *International Journal of Urban and Regional Research*, *17*(3), 366–83.

Wacquant, L. (1995). The ghetto, the state and the new capitalist economy. In P. Kasinitz (Ed.), *Metropolis: Center and symbol of our times* (pp. 418–49). New York: New York University Press.

Wacquant, L. (1996). Red belt, black belt: Racial division, class inequality and the state in the French urban periphery and the American ghetto. In E. Mingione (Ed.), *Urban Poverty and the Underclass: A reader* (pp. 234–74). Oxford: Blackwell.

Wacquant, L. (1997). Three pernicious premises in the study of the American ghetto. *International Journal of Urban and Regional Research*, *21*(2), 341–53.

Wacquant, L. (1999). Urban marginality in the coming millennium. *Urban Studies*, *36*(10), 1639–47.

Wacquant, L. (2007). Territorial stigmatization in the age of advanced marginality. *Thesis Eleven*, *91*(1), 66–77.

Wacquant, L. J. D. (2008). *Urban Outcasts: A comparative sociology of advanced marginality.* Cambridge: Polity Press.

Wacquant, L. J. D. (2009). *Punishing the Poor: The neoliberal government of social insecurity. Politics, history, and culture.* Durham, NC: Duke University Press.

Wacquant, L. (2010a). Class, race & hyperincarceration in revanchist America. *Daedalus, 139*(3), 74–90.

Wacquant, L. (2010b). Urban desolation and symbolic denigration in the hyper-ghetto. *Social Psychology Quarterly, 73*(3), 215–19.

Wacquant, L. J. D., & Wilson, W. J. (2013). The cost of racial and class exclusion in the inner city. In J. Lin & C. Mele (Eds.), *The Urban Sociology Reader* (2nd ed., pp. 182–91). London: Routledge.

Wagner, U., van Dick, R., Pettigrew, T. F., & Christ, O. (2003). Ethnic prejudice in East and West Germany: The explanatory power of intergroup contact. *Group Processes & Intergroup Relations, 6*(1), 22–36.

Waldinger, R. (1993). The ethnic enclave debate revisited. *International Journal of Urban and Regional Research, 17*(3), 444–452.

Wallerstein, I. M. (1991). *Geopolitics and Geoculture: Essays on the changing world-system.* Cambridge: Cambridge University Press.

Wang, Y., & Scott, S. (2008). Illegal farmland conversion in China's urban periphery: Local regime and national transitions. *Urban Geography, 29*(4), 327–47.

Ward, J. (1975). Skid row as a geographic entity. *Professional Geographer, 27*(3), 286–96.

Ward, K. (1996). Rereading urban regime theory: A sympathetic critique. *Geoforum, 27*(4), 427–38.

Warner, B. D., & Rountree, P. W. (1997). Local social ties in a community and crime model: Questioning the systemic nature of informal social control. *Social Problems, 44*(4), 520–36.

Waters, M. (1995). *Globalization.* London: Routledge.

Watson, S. (2002). The public city. In J. Eade & C. Mele (Eds.), *Understanding the City. Contemporary and future perspectives* (pp. 49–65). Oxford: Blackwell.

Watson, S. (2010). City A/Genders. In G. Bridge & S. Watson (Eds.), *The Blackwell City Reader* (2nd ed., pp. 237–42). Oxford: Blackwell.

Watson, S., & Gibson, K. (Eds.) (1995). *Postmodern cities and spaces.* Oxford: Blackwell.

Watt, P. (2009). Living in an oasis: Middle-class disaffiliation and selective belonging in an English suburb. *Environment and Planning A, 41*(12), 2874–92.

Weber, M. (1958). *The City.* Glencoe, IL: Free Press.

Weaver, R.C. (1940). Racial Policy in Public Housing. *Phylon (1940–1956)* 1(2): 149–161.

Weber, M. (1968). *Economy and Society: An outline of interpretive sociology.* New York: Bedminster Press.

Weber, M. (1988). *Gesammelte Aufsätze zur Wissenschaftslehre.* Tübingen: Mohr.

Webster, C. (2001). Gated cities of tomorrow. *Town Planning Review, 72*(2), 149–70.

Wellman, B. (Ed.) (1999). *Networks in the Global Village: Life in contemporary communities.* Boulder, CO: Westview Press.

Wellman, B., & Leighton, B. (1979). Networks, neighborhoods, and communities: Approaches to the study of the community question. *Urban Affairs Review, 14*(3), 363–90.

Wessel, T. (2000). Social polarization and socio-economic segregation in a welfare state: The case of Oslo. *Urban Studies, 37*(11), 1947–67.

Western, J. (2010). Just how different? Loïc Wacquant's Chicago-Paris comparisons. *Urban Geography, 31*(2), 175–8.

Wetzstein, S. (2007). *Economic Governance for a Globalising Auckland? Political projects, institutions and policy* (dissertation). University of Auckland, Auckland.

Whitzman, C. (2004). Safer cities, gender mainstreaming, and human rights. In R. La Paz (Ed.), *Report of Valladolid 2004: The Right to Safety and the City* (pp. 23–7). Valladolid: University of Valladolid, School of Architecture.

Whyte, W. F. (1981 [1943]). *Street Corner Society: The social structure of an Italian slum* (3rd ed., rev. and expanded). Chicago: University of Chicago Press.

Whyte, W. H. (2004). *The Social Life of Small Urban Spaces* (3rd edition). New York: Project for Public Spaces.

Williams, M. D. (1981). *On the Street Where I Lived: Case studies in cultural anthropology.* New York: Holt, Rinehart and Winston.

Williams, T. (1990). *The Cocaine Kids: The inside story of a teenage drug ring.* New York: Da Capo Press.

Williamson, T., Imbroscio, D., & Aplerovitz, G. (2005). The challenge or urban sprawl. In N. Kleniewski (Ed.), *Cities and Society* (pp. 303–29). Oxford: Blackwell.

Willmott, P., & Young, M. (1967). *Family and Class in a London suburb.* London: NEL Mentors.

Wilson, A. (1989). Mathematical models and geographical theory. In D. Gregory & R. Walford (Eds.), *Horizons in Human Geography* (pp. 29–47). Basingstoke: Macmillan.

Wilson, W. J. (1987). *The Truly Disadvantaged: The inner city, the underclass, and public policy.* Chicago: University of Chicago Press.

Wilson, E. (1991). *The Sphinx in the City: Urban life, the control of disorder, and women.* Berkeley: University of California Press.

Wilson, J. Q., & Kelling, G. L. (1982). Broken windows. *Atlantic Monthly*, 249(3), 29–38.

Wilson, W. J. (1996). *When Work Disappears: The world of the new urban poor*. New York: Knopf.

Wimmer, A. & Glick-Schiller, N. (2002). Methodological nationalism and beyond: Nation-state building, migration and the social sciences. *Global Networks*, 2(4), 301–34.

Winlow, S. (2001). *Badfellas: Crime, tradition and new masculinities*. Oxford: Berg.

Wirth, L. (1928). *The Ghetto*. Chicago: University of Chicago Press.

Wirth, L. (1938). Urbanism as a way of life. *American Journal of Sociology*, 44(1), 1–24.

Wood, A. M. (1996). Analysing the politics of local economic development: Making sense of cross-national convergence. *Urban Studies*, 33(8), 1281–95.

Wood, A. M. (2004). Domesticating urban theory? US concepts, British cities and the limits of cross-national applications. *Urban Studies*, 41(11), 2103–18.

Wolff, K. H. (Ed.) (1950). *The Sociology of Georg Simmel*. New York: Free Press.

World Bank (2008). *Reshaping Economic Geography: World development report 2009*. Washington, DC: World Bank.

Wrench, J., & Solomos, J. (Eds.) (1993). *Racism and Migration in Western Europe*. Oxford: Berg.

Wright, G. (2011). Women's aspirations and the home: Episodes in American feminist reform. In S. S. Fainstein & S. Campbell (Eds.), *Readings in Urban Theory* (3rd ed., pp. 147–60). Oxford: Blackwell.

Yang, Y.-R., & Chang, C.-H. (2007). An urban regeneration regime in China: A case study of urban redevelopment in Shanghai's Taipingqiao area. *Urban Studies*, 44(9), 1809–26.

Yinger, J. M. (1960). Contraculture and subculture. *American Sociological Review*, 25(5), 625–35.

Yinger, M. (1986). Intersecting strands in the theorisation of race and ethnic relations. In J. Rex & D. Mason (Eds.), *Theories of Race and Ethnic Relations* (pp. 20–41). Cambridge: Cambridge University Press.

Young, M., & Willmott, P. (1979). *Family and Kinship in East London*. Harmondsworth: Penguin.

Young, R. J. C. (1990). *White Mythologies: Writing history and the West*. London: Routledge.

Young, R. J. C. (2000). Deconstruction and the postcolonial. In N. Royle (Ed.), *Deconstructions: A user's guide* (pp. 187–210). Basingstoke: Palgrave.

Yücesoy, E. Ü. (2006). *Everyday Urban Public Space: Turkish immigrant women's perspective*. Apeldoorn: Het Spinhuis.

Zhang, T. (2002). Urban development and a socialist pro-growth coalition in Shanghai. *Urban Affairs Review, 37*(4), 475–99.

Zheng, J. & Hui, D. (2007). *Making Creative Industry Parks in Shanghai: The urban regime and the 'creative class'*. Hong Kong: University of Hong Kong.

Zhou, M. (1997). Growing up American: The challenge confronting immigrant children and children of immigrants. *Annual Review of Sociology, 23*(1), 63–95.

Zhu, J. (1999). Local growth coalition: The context and implications of China's gradualist urban land reforms. *International Journal of Urban and Regional Research, 23*(3), 534–48.

Zijderveld, A. (1991). *De samenleving als schouwspel: Een sociologisch leer- en leesboek* (2nd ed.). Utrecht: Lemma.

Zincone, G., Penninx, R., & Borkert, M. (Eds.) (2011). *Migration Policymaking in Europe: The dynamics of actors and contexts in past and present*. Amsterdam: Amsterdam University Press.

Zorbaugh, H. W. (1930). *The Gold Coast and the Slum*. Chicago: University of Chicago Press.

Zukin, S. (1980). A decade of the new urban sociology. *Theory and Society, 9*(4), 575–601.

Zukin, S. (1991). The hollow center. U.S. cities in the global era. In A. Wolfe (Ed.), *America at Century's End* (pp. 245–61). Berkeley: University of California Press.

Zukin, S. (2010). Gentrification: Culture and capital in the urban core. In L. Lees, T. Slater, & E. K. Wyly (Eds.), *The Gentrification Reader* (pp. 220–32). London: Routledge.

Zukin, S. (2013). Whose culture? Whose city? In J. Lin & C. Mele (Eds.), *The Urban Sociology Reader* (2nd ed., pp. 349–57). London: Routledge.

Index